SQL Queries 2012 Joes 2 Pros® Volume 1

The SQL Queries 2012 Hands-On Tutorial for Beginners

(SQL Exam Prep Series 70-461 Volume 1 of 5)

By

Rick A. Morelan
MCDBA, MCTS, MCITP, MCAD, MOE, MCSE, MCSE+I

Pinal Dave
Founder of SQLAuthority.com

EAN: 978-1-939666-12-3

Rick A. Morelan
INFO@JOES2PROS.COM

Table of Contents

About the Authors

Rick Morelan

In 1994, you could find Rick Morelan braving the frigid waters of the Bering Sea as an Alaskan commercial fisherman. His computer skills were non-existent at the time, so you might figure such beginnings seemed unlikely to lead him down the path to SQL Server expertise at Microsoft. However, every computer expert in the world today woke up at some point in their life knowing nothing about computers.

Making the change from fisherman seemed scary and took daily schooling at Catapult Software Training Institute. Rick got his lucky break in August of 1995, working his first database job at Microsoft. Since that time, Rick has worked more than 10 years at Microsoft and has attained over 30 Microsoft technical certifications in applications, networking, databases and .NET development.

At the time of this writing, Rick has authored, or co-authored six books related to SQL Server in the highly recognized technical series known as Joes 2 Pros.

- *Beginning SQL Joes 2 Pros: The SQL Hands-On Guide for Beginners*
  ISBN 1-4392-5317-X
- *SQL Queries Joes 2 Pros: SQL Query Techniques for Microsoft SQL Server 2008*
  ISBN 1-4392-5318-8
- *SQL Architecture Basics Joes 2 Pros: Core Architecture Concepts*
  ISBN: 1-4515-7946-2
- *SQL Programming Development Joes 2 Pros: Programming & Development for Microsoft SQL Server 2008*
  ISBN: 1-4515-7948-9
- *SQL Interoperability Joes 2 Pros: SQL 2008 Techniques with XML, C#, and PowerShell*
  ISBN: 1-4515-7950-0
- *SQL Wait Stats Joes 2 Pros: SQL Performance Tuning Techniques Using Wait Statistics, Types & Queues*
  ISBN: 1-4662-3477-6

His books are used the world over by individuals and educators to help people with little experience learn these technical topics and gain the ability to earn a Microsoft certification or have the confidence to do well in a job interview with their new found knowledge.

Rick's speaking engagements have included SQL PASS, SQL Saturdays and SQL Server Intelligence Conferences. In addition to these speaking engagements Rick gives back to the community by personally teaching students at both Bellevue Community College and for MoreTechnology in Redmond, WA.

Pinal Dave

Pinal Dave is a technology enthusiast and avid blogger. Prior to joining Microsoft, his outstanding community service helped to earn several awards, including the Microsoft Most Valuable Professional in SQL Server Technology (3 continuous years) and the Community Impact Award as an Individual Contributor for 2010.

Playing an active role in the IT industry for over eight years, his career has taken him across the world working in both India and the US, primarily with SQL Server Technology, from version 6.5 to its latest form. His early work experience includes being a Technology Evangelist with Microsoft and a Sr. Consultant with SolidQ, and he continues to work on performance tuning and optimization projects for high transactional systems.

Pinal's higher education degrees include a Master of Science from the University of Southern California, and a Bachelor of Engineering from Gujarat University. In addition to his degrees, Pinal holds multiple Microsoft certificates and helps to spread his knowledge as a regular speaker for many international events like TechEd, SQL PASS, MSDN, TechNet, and countless user groups.

At the time of this writing, Pinal has co-authored three SQL Server books:

- SQL Server Programming
- SQL Wait Stats
- SQL Server Interview Questions and Answers

Pinal's passion for the community drives him to share his training and knowledge and frequently writes on his blog http://blog.SQLAuthority.com covering various subjects related to SQL Server technology and Business Intelligence. As a very active member of the social media community it is easy to connect with him using one of these services:

- Twitter: http://twitter.com/pinaldave
- Facebook: http://facebook.com/SQLAuth

When he is not in front of a computer, he is usually travelling to explore hidden treasures in nature with his lovely daughter, Shaivi, and very supportive wife, Nupur.

Acknowledgements from Rick Morelan

As a book with a supporting web site, illustrations, media content and software scripts, it takes more than the usual author, illustrator and editor to put everything together into a great learning experience. Since my publisher has the more traditional contributor list available, I'd like to recognize the core team members:

Editor: Lori Stow
Technical Editor: Richard Stockhoff
Technical Review: Tony Smithlin
Software Design Testing: Richard Stockhoff
User Acceptance Testing: Sandi Howard
Index: Richard Stockhoff

Thank you to all the teachers at Catapult Software Training Institute in the mid-1990s. What a great start to open my eyes. It landed me my first job at Microsoft by August of that year. A giant second wind came from Koenig-Solutions, which gives twice the training and attention for half the price of most other schools. Mr. Rohit Aggarwal is the visionary founder of this company based in New Delhi, India. Rohit's business model sits students down one-on-one with experts. Each expert dedicates weeks to help each new IT student succeed. The numerous twelve-hour flights I took to India to attend those classes were pivotal to my success. Whenever a new generation of software was released, I got years ahead of the learning curve by spending one or two months at Koenig.

Dr. James D. McCaffrey at Volt Technical Resources in Bellevue, Wash., taught me how to improve my own learning by teaching others. You'll frequently see me in his classroom because he makes learning fun. McCaffrey's unique style boosts the self-confidence of his students, and his tutelage has been essential to my own professional development. His philosophy inspires the *Joes 2 Pros* curriculum.

Preface

How do you build a raging fire of learning from a single spark of curiosity? If you take that little spark and add some paper, a few twigs and a stick, eventually even the largest log can be tossed on to the raging fire. You, too, can evolve from flame to firestorm, from Joe to Pro, when you take the steps outlined in this book. Regardless of your skill level, this is the ideal way to learn.

Viewing a large and unruly database that someone else wrote is like throwing a huge log directly onto a match. What if that large database, which included complex relations, started off as a smaller database with just three tables and 12 employees? You will learn how to build that large database one chapter at a time over the course of studying these Joes 2 Pros books. When you are a part of building something, you comprehend each new level of complexity that is added. Afterward, you're able to stand back and say, "I built that!" Your *Joes 2 Pros* journey will soon make databases appear fun and familiar.

Introduction

Does the following story sound familiar to you? The first SQL book I bought left me confused and demoralized at chapter one. Enrolling in my first class totally overwhelmed me and left me nearly hopeless – and with only a partial tuition refund. Progress was expensive and slow. Countless times I was tempted to give up.

After years of trial and error, I finally got into my groove. While grinding away at my own work with SQL, those key "ah-ha" moments and insights eventually came. What took me over five years of intense study is now a high tide that lifts my students to the same level in just a few months.

Each lesson and chapter builds sequentially. The labs have been created and delivered by me over several years of teaching SQL. If a lab offered one of my classrooms an exciting "ah-ha" experience with students leaning forward on every word and demo, it's a keeper. However, when a lab caused more of a trance or tilted squint, it was discarded or revised with a better approach. The labs in this book are the end result, and each one consistently elicits "ah-ha" moments in my classes.

This book follows what students told me worked for them and launched their careers. This curriculum has helped many people achieve their career goals. If you would like to gain the confidence that comes with really knowing how to get things done, this book is your ticket. This book offers the following ways to help:

Most learning for the money: What if you could get more from this book than the average $1,800 class? Perhaps there is even more material here – proven teaching tools presented by someone whose goal is for you to succeed and achieve a high level of SQL knowledge and proficiency. More importantly, you can learn SQL with demos and practice. When you finish this book, you will be reading and writing in SQL with ease. This book can easily give you more than a typical 18-hour class costing $1,800.

Truly getting it: Is there a better way to learn SQL than from a giant book of concepts with only a few examples? You bet there is, and you're reading it. Just wait until you finish the Points to Ponder section of each chapter. It exists in written and video format to bring life and action to concepts. The Points-to-Ponder section represents a wrap-up of each chapter, which is like getting 10 pages of lengthy reading into one. This is a concise way to finalize the new points you have just used.

Downloadable files bring text to life: Answer keys, quiz games and setup scripts will prepare your SQL Server for the practices that will hone your skills. The files can be found at www.Joes2Pros.com.

Bug Catcher game reviews: After you have run the right code several times, you are ready to write code and help others do the same by spotting errors in code samples. Each chapter's interactive Bug Catcher section highlights common mistakes people make and improves your code literacy. In the classroom setting, this segment is a fun chapter wrap-up game with a wireless buzzer system. Try this game at home for yourself.

This book is an essential tool. When used correctly, you can determine how far and fast you can go. It has been polished and tuned for your use and benefit. In fact, this is the book I really wished was in my possession years ago when I was learning about SQL. What took me years of struggle to learn can now be yours in only months in the form of efficient, enjoyable and rewarding study.

Skills Needed for this Book

SQL stands for Structured Query Language. Since SQL uses English words like select, set and where, SQL statements can be created using basic English. Beyond that you only need to be able to turn on your computer, click a mouse, type a little, and navigate to files and folders.

You should be able to install SQL Server on your computer. Your options are to search the internet for a free download or buy a licensed copy. The official download site gets updated to a new location constantly. To get the most current installation steps go to the www.Joes2Pros.com site.

The preferred option is to get the Microsoft SQL Server 2012 Developer edition for under $50. The Joes2Pros site has a link to make this purchase. Microsoft offers a real bargain for students learning how to use SQL Server. For only $50 you can install and use the fully-enabled Developer edition as long as you agree to use it only for your own learning and to create your own code. This is an outstanding deal considering that businesses generally spend $10,000 to obtain and implement SQL Server Enterprise. More on these options and installation instructions can be found on the Joes2Pros.com site.

About this Book

For those of you who have read my 2008 series for the 70-433 exam you will find a lot of the same material from the 2008 series in this series. This is because much of the 70-461 test covers the same material as the 70-433. I have added material that is new to the test and removed material that is no longer relevant. If you have already read this series or have already passed the 70-433 exam you may choose to read my book which covers only the changes from 70-433 to 70-461. This book will be released in November 2012.

Most of the exercises in this book are designed around proper database practices in the workplace. The workplace also offers common challenges and process changes over time. For example, it is good practice to use numeric data for IDs. If you have ever seen a Canadian postal code (zip code), you see the need for character data in relational information. You will occasionally see an off-the-beaten-path strategy demonstrated so you know how to approach a topic in a job interview or workplace assignment.

To put it simply, there is a recipe for success and you can choose your own ingredients. Just learn the lesson, do the lab, view Points to Ponder, and play the review game at the end of each chapter.

Words from the Real World

Real world scenarios are much different than learning concepts or doing labs at your own pace. This book is written to keep these real world needs in focus. Each chapter is designed and organized after careful review of these needs and based on surveying real SQL developers and hiring managers.

Data retrieval is the most common task performed by any developer. Data is the key and there are three chapters (2, 3, and 4) dedicated to retrieving data the optimal way. Chapter 2 and 3 teaches the developer how to write proper queries and chapter 4 addresses the real world problems like unmatched queries and joins.

Chapter 5 and Chapter 6 will address scripting with DDL and DML statements. Many production databases have been wiped out clean as developers accidently, or mistakenly executed a DELETE command without using a WHERE clause. Updating and deleting data is a very essential task and should be performed by an experienced SQL developer or DBA. Performance becomes a very essential issue when dealing with multiple table operations. Chapter 7 discusses precisely the same concept of maintaining tables and populating them very fast.

It is very common to write T-SQL code or scripts and then forget about them when moving on to the next task. When looking at any executing code written in-line with an application, it often has very interesting characteristics as it was most likely built in multiple phases. Some parts of the code may come from variables and others from parameters passed in from an application. This is integrally built with an enumeration of the application. This is fine, as long as everything works.

Performance problems often begin with code written very quickly and easily, and then becomes the biggest headache for everybody. This is complicated even further when the code is not centralized, making it difficult to locate problems. Stored procedures often come in handy to building centralized code, but the real help it provides is with performance and security. Chapter 8 covers stored procedure and additional enhancements in detail.

How would we feel if our ATM debits the amount from our account, but refuses to give the cash withdrawal to us? We would not be very happy. The reason this type of situation does not occur is because there is a transaction control for this very important process. Chapter 9 discusses how transaction control works with SQL Server. It is recommended to only use when needed, since overuse of the transaction control can negatively affect SQL Server performance.

Security is an extremely important aspect when designing a real world database. It is essential to control access to the data, as well who should not see the data. Chapter 10 discusses basic security measures. Chapter 11 shares important tips to be more effective and successful in the workplace. When we are working with multiple developers in a team, it is essential to maintain some level of discipline and also it is a good idea to have best practices in the place. Chapter 12 is a quick summary of the whole book.

How to Use this Book

Chapter one of this book helps you become familiar with what a database is and introduce basic SQL Server terms. You can read this first chapter without installing SQL Server since.

Some readers will already have SQL Server installed on their computer and simply want to know how to set up the labs. Other readers need to learn how to install SQL Server and then learn how to set up the labs.

There is a video on the Joes2Pros website that can be watched while online, or downloaded and watched offline that demonstrates how to install SQL Server on a computer. If SQL Server 2012 is already installed on a computer, then open your favorite web browser and type www.Joes2Pros.com to be taken directly to the website for this book series *and follow the download instructions.*

Taking the practice quizzes is another great use of this book. Some multiple choice questions may only have one answer, while others will require multiple answers. There is a standard that most tests have adopted, that is good for you to know as you study and prepare.

Here is an example of a question with a single answer:

1.) What is the result of the equation: 2 + 3?

O a. 2
O b. 3
O c. 5

The correct answer to question #1 is (c). Notice that each choice has a round bubble symbol to the left of the letter selection. This symbol means that there will only be a single answer for this question.

Sometimes a question will have more than one correct answer, and for these multiple-answer types of questions, a square box symbol is shown to the left of the letter selection. An example of this is shown below in question #2.

2.) Which numbers in the following list are greater than 2?

□ a. 0
□ b. 2
□ c. 3
□ d. 4

The correct answers to question #2 are (c) and (d). Notice that each choice has a square box symbol to the left of the letter selection. This symbol means that there will be more than one answer for this question.

I'm often asked about the Points to Ponder feature, which is popular with both beginners and experienced developers. Some have asked why I don't simply call it a Summary Page. While it's true that the Points to Ponder page generally captures key points from each section, I frequently include options or technical insights not contained in the section. Often these are points which my students have found helpful and will likely enhance your understanding of SQL Server.

These books are also available as video books. To see the latest in this learning format visit the www.Joes2Pros.com website and click on Videos. Many of our students find that using the text and video together often help in their learning.

How to Use the Downloadable Labs

To help get you started, the first three chapters are in video format for free downloading. Videos show labs, demonstrate concepts, and review Points to Ponder along with tips from the appendix. Ranging from 3-15 minutes in length, they use special effects to highlight key points. You can go at your own pace and pause or replay within lessons as needed. To make knowing where to start even easier, the videos were named alphabetically. You don't even need to refer to the book to know what order they can be viewed. There is even a "Setup" video that shows you how to download and use all other files.

Clear content and high-resolution multimedia videos coupled with code samples will make learning easy and fun. To give you all this and save printing costs, all supporting files are available with a free download from www.Joes2Pros.com. The breakdown of the offerings from these supporting files is listed below:

Answer keys: The downloadable files also include an answer key. All exercise lab coding answers are available for peeking if you get really stuck.

Resource files: If you are asked to import a file into SQL, you will need that resource file. Located in the resources sub-folder from the download site are your practice lab resource files. These files hold the few non-SQL script files needed for some labs.

Lab setup files: SQL Server is a database engine and we need to practice on a database. The Joes 2 Pros Practice Company database is a fictitious travel booking company that has been shortened to the database name of JProCo. The scripts to set up the JProCo database can be found here.

Chapter review files: Ready to take your new skills out for a test drive? We have the ever popular Bug Catcher game located here.

DVD or Videos as a Companion

Training videos: These books are also available for sale as video books. In these videos I guide you through the lesson of each section of the book. Every lab of every chapter of this book series have multimedia steps recorded into videos. The content of the five book series fits into 10 DVDs. When comparing prices, you will find the costs are much less than the existing ad-hoc options on the market today.

If you have done some shopping around you will have noticed there are video training sets that cost over $300. You might also have seen single certification books for $60 each. Do the math and you see one book from other leading publishers will set you back nearly $400.

What this Book is Not

This book will start you off on the cornerstones of the language behind SQL. It will cover the most commonly used keywords. In short, this book won't attempt to 'boil the ocean' by teaching you every single keyword and command in SQL. However, you will become advanced enough at using the ones covered in this series to qualify for working in positions requiring SQL Server knowledge. In your continued study of SQL Server through more advanced books, you will acquire more of these keywords and continually add to your fluency of programming with SQL on your way to becoming a SQL expert.

This is not a memorization book. Rather, this is a skills book to make part of preparing for the MCTS 70-461 certification test a familiarization process. This book prepares you to apply what you have learned to answer SQL questions in the job setting. The highest hopes are that your progress and level of SQL knowledge will soon have business managers seeking your expertise to provide the reporting and information vital to their decision making. It's a good feeling to achieve and to help others at the same time. Many students commented that the training method used in *Joes 2 Pros* was what finally helped them achieve their goal of certification.

When you go through the *Joes 2 Pros* book series and really know this material, you deserve a fair shot at SQL certification. Use only authentic testing engines drawing on your skill. Show you know it for real. At the time of this writing, MeasureUp® at http://www.measureup.com provides a good test preparation simulator. The company's test pass guarantee makes it a very appealing option.

Chapter 1. Introduction to Databases

Structured Query Language (SQL) is the most used database language across the world. SQL contains words you will recognize as common English words. Often students ask me, "What's the difference between SQL and SQL Server?" My reply is simple: "If you were going to live and work in Germany, you'd be better off if you could speak German. If you're going to SQL Server-land, you'd better learn to speak the Structured Query Language or SQL". In other words, SQL Server is the name of the environment. SQL is the programming language that is spoken or used in that environment. Before all that, let's examine the hullabaloo about databases.

READER NOTE: *It is not necessary to have any version of SQL Server 2012 installed on a computer to learn from this chapter on Introduction to Databases. Please review the SQL Server installation video available at www.Joes2Pros.com when ready to move on to Chapter 2. Also, on our site there is a selection of free videos to watch to help you get started. Our entire video instruction library is available via online subscription and DVD.*

About Databases

If someone were to approach us claiming to have a database and then hands over a shoebox full of receipts, would we accept this as a database? A database is a collection of related information. Here is a list of some common collection of items that can be considered to be a database:

- An address book.
- A telephone book.
- A report card.
- A checkbook.
- A family tree.
- A diary.

Data vs. Information

A shoebox full of receipts will not provide much vocational advancement. So, what's the buzz about SQL? The things SQL can do that the shoebox can't do are critical. SQL organizes stored data in a meaningful way and allows us to easily retrieve only the information we need. These capabilities allow businesses to make decisions with that information.

OK, let's say we are just as fast at pulling receipts from the shoebox as SQL is at pulling data from a database. So, what else does SQL have to offer? Well, the shoebox of receipts may be in US dollars. Try asking that shoebox for the equivalent value in Canadian dollars at today's exchange rate. In this case, we are asking for information not even stored inside the shoebox. SQL can take existing data, apply directions or calculations to the data, and the final result can even be information that isn't directly stored in the database, but derived from the data contained within it.

This gets us to the definitions of data and information. Data is what is being stored in a database, such as raw numbers, text or images. Information is what we look at and often build into business reports. In other words, information is data that is processed or structured in such a way as to have true value to the user. It's useful for businesses to have the right information quickly, and SQL is a true master at turning data into information.

A Simple Database

By looking at the handwritten shopping list on this page (Figure 1.1) we can tell which items to purchase and what will be in the bag when we leave the store.

Which is the cheapest item? Which is the most expensive one? What does the third item cost?

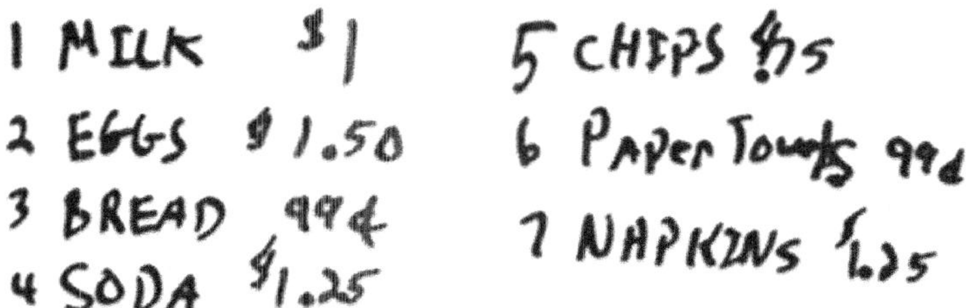

Figure 1.1 An example of a flat database.

To answer these questions, we use tools we learned in school like grouping, filtering, pattern recognition, and calculations. The SQL language uses these same tools to answer these questions. The difference is that humans can only query short lists, while SQL has the power to query trillions of records in multiple related lists from databases that do not even need to be on the same continent! Plus, SQL Server returns answers as result sets in mere nanoseconds. So, if we know how to answer a question, we can build a SQL query to answer the same type of question for us, only faster and with more reliability.

Computer languages are literal and numerical. Imagine that we have an appetite and you ask a computer, "What's a good snack?" The computer might answer, '5'. Whereas, a human would most likely interpret the language and reply, Chips.

The handwritten shopping list has seven items in it. The most expensive item listed is Eggs. The cheapest item is Chips. Item 3 costs 99 cents and is listed as Bread. The item on the list that costs one dollar is named Milk.

A database will store this shopping list (Figure 1.1), as seven rows of information, with three columns. The columns in this figure are not named but the first column lists the item number and could be named ItemNumber. The item Description column follows. Finally, we have a column that would logically be named Price.

Part of what we must know is how to translate SQL 'Geek Speak' into plain English. We must learn to translate business storage and reporting goals into valid SQL statements.

Database Geek Speak

Simple databases, such as shopping lists, use plain English. SQL Server can lay them out just as simply in a form that looks like a grid or spreadsheet.

In plain English, the shopping list written by a human in Figure 1.1 appears to have two columns each containing a row with groups of items. SQL Server will logically interpret these groups of items as having three columns and seven rows, as seen in Figure 1.2. The first column is the ItemNumber. The second column is named Description. The name of the third column is Price. Our first row has an ItemNumber of 1, a Description of Milk, and a Price that equals one dollar.

Results | Messages

	ItemNumber	Description	Price
1	1	Milk	1.00
2	2	Eggs	1.50
3	3	Bread	0.99
4	4	Soda	1.25
5	5	Chips	0.75
6	6	PaperTowels	0.99
7	7	Napkins	1.25

Query executed successfully. | RENO (11.0 RTM) | Reno\j2p (54) | dbBasics | 00:00:00 | 7 rows

Figure 1.2 A database table representing the shopping list from Figure 1.1.

In geek speak, a collection of columns and rows of data is called a table. We can see an example of what this looks like in Figure 1.2, which is a screen capture of the results from querying the ShoppingList table with SQL Server.

Our table named ShoppingList is much easier to read than the list written by hand on a napkin shown in Figure 1.1. This table currently has seven rows. Calling them rows is just fine in geek speak, although a few hardcore SQL folks might insist on calling them records. So, seven rows are the same as seven records.

The correct word for vertically stored data is a column. Geek speak allows for two naming choices, column or field. We can see that the ShoppingList table has three columns or we can just as easily call them three fields.

Each record (row) in our table has an ItemNumber, a Description and a Price, and each record has three fields. In geek speak we would say, "This table is populated with seven records". Since we do not know the values that might be contained in the next record (eighth record), these values are unknown. Each of the three cells in this potential record contains something called a NULL value. It is important to not confuse a NULL value with a value of zero, as they are absolutely not the same thing. Zero is a specific value that calculations can be performed on. NULL means we do not know what the value is at all and therefore, no calculations can be performed against it. The next record could be anything. Maybe it's going to be Sugar at $1.75, or Gum at $1.10. For now, just think of NULL as unknown or not specified, but anything is possible later. NULLs will be covered more deeply later in this book.

After records are placed in a table, we can delete all or some of them. If we were to delete one record in the ShoppingList table, we would have six records left in the table. If we were to delete all of the records, the table would be unpopulated.

Once again, the ShoppingList table has three fields. The first field name in this table is ItemNumber. The second field name is Description. The third field name is Price. Oftentimes the first field is numeric and helps us prevent duplicates. For example, we don't want to have two items named number 4. A business might have two employees named David, but each has a different employee number.

The fields offer us more than just a name or label atop the data. We can see that ItemNumber contains integer data, Description contains alphabetical data, and Price contains decimals (Figure 1.2). It seems clear which type of data is acceptable for each field of any given record. In SQL Server, database fields are constrained so that they accept only a specified data type. The way this table is set up, if we accidently typed in sugar for the price field when entering a new record, SQL Server will not accept the entry. Fields are protected or *constrained* using data types. We can enter different numbers for Price like 1.95 or 22.50, so long as they match the data type accepted by that field.

The point where a field (column) and row (record) meet contains a single *value*. A value sits inside what looks like a spreadsheet cell and acts similarly. In a table with three fields and seven rows, we would have 21 values.

When turning data into viewable information, we often place it in a grid format just like we see in Figure 1.2, although we rarely refer to this information as a grid, rather we usually call it a 'record set' or 'result set'.

Database Management Systems

What is a Database Management System? Well, it's not a shoebox full of receipts. Databases just store data. If the data is valuable and our decisions are driven by information, we may want a system that can provide quick reporting. The value of our data may dictate a system which backs up daily or even hourly.

A database management system like SQL Server can protect all the data it contains. Most importantly, we get to see exactly what we want as data turns into information. Information is data laid out in a way that can be viewed for business decisions.

Most databases have many tables, and those tables often relate to each other. Since SQL Server is a management system with related tables, it is called a Relational Database Management System or RDBMS. A shopping list is just a database. SQL Server is an RDBMS.

The true power in the RDBMS is when it is necessary to tabulate the weekend gross receipts for the latest weekend action movie across the nation. Do we really want to ship all the ticket stubs from every box office across the country to a central accounting desk and then count the piles of receipts? No. Fortunately, the movie industry uses an RDBMS so that by Monday morning it instantly knows the amount for the weekend gross receipts. This is the true power of turning data into information.

SQL at Your Service

In addition to being the most popular RDBMS, SQL Server is an extremely powerful program. It is like a software application, but falls under a different category we need to understand.

We are all familiar with applications. We run them, use them, and see them on the task bar when changing programs. Our computer runs application like processes to check for network connections and dozens of other processes to make things flow. These supporting applications and processes probably don't need to take up room on the taskbar. We need to keep our work area free for user applications.

Applications or processes that run invisibly are in fact called Windows services. Think of a service as an application that can run without a user interface. A service has one other handy distinction from an application, and a little background information on applications will clarify this distinction. Just share a machine with someone and notice the differences between the desktop themes. A co-worker, who likes everything pink, may open a popular spreadsheet to a pink theme, while we log into a spreadsheet with the default theme. Applications are customizable for different users. Nevertheless, regardless of who is logged onto the machine, the networking service had better run just fine.

Services are like applications that are running on the machine regardless of who is logged on. SQL Server is a service. Actually, SQL Server is a collection of services that run together. SQL Server services run invisibly in the background on our computer.

Since SQL Server runs invisibly, we might wonder how to manage it. The creator of a service often provides a special way to interact with the service. We must use a window to talk to a service, and in the case of Microsoft SQL Server 2005, 2008, and 2012 we use something called Management Studio. This is easier to say than the full name of Microsoft SQL Server Management Studio. Typically, we hear the phrase "Open SQL Server," when what we are actually being asked to accomplish, is to open Management Studio to a SQL service that is probably already running.

On our SQL Server machine it is likely that the SQL Server service is one of many Windows services. We can take a moment learning how to view all the invisible services that are running on our computer. Press the keyboard button with the Windows symbol ⊞ + the letter 'R' to open the '***Run***' dialog box (typically opens in the lower left-hand corner of the desktop window). Type the word 'services.msc' in this dialog box to open the '***Services***' dialog box.

When the Services dialog box opens, we can see that there is a long list of services sorted in alphabetical order (Figure 1.3 shows the standard tab selected). It will be necessary to scroll down to find the SQL Services grouped together.

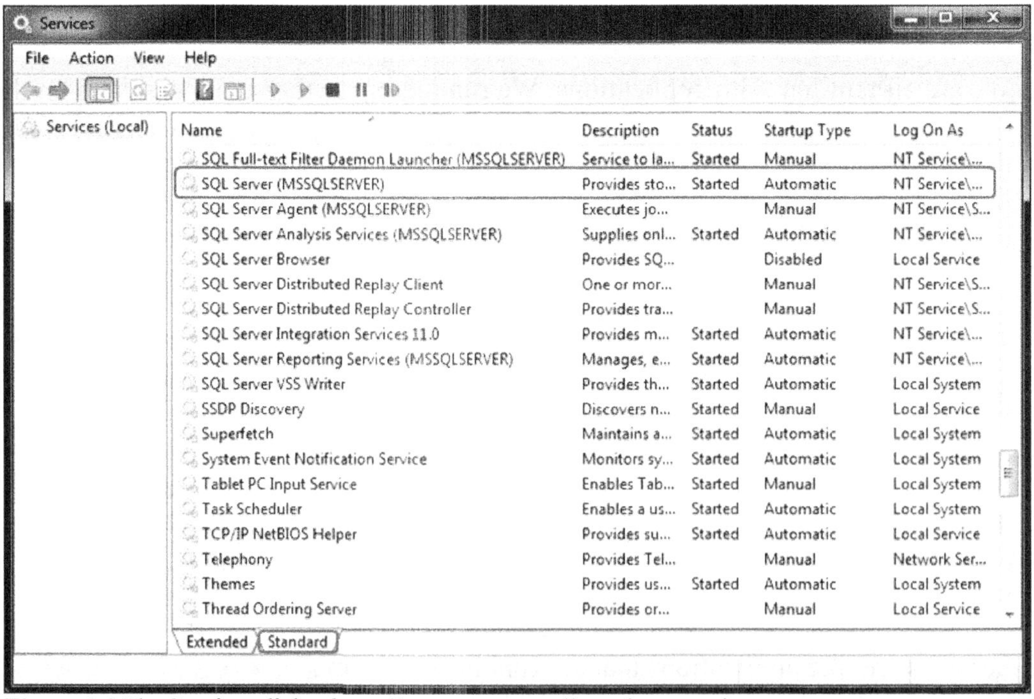

Services

File Action View Help

Services (Local)

Name	Description	Status	Startup Type	Log On As
SQL Full-text Filter Daemon Launcher (MSSQLSERVER)	Service to la...	Started	Manual	NT Service\...
SQL Server (MSSQLSERVER)	Provides sto...	Started	Automatic	NT Service\...
SQL Server Agent (MSSQLSERVER)	Executes jo...		Manual	NT Service\S...
SQL Server Analysis Services (MSSQLSERVER)	Supplies onl...	Started	Automatic	NT Service\...
SQL Server Browser	Provides SQ...		Disabled	Local Service
SQL Server Distributed Replay Client	One or mor...		Manual	NT Service\S...
SQL Server Distributed Replay Controller	Provides tra...		Manual	NT Service\S...
SQL Server Integration Services 11.0	Provides m...	Started	Automatic	NT Service\...
SQL Server Reporting Services (MSSQLSERVER)	Manages, e...	Started	Automatic	NT Service\...
SQL Server VSS Writer	Provides th...	Started	Automatic	Local System
SSDP Discovery	Discovers n...	Started	Manual	Local Service
Superfetch	Maintains a...	Started	Automatic	Local System
System Event Notification Service	Monitors sy...	Started	Automatic	Local System
Tablet PC Input Service	Enables Tab...	Started	Manual	Local System
Task Scheduler	Enables a us...	Started	Automatic	Local System
TCP/IP NetBIOS Helper	Provides su...	Started	Automatic	Local Service
Telephony	Provides Tel...		Manual	Network Ser...
Themes	Provides us...	Started	Automatic	Local System
Thread Ordering Server	Provides or...		Manual	Local Service

Extended Standard

Figure 1.3 The Services dialog box allows access to all services running on a computer.

To take a closer look at the options available, we need to locate the service named **SQL Server (MSSQLSERVER)** and then double-click on the name to open a dialog box for controlling this service (this service has a red box outlined around it in Figure 1.3). Depending on the version of SQL Server on our computer and what options were chosen when it was installed, the number of SQL services listed can vary dramatically. The machine in this example has a full installation of SQL Server 2012, which includes features like, SSIS, SSRS, and SSAS.

We can control nearly every aspect of the SQL Server service from this dialog box (Figure 1.4), including Start, Stop, Pause, Resume, and even when it starts with the Startup type option. Any of these actions can be performed without rebooting the computer.

Looking at Figure 1.4, we can see the SQL Server service is already up and running and that it starts automatically when the computer is booted. This is the default setting, since we can only use SQL Server and all of its tools when this service is running. We do not want to make any changes here, so click the 'Cancel' button to exit the dialog box without affecting any of the default settings.

Figure 1.4 Controlling how a SQL Server service operates.

Chapter Glossary

Column: A field in a database table.

Database: A collection of objects to store and retrieve data.

Database Management System: A set of software components and programs that creates, maintains, and controls access to a database.

Data type: An attribute of a field that tells SQL Server what kind of data it may accept. Examples include integers, dates and characters.

Field: A column in a database table.

Information: The data and calculation you choose to view from a database, usually for business purposes.

Management Studio: The user interface to talk with SQL Server services.

NULL: Unknown or unspecified values.

Populated: A term used to describe a table that contains data.

Query: A question asked to get information from data in a database.

RDBMS: Relational Database Management System is a tool that allows for safe storage of data and quick retrieval of important business information.

Record: A row of data in a table.

Record Set: The set of data returned as an answer to a query.

Result Set: Another term for record set.

Service: A process, much like an application, that runs in the background of your system.

SQL: Structured Query Language.

T-SQL: Transact Structured Query Language is the computer programming language based on the SQL standard and used by Microsoft SQL Server to create databases, populate tables and retrieve data.

[NOTES]

Chapter 2. Basic Queries

We now know that a database consists of the data stored inside it. By using the SELECT command we can choose which stored data to retrieve and view as information. In case you are an intermediate level student and simply skimmed the first chapter, here is a one sentence recap: "*Data* is items like numbers, text, and images stored and *information* is what and how we choose to view it". For example, our manager asks to send her a report of books sold last week. If we viewed the raw data in the company's massive sales database, we would see an enormous amount of detail (such as title, author, price, ISBN, language, weight, quantity remaining in inventory, etc.) for every book sold. However, what our manager wants to see is key information regarding last week's sales, such as the total amount of sales expressed in US dollars, the total number of books, a comparison of last week's total sales versus the prior week's total sales, and the top ten titles sold during this time period.

The way you retrieve data to get what our manager wants is to write a query starting with the word SELECT. This chapter will show the core elements for the most commonly used keywords we use to retrieve data from the RDBMS known as SQL Server 2012.

READER NOTE: *Before beginning this chapter, verify that SQL Server 2012 is installed on the computer and that it will connect to the Database Engine.*

Please run the SQLQueries2012Vol1Chapter2.0Setup.sql script in order to follow along with the examples in the first section of Chapter 2. All scripts mentioned in this chapter may be found at www.Joes2Pros.com.

If you need help running the script, please watch the video on setting up labs from the Joes2Pros web site.

Database Context

If you were to ask your best friend for their age you might get a different result than if you asked your child the same question. "How many employees work at your company?" could be a query. If you were working on a database for a pet store and looked for a list of employees, your results would differ greatly from the same query on the database of a giant global corporation. If you create the perfect query in the wrong database, it may run without error messages. When you query the right database, you get the information you need. Set your database context before you run your query.

In my career, every single server I've encountered has had many databases. You will find the same to be true and perhaps already have.

The Object Explorer inside Management Studio talks with the SQL Server service and finds all your databases. Databases appear as gold cylinders inside the Object Explorer window. In Figure 2.1we see three databases, identified by the golden cylinder icon, named dbBasics, dbTester and JProCo.

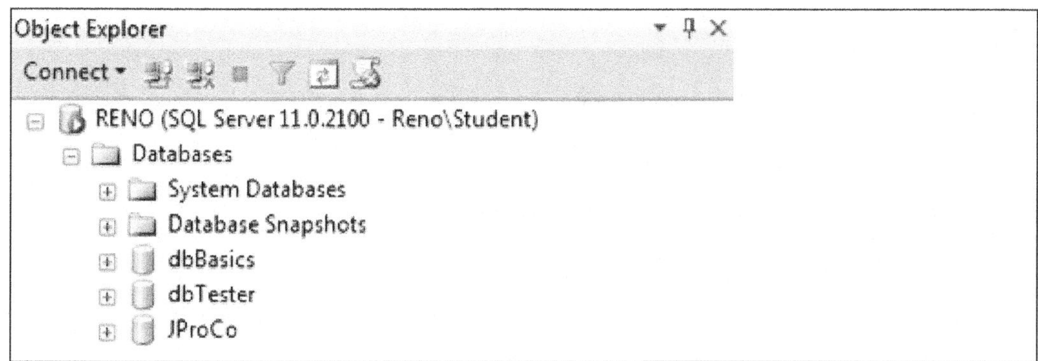

Figure 2.1 Databases appear as a gold cylinder icon inside the Object Explorer.

The data inside these three databases are different. When looking for information, we usually write a query on only one database at a time. Database context refers to which database we are running the current query against. Always remember to set the database context before running a query.

Notice the left side of Figure 2.2 shows the Object Explorer. The right side of the figure is a Query Window. A Query Window can have only one database context set at a time. If we look at the toolbar above both windows, we can see it is set to JProCo. We can change this connection by clicking the drop-down list control and selecting the desired database from the list.

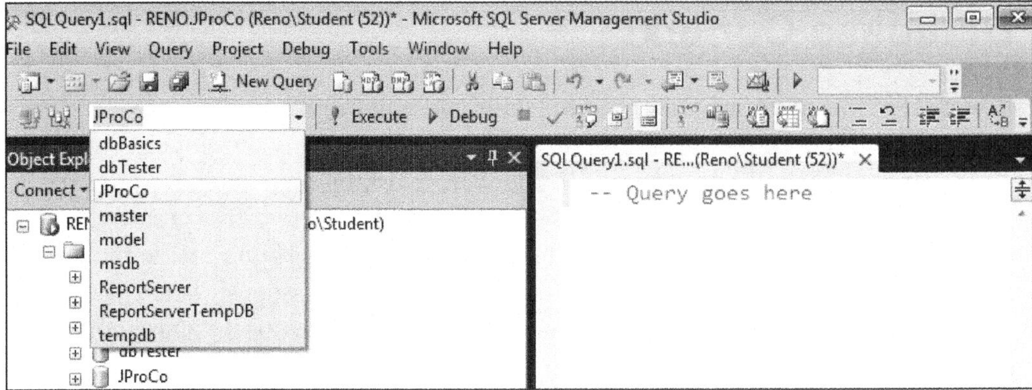

Figure 2.2 SQL Server Management Studio with database context set to the JProCo database.

There is always a risk that we will accidently run a query using the wrong database context. To help avoid this situation, we can simply change the database context to the correct database. The most consistent way to accomplish this is with a SQL statement in the Query Window. If we want to set or change the database context to the dbBasics database, we can type the USE statement below:

```
USE dbBasics
GO
```

Running this SQL statement is the preferred way to modify a database context. Alternatively, using the drop-down list works just as well (Figure 2.2). However, the code method is best when writing code that we plan to reuse, particularly when working on a team that shares SQL scripts.

When sharing code, we want others to be in the correct database when it runs. Placing the USE statement before any other code in a query, will set the database context allowing the rest of the query to run correctly. Press the F5 key or click the Execute button in the toolbar to run this USE statement query (Figure 2.3).

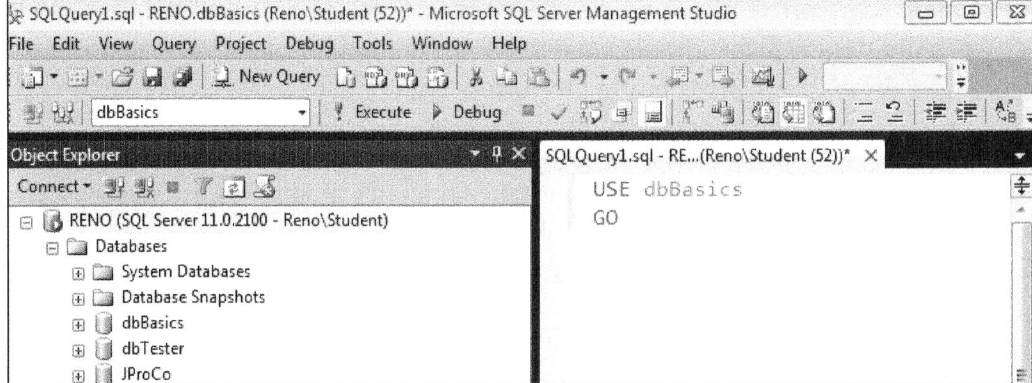

Figure 2.3 Setting the database context to dbBasics with a USE statement and running the query.

This SQL code (USE statement) tells the SQL Server service to look inside the dbBasics database for the data requested by any code that follows after it. The word GO means the statement above it must finish before moving on to any code that follows it. So, the GO keyword really means stop, finish and then go. This is a safety feature since the next statement is dependent on the database context already being set to dbBasics. If we're not in dbBasics, we can't query dbBasics. Modern systems are capable of running many lines of code at the same time. The GO keyword limits this ability by making sure the USE statement above it is completely finished before proceeding to the next line.

Single Table Queries

When we want information from a database, we write a query, such as SELECT *data* FROM *TableName*. In English we might say, "Show me the information!"

Let's write a simple query. We will use the dbBasics database context and request all records and all fields be returned from the ShoppingList table. The keyword SELECT requests information to be displayed and the asterisk (*) sign is a shortcut for all the field names. The keyword FROM chooses a specific table.

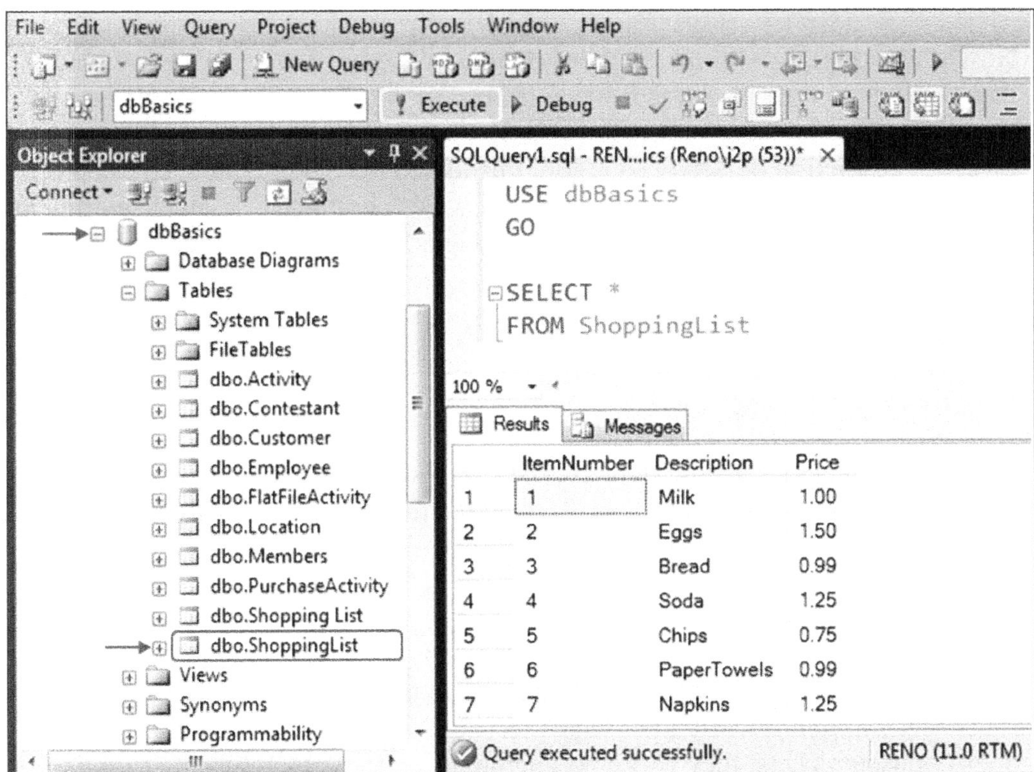

Figure 2.4 A query that requests all records and all fields from the ShoppingList table.

We are able to run this query to retrieve the information by either clicking on the '! **Execute**' button in the toolbar above the Query Window, or by pressing the F5 button on our keyboard (some keyboard configurations require pressing the fn (function) + F5 keys simultaneously).

When we look at the results pane in the lower right-hand portion of Figure 2.4, the results are exactly the same as those shown in Figure 1.1. In fact, we just built the exact same query as the one used in Chapter One to produce this screenshot. That was simple and easy!

Basic Query Syntax

A simple guide to what the words in a basic SQL query mean was neatly summarized by a group of students in one of my weekend classes. They insisted it be added to the book, so to honor their request, here is the code sample:

```
USE dbBasics                --choose DATABASE Context
GO                          --complete USE statement

SELECT *                    --choose Field(s) to display
FROM ShoppingList           --choose Table(s) containing fields
```

Now is a good time to point out words can be placed in a Query Window that have nothing to do with the SQL code itself. We can write non-SQL words and notes like "I wrote this query today" above the SELECT statement. In order to do this, we must tell SQL Server to ignore this text since it's not intended to be code. In fact, it should be non-executing code known as comments. To make comments, we need to begin the line with two-hyphen signs, one after the other with no spaces between them. Change the database context back to JProCo with the drop-down window in the toolbar and then run use this example of code:

```
--This is my latest query
SELECT * FROM Location
```

The code above runs fine in JProCo. The first line is ignored by SQL because of the double hyphens. It's there only for the benefit of the human eye reading it. This is a useful way to make notes that later provide us or our team with key hints or details explaining what the code is attempting to accomplish.

Table names can optionally have square brackets around them, and will not change the result set. Changing back to the dbBasics context, we can run the following two queries. Although one query uses square brackets and the other does not use brackets, they will both operate identically, by returning a result set.

```
SELECT * FROM [ShoppingList]
SELECT * FROM ShoppingList
```

When coding, we rarely use square brackets because it requires extra typing. The only time it is helpful is when we can't tell when a table name starts or stops. For this demo, the dbBasics database has two identical tables named 'ShoppingList' and 'Shopping List'. The latter contains a space in its name, which is generally a bad naming practice for any database object. For situations like this, we must use a delimiter, such as square brackets. Without these delimiters, SQL Server will think the table is named 'Shopping' and there is a command named 'List', which it does not recognize and will result in an error message (Figure 2.5).

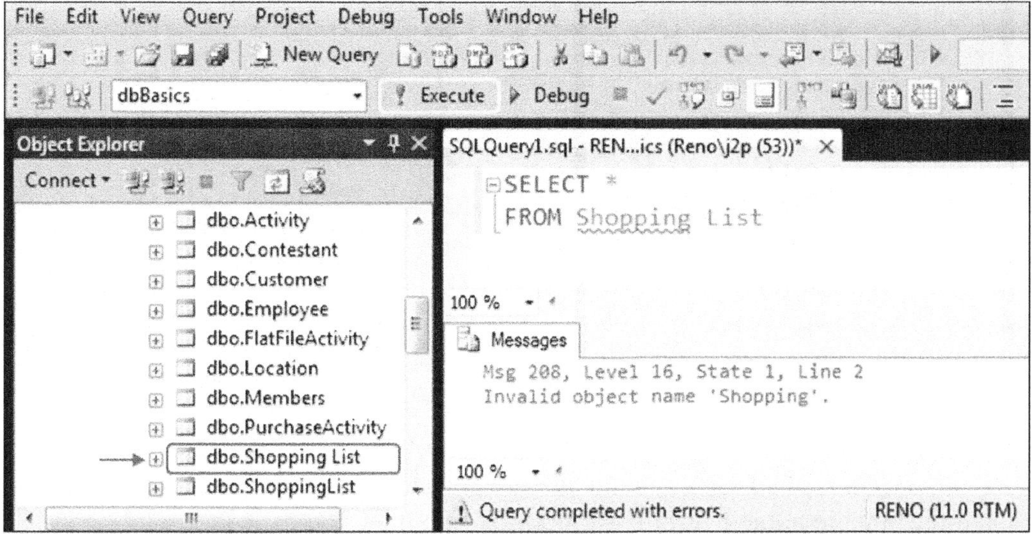

Figure 2.5 A table with a space in the name will not run without using square bracket delimiters.

Of course, as shown in the two earlier queries, we can put square brackets around any table. In fact, code that is automatically generated by SQL Server always creates these delimiters for every object in the database. The only time we must use the square bracket delimiters is when table names are separated by a space, have the same name as a SQL Server keyword (bad idea), or otherwise named in a way that is not obvious or easily interpreted by SQL Server.

We can easily correct this error message by placing square bracket delimiters around the 'Shopping List' table name. Once this is complete, the query will successfully run without an error (Figure 2.6) and we will get the same seven records in our result set, as the first query using the ShoppingList table (no space).

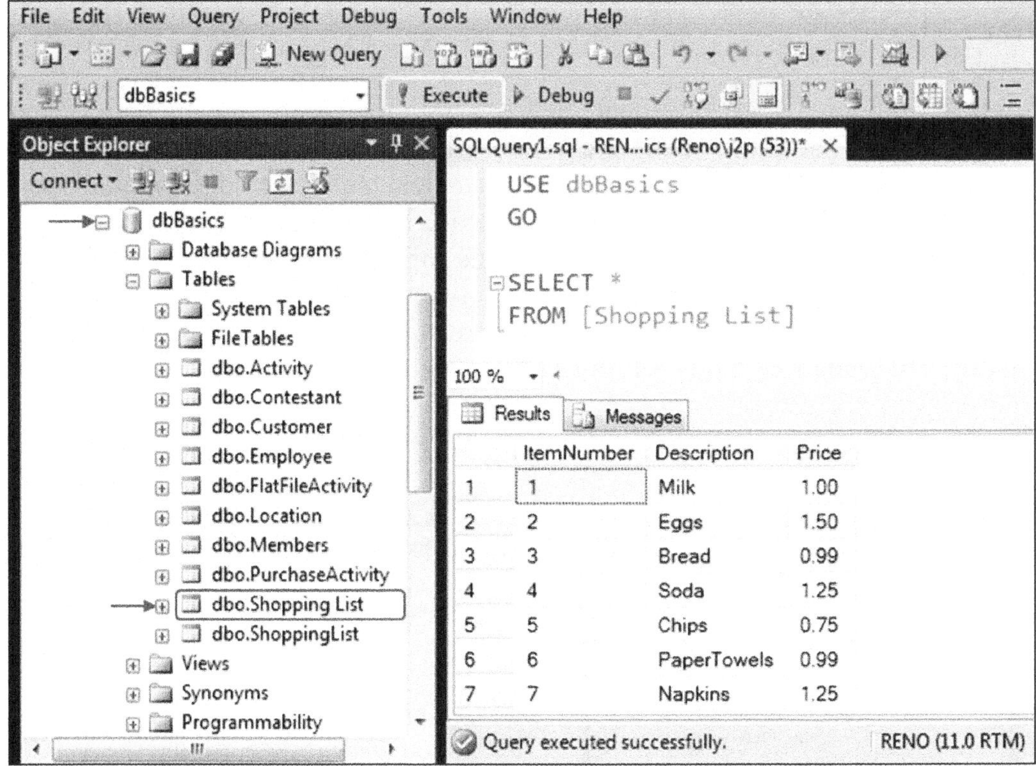

Figure 2.6 Delimiting a table whose name includes a space will allow the query to run.

Using delimiters for table names helps us in another way, too. As previously mentioned, it is a bad idea to name a table after known SQL Server keywords. For example, a table named 'From' would look like this:

```
SELECT * FROM From
```

The vocabulary of SQL Server has grown over the years, and new keywords are continually added to the existing list. Take an example where a company database that keeps track of charity grants is named 'Grant'. The company upgrades to a newer version of SQL Server where Grant is now a keyword used to administer database permissions. The following code would create problems:

```
SELECT * FROM Grant
```

In this case, SQL Server interprets the word 'Grant' as a keyword. We can tell this is happening because the word 'Grant' appears in the color blue (just like the keywords SELECT and FROM). We can solve all conflicts between a table name and keyword(s) by using square bracket delimiters. By placing these delimiters around the Grant table name, SQL Server will know that this is not a keyword.

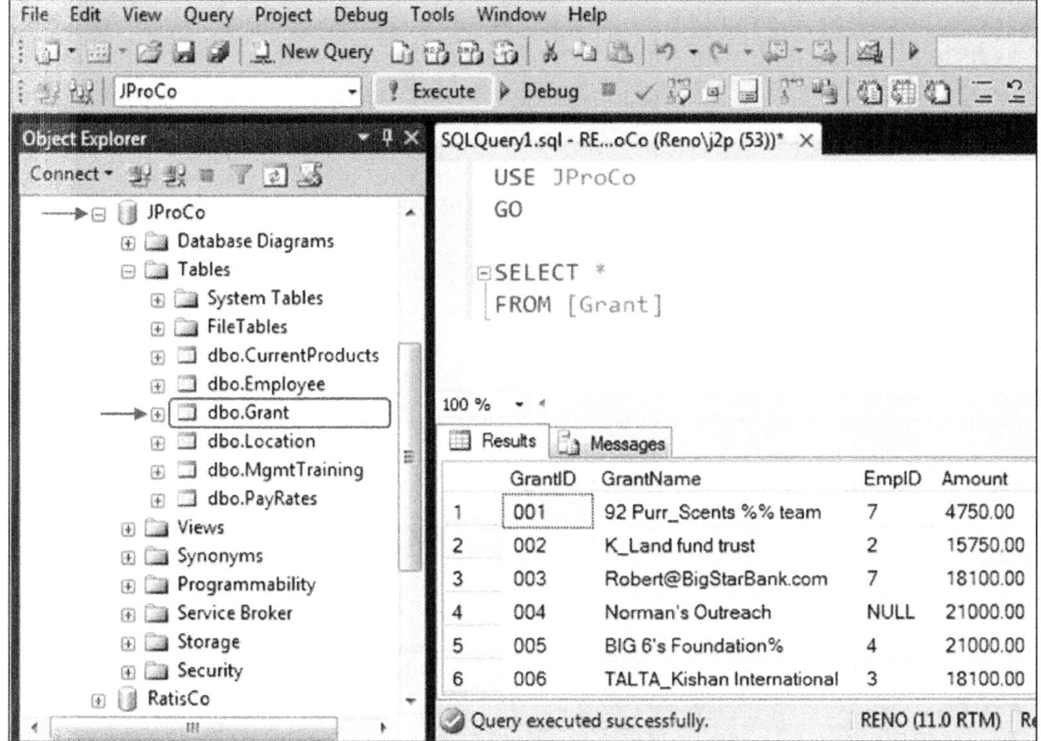

Figure 2.7 Delimiters instruct SQL Server that [Grant] is a table, not the keyword GRANT.

Square brackets work on all database objects, so we could place square brackets around the [Employee] table, if we wanted to. This means delimiters can be used for field names. For example: the Location table in the JProCo database has a field named 'state'. STATE is a keyword first introduced with SQL Server 2008. There's more on selecting fields later in this chapter.

Over time, we will find that in reality, delimiters are only necessary on rare occasions, as most database objects are created using proper naming practices.

Exact Matching

There is a big difference between selecting everything and being selective. When questioning the business importance of database systems, we need only to look at what a highly profitable search engine company does every day. The world has billions of websites and when we want a search narrowed down to just a few sites of interest, the database a search engine company uses will make the necessary calculations based on our unique search query and make the selections best suited for our needs. This information is presented as a plethora of links, enticing us to click on them and visit a specific website, which drives revenue created by the search engine company's advertising business.

Trying to obtain information by looking at all records in a table is about as useful as trying to look at all web sites on the internet to find what we want. Instead, the preferred way is to add criteria to a query. With criteria we can deliver the exact information that is needed. All queries must have the SELECT and FROM keywords together to be valid. We also have other choices available, such as the WHERE clause, which is the most common optional keyword.

When we query the entire ShoppingList table we have two items which cost $1.25. It's easy to spot two records out of seven with our own eyes. However, finding two records from a million with our own eyes is like looking for a needle in a haystack. So, let's tunnel through that haystack with the WHERE clause. We want to limit our result set based on the Price field being exactly $1.25. This is accomplished by adding this specific criteria immediately after the WHERE clause (Figure 2.8).

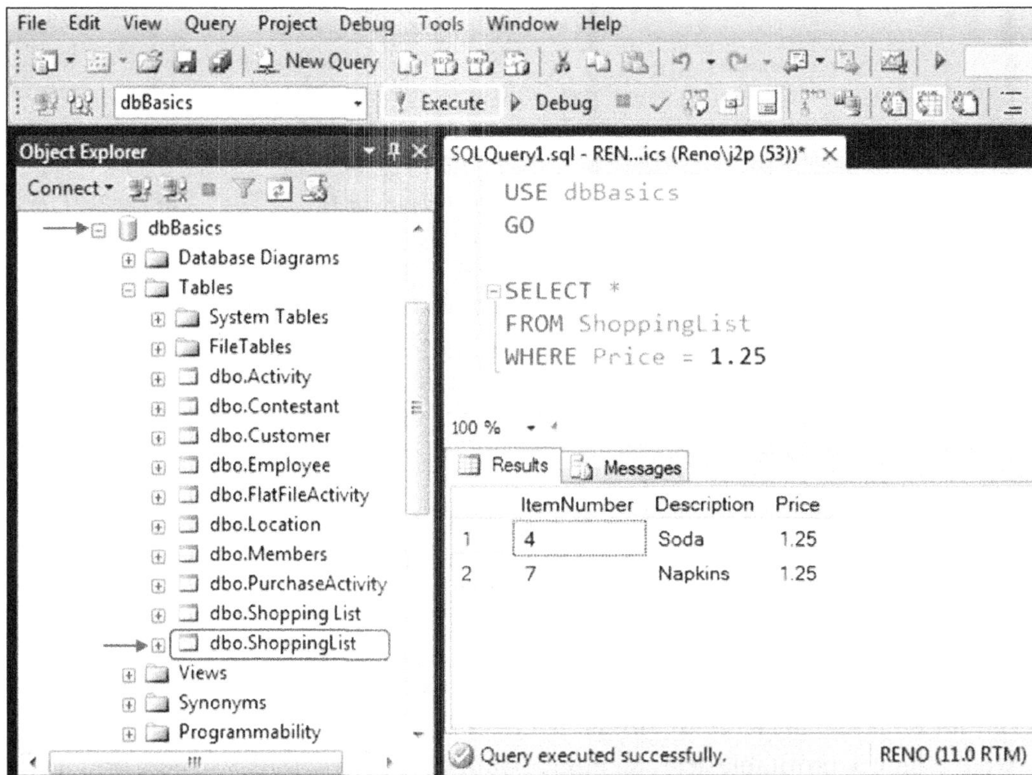

Figure 2.8 The WHERE clause limits the number of records in your result set.

The perfect tool for filtering data, is the WHERE clause. There are still seven records contained in the [ShoppingList] table, even though the number of records in the result set of our query is now two.

Any type of data can be filtered by the WHERE clause. If we wanted to see all people in the Employee table of the JProCo database, with a first name of David, we can use the WHERE clause with this criteria. It is important to know that we must enclose any characters or words in a set of single quotation marks.

The query seen in Figure 2.9 uses a WHERE clause to filter on the FirstName field looking for all values that are equal to David. We have data represented by twelve records stored in the Employee table. The WHERE clause will show only those records that exactly match the criteria we give it and expects a logical statement to evaluate each record. This logical statement (FirstName = 'David') is commonly known as a *predicate*. By predicating on the FirstName field, our goal is to filter the results to provide us with only the information that we want to see.

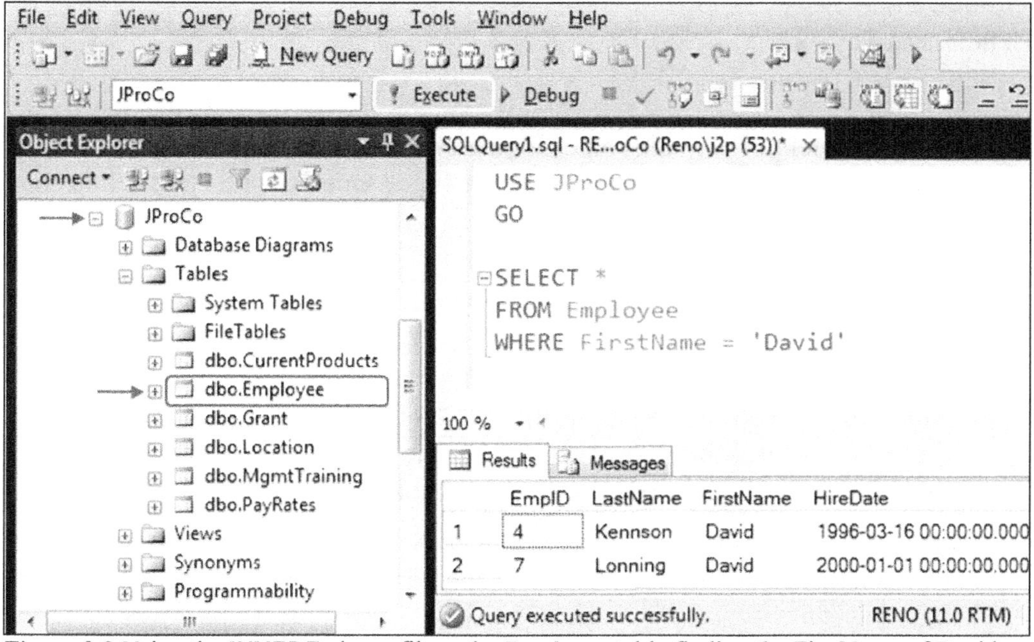

Figure 2.9 Using the WHERE clause filters the Employee table finding the FirstName of David.

Let's try running the next few examples by ourselves, checking the results after completing each query. Use the JProCo database context for these examples.

Of the twelve employees, we have ten who are not named David. The reverse of this query will show all records that don't have David as a FirstName:

```
SELECT *
FROM Employee
WHERE FirstName != 'David'
```

When we place an exclamation point before the equals sign it means ‘Not Equals’. This will filter all exact matches out of the result set. In versions of SQL Server previous to SQL Server 2008, the ‘< >’ operator was used as ‘Not Equals,’ as shown in the next code sample.

```
SELECT *
FROM Employee
WHERE FirstName <> 'David'
```

The risk in using the ‘< >’ operator is that it looks exactly like an HTML or XML tag. When SQL Server needs to talk with other languages, it’s better to use ‘! =’ operator for ‘Not Equals’ as shown in this code sample:

```
SELECT *
FROM Employee
WHERE FirstName != 'David'
```

Using the ‘=’ operator provides an exact match. What if we wanted to look for all the values of Lisa or David in the FirstName field? One option is to use this code:

```
SELECT *
FROM Employee
WHERE FirstName = 'Lisa'
OR FirstName = 'David'
```

This works fine, except for the logical rule that only allows for one exact match after the ‘=’ operator. Some people like using the equals sign and simply write an additional line for each criterion that they are looking for.

To enumerate a set of exact matches in a query with a single criterion requires the use of the **IN** operator. The code below is another way to find the same result set:

```
SELECT *
FROM Employee
WHERE FirstName IN ('Lisa', 'David')
```

What if you wanted to find everyone in the company except for Lisa and David? By putting the word NOT in front of the IN operator we give the opposite result. Since there are twelve employees and three are named Lisa or David, there will be nine employees who are not named Lisa or David. The code below is an example of how to use the NOT IN operator when specifying a list:

```
SELECT *
FROM Employee
WHERE FirstName NOT IN ('Lisa', 'David')
```

Lab 2.1: Single Table Queries

Lab Prep: Each lab has one or more Skill Checks. Start with Skill Check 1 and proceed until reaching the Points to Ponder section.

Before beginning this lab, verify that SQL Server 2012 is properly installed and operating. Before running the lab setup script for resetting the database (SQLQueries2012Vol1Chapter2.1Setup.sql), please make sure to close all query windows within SSMS. An open query window pointing to a database context can lock that database preventing it from updating when the script is executing. A simple way to assure all query windows are closed, is to exit out of SSMS, then open a new instance of SSMS, and lastly run the setup script.

Skill Check 1: Write a query that displays a result set of all records and all fields from the CurrentProducts table of the JProCo database. When done the results should resemble those shown in Figure 2.10.

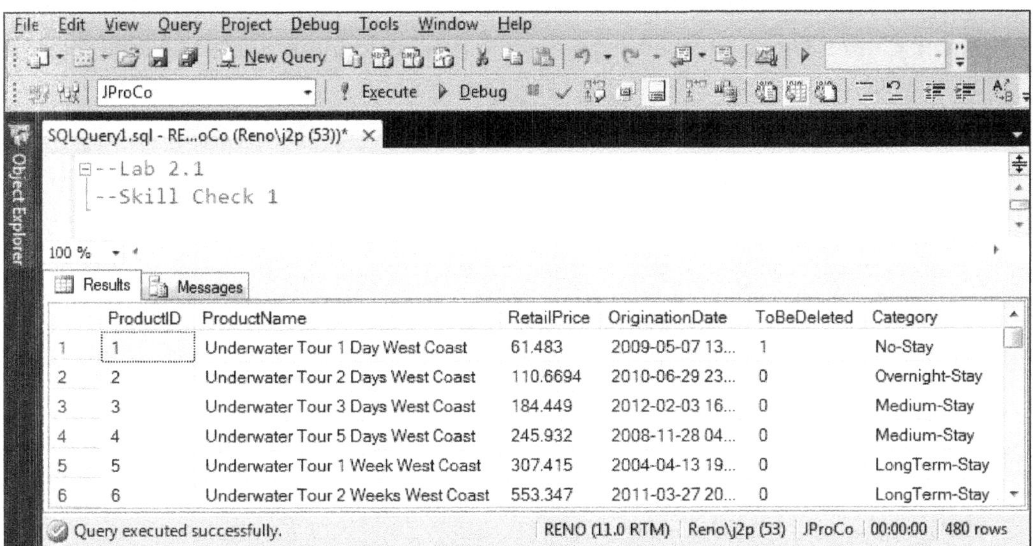

Figure 2.10 The Skill Check 1 query of the CurrentProducts table should produce 480 records.

Skill Check 2: In the JProCo database, write a query that shows all records and all fields from the [Grant] table. The result set should produce 10 records.

Skill Check 3: In the JProCo database, write a query that shows all records and all fields from the [Grant] table that have an amount of $21,000. The result set should produce two records.

Skill Check 4: Write a query that displays a result set for all records and fields from the Location table in the JProCo database that are located in the state of Washington. When done the results should resemble those shown in Figure 2.11.

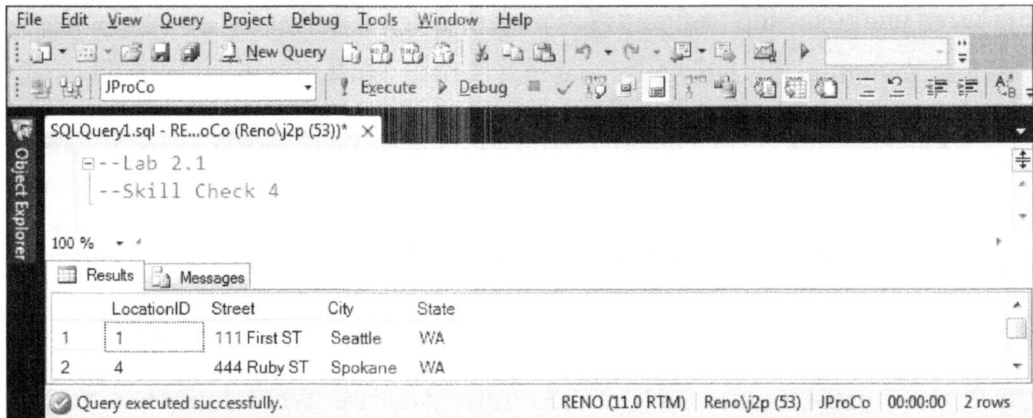

Figure 2.11 Skill Check 4 query shows two records with locations in Washington (WA).

Answer Code: The T-SQL code to this lab can be found in the downloadable files in a file named Lab2.1_SingleTableQueries.sql.

Points to Ponder - Single Table Queries

1. A query written in the SQL language is a request for information created from data stored in a table within a database.
2. Microsoft SQL Server uses the Transact Structured Query Language (T-SQL) standard for writing database queries.
3. Database context refers to which database to run the current query against.
4. The FROM clause tells SQL which table or tables contain searchable data.
5. When writing a SQL query, if a letter is missed, a punctuation mark forgotten, or a spelling error is made, SQL Server returns an error message.

Using Criteria

I remember a few years ago walking into a restaurant & bar at the airport during a long layover. The greeter at the entrance asked me, "Are you 21?" By this time I was in my early 40's. At first it seemed strange to set up a business only allowing people who are exactly 21 years old. What business would allow someone to eat only if they were exactly 21 years old? I looked around and saw many senior citizens and clearly there were people who were far older than 21 enjoying their meal. So, leaving my SQL Server brain behind, I immediately knew that she did not need my age to exactly match 21 years old she wanted it to be 21 or higher. So I answered, "Yes" to the question and was allowed into the restaurant.

Numeric Ranges

As we learned in the first section of this chapter, any query with a WHERE clause uses matching criteria to find the data we need. This is a great way to find all grants worth exactly $20,000 or people who are exactly 18 years old. When working with numbers we are often looking for some cutoff, like needing to be over 18 or any grant over $20,000.

Looking at the Grant table, we notice there are values for the Amount field as low as $4,750 and as high as $41,000 (Figure 2.12).

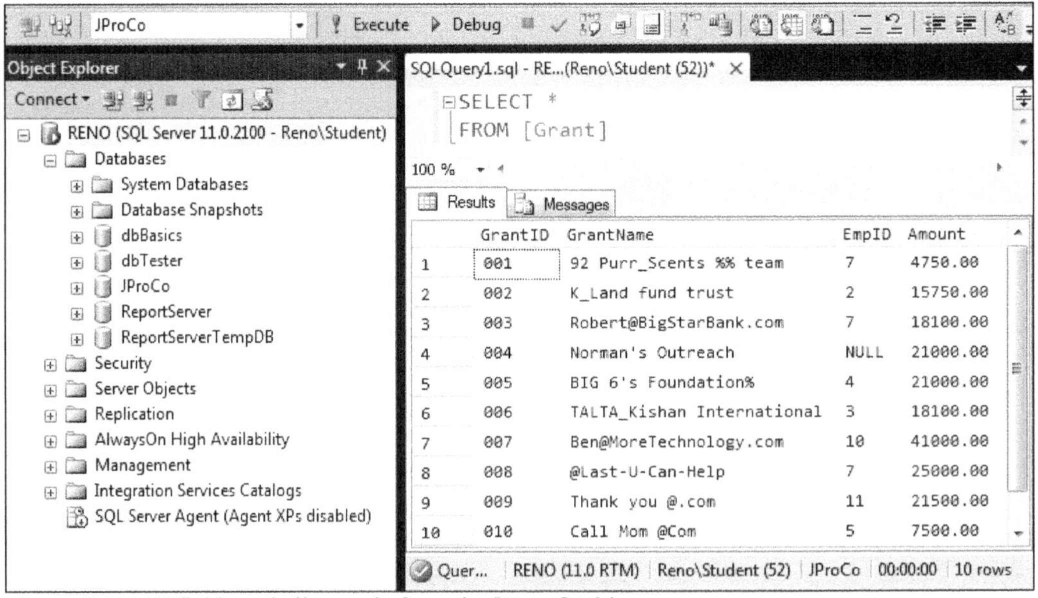

Figure 2.12 All fields and all records from the [Grant] table.

There are many values for grants over $20,000 in the Amount field. In the following query we use a 'greater than' operator to find values over 20000:

```
SELECT *
FROM [GRANT]
WHERE Amount > 20000
```

There are also multiple grants under $20,000 in the Amount field. The following query uses a 'less than' operator to find these values under 20000:

```
SELECT *
FROM [GRANT]
WHERE Amount < 20000
```

We need to be careful when looking for amounts over $21,000 (Figure 2.13), because we have some Amount values that are exactly $21,000. Using a greater than '>' operator will not include this amount, but a greater than or equal to '>=' operator will include the amount matching $21,000.

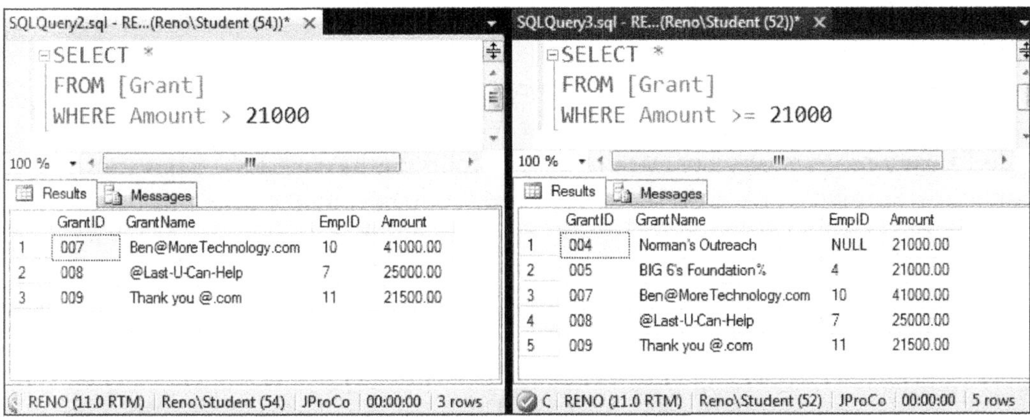

Figure 2.13 Result sets for 'greater than' vs. 'greater than or equal to' operators.

When someone asks us to pick a number between one and ten, what are valid answers? Zero would be out of range. How about an edge case answer of one? Is one between one and ten? Yes! When we use the word between in everyday life the numbers on the edge are considered inclusive. The same is true with the BETWEEN operator in SQL Server.

After the WHERE clause, we can place a BETWEEN operator with the AND operator to specify two numbers that define a range. When looking for values between 21000 and 30000 in the Amount field, we get four records in our result set as seen in Figure 2.14.

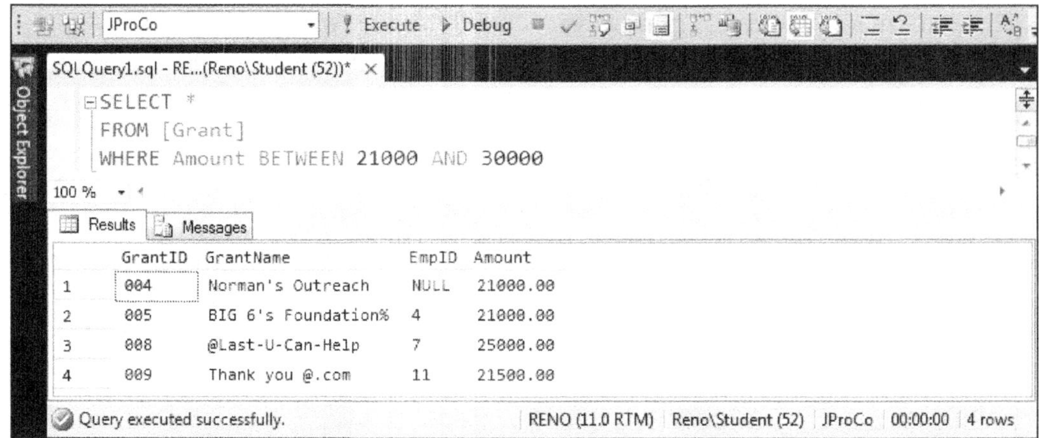

Figure 2.14 Using BETWEEN with AND to find a range of values.

Notice that two of the results are exactly 21000. Using a BETWEEN operator offers results that are inclusive of the numbers in the predicate.

Field Selection Lists

Since we rarely need to see all the records in a table we often use the WHERE clause to limit the result set to just what we are interested in seeing. We simply don't want more records to sift through than necessary and just want to see what matters. Similarly, it is also possible to see too many fields in a set of results. When this happens, we need a way to limit the number of columns returned in our result set.

So far all of our queries have used the asterisk * sign right after the SELECT clause. This is both handy and common for an initial look at the information in a table, or when building more complicated queries. The asterisk sign frees us from needing to know the names of the fields. One drawback to this method is all fields are returned in the query. Oftentimes we only want a few specific fields in our result set.

SQL Server allows tables with up to 1024 fields. That is a lot of information to try viewing at once and would require a great deal of scrolling. If we wanted to see only some of these fields, we can pick them individually. Simply itemize the field list in the SELECT clause. Of course, to accomplish this task we need to know the names of the available fields.

The Employee table of the JProCo database has seven fields (Figure 2.15). A few more fields and we would need to scroll right or left to view all the information.

```
SELECT *
FROM Employee
```

	EmpID	LastName	FirstName	HireDate	Locati...	ManagerID	Status
1	1	Adams	Alex	2001-01-01 00:00:00.000	1	11	NULL
2	2	Brown	Barry	2002-08-12 00:00:00.000	1	11	NULL
3	3	Osako	Lee	1999-09-01 00:00:00.000	2	11	NULL
4	4	Kennson	David	1996-03-16 00:00:00.000	1	11	Has Tenure
5	5	Bender	Eric	2007-05-17 00:00:00.000	1	11	NULL
6	6	Kendall	Lisa	2001-11-15 00:00:00.000	4	4	NULL
7	7	Lonning	David	2000-01-01 00:00:00.000	1	11	On Leave
8	8	Mars...	John	2001-11-15 00:00:00.000	NULL	4	NULL
9	9	Newton	James	2003-09-30 00:00:00.000	2	3	NULL
10	10	O'Haire	Terry	2004-10-04 00:00:00.000	2	3	NULL
11	11	Smith	Sally	1989-04-01 00:00:00.000	1	NULL	NULL
12	12	O'Neil	Barbara	1995-05-26 00:00:00.000	4	4	Has Tenure

Query executed successfully. RENO (11.0 RTM) Reno\Student (52) JProCo 00:00:00 12 rows

Figure 2.15 Using the SELECT * (asterisk) displays all fields in the table.

By listing the FirstName and LastName fields separated by a comma, we will only get two fields in our result set (Figure 2.16).

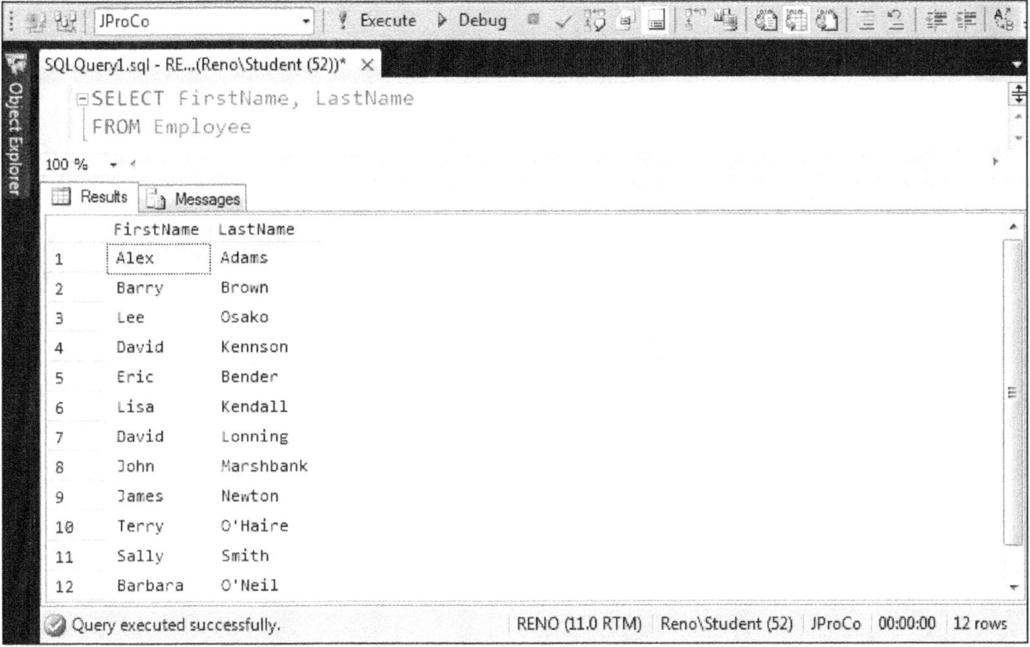

```
SELECT FirstName, LastName
FROM Employee
```

	FirstName	LastName
1	Alex	Adams
2	Barry	Brown
3	Lee	Osako
4	David	Kennson
5	Eric	Bender
6	Lisa	Kendall
7	David	Lonning
8	John	Marshbank
9	James	Newton
10	Terry	O'Haire
11	Sally	Smith
12	Barbara	O'Neil

Query executed successfully. RENO (11.0 RTM) Reno\Student (52) JProCo 00:00:00 12 rows

Figure 2.16 Choosing specific fields in the SELECT list to show FirstName and LastName only.

We now know that we can choose to display only the fields we wish to view by specifically listing them in the SELECT clause, separated by commas, one after the other. We can list one, many or all the fields available from any table listed in the FROM clause. Of course, it's easier to type '*' than to know and type out all those names separated by commas.

We can optionally use a two-part name of the field by listing the table identifier and then the field identifier separated by a '.' (symbol for a period). This requires extra typing, which we will learn how to avoid in Chapter 4.

Using two-part names for fields uses the syntax, *TableName.FieldName*. This means that Employee.FirstName and Employee.LastName (Figure 2.17) gives us the same results as specifying the FirstName and LastName fields (Figure 2.16).

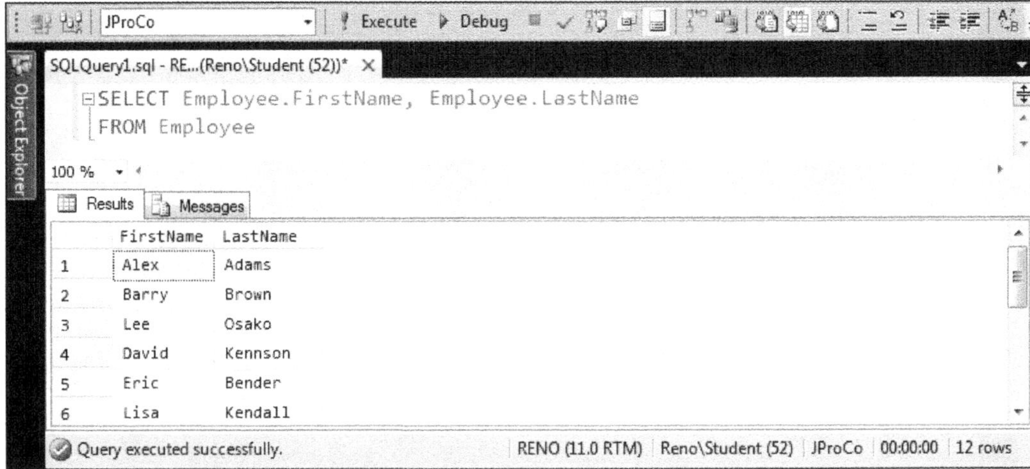

Figure 2.17 Field SELECT list using the two-part naming convention of *TableName.FieldName*.

Field names can clash with an existing keyword. For example, the Location table has a field named State. Placing the square bracket delimiters around the [State] field tells SQL Server we're referring to an object and not the keyword command. The following example demonstrates a query for the Street, City and State fields.

```
SELECT Street, City, [State]
FROM Location
```

Anatomy of a SQL Query

Remember that query keyword order must be followed in our SQL code. Here is the full breakdown for the anatomy of a basic query:

```
USE JProCo                       --Choose the database
GO                               --GO finishes the USE statement

SELECT FirstName, LastName --Choose the field(s)
FROM Employee                    --Choose the table(s)
WHERE FirstName = 'Lisa'         --Filter the result set
```

Lab 2.2: Using Criteria

Lab Prep: Each lab has one or more Skill Checks. Start with Skill Check 1 and proceed until reaching the Points to Ponder section.

Before beginning this lab, verify that SQL Server 2012 is properly installed and operating. Before running the lab setup script for resetting the database (SQLQueries2012Vol1Chapter2.2Setup.sql), please make sure to close all query windows within SSMS. An open query window pointing to a database context can lock that database preventing it from updating when the script is executing. A simple way to assure all query windows are closed, is to exit out of SSMS, then open a new instance of SSMS, and lastly run the setup script.

Skill Check 1: Write a query to show all records from the CurrentProducts table of the JProCo database with a retail price more than $1,100.00. When done, the result set should resemble Figure 2.18.

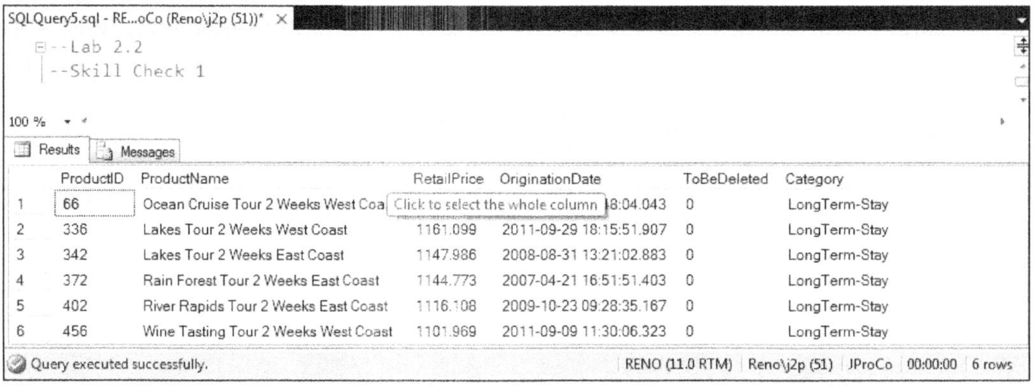

SQLQuery5.sql - RE...oCo (Reno\j2p (51))*

```
--Lab 2.2
--Skill Check 1
```

100 %

Results | Messages

	ProductID	ProductName	RetailPrice	OriginationDate	ToBeDeleted	Category
1	66	Ocean Cruise Tour 2 Weeks West Coa	Click to select the whole column	8:04.043	0	LongTerm-Stay
2	336	Lakes Tour 2 Weeks West Coast	1161.099	2011-09-29 18:15:51.907	0	LongTerm-Stay
3	342	Lakes Tour 2 Weeks East Coast	1147.986	2008-08-31 13:21:02.883	0	LongTerm-Stay
4	372	Rain Forest Tour 2 Weeks East Coast	1144.773	2007-04-21 16:51:51.403	0	LongTerm-Stay
5	402	River Rapids Tour 2 Weeks East Coast	1116.108	2009-10-23 09:28:35.167	0	LongTerm-Stay
6	456	Wine Tasting Tour 2 Weeks West Coast	1101.969	2011-09-09 11:30:06.323	0	LongTerm-Stay

Query executed successfully. | RENO (11.0 RTM) | Reno\j2p (51) | JProCo | 00:00:00 | 6 rows

Figure 2.18 Skill Check 1 query shows six records from the CurrentProducts table.

Skill Check 2: Write a query from the [Grant] table of the JProCo database with the following specifications:

- o Show all fields.
- o Show the four records that have an amount between 7,500 and 20,000.

When done, the result set should resemble Figure 2.19.

SQLQuery5.sql - RE...oCo (Reno\j2p (51))*

```
--Lab 2.2
--Skill Check 2
```

100 %

Results | Messages

	GrantID	GrantName	EmpID	Amount
1	002	K_Land fund trust	2	15750.00
2	003	Robert@BigStarBank.com	7	18100.00
3	006	TALTA_Kishan International	3	18100.00
4	010	Call Mom @Com	5	7500.00

Query executed successfully. | RENO (11.0 RTM) | Reno\j2p (51) | JProCo | 00:00:00 | 4 rows

Figure 2.19 Skill Check 2 returns four records for an Amount field range of 7500-20000.

Skill Check 3: Write a query from the Employee table of the JProCo database with the following specifications:

- o Show just the FirstName, LastName, and HireDate fields.
- o Show the three employee records having a first name of David or James.

When done, the result set should resemble Figure 2.20.

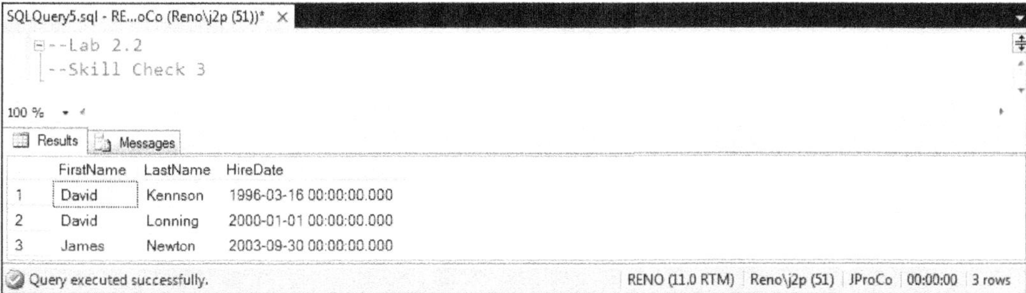

SQLQuery5.sql - RE...oCo (Reno\j2p (51))*

```
--Lab 2.2
--Skill Check 3
```

100 %

Results | Messages

	FirstName	LastName	HireDate
1	David	Kennson	1996-03-16 00:00:00.000
2	David	Lonning	2000-01-01 00:00:00.000
3	James	Newton	2003-09-30 00:00:00.000

Query executed successfully. | RENO (11.0 RTM) | Reno\j2p (51) | JProCo | 00:00:00 | 3 rows

Figure 2.20 Skill Check 3 shows the three records with a FirstName of David or James.

Skill Check 4: Write a query from the Employee table of the JProCo database with the following specifications:

- o Show all fields.
- o Show the two employee records with a status equal to 'Has Tenure'.

When done, the result set should resemble Figure 2.21.

SQLQuery5.sql - RE...oCo (Reno\j2p (51))* ×

```
--Lab 2.2
--Skill Check 4
```

100 %

Results | Messages

	EmpID	LastName	FirstName	HireDate	LocationID	ManagerID	Status
1	4	Kennson	David	1996-03-16 00:00:00.000	1	11	Has Tenure
2	12	O'Neil	Barbara	1995-05-26 00:00:00.000	4	4	Has Tenure

Query executed successfully. | RENO (11.0 RTM) | Reno\j2p (51) | JProCo | 00:00:00 | 2 rows

Figure 2.21 Your query in Skill Check 4 should show two records.

Answer Code: The T-SQL code to this lab can be found in the downloadable files in a file named Lab2.2_UsingCriteria.sql.

Points to Ponder - Using Criteria

1. Always maintain the following query keyword order: SELECT, FROM, and WHERE.
2. A SELECT clause with an '*' (asterisk) will choose all available fields.
3. To see only a subset of fields in a query, make sure to itemize each field name, separated by commas, after the SELECT clause.
4. The WHERE clause is handy for filtering records to only the information that is needed by the user.
5. The WHERE clause in a SELECT statement is optional. By omitting the WHERE clause, all records in a table are returned in the result set.
6. Changing the WHERE clause affects the records shown in the result set.
7. The WHERE keyword is followed by a logical expression. This logical expression is called a predicate.
8. Using the equal '=' sign finds exact matches to the criteria.

Pattern Matching

What do the names Brian and Bo have in common? They both start with the letter 'B'. Yes, there are other similarities, but let's go with the most obvious. Using the '=' operator with the letter 'B', wouldn't find either name. The query would look for the name 'B,' which is only one letter long and produces an empty result set. A query that searches for a partial match needs an approximate logical operator combined with something called a *wildcard* character to return a result set.

The operator that allows for an approximate predicate is ***LIKE***. The LIKE operator allows us to perform special relative searches to filter the result set.

To find everyone with a FirstName beginning with the letter 'B', we will need to predicate on the letter 'B' followed by a wildcard character, which allows for any number of characters to follow it. For example: WHERE FirstName LIKE 'B%' is the proper format for finding all FirstName fields with a value (name) beginning with the letter 'B' (Figure 2.22).

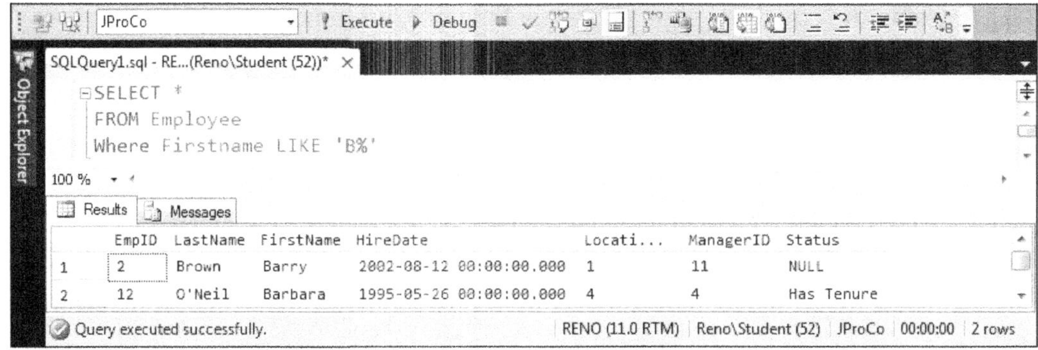

Figure 2.22 Using LIKE allows for a wildcard in your predicate.

Reader Note: *SQL Server does not care if the FirstName value (name) is Barry or barry, as it is case insensitive by default (unless this setting has been intentionally changed). This means that SQL Server merely looks at the letters themselves, not which case they are, to determine if there is a match in the predicate. EXAMPLE: Predicating on a FirstName using these spellings, 'Barry', 'BARRY', 'barry', 'baRRy', 'barrY' will all return the same results.*

The % wildcard character represents any number of characters of any length. Let's find all first names that end in the letter 'A'. By using the percentage '%' sign with the letter 'A', we achieve this goal using the code sample below:

```
SELECT *
FROM Employee
WHERE FirstName LIKE '%A'
```

Lisa and Barbara both end in the letter 'A'. In this example, a capital letter 'A' was used and it found all FirstName records ending in 'A', even if the letter was in lower case.

Lisa has three characters before the ending letter 'A' while Barbara has six. The '%' wildcard can mean one character, three, nine or even zero characters. If the FirstName value is the letter 'A', then it would also appear in this result set.

The next goal is to find records with FirstName values where the letter 'A' is the second letter. We want exactly one character of any type followed by an 'A', then any number of letters afterwards. The wildcard sign representing exactly one character is the underscore '_' sign.

Writing a query searching for one character before the letter 'A', and any amount of characters afterward will find David, James and several others (Figure 2.23). The '%' sign wildcard can represent many characters while the '_' sign wildcard always represents exactly one character.

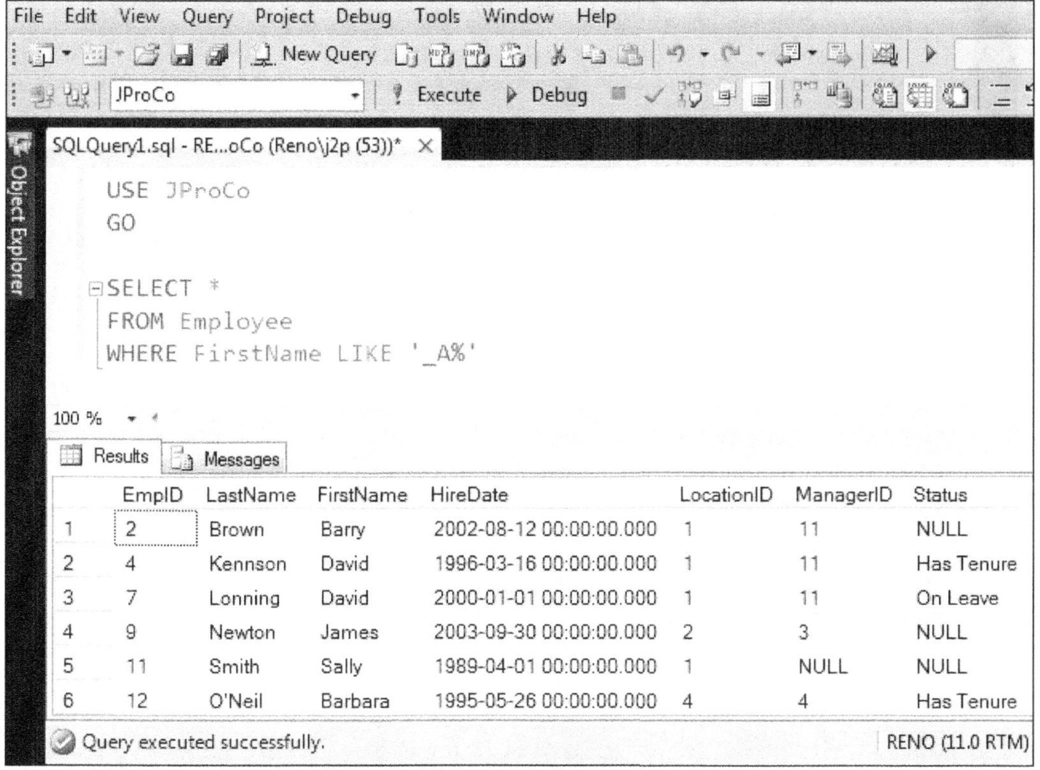

Figure 2.23 The underscore wildcard will find exactly one character.

Querying Pattern Ranges

To find all FirstName values beginning with the letters 'A' or 'B' we can use two predicates in our WHERE clause, by separating them with the *OR* statement.

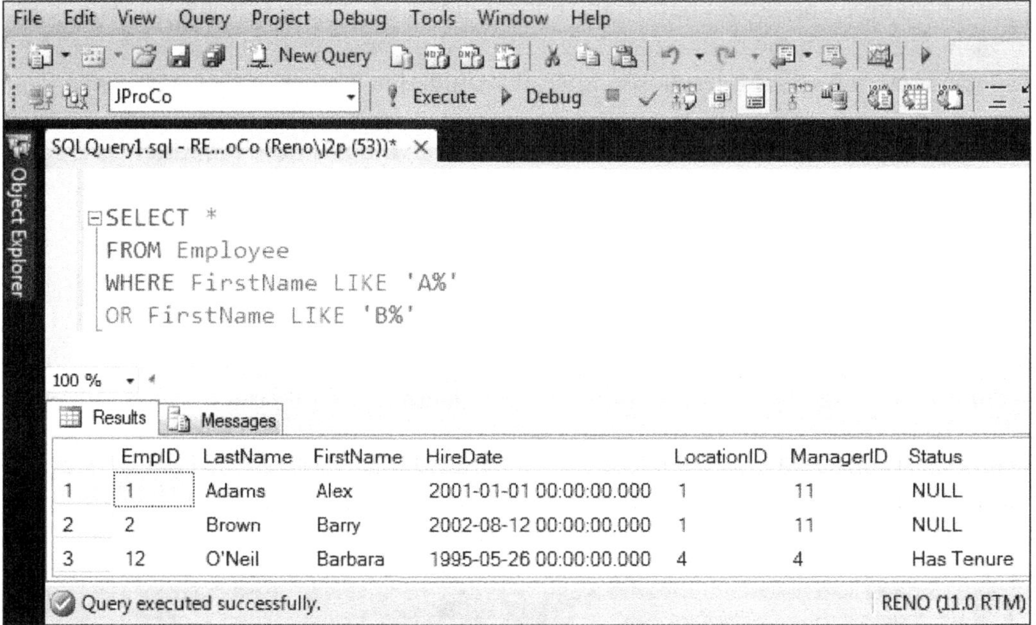

	EmpID	LastName	FirstName	HireDate	LocationID	ManagerID	Status
1	1	Adams	Alex	2001-01-01 00:00:00.000	1	11	NULL
2	2	Brown	Barry	2002-08-12 00:00:00.000	1	11	NULL
3	12	O'Neil	Barbara	1995-05-26 00:00:00.000	4	4	Has Tenure

Figure 2.24 Using the OR operator to find FirstName values starting with letters A or B.

Finding names beginning with an 'A' or 'B' is easy and this works fine until we want a larger range of letters as in the example below for 'A' thru 'K':

```
SELECT *
FROM Employee
WHERE FirstName Like 'A%'
OR FirstName Like 'B%'
OR FirstName Like 'C%'
OR FirstName Like 'D%'
OR FirstName Like 'E%'
OR FirstName Like 'F%'
OR FirstName Like 'G%'
OR FirstName Like 'H%'
OR FirstName Like 'I%'
OR FirstName Like 'J%'
OR FirstName Like 'K%'
```

The previous query does find FirstName values beginning with the letters 'A' thru 'K'. However, when a query requires a large range of letters, the LIKE operator has an even better option. Since the first letter of the FirstName field can be 'A', 'B', 'C', 'D', 'E', 'F', 'G', 'H', 'I', 'J' or 'K', simply list all these choices inside a set of square brackets followed by the '%' wildcard, as in the example below:

```
SELECT *
FROM Employee
WHERE FirstName Like '[ABCDEFGHIJK]%'
```

A more elegant example of this technique recognizes that all these letters are in a continuous range, so we really only need to list the first and last letter of the range inside the square brackets, followed by the '%' wildcard allowing for any number of characters after the first letter in the range (Figure 2.25).

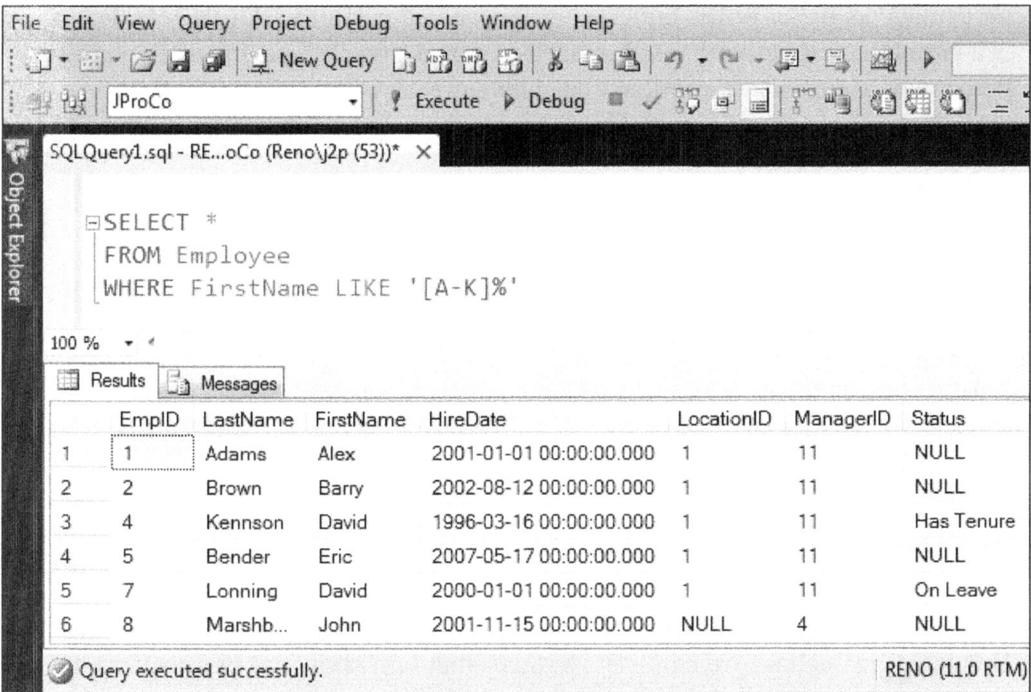

	EmpID	LastName	FirstName	HireDate	LocationID	ManagerID	Status
1	1	Adams	Alex	2001-01-01 00:00:00.000	1	11	NULL
2	2	Brown	Barry	2002-08-12 00:00:00.000	1	11	NULL
3	4	Kennson	David	1996-03-16 00:00:00.000	1	11	Has Tenure
4	5	Bender	Eric	2007-05-17 00:00:00.000	1	11	NULL
5	7	Lonning	David	2000-01-01 00:00:00.000	1	11	On Leave
6	8	Marshb...	John	2001-11-15 00:00:00.000	NULL	4	NULL

Figure 2.25 Using square brackets with LIKE to find FirstName values in the range from A-K.

Reader Note: *A predicate that uses a range will not work with the '=' operator (equals sign). It will neither raise an error, nor produce a result set.*

```
--Bad query (will not error or return any records)
SELECT *
FROM Employee
WHERE FirstName = '[A-K]%'
```

We have now discovered that a range of characters can be found using LIKE accompanied with the appropriate characters inside square brackets. The '%' wildcard is used when working with a string pattern and must be enclosed in single quotes. Simply place the starting letter followed by a hyphen and then the ending letter of the range inside a set of brackets and single quotes followed by the '%' wildcard (Figure 2.25).

Notice that Alex is in this result set. This is because 'A' is considered to be in the [a-k] range. The same logic applies to John. There is a similar trick we can use when working with a range of numbers.

Querying Special Characters

We learned about two special characters earlier called wildcards. When using the percentage sign '%' or the underscore '_' we can perform relative searches. There is a GrantName field with a value of '92 Purr_Scents %% team' which has two percentage signs as part of the name. There are also other values in the GrantName field containing the percentage sign.

How do we search for a percentage sign? Do we simply place a wildcard '%' on either side of it? No. SQL Server will interpret this as a request to search for three wildcards and return all records as seen in the query below:

```
--Bad pattern logic (finds all records)
SELECT *
FROM [GRANT]
WHERE GrantName LIKE '%%%'
```

So, we need a method of identifying a literal percentage sign as being different from a wildcard '%' sign. Help is on the way again with the square bracket! In this case, we place the literal percentage sign inside the square brackets and then surround the square brackets with the '%' wildcards on either side.

By using this method we can write a query that will show the two records having a percentage sign within the GrantName field (Figure 2.26). In this example, the square brackets tell SQL Server to interpret the '%' sign inside of them as a literal percentage sign and not a wildcard character.

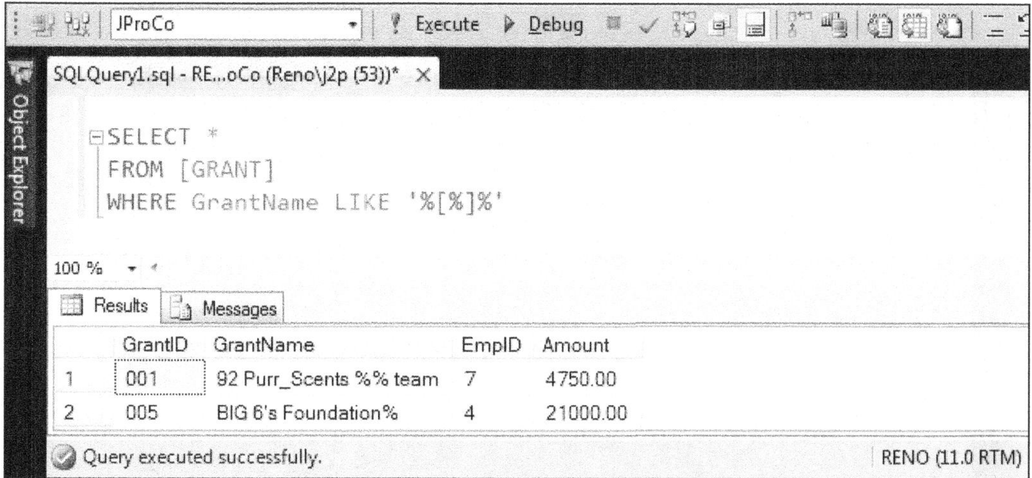

Figure 2.26 Finding a literal '%' sign in a relative search predicate.

There is a GrantName with a value of 'K_Land fund trust' containing an actual underscore in the name. There are other grants with underscores as well. How do we search for an underscore sign? Do we simply place the '%' wildcard on each side? No. SQL Server will interpret this as a request to search for all records with one or more characters in the GrantName field, as seen in the following query:

```
--Bad pattern logic (finds all records
--with one or more characters)
SELECT *
FROM [GRANT]
WHERE GrantName LIKE '%_%'
```

So, we have three special characters ('%' and '_') in the predicate without a single literal underscore sign. Once again, square brackets are to the rescue! We need to place the literal underscore inside a set of square brackets, and then surround the brackets by a '%' wildcard on either side.

By running the query shown in Figure 2.27, we can see the three records in the [Grant] table that have an underscore somewhere in the GrantName field. This example instructs SQL Server that the underscore sign inside the square brackets is a literal underscore and not a '_' wildcard character.

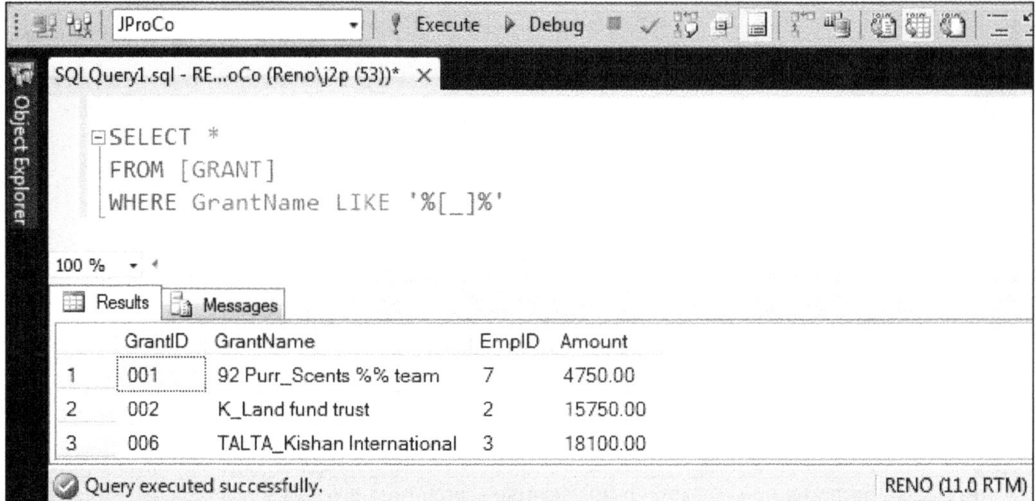

Figure 2.27 Finding a literal _ sign using a relative search predicate.

What if we want to find values that have an apostrophe (single quote sign) in the GrantName fields, such as 'Norman's Outreach'? Everything inside single quotes after the LIKE operator evaluates every record and returns a result set.

Remember that words or characters in SQL Server must be enclosed within a ***pair*** of single quotes. In this example, the first single quote marks the beginning of a string and the next single quote marks the end of a string. Everything between these single quotes is part of the search string. Everything before the first single quote and after the second single quote is not part of the search string. So a pair of single quote marks, act as delimiters for the string pattern we are searching for.

This presents a new challenge. The following query will produce a syntax error.

```
--Bad query syntax results in an error.
SELECT *
FROM [GRANT]
WHERE GrantName LIKE '%'%'
```

The problem lies in the fact that SQL Server follows the rule that any predicate based on a string is completed after the second single quote is found. In other words, SQL Server interprets any character after the second single quote as an error in the code it is trying to execute. Thus, our intentions with this code are either lost or misunderstood in the translation from human to computer.

To have SQL Server interpret a predicate searching for a literal single quote, we need to precede it with another single quote, as shown in Figure 2.28.

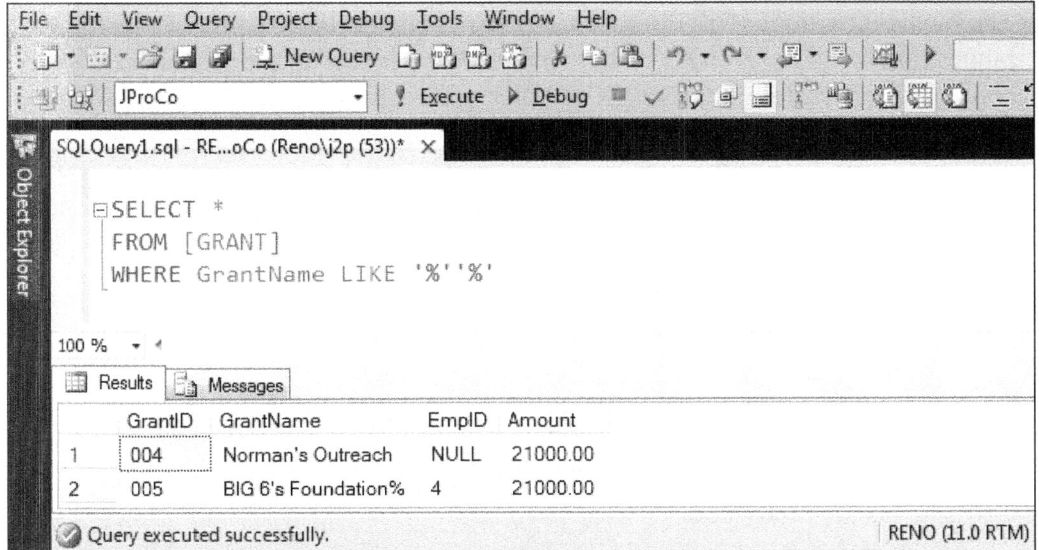

	GrantID	GrantName	EmpID	Amount
1	004	Norman's Outreach	NULL	21000.00
2	005	BIG 6's Foundation%	4	21000.00

Figure 2.28 Two single quotes enclosed by '%' filters a result set for an apostrophe.

We now have two records with a single quote in the result set. To view all names without a single quote (apostrophe) we simply change the LIKE operator to a NOT LIKE operator in the WHERE clause.

Square Bracket Exclusions

So far, all of our pattern matching queries have searched for an item based either on what it is like or not like. For example: Finding all the names starting with the letter 'O', would use LIKE 'O%' for the predicate. Finding all names that do not start with the letter 'O', would use NOT LIKE 'O%' for the predicate to return the proper result set.

What if we wanted to find every name with a first letter beginning with an 'O', and the second letter cannot be an 'S'. In other words, the search results would not contain any names like Osborn or Osmond, although it would contain the name Olsen. To accomplish this, we would want to use code like the sample shown here:

```
--First letter is 'O' and the second letter is not 'S'
SELECT *
FROM Employee
WHERE LastName LIKE 'O[^S]%'
```

The carrot sign '^' instructs SQL Server to ignore values that match this pattern. We can use this feature with a range of values as well.

The next code sample will eliminate any name where the second letter is in the range from 'A' thru 'Z'. Okay, that covers all the letters in the alphabet. What could possibly be left in the result set after ignoring the entire alphabet as the second character in the LastName field? Let's run the code shown here and find out what records are shown for this query.

```
--First letter is O and second letter is not A-Z
SELECT *
FROM Employee
WHERE LastName LIKE 'O[^A-Z]%'
```

Aha! We can find names with special characters immediately after the first letter in a LastName. So, any names like O'Neil, O'Dowd, or O'Shannon are perfectly acceptable results in this query, as the second character is not a letter from 'A' thru 'Z'. That is pretty cool!

Lab 2.3: Pattern Matching

Lab Prep: Each lab has one or more Skill Checks. Start with Skill Check 1 and proceed until reaching the Points to Ponder section.

Before beginning this lab, verify that SQL Server 2012 is properly installed and operating. Before running the lab setup script for resetting the database (SQLQueries2012Vol1Chapter2.3Setup.sql), please make sure to close all query windows within SSMS. An open query window pointing to a database context can lock that database preventing it from updating when the script is executing. A simple way to assure all query windows are closed, is to exit out of SSMS, then open a new instance of SSMS, and lastly run the setup script.

Skill Check 1: In the JProCo context, write a query that displays all records and fields from the CurrentProducts table that have the letter 'X' somewhere in the ProductName field. When done, the results should resemble Figure 2.29.

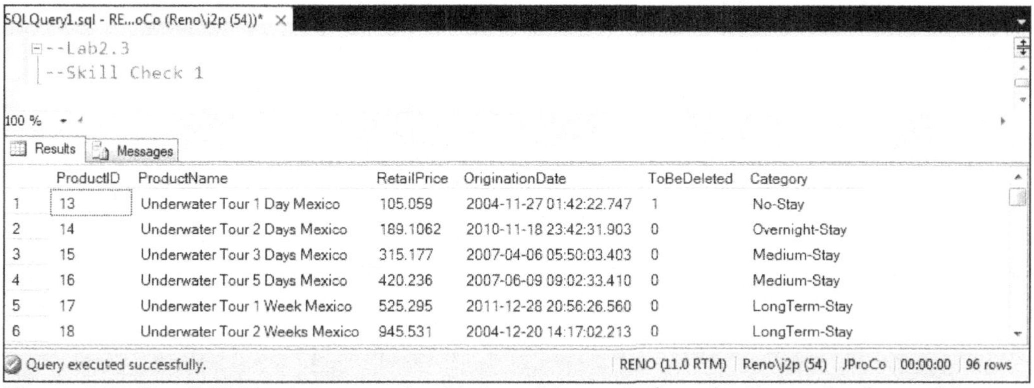

SQLQuery1.sql - RE...oCo (Reno\j2p (54))*

```
--Lab2.3
--Skill Check 1
```

100 %

Results | Messages

	ProductID	ProductName	RetailPrice	OriginationDate	ToBeDeleted	Category
1	13	Underwater Tour 1 Day Mexico	105.059	2004-11-27 01:42:22.747	1	No-Stay
2	14	Underwater Tour 2 Days Mexico	189.1062	2010-11-18 23:42:31.903	0	Overnight-Stay
3	15	Underwater Tour 3 Days Mexico	315.177	2007-04-06 05:50:03.403	0	Medium-Stay
4	16	Underwater Tour 5 Days Mexico	420.236	2007-06-09 09:02:33.410	0	Medium-Stay
5	17	Underwater Tour 1 Week Mexico	525.295	2011-12-28 20:56:26.560	0	LongTerm-Stay
6	18	Underwater Tour 2 Weeks Mexico	945.531	2004-12-20 14:17:02.213	0	LongTerm-Stay

Query executed successfully. | RENO (11.0 RTM) | Reno\j2p (54) | JProCo | 00:00:00 | 96 rows

Figure 2.29 The Skill Check 1 query should show 96 records from the CurrentProducts table.

Skill Check 2: Write a query from the CurrentProducts table of the JProCo database with the following specifications:

- o Show only the ProductName, RetailPrice and Category fields.
- o Show the records where the first letter of the ProductName starts with the letters 'A' thru 'C'.

When done, the results should resemble Figure 2.30.

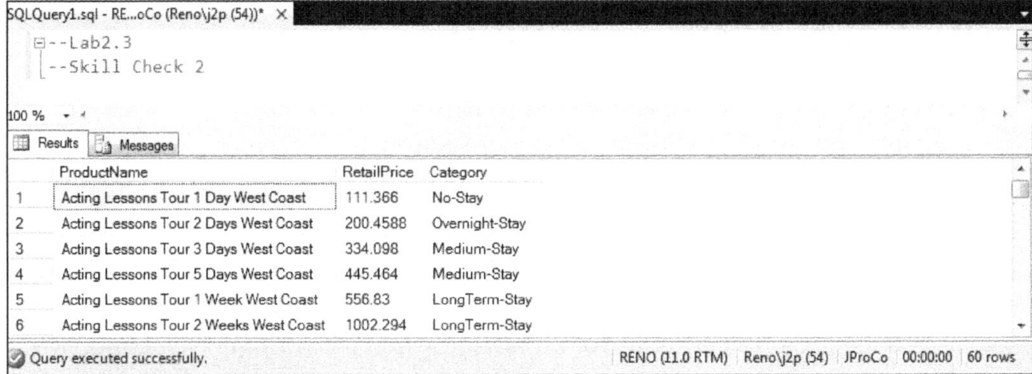

Figure 2.30 Skill Check 2 query results should show 60 records.

Skill Check 3: Write a query from the [Grant] table of the JProCo database with the following specifications:

- Show all fields.
- Show the three records that have an underscore in their grant names.

When done, the results should resemble Figure 2.31.

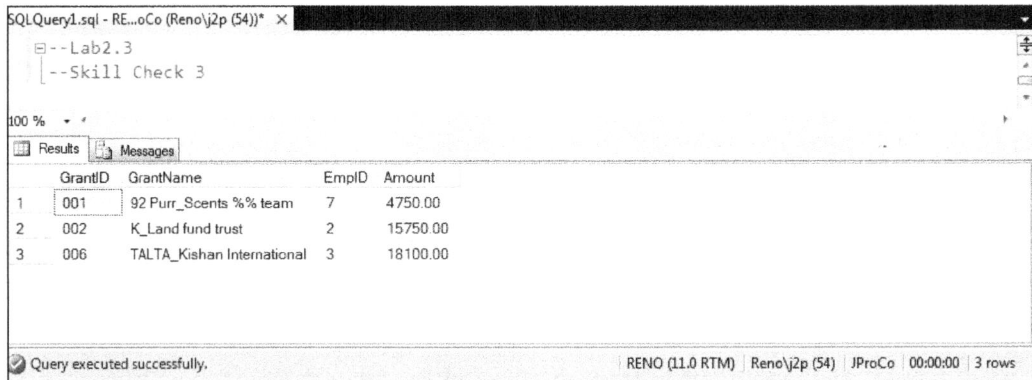

Figure 2.31 Skill Check 3 query results should show three records.

Skill Check 4: Write a query from the [Grant] table of the JProCo database with the following specifications:

- Show all fields.
- Show the two grant records that have the character 'O' as the second letter in the GrantName field.

When done, the screen should resemble Figure 2.32.

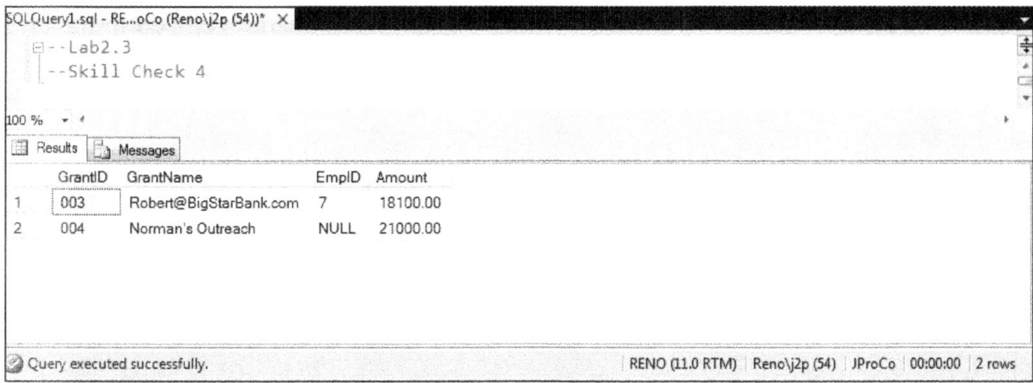

	GrantID	GrantName	EmpID	Amount
1	003	Robert@BigStarBank.com	7	18100.00
2	004	Norman's Outreach	NULL	21000.00

Figure 2.32 Skill Check 4 query should show two records.

Skill Check 5: Imagine we have been asked to create a result set from the JProCo database, where we must create a record set showing all grants that were funded by someone with a valid .com email address. To succeed, we will need to use wildcards with the following information:

- Look for the '@' sign somewhere in the name.
- The e-mail address name should end in .com
- Make sure at least one character exists before the '@' sign.
- Make sure at least one character exists between the '@' and the .com
- Ensure there are no spaces in the GrantName.

When done, the results should resemble Figure 2.33.

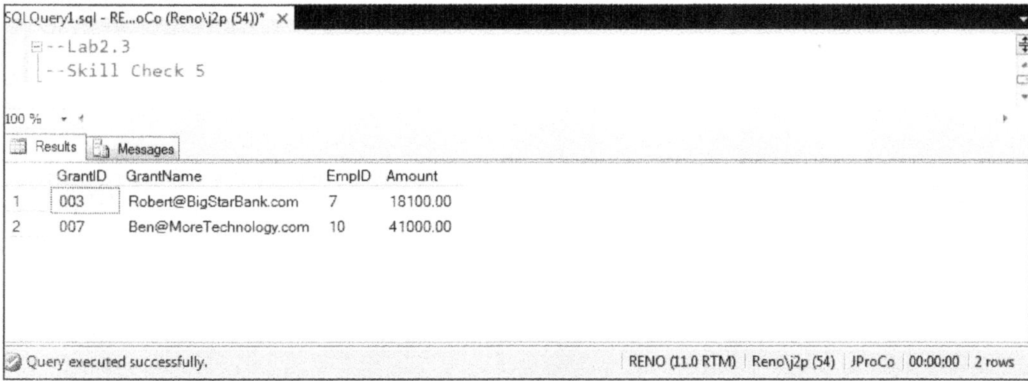

	GrantID	GrantName	EmpID	Amount
1	003	Robert@BigStarBank.com	7	18100.00
2	007	Ben@MoreTechnology.com	10	41000.00

Figure 2.33 The results for Skill Check 5 should show two records.

Skill Check 6: Show all employees whose LastName does not start with the letter 'O' and has the letter 'A' somewhere after the first letter. Only display the FirstName and LastName fields. To succeed, use wildcards with the following information:

- The first letter of the LastName cannot be an 'O'.
- The LastName must have the letter 'A' appearing after the first letter.
- Show only the FirstName and LastName fields.

	FirstName	LastName
1	Alex	Adams
2	Lisa	Kendall
3	John	Marshbank

Figure 2.34 Skill Check 6 results show 3 records.

Answer Code: The T-SQL code to this lab can be found in the downloadable file named Lab2.3_PatternMatching.sql.

Points to Ponder - Pattern Matching

1. Wildcard characters such as '%' and '_' can be used in a WHERE clause.
2. The '%' (percent sign) is the most common wildcard. This sign represents any number of characters. For example, **WHERE FirstName LIKE '%N'** would find a name that ends in 'N' regardless of how long the name is. Examples may include Ann, MaryAnn and Dean among others.
3. The '%' sign can even represent zero characters. For example, **'%A%'** would find Alex and Lisa.
4. The SQL Server operator, LIKE can be used to return a range of names, such as those beginning with a letter ranging from 'A' thru 'M'. For example, **WHERE FirstName LIKE '[a-m]%'**
5. To exclude a value from a pattern match search, use the '^' (carrot sign) in square brackets followed by the value or values to be omitted. For example, **LIKE '[^O]%'** gets all names not starting with the letter 'O'.
6. To have SQL Server interpret '%' as a literal percentage sign and not as a wildcard, place the literal percentage sign inside square brackets and surround the square brackets on either side with the wildcard '%'. For example, **LastName LIKE '%[%]%'.** This technique can be used to search for names that include these special signs like the password R%per!est and all other names with a percent sign in them.

Chapter Glossary

BETWEEN Operator: An operator used in SQL selects a range of data between two values.

Clause: A type of keyword used for a query. SELECT is both a clause and a keyword.

Database Context: Refers to which database you are running the current query against.

Delimiter: A character which separates one object or entity from another.

Filter: A clause that limits the records in your query results.

FROM: A keyword which chooses the table you're querying for the information.

IN: An operator used to enumerate a set of exact matches in your query.

Keyword: A word built into the SQL language.

LIKE: An operator that allows a relative search to filter a result set for a specified pattern in a column.

Operator: Words or signs used by SQL to make calculations or evaluations. Some commonly used operators are AND, OR, '<', '>' and '='.

Predicate: A logical statement used to evaluate to TRUE, FALSE, or UNKNOWN for each record.

SELECT: A SQL command used to choose which fields to return in a result set.

WHERE (clause): The most common optional keyword used to filter result sets.

Wildcard: Special characters that are used in conjunction with the LIKE keyword to match patterns for a result set.

Review Quiz - Chapter Two

1.) Which SQL clause helps you to limit the number of records you see in a query from a single table?

O a. FROM

O b. WHERE

O c. IF

O d. SELECT

2.) Which wildcard usage will help you find all last names starting with R?

O a. WHERE LastName = 'R%'

O b. WHERE LastName = '%R'

O c. WHERE LastName LIKE 'R%'

O d. WHERE LastName LIKE '%R'

3.) The SELECT clause in a query on a single table is…

O a. Optional

O b. Required

4.) Which keyword filters or reduces the number of fields in your query?

O a. ON

O b. WHERE

O c. IF

O d. SELECT

5.) What comes right after the SELECT clause?

O a. The predicate

O b. The list of fields

O c. The list of records

6.) What comes right after the FROM clause?

O a. The predicate

O b. The list of fields

O c. The list of records

O d. The table or tables

O e. The data type

7.) You want to find all first names that start with the letters A-M in your Customer table. Which SQL code would you use?

O a.
```
SELECT * FROM Customer
WHERE FirstName <= 'm%'
```
O b.
```
SELECT * FROM Customer
WHERE FirstName  = 'a-m%'
```
O c.
```
SELECT * FROM Customer
WHERE FirstName LIKE 'a-m%'
```
O d.
```
SELECT * FROM Customer
WHERE FirstName  = '[a-m]%'
```
O e.
```
SELECT * FROM Customer
WHERE FirstName LIKE '[a-m]%'
```

8.) What comes right after the WHERE clause?

O a. The predicate
O b. The list of fields
O c. The list of records
O d. The table or tables
O e. The data type

9.) You want to find all scores for contestants who scored in the range of 20-30 points. Which SQL code would you use?

O a.
```
SELECT * FROM contestant
WHERE score BETWEEN 20 OR 30
```
O b.
```
SELECT * FROM contestant
WHERE score BETWEEN 20 AND 30
```
O c.
```
SELECT * FROM contestant
WHERE score IS BETWEEN 20 AND 30
```
O d.
```
SELECT * FROM contestant
WHERE score MIDDLE RANGE (20,30)
```

10.) You want to find all first names that have the letter A as the second letter and do not end with the letter Y. Which SQL code would you use?

O a.
```
SELECT * FROM Employee
WHERE FirstName LIKE '_A% ' AND FirstName NOT LIKE 'Y%'
```
O b.
```
SELECT * FROM Employee
WHERE FirstName LIKE '_A% ' AND FirstName NOT LIKE '%Y'
```
O c.
```
SELECT * FROM Employee
WHERE FirstName LIKE 'A_% ' AND FirstName NOT LIKE 'Y%'
```

11.) You work for a commercial certificate authority (CA) to track safe internet business. You have a table named ApprovedWebSites. Some are 'ftp://' sites and some are 'http://' sites. You want to find all approved '.org' sites listed in the URLName field of the ApprovedWebSites table. All URL names will have the '://' with at least one character before them. All sites will have at least one character after the '://' and before the '.org' at the end. What code will give you all '.org' records?

O a.
```
SELECT * FROM ApprovedWebSites
WHERE URLName LIKE '%://%[.org]'
```
O b.
```
SELECT * FROM ApprovedWebSites
WHERE URLName LIKE '_%org'
```
O c.
```
SELECT * FROM ApprovedWebSites
WHERE URLName LIKE '%://%.org'
```
O d.
```
SELECT * FROM ApprovedWebSites
WHERE URLName LIKE '_%://_%.org'
```

Answer Key

1.) The FROM clause lists the table or tables you are using but does not limit its records so (a) is incorrect. The IF keyword is used for finding running conditions and not inside of queries (see Chapter 5), therefore (c) is also incorrect. SELECT limits the number of fields (not records) returned so it's not (d). The WHERE clause creates criteria and limits the records in your result set so (b) is the right answer.

2.) The = sign does not use wildcards so both (a) and (b) are incorrect. Putting the % before the 'R' would give you a name ending in R, so (d) is also incorrect. R% means a string where the first character is 'R' followed by any number of characters (even zero) so (c) would be the correct answer.

3.) Because every query starts with SELECT, it is not an optional word; therefore (a) is incorrect. Given that all queries start with SELECT, it must be required; making (b) the correct answer.

4.) ON is used to define the criteria for joining two tables (see Chapter 3), so (a) is incorrect. The WHERE clause creates criteria that limits the *records* in your result set so (b) is also wrong. The IF keyword is used for finding running conditions and not inside of queries (see Chapter 5), therefore (c) is also incorrect. Since you list the specific fields you would like displayed in your result immediately following the SELECT keyword, it is limiting the number of fields returned so (d) is the correct answer here.

5.) 'The predicate' is the equation following the WHERE keyword which defines criteria for filtering records so (a) is wrong. 'The list of records' makes up our result set which is usually displayed on screen thus making (c) wrong too. The correct answer is (b) since the SELECT keyword filters the number of fields.

6.) 'The predicate' is the equation following the WHERE keyword which defines criteria for filtering records so (a) is wrong. The SELECT keyword is followed by 'The list of fields' which makes (b) wrong too. 'The list of records' makes up our result set which is usually displayed on screen thus making (c) wrong too. 'The data type' is used when defining fields while creating tables so (e) is also incorrect. FROM lists 'the table or tables' you are using making (d) the correct answer.

7.) Wildcards (%) only work with the LIKE keyword so (a), (b) and (d) are all incorrect. LIKE 'a-m%' would only match strings where the first three characters are 'a-m' so (c) is also wrong. The correct answer is (e) because the predicate uses the LIKE keyword and ends in %, meaning zero or more characters following the first character, which has its range defined correctly with [a-m].

8.) 'The list of fields' follows the SELECT keyword so (b) is incorrect. 'The list of records' makes up our result set making (c) wrong too. 'The table or tables' follows the FROM clause to determine which tables to look in so (d) is also incorrect. 'The data type' is used when defining fields while creating tables so (e) is also incorrect. 'The predicate' is the equation immediately following the WHERE keyword which defines criteria for filtering records so (a) is correct.

9.) BETWEEN uses the AND operator so (a) is incorrect because it used the OR operator. The IS operator is not used with the BETWEEN operator so (c) is also incorrect. There is no such operator as MIDDLE RANGE so (d) is wrong too. The BETWEEN operator requires the AND operator but does not need the IS operator so (b) is correct.

10.) When pattern matching, the use of NOT LIKE 'Y%' only ensures that the first character in the string is not 'Y' so it does not check to see what the string ends in so (a) and (c) are both wrong. The use of LIKE '_A%' will match strings with any character in the first position followed by 'A' followed by zero or more characters; the use of NOT LIKE '%Y' ensures that the last character in the string is not 'Y' so (b) is correct.

11.) The wildcard '%' can match zero characters so (a) is wrong because it would match a string starting with '://'. The pattern we need to match must include '://' and (b) doesn't include this so it is wrong too. The wildcard '%' can match zero characters so (c) is wrong because it would also match a string starting with '://'. The two wildcards '_' and '%' used side by side ensure that a pattern contains at least one character immediately followed by zero or more characters; therefore (d) is the correct answer.

Bug Catcher Game

To play the Bug Catcher game, run the BugCatcher_Chapter2.pps from the BugCatcher folder of the companion files. You can obtain these files from the www.Joes2Pros.com web site.

[NOTES]

Chapter 3. Viewing Combined Information

We have all probably had a situation where someone asks, "Can you look this up for me?" Maybe we were given a person's name, but not their phone number. When we only have part of the information, but need more related information, we are effectively joining data together from different sources. When joining data we are putting the information into one viewable location. The data may even physically reside in a separate area. For example, the phone number is still in the phone book even after we write it down on a memo pad. Joining data leaves the original data where it started, but shows us all the information together as one consolidated report. This chapter explores how to select data from two related tables into one result set.

As a SQL Developer, it is common to use two or more tables in a single query. No matter how many tables are in a query, it will appear as one result set. Joining tables is one of the most common ways to turn separated data into consolidated information for reports. In this chapter we will learn how to discern relationships between tables and queries and place them into a single report.

READER NOTE: *Please run the SQLQueries2012Vol1Chapter3.0Setup.sql script in order to follow along with the examples in the first section of Chapter 3. All scripts mentioned in this chapter may be found at www.Joes2Pros.com.*

Database Complexity

There are two types of database complexity. The first type is a flat file database, which is a single list that does not relate to any other list. A flat file database cannot go beyond a single table of data.

The second type is called a relational database. If we had a list of students from school and wanted to keep track of their parents and legal guardians, we might need to add a second list. These lists are related to one another. This allows the school administration to look up a student's parental information when needed. Tables that relate to one another and reside in one managing system are part of a relational database.

Recall from the Geek Speak section of Chapter One, that lists are called tables in SQL Server. This is a benefit to us, because SQL Server thrives on allowing us to query one table, or look at a result set having relationships between several tables.

Relational Data

When was the last time we received a vague answer to a question? For most of us, it happens every day. Let's say we asked someone where they worked. We are anticipating a response that may include a city name or address, except the answer we actually get is, "I work at headquarters". While this is an accurate answer, it is not the detailed answer we wanted to know.

After detecting a slight New England accent from James Newton, we decide to look him up in the Employee table and discover that he works at LocationID 2. In what City or State is this mysterious LocationID 2 located? A quick query of the Location table shows us the following data (Figure 3.1).

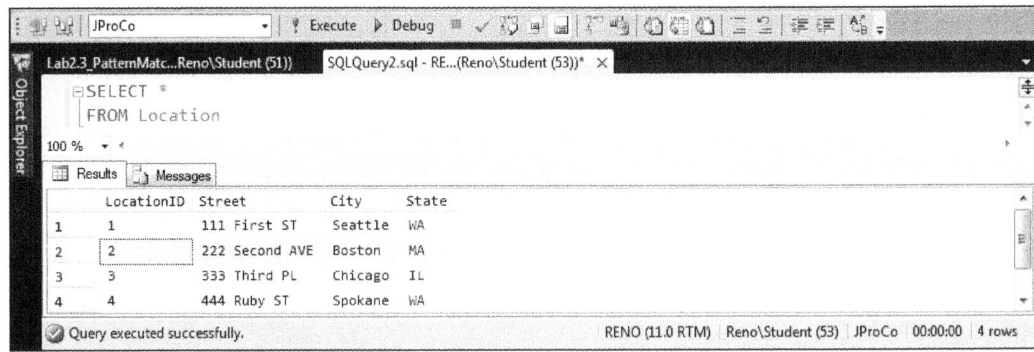

Figure 3.1 All records and fields from the Location table of JProCo.

Now, each time we see an employee listed for LocationID 2 we know the Street, City and State information for where they work. Why not just store this City, State, and Street information in the Employee table? In fact, why not put all of our data in one giant table so we only have one place to go to get our information? That is a common interview question about database design, so let's review a few database design best practices to add to our interviewing arsenal.

One reason is a lot of space in memory is saved by not replicating all three data items for each employee in a table. Another reason for having location fields only in the Location table is that it saves us time as well. For example: What would happen if the office at LocationID 2 physically moved from Boston to a new building in nearby Cambridge? If all the data were in a giant table, then we would have to update every Street, City and State for each employee individually. This is a very tedious task that leaves a great deal of room for errors and inconsistency in how the data is entered. Placing the LocationID field only in the Location table means all employees with LocationID 2 map to an update we can make just once.

So, how do we find an employee's address if the information is spread between two tables? Each table has a LocationID field inside it. We can then use a two-part identifier (from Chapter 2), to distinguish them as the Employee.LocationID field corresponds to the Location.LocationID field.

Refer to Figure 3.2 for a look at Alex Adams and Barry Brown. These employees both work at LocationID 1. If we were new to the company and only had access to the Employee table, we would not have enough detailed information to send a parcel to Alex Adams. What if we put two tables next to one another on our screen? By physically drawing a line from the Employee.LocationID field to the Location.LocationID field we can get more location details for each employee. LocationID 1 is located at 111 First ST in Seattle, WA (Figure 3.2).

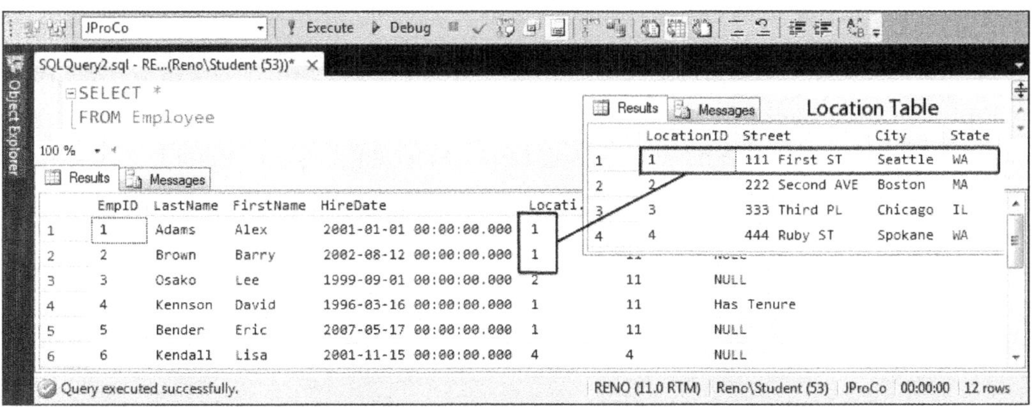

Figure 3.2 The Employee and Location tables are correlated on the LocationID field.

What about a global company with locations in all 50 states and over 100 different countries? We will have many records in our Location table and probably will not be able to look at both tables very efficiently on one screen.

How can we effectively see information in two different tables at the same time? Our ultimate goal is to show the Employee and Location information in one result set (Figure 3.3). Since we have not learned the code on how to do this yet, it is not shown in this figure. The results shown are the goal of the upcoming example.

Results | Messages

	EmpID	LastName	FirstName	HireDate	LocationID	ManagerID	Status	LocationID	Street	City	State
1	1	Adams	Alex	2001-01-01 00:00:00.000	1	11	NULL	1	111 First ST	Seattle	WA
2	2	Brown	Barry	2002-08-12 00:00:00.000	1	11	NULL	1	111 First ST	Seattle	WA
3	3	Osako	Lee	1999-09-01 00:00:00.000	2	11	NULL	2	222 Second AVE	Boston	MA
4	4	Kennson	David	1996-03-16 00:00:00.000	1	11	Has Tenure	1	111 First ST	Seattle	WA
5	5	Bender	Eric	2007-05-17 00:00:00.000	1	11	NULL	1	111 First ST	Seattle	WA
6	6	Kendall	Lisa	2001-11-15 00:00:00.000	4	4	NULL	4	444 Ruby ST	Spok...	WA

Query executed successfully. | RENO (11.0 RTM) | Reno\j2p (53) | JProCo | 00:00:00 | 11 rows

Figure 3.3 Two related tables showing as one result set.

Inner Joins

So far, we have learned that each query can have only one result set and will only allow a single FROM clause. How can we place two tables in one FROM clause? We can include many tables in one FROM clause by using a JOIN clause. The most common type of a join is called the INNER JOIN.

Reader Note: *Prior to SQL Server 2008, the limit was 256 tables. The number of tables you can now join is limited only by available resources.*

An INNER JOIN clause allows us to join multiple tables in a single query, although it requires a specific condition in order for it to work correctly. We must ensure that the INNER JOIN statement has two tables with at least one common or overlapping field. We already know the Employee and Location tables share a common field (LocationID). The relationship is between Employee.LocationID and Location.LocationID, so we instruct SQL Server that the INNER JOIN is on this field and voila! We have combined two tables into one result set.

```
SELECT *
FROM Employee
```

Location Table

	LocationID	Street	City	State
1	1	111 First ST	Seattle	WA
2	2	222 Second AVE	Boston	MA
3	3	333 Third PL	Chicago	IL
4	4	444 Ruby ST	Spokane	WA

	EmpID	LastName	FirstName	HireDate	Locati...		
1	1	Adams	Alex	2001-01-01 00:00:00.000	1		
2	2	Brown	Barry	2002-08-12 00:00:00.000	1		
3	3	Osako	Lee	1999-09-01 00:00:00.000	2	11	NULL
4	4	Kennson	David	1996-03-16 00:00:00.000	1	11	Has Tenure
5	5	Bender	Eric	2007-05-17 00:00:00.000	1	11	NULL
6	6	Kendall	Lisa	2001-11-15 00:00:00.000	4	4	NULL

Query executed successfully. RENO (11.0 RTM) Reno\Student (53) JProCo 00:00:00 12 rows

Figure 3.4 The LocationID field is a common field between the Employee and Location tables.

Every time a value is found in Employee.LocationID, the inner join searches for the matching record in the Location.LocationID field. If a match is found, data from both tables are displayed as a single record. Both tables will show all their fields if we type SELECT * at the beginning of our query.

In looking at the Grant table we can see 'Ben@MoreTechnology.com' is the GrantName with the largest value (41000) in the Amount field (Figure 3.5).

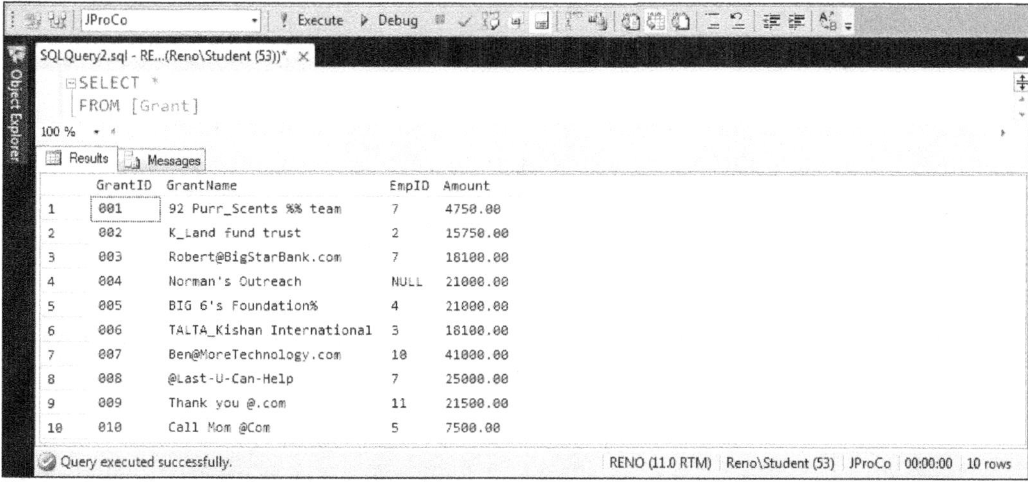

```
SELECT *
FROM [Grant]
```

	GrantID	GrantName	EmpID	Amount
1	001	92 Purr_Scents %% team	7	4750.00
2	002	K_Land fund trust	2	15750.00
3	003	Robert@BigStarBank.com	7	18100.00
4	004	Norman's Outreach	NULL	21000.00
5	005	BIG 6's Foundation%	4	21000.00
6	006	TALTA_Kishan International	3	18100.00
7	007	Ben@MoreTechnology.com	10	41000.00
8	008	@Last-U-Can-Help	7	25000.00
9	009	Thank you @.com	11	21500.00
10	010	Call Mom @Com	5	7500.00

Query executed successfully. RENO (11.0 RTM) Reno\Student (53) JProCo 00:00:00 10 rows

Figure 3.5 All records from the Grant table.

The employee who made that procurement has an EmpID of 10. What if we wanted to find more information about this employee. Is this employee a man or woman? When was this employee hired?

We are unable to get answers to detailed questions about this employee, without looking beyond the Grant table.

For visual purposes, let's put these two tables next to one another. We can see that the EmpID field correlates data between these two tables. Grant.EmpID equates to Employee.EmpID. If we look at EmpID 10 on both tables, we can see Terry O'Haire is the employee who found the $41,000 grant Amount (Figure 3.6).

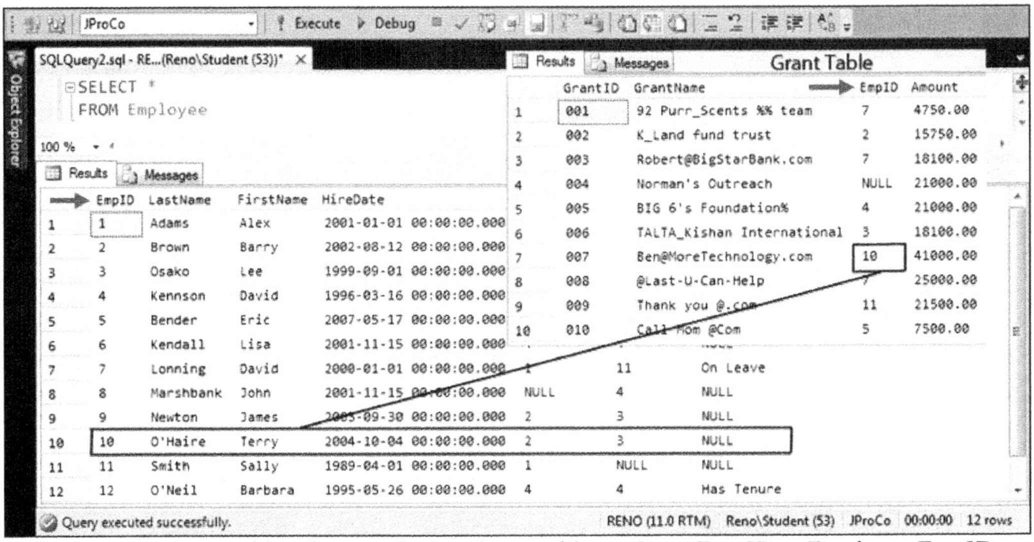

```
SELECT *
FROM Employee
```

	EmpID	LastName	FirstName	HireDate			
1	1	Adams	Alex	2001-01-01 00:00:00.000			
2	2	Brown	Barry	2002-08-12 00:00:00.000			
3	3	Osako	Lee	1999-09-01 00:00:00.000			
4	4	Kennson	David	1996-03-16 00:00:00.000			
5	5	Bender	Eric	2007-05-17 00:00:00.000			
6	6	Kendall	Lisa	2001-11-15 00:00:00.000			
7	7	Lonning	David	2000-01-01 00:00:00.000	1	11	On Leave
8	8	Marshbank	John	2001-11-15 00:00:00.000	NULL	4	NULL
9	9	Newton	James	2003-09-30 00:00:00.000	2	3	NULL
10	10	O'Haire	Terry	2004-10-04 00:00:00.000	2	3	NULL
11	11	Smith	Sally	1989-04-01 00:00:00.000	1	NULL	NULL
12	12	O'Neil	Barbara	1995-05-26 00:00:00.000	4	4	Has Tenure

Grant Table

	GrantID	GrantName	EmpID	Amount
1	001	92 Purr_Scents %% team	7	4750.00
2	002	K_Land fund trust	2	15750.00
3	003	Robert@BigStarBank.com	7	18100.00
4	004	Norman's Outreach	NULL	21000.00
5	005	BIG 6's Foundation%	4	21000.00
6	006	TALTA_Kishan International	3	18100.00
7	007	Ben@MoreTechnology.com	10	41000.00
8	008	@Last-U-Can-Help	7	25000.00
9	009	Thank you @.com	11	21500.00
10	010	Call Mom @Com	5	7500.00

Query executed successfully. RENO (11.0 RTM) Reno\Student (53) JProCo 00:00:00 12 rows

Figure 3.6 The Grant table relates to the Employee table on Grant.EmpID to Employee.EmpID.

Again, placing these two small tables side by side and analyzing them can work, but it's time-consuming and not very efficient, especially if we have two very large tables. Instead, we can use SQL Server to put both tables into one result set. Putting information into one report is of great value to businesses.

Reader Note: *The tables in Figure 3-6 share the common field of EmpID. Knowing this is a key step.*

To put all these records into one result set, we will need both tables in the FROM clause and a join requires a field that corresponds to both tables. The ON clause after the INNER JOIN is how we show this relationship.

Looking closely at Figure 3.6 and Figure 3.7 we can see something unusual that might cause us to be cautious when using an INNER JOIN. There are ten grants in the Grant table, but the INNER JOIN only returned nine records. Thus, an INNER JOIN can produce what seems to be a loss of data. We will explore how to know when this will happen and when it is necessary to use a different type of join.

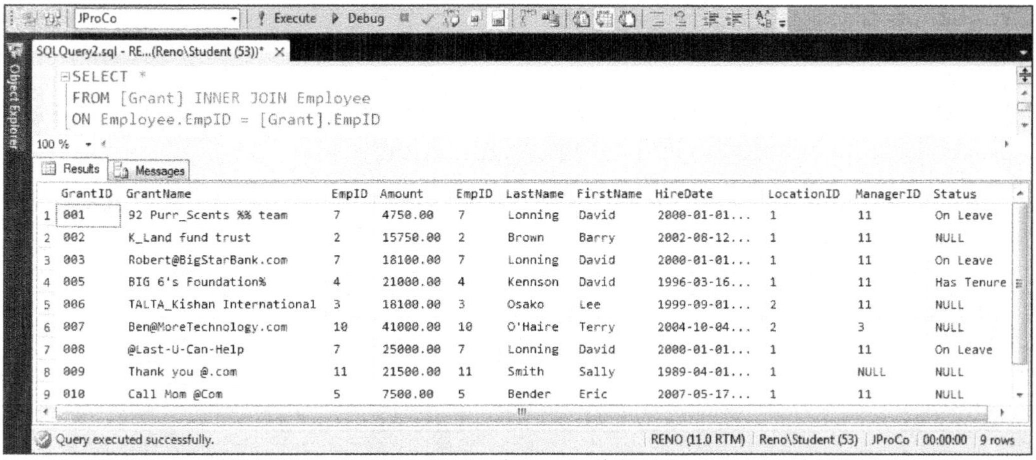

```
SELECT *
FROM [Grant] INNER JOIN Employee
ON Employee.EmpID = [Grant].EmpID
```

	GrantID	GrantName	EmpID	Amount	EmpID	LastName	FirstName	HireDate	LocationID	ManagerID	Status
1	001	92 Purr_Scents %% team	7	4750.00	7	Lonning	David	2000-01-01...	1	11	On Leave
2	002	K_Land fund trust	2	15750.00	2	Brown	Barry	2002-08-12...	1	11	NULL
3	003	Robert@BigStarBank.com	7	18100.00	7	Lonning	David	2000-01-01...	1	11	On Leave
4	005	BIG 6's Foundation%	4	21000.00	4	Kennson	David	1996-03-16...	1	11	Has Tenure
5	006	TALTA_Kishan International	3	18100.00	3	Osako	Lee	1999-09-01...	2	11	NULL
6	007	Ben@MoreTechnology.com	10	41000.00	10	O'Haire	Terry	2004-10-04...	2	3	NULL
7	008	@Last-U-Can-Help	7	25000.00	7	Lonning	David	2000-01-01...	1	11	On Leave
8	009	Thank you @.com	11	21500.00	11	Smith	Sally	1989-04-01...	1	NULL	NULL
9	010	Call Mom @Com	5	7500.00	5	Bender	Eric	2007-05-17...	1	11	NULL

Query executed successfully. RENO (11.0 RTM) Reno\Student (53) JProCo 00:00:00 9 rows

Figure 3.7 Grant and Employee INNER JOIN shows 9 of the 10 grants matching on EmpID.

The GrantName, 'Norman's Outreach' was an online registration, so no employee is listed as receiving credit for obtaining this grant (See Figure 3.6 where EmpID is NULL). This record has a NULL value. We briefly talked about NULL values in Chapter One. Nulls will ***never*** match records in another table. Since no match was found, the record containing the 'Norman's Outreach' grant is not included in the result set.

The core behavior of an INNER JOIN is to only include records when an exact match is found in both tables. Unmatched records are left out of the result set.

Lab 3.1: Inner Joins

Lab Prep: Each lab has one or more Skill Checks. Start with Skill Check 1 and proceed until reaching the Points to Ponder section.

Before beginning this lab, verify that SQL Server 2012 is properly installed and operating. Before running the lab setup script for resetting the database (SQLQueries2012Vol1Chapter3.1Setup.sql), please make sure to close all query windows within SSMS. An open query window pointing to a database context can lock that database preventing it from updating when the script is executing. A simple way to assure all query windows are closed, is to exit out of SSMS, then open a new instance of SSMS, and lastly run the setup script.

Skill Check 1: In a single query, show the employees and cities where they work. Join the Employee and Location tables of the JProCo database on the field they share in common (LocationID). The field selection list should only include FirstName, LastName, City and State. When done, the results should have 11 records and resemble Figure 3.8.

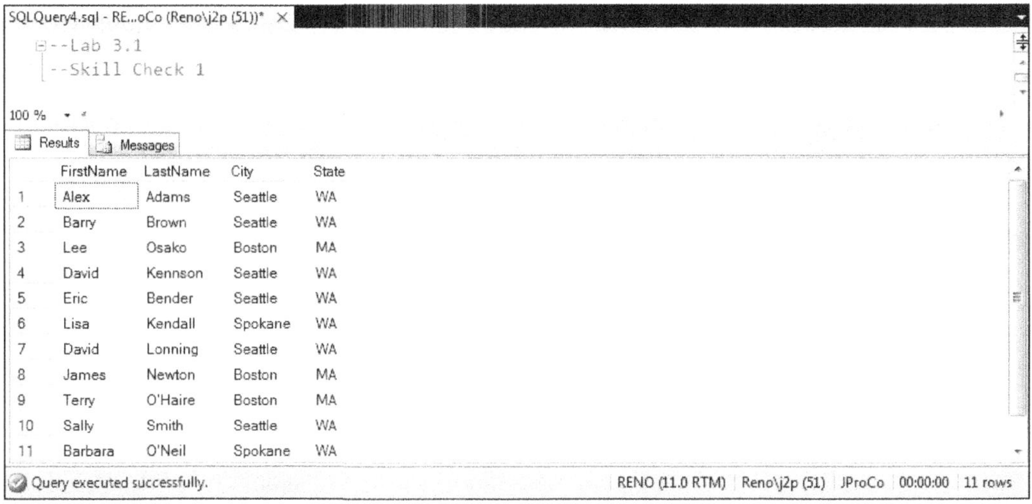

	FirstName	LastName	City	State
1	Alex	Adams	Seattle	WA
2	Barry	Brown	Seattle	WA
3	Lee	Osako	Boston	MA
4	David	Kennson	Seattle	WA
5	Eric	Bender	Seattle	WA
6	Lisa	Kendall	Spokane	WA
7	David	Lonning	Seattle	WA
8	James	Newton	Boston	MA
9	Terry	O'Haire	Boston	MA
10	Sally	Smith	Seattle	WA
11	Barbara	O'Neil	Spokane	WA

Figure 3.8 Skill Check 1 shows all employees and where they work.

Skill Check 2: The Grant table has an EmpID field. List all Employees' first and last names next to the grants they have found. Show the FirstName, LastName, GrantName and Amount fields. When done, the results should have 9 records and resemble Figure 3.9.

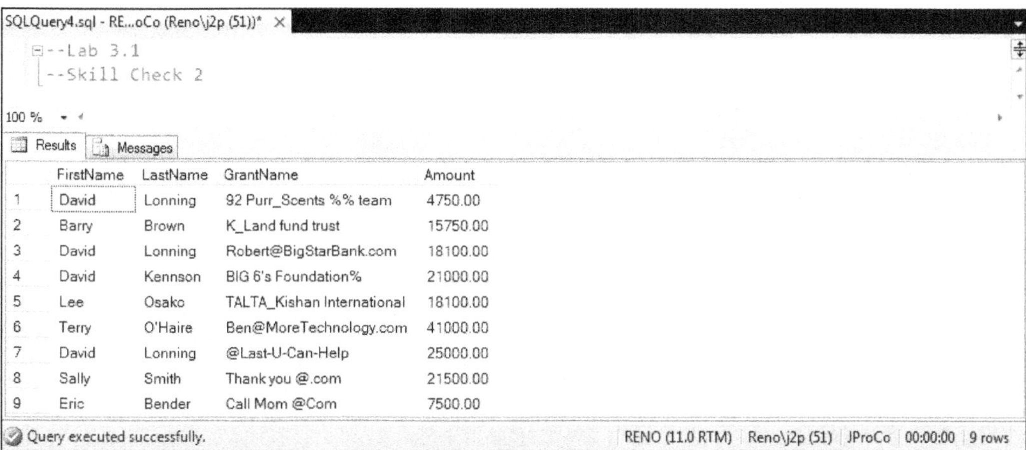

SQLQuery4.sql - RE...oCo (Reno\j2p (51))*

```
--Lab 3.1
--Skill Check 2
```

	FirstName	LastName	GrantName	Amount
1	David	Lonning	92 Purr_Scents %% team	4750.00
2	Barry	Brown	K_Land fund trust	15750.00
3	David	Lonning	Robert@BigStarBank.com	18100.00
4	David	Kennson	BIG 6's Foundation%	21000.00
5	Lee	Osako	TALTA_Kishan International	18100.00
6	Terry	O'Haire	Ben@MoreTechnology.com	41000.00
7	David	Lonning	@Last-U-Can-Help	25000.00
8	Sally	Smith	Thank you @.com	21500.00
9	Eric	Bender	Call Mom @Com	7500.00

Query executed successfully. RENO (11.0 RTM) Reno\j2p (51) JProCo 00:00:00 9 rows

Figure 3.9 Skill Check 2 displays all grants found by employees and their names.

Skill Check 3: Set the database context to the dbBasics database. The Activity table shows the books which have been checked out and the Library card number of the library patron who checked it out.

Join the Activity table to the Members table to see the books and the member details of who checked it out. When done, the results should have 7 records and resemble those shown in Figure 3.10.

SQLQuery4.sql - REN...ics (Reno\j2p (51))*

```
--Lab 3.1
--Skill Check 3
```

	LibraryCardNo	Book	LibraryCardNo	fName	lName	Address	Gender	DOB
1	1001	Dust Bowl	1001	Tom	Larson	312 Costa Ave	M	1971-08-16 00:00:00.000
2	1001	How to Fix Things	1001	Tom	Larson	312 Costa Ave	M	1971-08-16 00:00:00.000
3	1003	Yachting for dummies	1003	Susan	Pederson	4515 Tolo Rd	F	1942-04-04 00:00:00.000
4	1005	How to marry a millionaire	1005	Larry	Kimball	1908 S Huson	M	1966-03-05 00:00:00.000
5	1005	Spice world	1005	Larry	Kimball	1908 S Huson	M	1966-03-05 00:00:00.000
6	1005	Juice Master tells all	1005	Larry	Kimball	1908 S Huson	M	1966-03-05 00:00:00.000
7	1006	Doctor Doctor	1006	Phil	Coleman	655 Rubber Rd	M	1940-07-09 00:00:00.000

Query executed successfully. RENO (11.0 RTM) Reno\j2p (51) dbBasics 00:00:00 7 rows

Figure 3.10 Skill Check 3 shows Library members and all the books they have checked out.

Skill Check 4: In the dbBasics database, join the PurchaseActivity and Customer tables together. Narrow the field selection list to only include the Date, Item, Price and CustomerName fields. When done, the results should contain 11 records and resemble Figure 3.11.

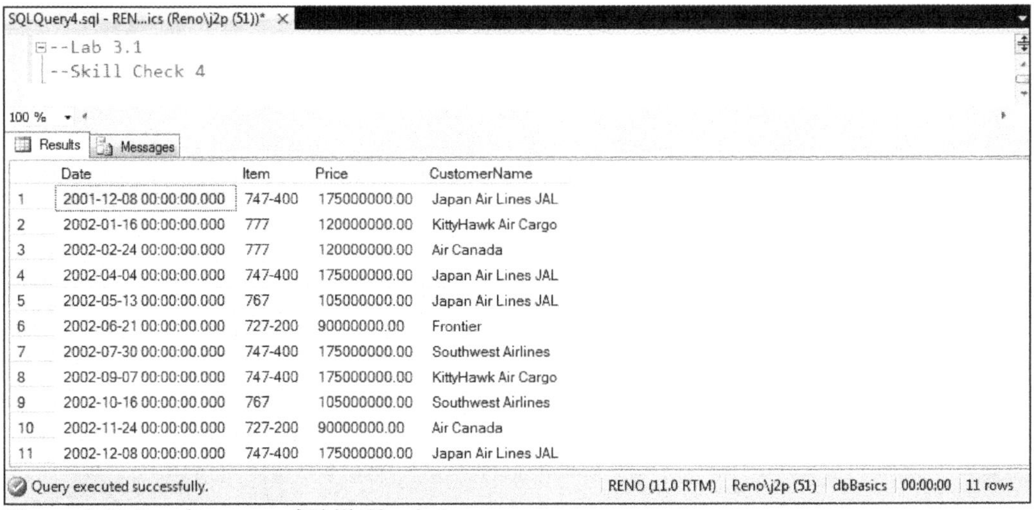

SQLQuery4.sql - REN...ics (Reno\j2p (51))*

```
--Lab 3.1
--Skill Check 4
```

100 %

Results | Messages

	Date	Item	Price	CustomerName
1	2001-12-08 00:00:00.000	747-400	175000000.00	Japan Air Lines JAL
2	2002-01-16 00:00:00.000	777	120000000.00	KittyHawk Air Cargo
3	2002-02-24 00:00:00.000	777	120000000.00	Air Canada
4	2002-04-04 00:00:00.000	747-400	175000000.00	Japan Air Lines JAL
5	2002-05-13 00:00:00.000	767	105000000.00	Japan Air Lines JAL
6	2002-06-21 00:00:00.000	727-200	90000000.00	Frontier
7	2002-07-30 00:00:00.000	747-400	175000000.00	Southwest Airlines
8	2002-09-07 00:00:00.000	747-400	175000000.00	KittyHawk Air Cargo
9	2002-10-16 00:00:00.000	767	105000000.00	Southwest Airlines
10	2002-11-24 00:00:00.000	727-200	90000000.00	Air Canada
11	2002-12-08 00:00:00.000	747-400	175000000.00	Japan Air Lines JAL

Query executed successfully. | RENO (11.0 RTM) | Reno\j2p (51) | dbBasics | 00:00:00 | 11 rows

Figure 3.11 Result screen of Skill Check 4.

Answer Code: The T-SQL code to this lab can be found from the downloadable files named Lab3.1_InnerJoins.sql.

Points to Ponder - Inner Joins

1. Tables with related fields can be used together in a single query using a join.
2. An INNER JOIN only returns a result set with exact matches on a field in two or more tables.
3. An INNER JOIN is the default join type. If the keyword INNER is omitted from the join clause of a query, SQL Server defaults to an INNER JOIN.

Outer Joins

Being able to understand how an INNER JOIN works makes it much easier to learn how an OUTER JOIN works. They both display records found by a match between two tables. Both types of joins require us to specify the matching field(s) in an ON clause. The primary difference is that an OUTER JOIN will find records that an INNER JOIN omits from its result set.

In the JProCo database, the Employee table has 12 records and the Location table has 4 records. A query using a FULL OUTER JOIN will return 13 records. It looks like this type of join can produce a result set with more records than either table contains individually.

Left Outer Joins

Before we begin writing an OUTER JOIN query, we need to state the goal for what records we want to see in the query result set. There is a record in the Employee table for an employee who works remotely and has a NULL value for the LocationID. Also, there is a location under construction in Chicago that has not had any employees assigned to it yet, so it is not in the Employee table at all.

Are we looking for an employee report or a location report? In an employee report, it's alright if Chicago does not show in the results. We simply need a list of all employees from the Employee table. Thus, the OUTER JOIN must favor the Employee table to ensure that all employee records are shown (Figure 3.12).

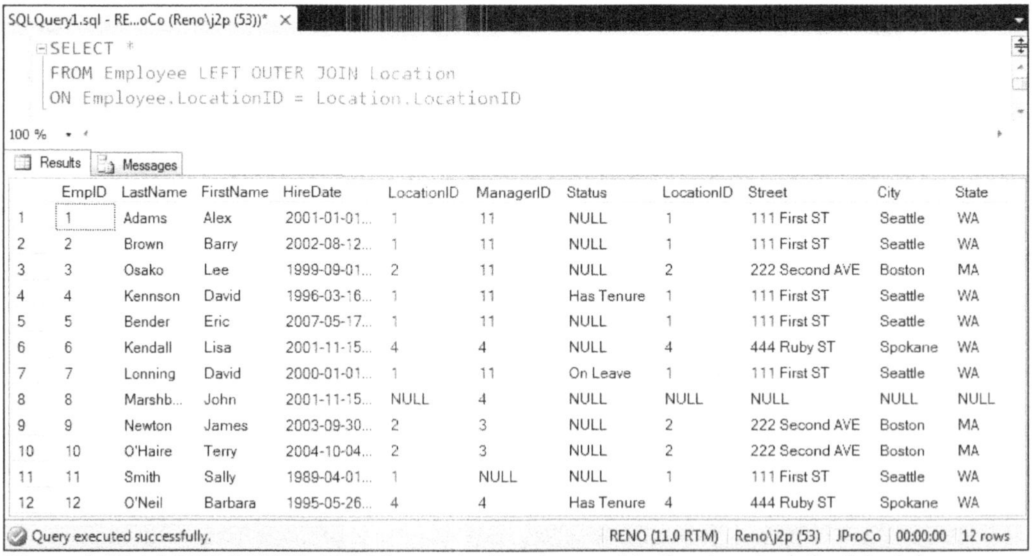

SQLQuery1.sql - RE...oCo (Reno\j2p (53))* ×

```
SELECT *
FROM Employee LEFT OUTER JOIN Location
ON Employee.LocationID = Location.LocationID
```

100 %

Results | Messages

	EmpID	LastName	FirstName	HireDate	LocationID	ManagerID	Status	LocationID	Street	City	State
1	1	Adams	Alex	2001-01-01...	1	11	NULL	1	111 First ST	Seattle	WA
2	2	Brown	Barry	2002-08-12...	1	11	NULL	1	111 First ST	Seattle	WA
3	3	Osako	Lee	1999-09-01...	2	11	NULL	2	222 Second AVE	Boston	MA
4	4	Kennson	David	1996-03-16...	1	11	Has Tenure	1	111 First ST	Seattle	WA
5	5	Bender	Eric	2007-05-17...	1	11	NULL	1	111 First ST	Seattle	WA
6	6	Kendall	Lisa	2001-11-15...	4	4	NULL	4	444 Ruby ST	Spokane	WA
7	7	Lonning	David	2000-01-01...	1	11	On Leave	1	111 First ST	Seattle	WA
8	8	Marshb...	John	2001-11-15...	NULL	4	NULL	NULL	NULL	NULL	NULL
9	9	Newton	James	2003-09-30...	2	3	NULL	2	222 Second AVE	Boston	MA
10	10	O'Haire	Terry	2004-10-04...	2	3	NULL	2	222 Second AVE	Boston	MA
11	11	Smith	Sally	1989-04-01...	1	NULL	NULL	1	111 First ST	Seattle	WA
12	12	O'Neil	Barbara	1995-05-26...	4	4	Has Tenure	4	444 Ruby ST	Spokane	WA

Query executed successfully. | RENO (11.0 RTM) | Reno\j2p (53) | JProCo | 00:00:00 | 12 rows

Figure 3.12 A LEFT OUTER JOIN favors the Employee table listed to the left of the join.

The query shown in Figure 3.12 is written in a way to help illustrate that the Employee table is to the left of the Location table. Since we want all employees to be included in our results, we need to use a *LEFT OUTER JOIN*. Notice, that John Marshbank, JProCo's remote worker, appears in this result set. When filtering data, a LEFT OUTER JOIN will first return all records from the table on the left and then tries to find matches with the table on the right.

In this example, all employees are shown and then the matches for the LocationID field from the Location table are populated and displayed. By looking closer at the results shown in Figure 3.12, we see all fields from the left table (Employee) are sorted by EmpID, and all the fields from the right table (Location) are displayed by aligning values of the matching LocationID fields.

Right Outer Joins

A notification from OSHA states they are going to inspect all JProCo buildings, and we need to provide location details for our buildings. They also want to know which employees work in these buildings. Since John Marshbank works remotely, they have no interest in him. They want to inspect each building even if it is under construction and no employees work there.

To show all records from the table on the right, we need a *RIGHT OUTER JOIN* (Figure 3.13). Since the right outer join favors the Location table in this query, all locations will be displayed. Because LocationID 3 (Chicago) does not appear in the Employee table its fields are assigned NULL values.

SQLQuery1.sql - RE...oCo (Reno\j2p (53))*

```
SELECT *
FROM Employee RIGHT OUTER JOIN Location
ON Employee.LocationID = Location.LocationID
```

100 %

Results | Messages

	EmpID	LastName	FirstName	HireDate	LocationID	ManagerID	Status	LocationID	Street	City	State
1	1	Adams	Alex	2001-01-01...	1	11	NULL	1	111 First ST	Seattle	WA
2	2	Brown	Barry	2002-08-12...	1	11	NULL	1	111 First ST	Seattle	WA
3	4	Kennson	David	1996-03-16...	1	11	Has Tenure	1	111 First ST	Seattle	WA
4	5	Bender	Eric	2007-05-17...	1	11	NULL	1	111 First ST	Seattle	WA
5	7	Lonning	David	2000-01-01...	1	11	On Leave	1	111 First ST	Seattle	WA
6	11	Smith	Sally	1989-04-01...	1	NULL	NULL	1	111 First ST	Seattle	WA
7	3	Osako	Lee	1999-09-01...	2	11	NULL	2	222 Second AVE	Boston	MA
8	9	Newton	James	2003-09-30...	2	3	NULL	2	222 Second AVE	Boston	MA
9	10	O'Haire	Terry	2004-10-04...	2	3	NULL	2	222 Second AVE	Boston	MA
10	NULL	NULL	NULL	NULL	NULL	NULL	NULL	3	333 Third PL	Chicago	IL
11	6	Kendall	Lisa	2001-11-15...	4	4	NULL	4	444 Ruby ST	Spokane	WA
12	12	O'Neil	Barbara	1995-05-26...	4	4	Has Tenure	4	444 Ruby ST	Spokane	WA

Query executed successfully. | RENO (11.0 RTM) | Reno\j2p (53) | JProCo | 00:00:00 | 12 rows

Figure 3.13 The RIGHT OUTER JOIN shows all locations, even if nobody works there.

Notice the EmpID values are no longer in order and it is the LocationID values from 1 to 4 that determine how the results are sorted. This is because the right table (Location) is the dominant table finding records matching on LocationID. All the records from the right table (Location) are shown, including Chicago.

Full Outer Joins

When we want to see all employees with information obtained from both the Employee table and the Location table, including employees without a location, a LEFT OUTER JOIN works great. Using these same tables, if we want to see all locations, even those without employees, a RIGHT OUTER JOIN will give us the results we need for our location report.

If we wanted to see all employees and all locations regardless of whether each employee matches to a location and regardless of whether each location matches to an employee, we would use a *FULL OUTER JOIN* (Figure 3.14).

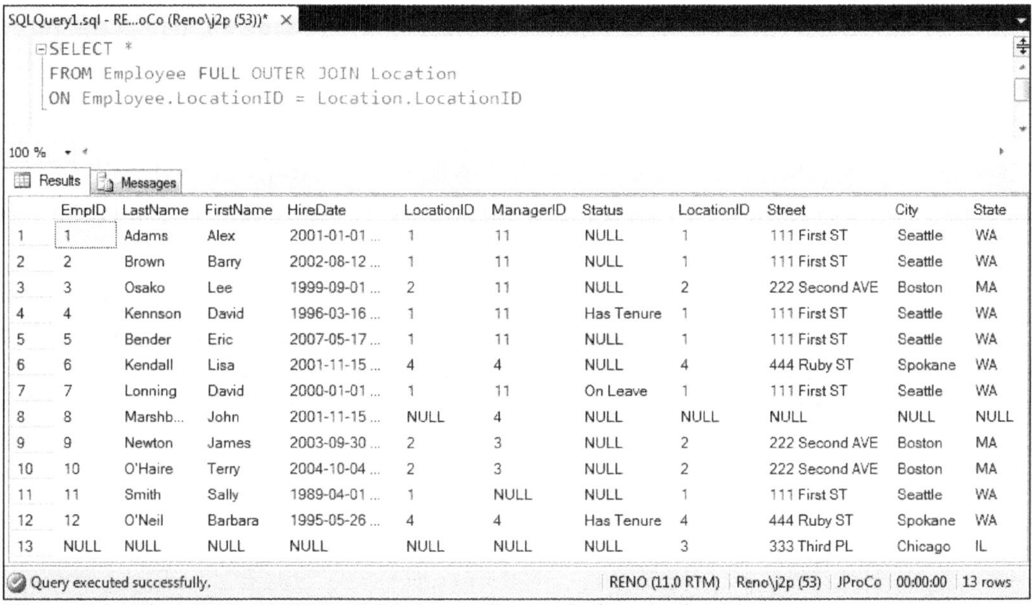

SQLQuery1.sql - RE...oCo (Reno\j2p (53))*

```
SELECT *
FROM Employee FULL OUTER JOIN Location
ON Employee.LocationID = Location.LocationID
```

100 %

Results | Messages

	EmpID	LastName	FirstName	HireDate	LocationID	ManagerID	Status	LocationID	Street	City	State
1	1	Adams	Alex	2001-01-01 ...	1	11	NULL	1	111 First ST	Seattle	WA
2	2	Brown	Barry	2002-08-12 ...	1	11	NULL	1	111 First ST	Seattle	WA
3	3	Osako	Lee	1999-09-01 ...	2	11	NULL	2	222 Second AVE	Boston	MA
4	4	Kennson	David	1996-03-16 ...	1	11	Has Tenure	1	111 First ST	Seattle	WA
5	5	Bender	Eric	2007-05-17 ...	1	11	NULL	1	111 First ST	Seattle	WA
6	6	Kendall	Lisa	2001-11-15 ...	4	4	NULL	4	444 Ruby ST	Spokane	WA
7	7	Lonning	David	2000-01-01 ...	1	11	On Leave	1	111 First ST	Seattle	WA
8	8	Marshb...	John	2001-11-15 ...	NULL	4	NULL	NULL	NULL	NULL	NULL
9	9	Newton	James	2003-09-30 ...	2	3	NULL	2	222 Second AVE	Boston	MA
10	10	O'Haire	Terry	2004-10-04 ...	2	3	NULL	2	222 Second AVE	Boston	MA
11	11	Smith	Sally	1989-04-01 ...	1	NULL	NULL	1	111 First ST	Seattle	WA
12	12	O'Neil	Barbara	1995-05-26 ...	4	4	Has Tenure	4	444 Ruby ST	Spokane	WA
13	NULL	NULL	NULL	NULL	NULL	NULL	NULL	3	333 Third PL	Chicago	IL

Query executed successfully. | RENO (11.0 RTM) | Reno\j2p (53) | JProCo | 00:00:00 | 13 rows

Figure 3.14 The FULL OUTER JOIN shows all records from both tables.

The Employee table has 12 records and the Location table has 4 records. A query using a FULL OUTER JOIN with these tables will return 13 records, showing all records from both tables at least one time each.

A FULL OUTER JOIN will show all matched ***and*** all unmatched records from both tables. So, this type of join can contain results with NULL values in the field(s) listed in the ON clause.

Here is another example of a FULL OUTER JOIN query returning all records from both tables. We need to find all employees with no grants and all grants with no employees by joining the Employee and Grant tables, as seen in Figure 3.15.

As expected, a query with a FULL OUTER JOIN finds all records whether they are matched or unmatched. Until now, none of our queries using a join have included a WHERE clause, so our results always included all possible records.

When filtering any type of a query using a WHERE clause, only the records that satisfy the criteria in the predicate will be included in the result set. By adding the statement, WHERE LocationID = 1 to the code shown in Figure 3.14, all records in the tables not matching this criteria would be removed from the result set. The original result set with 15 records will be reduced to the 10 records for the Seattle location. Without the WHERE clause, our result set includes all matched and unmatched records. Unmatched records between tables will show as NULL.

SQLQuery2.sql - (lo...(Reno\Student (51))*

```
SELECT *
FROM [Grant] FULL OUTER JOIN Employee
ON [Grant].EmpID = Employee.EmpID
```

100 %

Results | Messages

	GrantID	GrantName	EmpID	Amount	EmpID	LastName	FirstName	HireDate	LocationID	ManagerID	Status
1	001	92 Purr_Scents %%...	7	4750.00	7	Lonning	David	2000-01-0...	1	11	On Leave
2	002	K_Land fund trust	2	15750.00	2	Brown	Barry	2002-08-1...	1	11	NULL
3	003	Robert@BigStarBa...	7	18100.00	7	Lonning	David	2000-01-0...	1	11	On Leave
4	004	Norman's Outreach	NULL	21000.00	NULL	NULL	NULL	NULL	NULL	NULL	NULL
5	005	BIG 6's Foundation%	4	21000.00	4	Kennson	David	1996-03-1...	1	11	Has Tenure
6	006	TALTA_Kishan Inter...	3	18100.00	3	Osako	Lee	1999-09-0...	2	11	NULL
7	007	Ben@MoreTechnol...	10	41000.00	10	O'Haire	Terry	2004-10-0...	2	3	NULL
8	008	@Last-U-Can-Help	7	25000.00	7	Lonning	David	2000-01-0...	1	11	On Leave
9	009	Thank you @.com	11	21500.00	11	Smith	Sally	1989-04-0...	1	NULL	NULL
10	010	Call Mom @Com	5	7500.00	5	Bender	Eric	2007-05-1...	1	11	NULL

Query executed successfully. | (local) (11.0 RTM) | Reno\Student (51) | JProCo | 00:00:00 | 15 rows

Figure 3.15 The FULL OUTER JOIN between the Grant and Employee tables shows all records.

Filtering Multi-Table Queries

We now know that all outer join types show more records than an inner join type. Regardless of the type of join used in a query, the WHERE clause will filter the result set returning only the records that satisfy the criteria in the predicate. Does a JOIN clause filter records before the WHERE clause or vice versa? How can we anticipate what records will be returned by a query with a JOIN clause and a WHERE clause? The next section will explore the answers to these questions.

Filtering with Inner Joins

The following inner join with no criteria produces eleven records:

```
SELECT *
FROM Employee INNER JOIN Location
ON Employee.LocationID = Location.LocationID
```

Of the twelve employees, John Marshbank does not appear in the query result set, because he was already filtered out by the INNER JOIN. Can we use a WHERE clause to find John and bring him back into the result set? No. We can see from the query in Figure 3.16 that the result set is empty, even though we know there is a FirstName of John in the Employee table. Since the INNER JOIN has already eliminated this record from the result set, there is no longer a FirstName of John for the WHERE clause criteria to match, which produces an empty result set.

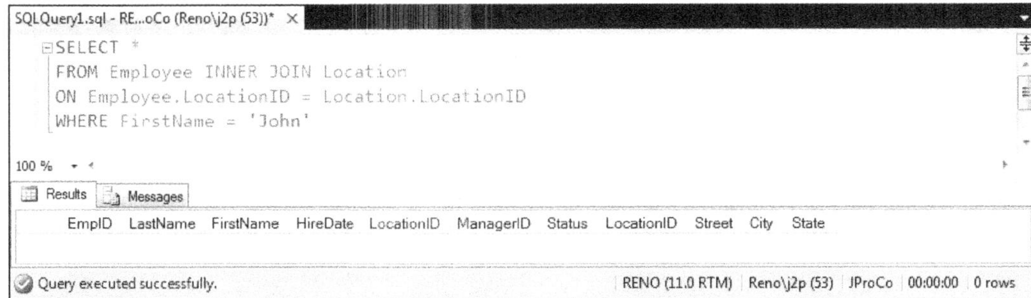

Figure 3.16 A WHERE clause cannot find records not included in an INNER JOIN.

Filtering with Outer Joins

Changing this query to a LEFT OUTER JOIN will always show all records from the Employee table, which makes the 12 records available for the WHERE clause criteria to find a match. The predicate is filtering on the FirstName equal to John, so our result set has the one Employee record matching the criteria (Figure 3.17).

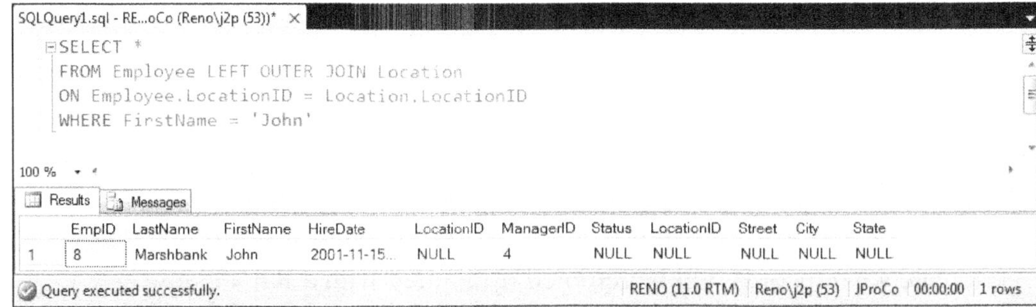

Figure 3.17 A WHERE clause can find records included in a LEFT OUTER JOIN.

Filtering with All Types of Joins

To know how filtering in a WHERE clause will work with any type of join we need to think of it much the same way as a single table query. The type of join being used will determine what records are available for a WHERE clause to use filtering criteria to find matches on. Think of the result set from the join portion of the query as a big table. If one or more records are available in this 'virtual table' for the WHERE clause to predicate on, then it will be displayed in the result set.

Follow this one simple rule: The records we are searching for must meet both the join and filtering criteria. If either process eliminates a record, it will not appear in our result set.

Lab 3.2: Outer Joins

Lab Prep: Each lab has one or more Skill Checks. Start with Skill Check 1 and proceed until reaching the Points to Ponder section.

Before beginning this lab, verify that SQL Server 2012 is properly installed and operating. Before running the lab setup script for resetting the database (SQLQueries2012Vol1Chapter3.2Setup.sql), please make sure to close all query windows within SSMS. An open query window pointing to a database context can lock that database preventing it from updating when the script is executing. A simple way to assure all query windows are closed, is to exit out of SSMS, then open a new instance of SSMS, and lastly run the setup script.

Skill Check 1: Set the database context to JProCo. Write a query that shows a list of records (grants) from the Grant table, plus the first and last names for the employees who acquired them. If a grant was not found by an employee, display a NULL where their names would have been.

This can be accomplished by joining the Employee and [Grant] tables together. Include the FirstName, LastName, GrantName and Amount fields in the selection list. When done, the results should have 10 records and resemble Figure 3.18.

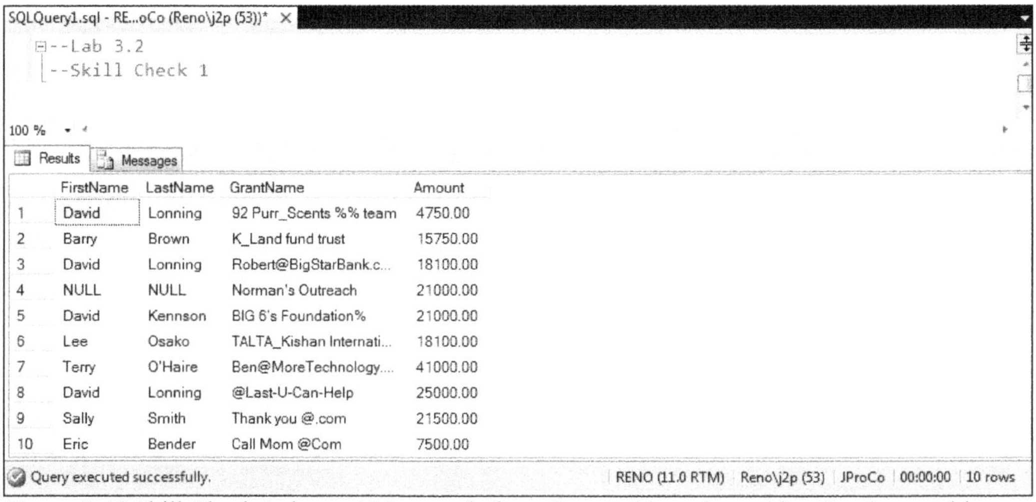

SQLQuery1.sql - RE...oCo (Reno\j2p (53))*

```
--Lab 3.2
--Skill Check 1
```

100 %

Results | Messages

	FirstName	LastName	GrantName	Amount
1	David	Lonning	92 Purr_Scents %% team	4750.00
2	Barry	Brown	K_Land fund trust	15750.00
3	David	Lonning	Robert@BigStarBank.c...	18100.00
4	NULL	NULL	Norman's Outreach	21000.00
5	David	Kennson	BIG 6's Foundation%	21000.00
6	Lee	Osako	TALTA_Kishan Internati...	18100.00
7	Terry	O'Haire	Ben@MoreTechnology....	41000.00
8	David	Lonning	@Last-U-Can-Help	25000.00
9	Sally	Smith	Thank you @.com	21500.00
10	Eric	Bender	Call Mom @Com	7500.00

Query executed successfully. | RENO (11.0 RTM) | Reno\j2p (53) | JProCo | 00:00:00 | 10 rows

Figure 3.18 Skill Check 1 shows ALL records from Grant table and matching Employee table.

Skill Check 2: Set the database context to JProCo. Write a query to show all employees and the grants that they have acquired. If they haven't found any grants, a NULL should appear next to their name.

This can be accomplished by joining the Employee and [Grant] tables together. Include the FirstName, LastName, GrantName and Amount fields in the selection list. When done, the results should have 14 records and resemble Figure 3.19.

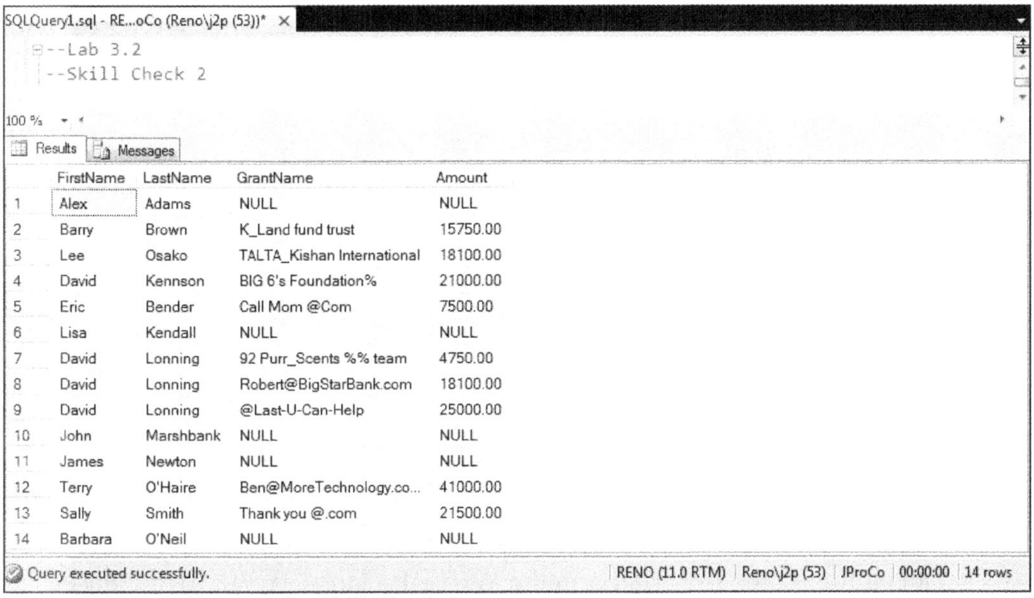

```
--Lab 3.2
--Skill Check 2
```

	FirstName	LastName	GrantName	Amount
1	Alex	Adams	NULL	NULL
2	Barry	Brown	K_Land fund trust	15750.00
3	Lee	Osako	TALTA_Kishan International	18100.00
4	David	Kennson	BIG 6's Foundation%	21000.00
5	Eric	Bender	Call Mom @Com	7500.00
6	Lisa	Kendall	NULL	NULL
7	David	Lonning	92 Purr_Scents %% team	4750.00
8	David	Lonning	Robert@BigStarBank.com	18100.00
9	David	Lonning	@Last-U-Can-Help	25000.00
10	John	Marshbank	NULL	NULL
11	James	Newton	NULL	NULL
12	Terry	O'Haire	Ben@MoreTechnology.co...	41000.00
13	Sally	Smith	Thank you @.com	21500.00
14	Barbara	O'Neil	NULL	NULL

Query executed successfully. RENO (11.0 RTM) Reno\j2p (53) JProCo 00:00:00 14 rows

Figure 3.19 Result screen for Skill Check 2.

Answer Code: The T-SQL code to this lab can be found in the downloadable files in a file named Lab3.2_OuterJoins.sql

Points to Ponder - Outer Joins

1. Outer joins can allow more records to be seen in your result set than just an equal record match list from the INNER JOIN.
2. There are three types of outer joins: LEFT OUTER JOIN, RIGHT OUTER JOIN and FULL OUTER JOIN.
3. In a left outer join, the table named before the join might have records that appear even if SQL Server finds no matching records in the table listed after the LEFT OUTER JOIN clause.
4. The table listed after the RIGHT OUTER JOIN might have records that appear even if no matching records are found in the table on the left of the join.
5. In full outer joins, all matches and unmatched records are displayed from both tables.
6. Using the word OUTER is optional. LEFT OUTER JOIN means the same thing as LEFT JOIN in a query.
7. Using the word INNER is optional. INNER JOIN means the same thing as JOIN in a query.
8. Regardless of the type of Join you use the records produced from the Join can be filtered by the criteria in the WHERE clause. A WHERE clause filters records after the JOIN clauses.

Chapter Glossary

Data Loss: An activity that you run on your system that deletes data you wanted to keep.

Flat File Database: A database with only one table. A text file or simple list is a flat file database.

INNER JOIN: Combines records from two or more tables where matching values are found.

Join Clause: The clause used to join tables in SQL.

Outer Join: Combines records from two or more tables and shows matching and unmatched values.

Relational Database: A database containing more than one table.

Review Quiz - Chapter Three

1.) Which sign says you want all fields from a table in a SELECT statement.

O a. _
O b. &
O c. %
O d. *

2.) The WHERE clause in a query on a single table is…

O a. Optional
O b. Required

3.) The FROM Clause in a query against a single table is…

O a. Optional
O b. Required

4.) Which record(s) will not return with the following WHERE clause? WHERE EmpName like '%T' (Choose all correct answers).

□ a. Thomas
□ b. Atwater
□ c. Tompter
□ d. TeeTee

5.) Which record will not return with the following WHERE clause?

```
WHERE LastName LIKE 'T%'
```

O a. Thomas
O b. Atwater
O c. Tompter
O d. TeeTee

6.) Which type of join would not show nulls as a match?

O a. INNER JOIN
O b. LEFT OUTER JOIN
O c. RIGHT OUTER JOIN
O d. FULL OUTER JOIN

7.) Which syntax would create an error?

O a. JOIN
O b. INNER JOIN
O c. INNER OUTER JOIN
O d. FULL JOIN
O e. FULL OUTER JOIN

8.) Look at the following SQL statement:

```
SELECT *
FROM Employee LEFT OUTER JOIN Location
ON Location.LocationID = Employee.LocationID
```

What will be displayed in the result set?

O a. All records where both tables match.
O b. All records in Employee including matches from Location.
O c. All records from Location including matches from Employee.
O d. The superset of both tables.

9.) You have a table named Employee. You write the following query:

```
SELECT * FROM Employee
```

You plan to join the Location table and fear there may be some employees with no location. You want to make sure that the query returns a list of all employee records. What join clause would you add to the query above?

O a.
```
LEFT JOIN Location
ON Employee.LocationID = Location.LocationID
```

O b.
```
RIGHT JOIN Location
ON Employee.LocationID = Location.LocationID
```

O c.
```
INNER JOIN Location
ON Employee.LocationID = Location.LocationID
```

O d.
```
FULL JOIN Location
ON Employee.LocationID = Location.LocationID
```

Answer Key

1.) The _ matches exactly one character when comparing strings, so (a) is wrong. '&' is not a wildcard and would only match another '&', so (b) is also wrong. '%' represents zero or more characters when pattern matching, so (c) is wrong. The correct answer is (d) because '*' represents every field in a table.

2.) The WHERE clause filters records from the result set, but not every result set needs to be filtered, so (b) is not correct. If all records need to be returned from a query, the table would not be filtered with a WHERE clause, so (a) is the correct answer.

3.) Running a query without knowing what tables to use is not possible, so (a) is not correct. Since the FROM clause tells the query which tables to look in, it is required making (b) the correct answer.

4.) Because '%' represents zero or more characters and the last character in the pattern to be matched is 'T' the only names that will be returned will end in 'T'. Since none of the names end in 'T', (a)Thomas, (b)Atwater, (c)Tompter and (d) TeeTee are all correct answers.

5.) Because '%' represents zero or more characters and the first character in the pattern to be matched is 'T' the only names that will be returned will start with 'T'. Three of the names do start with a 'T', so (a)Thomas, (c)Tompter and (d) TeeTee are all wrong. Since Atwater is the only one that does not start with a 'T', (b) is the correct answer.

6.) OUTER JOINs display mismatching records using NULL as a value for fields in records that otherwise would not have been returned, so (b), (c) and (d) are incorrect. INNER JOINs only displays records where the field from one table contains the same value as the field in the other table, so (a) is correct.

7.) Since JOIN is short for INNER JOIN both (a) and (b) are incorrect. Because FULL JOIN is short for FULL OUTER JOIN, both (d) and (e) are incorrect too. Because INNER and OUTER are two different types of JOIN they can't both be used on the same tables, so (c) is the right answer.

8.) An INNER JOIN will return 'All records where both tables match', so (a) is incorrect. RIGHT OUTER JOIN to Location would return 'All records from Location including matches from Employee', making (c) wrong too. A FULL OUTER JOIN would return 'The superset of both tables', so (d) is also wrong. Because Employee is on the left and Location is on the right of the LEFT OUTER JOIN operator, (b) is correct and will return 'All records in Employee including matches from Location'

9.) RIGHT JOIN Location ON Employee.LocationID = Location.LocationID will return all Location records including any matches from the Employee table, so (b) is wrong. INNER JOIN Location ON Employee.LocationID = Location.LocationID will only return the employee records that have a matching location, so (c) is wrong too. FULL JOIN Location ON Employee.LocationID = Location.LocationID will return the superset of both tables, making (d) incorrect. LEFT JOIN Location ON Employee.LocationID = Location.LocationID will return all employee records including any matches from the location table, making (a) the correct answer.

Bug Catcher Game

To play the Bug Catcher game, run the BugCatcher_Chapter3.pps from the BugCatcher folder of the companion files. You can obtain these files from the www.Joes2Pros.com website.

[NOTES]

Chapter 4. Query Strategies

As we get better at writing queries, there will be more people making requests for us to write them. Once we learn all the tricks, we'll begin to get the "Wow" reactions from managers and teammates. Of course, this means that we will also get to be a part of all the deadlines.

This chapter covers several ways to increase the bag of tricks available to us when writing queries, many of these techniques will help make our daily work life much easier as well. A few of the query strategies presented here will help us write robust and stable queries using fewer keystrokes. The first, and most important query strategy, will demonstrate how to write robust queries that won't break if the database changes. This usually requires some extra code, but the benefits make it well worth the effort.

READER NOTE: *Please run the SQLQueries2012Vol1Chapter4.0Setup.sql script in order to follow along with the examples in the first section of Chapter 4. All scripts mentioned in this chapter may be found at www.Joes2Pros.com.*

Query Writing Strategy

Here is something I have yet to find in any book. When enthusiastic SQL students do this, they experience a revelation. The number of errors drops significantly and the speed at writing complex queries increases immediately. Knowing how to narrow down what we are looking for amongst a vast list of choices helps immensely. Grabbing the right tables first and then the fields second is akin to grabbing the right menu before ordering an item from it. In fact, one student named Tim took this back to his team of SQL developers and they immediately implemented this process.

We are all used to following steps. Most of the time, actions are sequential from top to bottom or left to right. Other times we complete things in phases. The two phases we are going to use in this exercise apply to joining tables. This is easy to implement as we only need remember to organize first and clean up second.

When visiting a new restaurant, we will ask to see the menu, because we want to see all they have to offer. The odds are that we might be interested in half of the items, but only need a few dishes for our group at the table. Looking at the menu is like starting a query with a 'SELECT *' statement. Once we have looked at all the fields, we narrow our choice(s) to only the items we want at the time.

Sometimes restaurants have multiple menus. My favorite restaurant has a kids' menu, an adult menu, a gluten-free menu and a drink menu. These menus were each gathered at our table. Ultimately, in my head, a selection was narrowed to what was needed.

> **Phase I:** *Organize*. When building a new query from many tables, we often find ourselves wondering, "Where do I start?" First, lay the steps out by identifying which tables contain the essential data. Second, get all the table joins working with a basic 'SELECT *' statement. Third, add any basic filtering criteria.
>
> **Phase II:** *Itemize*. Once all joins and criteria, such as SELECT, FROM and WHERE are working, we are ready for Phase II. This entails going back and changing our 'SELECT *' to an itemized SELECT field list as the final step.

Let's explore how this two-phase process of Organize and then Itemize can be a big time-saver. We are going to use one of the challenges from the last lab. In Lab 3.2 (Outer Joins), Skill Check 2, we needed to get four fields from two different tables. If we were to list all four desired fields and test one table at time, we will get an error as seen on the right side of Figure 4.1.

In Figure 4.1 we write a SELECT statement and part of the FROM clause. When completed, the FROM clause will have two tables, but for now we just want to get the Location table working. By using the 'SELECT *' strategy, we remove any possible errors from line 1. From there, we can focus on the more complicated logic used for joining tables together. We can add tables one at a time until everything is working. This is the Organize phase.

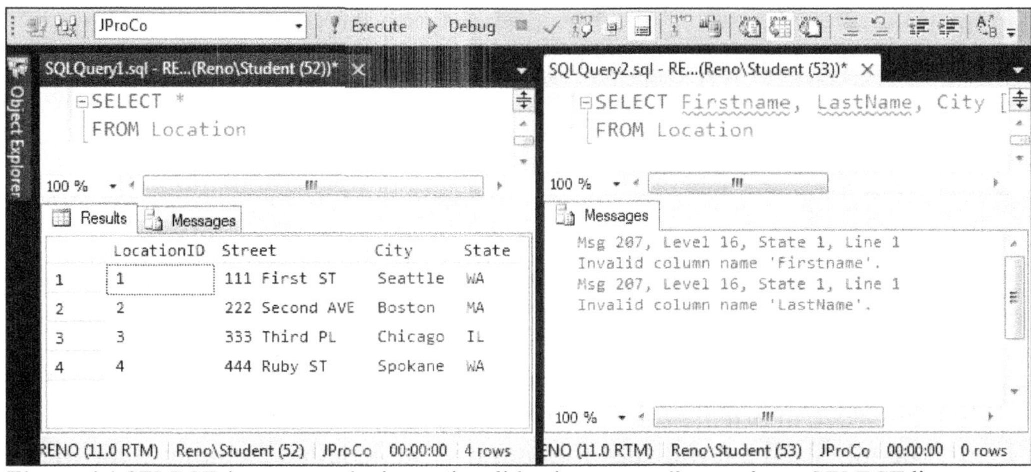

Figure 4.1 SELECT * never results in an "invalid column name" error, but a SELECT list can.

Reader Note: *SELECT * never results in an Error message stating "invalid column name", however; a SELECT list with itemized field(s) can have this error.*

After our query is organized and working, we can go back and itemize the SELECT field list to display only the fields that are necessary. This is done during Phase II (Itemize). The steps for this system are broken down as follows:

Phase I: *ORGANIZE* (write a SELECT * query statement with joins)

```
--Test first table logic
SELECT *
FROM Location
```

```
--Test second table with join
SELECT *
FROM Location INNER JOIN Employee
ON Location.LocationID = Employee.LocationID
```

```
--Test all tables with criteria
SELECT *
FROM Location INNER JOIN Employee
ON Location.LocationID = Employee.LocationID
WHERE [State] = 'WA'
```

Phase II: ***ITEMIZE*** (itemize the SELECT field list)

```
--Choose the fields
SELECT FirstName, LastName, City, [State]
FROM Location INNER JOIN Employee
ON Location.LocationID = Employee.LocationID
WHERE [State] = 'WA'
```

Since SELECT is always the first statement in a query, it's natural to want to write the field names before writing the FROM clause. However; we can save time and trouble by using the '*' until the entire query is working properly. When this is complete, it is very easy to itemize the field list, with the confidence of knowing it will not cause any problems.

READER NOTE: *Consistently using this two phase method for writing queries will prevent us from ever getting a field selection error again.*

Table Aliasing

When people ask me, "How did you do that?" oftentimes they are asking about ordinary work that got done quickly. This is great for deadlines. *Table aliasing* is a big saver of keystrokes. As we know, tables are listed in the FROM clause. We had to retype the table names again in the ON clause as seen in the code below:

```
SELECT *
FROM Location INNER JOIN Employee
ON Location.LocationID = Employee.LocationID
```

Setting Aliases

Our next goal is to get the FROM clause to refer to the Employee table as 'emp' and the Location table as 'loc'. It's like giving a nickname to a friend. They respond and use it, but their birth certificate still has the original name. In other words, the tables will not change names literally, but our query can use a shorter name. Simply alias the table name as another name in the FROM clause and we can then reuse the shorter name. Here is a SQL example:

```
SELECT *
FROM Location AS loc
INNER JOIN Employee AS emp
ON loc.LocationID = emp.LocationID
```

In this example, the payoff is only slightly obvious. As we write more and more complex queries, we will find that some queries will use a table name in dozens of places. It's far quicker to type *Loc* many times versus *Location.*

Using Aliases

At this point, we are probably not big fans of two-part field names in a query. In fact, the simple name seems to do the same thing with far fewer keystrokes. In comparing the two queries below, we see identical results.

```
--Simple Field Names
SELECT FirstName, LastName, [State]
FROM Location INNER JOIN Employee
ON Location.LocationID = Employee.LocationID
```

```
--Two-part Field Names
SELECT Employee.FirstName, Employee.LastName,
Location.[State]
FROM Location INNER JOIN Employee
ON Location.LocationID = Employee.LocationID
```

The truth is we have lucked out on all our past queries. The simple field name query from above is looking for FirstName from either table. Since there is a FirstName field in the Employee table only, FirstName must really mean Employee.FirstName, so SQL Server implicitly does this behind the scenes for us. The same is true with the [State] field. When SQL Server looks for the [State] field in the Employee table and realizes it isn't present, it does us the courtesy of pulling it in from the Location table.

Warning: *Please don't do any of the following steps regarding renaming fields. They are only for demonstration and assume a knowledge level discussed in Chapter 5 and Chapter 6. Enjoy the concept and feel free to come back and experiment after finishing this book.*

So far, we have been lucky. Everything has worked using the simple name. Why? Let's use an example. The Employee table has a Status field as seen in Figure 4.2.

```
SELECT *
FROM Employee
WHERE [Status] IS NOT NULL
```

	EmpID	LastName	FirstName	HireDate	LocationID	ManagerID	Status
1	4	Kennson	David	1996-03-16...	1	11	Has Tenure
2	7	Lonning	David	2000-01-01...	1	11	On Leave
3	12	O'Neil	Barbara	1995-05-26...	4	4	Has Tenure

3 rows

Figure 4.2 The Employee table has a Status field.

What if the Status field was renamed to [State] in the Employee table? We could end up with two table designs like the ones shown in Figure 4.3.

SQLQuery1.sql - RE...oCo (Reno\j2p (53))*

```
SELECT * FROM Employee
WHERE [State] IS NOT NULL
```

	EmpID	LastName	FirstName	HireDate	LocationID	ManagerID	State
1	4	Kennson	David	1996-03-16...	1	11	Has Tenure
2	7	Lonning	David	2000-01-01...	1	11	On Leave
3	12	O'Neil	Barbara	1995-05-26...	4	4	Has Tenure

Query executed successfully. RENO (11.0 RTM) Reno\j2p (53) JProCo 00:00:00 3 rows

SQLQuery2.sql - RE...oCo (Reno\j2p (55))*

```
SELECT *
FROM Location
```

	LocationID	Street	City	State
1	1	111 First ST	Seattle	WA
2	2	222 Second AVE	Boston	MA
3	3	333 Third PL	Chicago	IL
4	4	444 Ruby ST	Spokane	WA

RENO (11.0 RTM) Reno\j2p (55) JProCo 00:00:00 4 rows

Figure 4.3 The Employee table's Status field has been renamed to State. This move could lead to confusion as the Location table already has a State field with an entirely different meaning.

What happens when the Employee.Status field is renamed to the Employee.State field as shown in this code sample?

```
SELECT * FROM Employee
INNER JOIN Location
ON Employee.LocationID = Location.LocationID
```

	EmpID	LastName	FirstName	HireDate	LocationID	ManagerID	State	LocationID	Street	City	State
1	1	Adams	Alex	2001-01-01...	1	11	NULL	1	111 First ST	Seattle	WA
2	2	Brown	Barry	2002-08-12...	1	11	NULL	1	111 First ST	Seattle	WA
3	3	Osako	Lee	1999-09-01...	2	11	NULL	2	222 Second AVE	Boston	MA
4	4	Kennson	David	1996-03-16...	1	11	Has Tenure	1	111 First ST	Seattle	WA
5	5	Bender	Eric	2007-05-17...	1	11	NULL	1	111 First ST	Seattle	WA
6	6	Kendall	Lisa	2001-11-15...	4	4	NULL	4	444 Ruby ST	Spokane	WA

Query executed successfully. RENO (11.0 RTM) Reno\j2p (53) JProCo 00:00:00 11 rows

Figure 4.4 SELECT * displays the State fields from both the Location and Employee tables.

This brings up a question. If a SELECT field list includes [State], will SQL Server choose the Employee.State field or the Location.State field? The sheer risk of picking the wrong field means SQL Server will give an error message requesting more information. If we use a 'SELECT *' we will get both fields with no error.

When itemizing fields, we must specify exactly which ones we want. Suppose we want to include the [State] field in our report. If we use the simple name for a field when two fields with the same name exist, our list will be ambiguous and SQL Server displays an error message (Figure 4.5).

```
SELECT FirstName, LastName, City, [State]
FROM Employee INNER JOIN Location
ON Employee.LocationID = Location.LocationID
```

Messages
Msg 209, Level 16, State 1, Line 1 Ambiguous column name 'State'.
0 rows

Figure 4.5 SQL Server can't tell which [State] field you wish to see.

Notice the error message is coupled with an explanation that SQL Server does not make guesses for what field we want to see. The only time it allows simple field names in a multiple table query is when there is only one field with that name in either table. A good tip to remember is that a 'SELECT *' statement does not give ambiguous column name errors since it will display all fields.

We wanted the City and State fields displayed from the Location table. This error can be fixed by using a two-part field name. Let's modify the field selection list, to specify the Location.City and the Location.State fields with table aliases.

We used the Loc alias for the Location table in this query. Doing so allows us to use a shorter name each time we reference that table. This allows the State field to work in our query. We did not need to prefix the City field to get this query to work. Can you guarantee that tomorrow someone will not add a City field to the Employee table in your database to denote where the employee resides? This would break some of your queries.

You want to ensure that your queries will work today and into the future. A good way to do this is to use two-part names for all fields listed in your SELECT statement. This seems like extra typing which can be significantly reduced by using aliases.

```
SELECT FirstName, LastName, loc.City, loc.[State]
FROM Employee
INNER JOIN Location AS loc
ON Employee.LocationID = loc.LocationID
```

	FirstName	LastName	City	State
1	Alex	Adams	Seattle	WA
2	Barry	Brown	Seattle	WA
3	Lee	Osako	Boston	MA
4	David	Kennson	Seattle	WA
5	Eric	Bender	Seattle	WA
6	Lisa	Kendall	Spokane	WA
				11 rows

Figure 4.6 Using the Loc alias for the Location table to use the two-part names loc.City and loc.[State].

In Figure 4.7 we have changed every listed field to use the two-part name. The aliasing we did in our FROM clause allowed us to use the shorter names. Aliasing is a time-saving way to allow you to create robust and durable code more easily.

```
SELECT emp.FirstName, emp.LastName,
loc.city, loc.[state]
FROM Employee AS emp
INNER JOIN Location AS loc
ON emp.LocationID = Loc.LocationID
```

	FirstName	LastName	City	State
1	Alex	Adams	Seattle	WA
2	Barry	Brown	Seattle	WA
3	Lee	Osako	Boston	MA
4	David	Kennson	Seattle	WA
5	Eric	Bender	Seattle	WA
6	Lisa	Kendall	Spokane	WA
				11 rows

Figure 4.7 All four fields in the SELECT list are using two-part names.

Lab 4.1: Table Aliasing

Lab Prep: Each lab has one or more Skill Checks. Start with Skill Check 1 and proceed until reaching the Points to Ponder section.

Before beginning this lab, verify that SQL Server 2012 is properly installed and operating. Before running the lab setup script for resetting the database (SQLQueries2012Vol1Chapter4.1Setup.sql), please make sure to close all query windows within SSMS. An open query window pointing to a database context can lock that database preventing it from updating when the script is executing. A simple way to assure all query windows are closed, is to exit out of SSMS, then open a new instance of SSMS, and lastly run the setup script.

Skill Check 1: We are asked to show all employees who have found grants. This can be accomplished by joining the Employee and [Grant] tables in the JProCo database context.

Include the FirstName, LastName, GrantName and Amount fields in the selection list. Alias the Employee table as 'E' and the Grant table as 'G'. All four fields in the SELECT list must use the two-part field name identifier. When done, the results will have 9 records and resemble Figure 4.8.

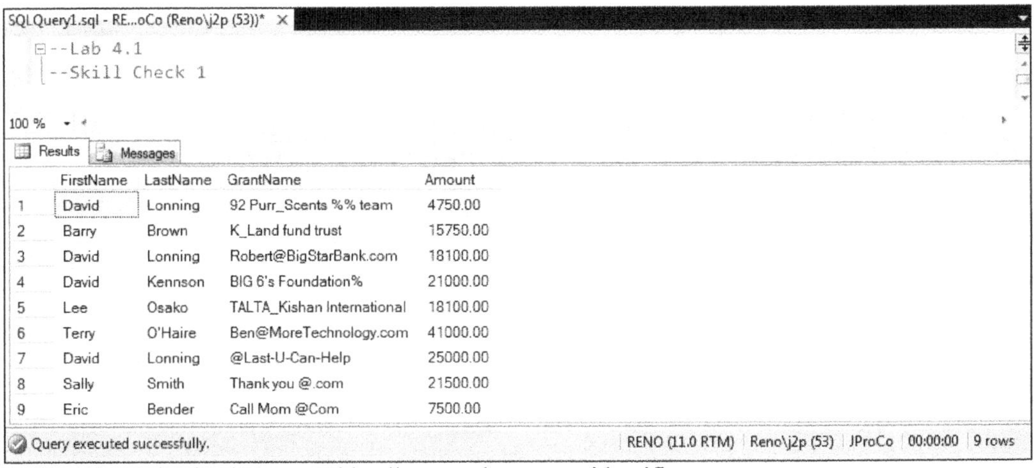

SQLQuery1.sql - RE...oCo (Reno\j2p (53))*

```
--Lab 4.1
--Skill Check 1
```

100 %

Results | Messages

	FirstName	LastName	GrantName	Amount
1	David	Lonning	92 Purr_Scents %% team	4750.00
2	Barry	Brown	K_Land fund trust	15750.00
3	David	Lonning	Robert@BigStarBank.com	18100.00
4	David	Kennson	BIG 6's Foundation%	21000.00
5	Lee	Osako	TALTA_Kishan International	18100.00
6	Terry	O'Haire	Ben@MoreTechnology.com	41000.00
7	David	Lonning	@Last-U-Can-Help	25000.00
8	Sally	Smith	Thank you @.com	21500.00
9	Eric	Bender	Call Mom @Com	7500.00

Query executed successfully. | RENO (11.0 RTM) | Reno\j2p (53) | JProCo | 00:00:00 | 9 rows

Figure 4.8 Skill Check 1 uses table aliases and two-part identifiers.

Skill Check 2: We are asked to show a list of employees and where they work, only if they work at one of the four locations. Display the FirstName, LastName, City and [State] fields. Alias the Employee table as 'emp' and the Location table as 'loc'. When done the result set should contain eleven records.

Answer Code: The T-SQL code to this lab can be found from the downloadable files named Lab4.1_TableAliasing.sql.

Points to Ponder - Table Aliasing

1. Databases, tables and columns have names. These names are called Identifiers. There is an Employee table in the JProCo database. This table is an object and the object's Identifier is Employee.
2. To alias a table, we use an abbreviation. SQL aliasing usually means a shorter name is being used than the original identifier.
3. Aliases must be declared immediately after the table's name in the FROM clause.
4. Once a table has an alias, the alias must be used wherever that table is referred to in the query.
5. The process of qualifying fields with two part names ensures that a query will be unambiguous.
6. The extra work of qualifying fields is reduced by using a shorter alias name instead of the complete table name.
7. Using the keyword AS when specifying an alias is optional, although it is considered a best practice, since it makes reading the code much easier.

Cartesian Result Sets

Sometimes we find tables that do not have a field relatable to any other table. Because of this, there is no way to perform a meaningful inner or outer type of join for reporting. There are times when we are really looking for combinations between tables rather than exact matches. The Cartesian combination of data coupled with the CROSS JOIN will be explored in this section.

Inner and outer join types are useful for finding records in related tables. These join types reflect the reality of our data. In contrast, a CROSS JOIN does not need related data to execute, making this type of join useful for exploring future possibilities. For example, at the beginning of a college semester, students may want to know what courses are required of them. Perhaps they have satisfied some of those requirements. The requirements apply to all students regardless of the coursework they have done so far. A CROSS JOIN simply returns all possible combinations of the record set data from the tables listed.

Using this type of join will display all combinations for a list of students and their course requirements. So, if 10 students need to take 3 required courses each, then the Cartesian result of this CROSS JOIN is 30 records. Each student will be listed three times in the result set, once for each required class.

This list details the courses each student must complete prior to graduation and has nothing to do with what they have actually done. The Cartesian result set is a combination of the information freshman students need to know to ensure their ability to graduate in the future.

Let us suppose that employees Alex Adams and Barry Brown from the JProCo database want to become managers. In JProCo, there is a list of management classes that aspiring managers must complete. This list is located in the JProCo MgmtTraining table.

We can query the Employee table using the EmpID numbers for Alex and Barry, and write a separate SELECT query of the MgmtTraining table to show both employees and the three required classes as seen in Figure 4.9.

```
SELECT * FROM Employee
WHERE EmpID IN (1,2)

SELECT * FROM MgmtTraining
```

	EmpID	LastName	FirstName	HireDate	LocationID	ManagerID	Status
1	1	Adams	Alex	2001-01-01 00:00:00.000	1	11	NULL
2	2	Brown	Barry	2002-08-12 00:00:00.000	1	11	NULL

	ClassID	ClassName	ClassDurationHours
1	1	Embracing Diversity	12
2	2	Interviewing	6
3	3	Difficult Negotiations	30

Query executed successfully. | RENO (11.0 RTM) | Reno\j2p (51) | JProCo | 00:00:00 | 5 rows

Figure 4.9 Two employees are in the first result set while three classes are in the second.

We don't know how many classes Alex or Barry have already taken. A third-party company has stored all of their registration information. Right now, we are more interested in supplying them with a list of requirements for their benefit. Using a CROSS JOIN will show the entire list of classes each aspiring employee must complete before being considered for JProCo management.

If Alex must complete three classes and Barry must complete the same three, combining the result sets from both queries would yield six records (2 * 3 = 6). We can verify this by looking at the results shown in Figure 4.10.

```
SELECT * FROM Employee
CROSS JOIN MgmtTraining
WHERE EmpID IN (1,2)
```

	EmpID	LastName	FirstName	HireDate	LocationID	ManagerID	Status	ClassID	ClassName	ClassDurationHours
1	1	Adams	Alex	2001-01-01...	1	11	NULL	1	Embracing Diversity	12
2	1	Adams	Alex	2001-01-01...	1	11	NULL	2	Interviewing	6
3	1	Adams	Alex	2001-01-01...	1	11	NULL	3	Difficult Negotiations	30
4	2	Brown	Barry	2002-08-12...	1	11	NULL	1	Embracing Diversity	12
5	2	Brown	Barry	2002-08-12...	1	11	NULL	2	Interviewing	6
6	2	Brown	Barry	2002-08-12...	1	11	NULL	3	Difficult Negotiations	30

Query executed successfully. | RENO (11.0 RTM) | Reno\j2p (51) | JProCo | 00:00:00 | 6 rows

Figure 4.10 A CROSS JOIN with 3 records from one table and 2 from another yields 6 records.

A CROSS JOIN does not show us the actual relationship between the tables. The list shown in Figure 4.10 does not tell us what classes Barry and Alex have taken. Instead, it simply shows all possible record combinations between two results and combines them into one record set. These tables often have nothing in common, or may have no common field upon which to join. Because of this trait, we do not need to specify an ON clause for a CROSS JOIN query.

Lab 4.2: Cross Joins

Lab Prep: Each lab has one or more Skill Checks. Start with Skill Check 1 and proceed until reaching the Points to Ponder section.

Before beginning this lab, verify that SQL Server 2012 is properly installed and operating. Before running the lab setup script for resetting the database (SQLQueries2012Vol1Chapter4.2Setup.sql), please make sure to close all query windows within SSMS. An open query window pointing to a database context can lock that database preventing it from updating when the script is executing. A simple way to assure all query windows are closed, is to exit out of SSMS, then open a new instance of SSMS, and lastly run the setup script.

Skill Check 1: In the JProCo database, there is an Employee table with twelve records and a Location table with four locations. Each employee has one location, although they can visit any of them.

Write a query to show the combinations of every employee and every location. Display the FirstName, LastName, City and State fields in the selection list. Alias the Employee table as 'E' and the Location table as 'L'. When done the results should reveal 48 records and resemble Figure 4.11.

	FirstName	LastName	City	State
1	Alex	Adams	Seattle	WA
2	Barry	Brown	Seattle	WA
3	Lee	Osako	Seattle	WA
4	David	Kennson	Seattle	WA
5	Eric	Bender	Seattle	WA
6	Lisa	Kendall	Seattle	WA
				48 rows

Figure 4.11 Skill Check 1 shows each employee combined with each possible location.

Answer Code: The T-SQL code to this lab can be found from the downloadable files named Lab4.2_CrossJoins.sql.

Points to Ponder - Cross Joins

1. A CROSS JOIN creates or finds all possible entity combinations.
2. There is no need for an ON clause with a CROSS JOIN.
3. The size of the result set created from a CROSS JOIN is determined by multiplying the number of records in the first and second table together.
4. A CROSS JOIN gives every combination of both tables. It is known as a Cartesian product or Cartesian result.
5. If one table had 12 records and the other had four, then the Cartesian result of these tables would be 48 records.
6. When Cartesian results are the desired goal, use a CROSS JOIN query.

Unmatched Records Queries

Try to recall from our earlier exercises that the JProCo database has two related tables with some unmatched records. For example, in the Employee table, John Marshbank has no LocationID for any of the JProCo locations. The LocationID field of the Employee table is used to map to the LocationID field of the Location table. Without even looking at the Location table we can identify the employee that would not be matched up to records in the Location table. All we need to do is find the NULL in the LocationID field.

With a single table query we can easily see that John Marshbank is the only employee without a location (Figure 4.12).

```
SELECT FirstName, LastName, LocationID
FROM Employee
```

	FirstName	LastName	LocationID
5	Eric	Bender	1
6	Lisa	Kendall	4
7	David	Lonning	1
8	John	Marshbank	NULL
9	James	Newton	2
10	Terry	O'Haire	2

12 rows

Figure 4.12 The Employee table shows which employee has a LocationID of NULL.

Whenever a table has relatable fields that allow NULLs, like LocationID, we need to be on the lookout for possible unmatched records in related tables.

```
SELECT *
FROM Location
```

	LocationID	Street	City	State
1	1	111 First ST	Seattle	WA
2	2	222 Second AVE	Boston	MA
3	3	333 Third PL	Chicago	IL
4	4	444 Ruby ST	Spokane	WA

4 rows

Figure 4.13 The Location table has no NULLs, although some locations may have no employees.

Looking at the Location table in Figure 4.13 we see all the data. In fact, this table does not allow NULLs for the LocationID field. Looking closer, we see there are no NULLs anywhere in the Location table. So does this mean that all locations have at least one employee? Perhaps that is not the case.

In an earlier exercise, we discovered that the location in Chicago is still under construction and has no employees. If we wanted to find all locations with no employees, we would run a query that finds unmatched records.

In this case, we need to join the Location table with the Employee table in order to determine the location where nobody yet works.

What type of join can we use to find unmatched records? Since NULLs are unable to pass thru the ON clause of an INNER JOIN, any records with a LocationID having a NULL will be dropped from the result set, so we won't see Chicago. An OUTER JOIN will show both the matched and the unmatched records, so we will be able to see every employee and their location (Figure 4.14).

```
SELECT *
FROM Location AS loc
LEFT OUTER JOIN Employee AS emp
ON loc.LocationID = emp.LocationID
```

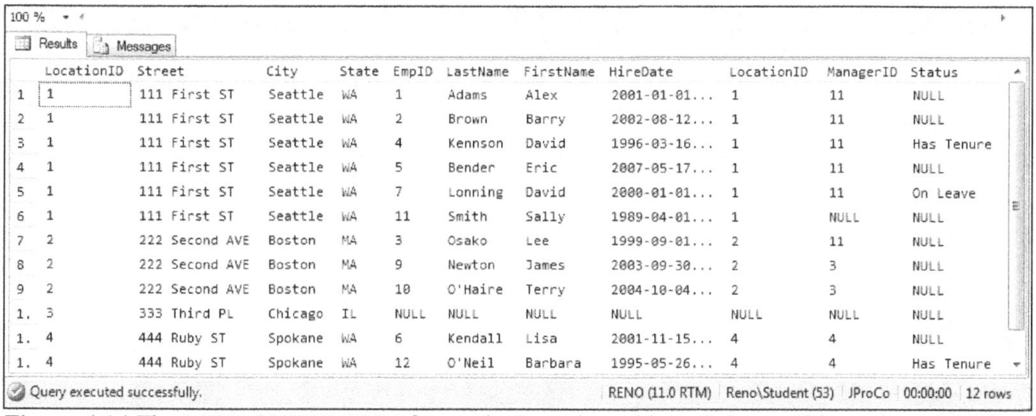

100 %

Results | Messages

	LocationID	Street	City	State	EmpID	LastName	FirstName	HireDate	LocationID	ManagerID	Status
1	1	111 First ST	Seattle	WA	1	Adams	Alex	2001-01-01...	1	11	NULL
2	1	111 First ST	Seattle	WA	2	Brown	Barry	2002-08-12...	1	11	NULL
3	1	111 First ST	Seattle	WA	4	Kennson	David	1996-03-16...	1	11	Has Tenure
4	1	111 First ST	Seattle	WA	5	Bender	Eric	2007-05-17...	1	11	NULL
5	1	111 First ST	Seattle	WA	7	Lonning	David	2000-01-01...	1	11	On Leave
6	1	111 First ST	Seattle	WA	11	Smith	Sally	1989-04-01...	1	NULL	NULL
7	2	222 Second AVE	Boston	MA	3	Osako	Lee	1999-09-01...	2	11	NULL
8	2	222 Second AVE	Boston	MA	9	Newton	James	2003-09-30...	2	3	NULL
9	2	222 Second AVE	Boston	MA	10	O'Haire	Terry	2004-10-04...	2	3	NULL
1.	3	333 Third PL	Chicago	IL	NULL	NULL	NULL	NULL	NULL	NULL	NULL
1.	4	444 Ruby ST	Spokane	WA	6	Kendall	Lisa	2001-11-15...	4	4	NULL
1.	4	444 Ruby ST	Spokane	WA	12	O'Neil	Barbara	1995-05-26...	4	4	Has Tenure

Query executed successfully. | RENO (11.0 RTM) | Reno\Student (53) | JProCo | 00:00:00 | 12 rows

Figure 4.14 The LEFT OUTER JOIN favors the Location table and shows Chicago has a NULL employee.

Seattle is listed many times. Chicago is listed once with no employee found. A NULL appears in the fields from the Employee table for Chicago. With the Location table on the left and the NULL located in the table on the right, we have part of an unmatched records query. To find just the records that don't match, we must look for only the NULL records in the table that the outer join does not favor. In this case, it's the Employee table.

A LEFT OUTER JOIN will show all unmatched records with a NULL value for the LocationID when the WHERE clause criteria looks for NULLs on this field in the non-dominant table. Unmatched record queries will return a result set displaying ***only*** the unmatched records between the two tables.

We can use a LEFT OUTER JOIN to filter our search condition criteria on a NULL LocationID value from the Employee table (right table), which will produce an unmatched records query. Since our query criterion specifies a LocationID that IS NULL in the Employee table, the only location to show in our result set will be Chicago (Figure 4.15).

```
SELECT *
FROM Location AS loc
LEFT OUTER JOIN Employee AS emp
ON loc.LocationID = emp.LocationID
WHERE emp.LocationID IS NULL
```

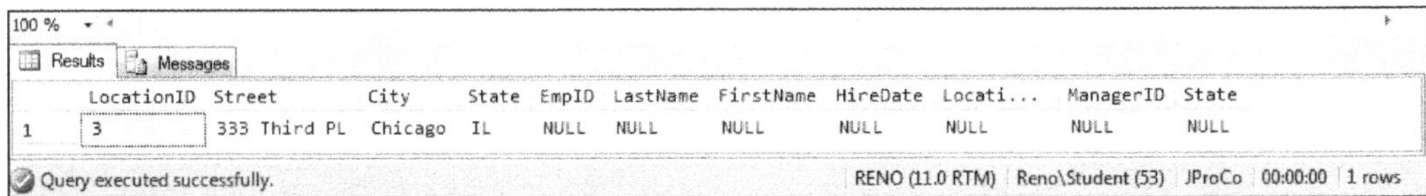

	LocationID	Street	City	State	EmpID	LastName	FirstName	HireDate	Locati...	ManagerID	State
1	3	333 Third PL	Chicago	IL	NULL	NULL	NULL	NULL	NULL	NULL	NULL

Query executed successfully. | RENO (11.0 RTM) | Reno\Student (53) | JProCo | 00:00:00 | 1 rows

Figure 4.15 A unmatched query where records from the left table find no records in the right table.

Lab 4.3: Unmatched Records Queries

Lab Prep: Each lab has one or more Skill Checks. Start with Skill Check 1 and proceed until reaching the Points to Ponder section.

Before beginning this lab, verify that SQL Server 2012 is properly installed and operating. Before running the lab setup script for resetting the database (SQLQueries2012Vol1Chapter4.3Setup.sql), please make sure to close all query windows within SSMS. An open query window pointing to a database context can lock that database preventing it from updating when the script is executing. A simple way to assure all query windows are closed, is to exit out of SSMS, then open a new instance of SSMS, and lastly run the setup script.

Skill Check 1: David Lonning and a few other employees have been great about finding grants. Some other employees have found none at all.

Write an unmatched records query to show all employees who have never found a grant. Show the FirstName, LastName and GrantName fields. When done, the results should resemble Figure 4.16.

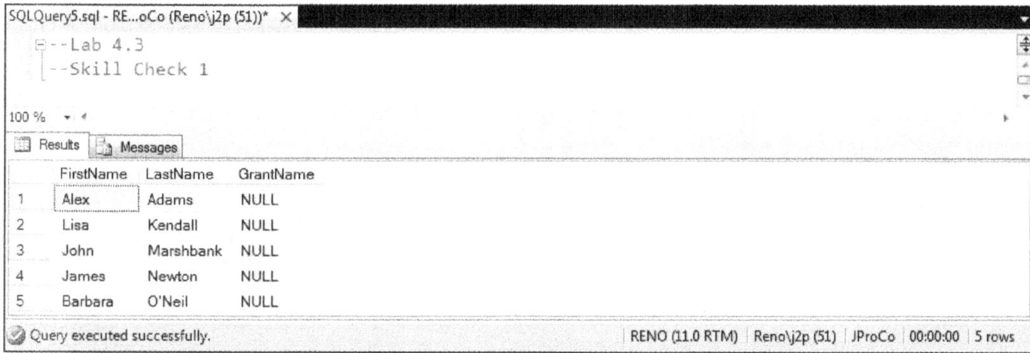

	FirstName	LastName	GrantName
1	Alex	Adams	NULL
2	Lisa	Kendall	NULL
3	John	Marshbank	NULL
4	James	Newton	NULL
5	Barbara	O'Neil	NULL

Figure 4.16 Skill Check 1 displays all employees that have not found a grant.

Answer Code: The T-SQL code to this lab can be found from the downloadable files named Lab4.3_UnmatchedRecordsQueries.sql.

Points to Ponder - Unmatched Records Queries

1. A LEFT OUTER JOIN and a RIGHT OUTER JOIN are useful for finding records when two sets of tables have unmatched values on the joined field.
2. When looking for NULL values, use the IS NULL operator rather than the equals comparison operator sign '= NULL'.
3. Using a WHERE clause adds search criteria to a query. The correct SQL syntax for a WHERE clause is: WHERE *<column name>* [*search condition criteria*]. In our unmatched records query example this clause reads **WHERE FirstName IS NULL**.
4. If all values in the joined fields match, the unmatched records query result set will return no records.

Chapter Glossary

Alias: An abbreviated name for a database object to save keystrokes while writing queries.

Cartesian Result: All combinations of records from all tables. If table A has five records and table B has 10 records, the Cartesian result set would be 50 records.

CROSS JOIN: A type of join that produces a Cartesian result set.

Unmatched Records Query: A technique used to find the records between tables that don't match.

Review Quiz - Chapter Four

1.) You want to change the database context to your JProCo database. Which code accomplishes this?

O a. GOTO JProCo
O b. USE JProCo
O c. GO JProCo
O d. SELECT JProCo

2.) You have two tables. Which type of join would produce the most number of records?

O a. INNER JOIN
O b. LEFT OUTER JOIN
O c. RIGHT OUTER JOIN
O d. FULL OUTER JOIN
O e. CROSS JOIN

3.) What is the correct way to alias the sales table?

O a. FROM Sales AS sl
O b. FROM sl AS Sales sl
O c. SELECT Sales AS sl

4.) Square brackets are required when…

O a. The table name conflicts with a keyword
O b. The table name is the same as another table.
O c. The table uses the same name as the database.
O d. To alias the table.

5.) What happens when you omit the word INNER from an INNER JOIN?

O a. You get an error message.
O b. The join becomes and outer join.
O c. The join operates as an inner join by default.

6.) Which of the following queries returns a true Cartesian result from the Employee and Location tables?

O a.
```
SELECT p.EmployeeID, T.[Name]
FROM Employee p
FULL OUTER JOIN Location t
WHERE t.TerritoryID = t.TerritoryID
```

O b.
```
SELECT P.EmployeeID, T.[Name]
FROM Employee p
CROSS JOIN Location t
WHERE t.TerritoryID = t.TerritoryID
```

O c.
```
SELECT P.EmployeeID, t.[Name]
FROM Employee p
CROSS JOIN Location t
WHERE t.TerritoryID != t.TerritoryID
```

O d.
```
SELECT p.EmployeeID, t.[Name]
FROM Employee p
CROSS JOIN Location t
```

Answer Key

1.) GOTO tells SQL Server to jump to a labeled piece of code to execute, so (a) is incorrect. GO tells SQL Server to finish processing the preceding code before continuing, making (c) incorrect too. SELECT is the first word in a query, so (d) is incorrect. USE JProCo will change the database context to the JProCo database, so (b) is correct.

2.) INNER JOIN will return only those records that have a matching value in a field common to both tables, limited to the number of records in the larger table, so (a) is wrong. LEFT OUTER JOIN will return every record in the left table and include any matches from the other table, limited to the number of records in the left table, so (b) is also wrong. RIGHT OUTER JOIN will return every record in the right table and include any matches from the other table, limited to the number of records in the right table, so (c) is wrong too. FULL OUTER JOIN will return every row from both tables including the mismatched records, limited to the sum of the records from each table making (d) wrong also. A CROSS JOIN will return every row in one table for each row in the other table creating a Cartesian result; the number of rows returned is the number of rows from the first table multiplied by the number of rows in the other, so (e) is the right one.

3.) 'FROM sl AS Sales sl' will alias the 'sl' table as 'Sales' then display a syntax error because of the second 'sl' making (b) wrong. 'SELECT Sales AS sl' will alias the 'Sales' field as 'sl', so (c) is also wrong. 'FROM Sales AS sl' will alias the 'Sales' table as 'sl', so (a) is correct.

4.) If 'The table name is the same as another table' we must fully qualify the name to refer to the correct table but square brackets are not needed, so (b) is not correct. If 'The table uses the same name as the database' then the table's fully qualified name is *[DatabaseName].[SchemaName].[ObjectName]* but square brackets are not needed, so (c) is also wrong. When 'The table name conflicts with a keyword' we can use square brackets to tell SQL Server we are referring to an object and not the keyword, so (a) is correct.

5.) Because JOIN is short for INNER JOIN there will be no error message so (a) is not correct. If OUTER is omitted from LEFT OUTER JOIN or RIGHT OUTER JOIN the join will work as an outer join, so (b) is also incorrect. The join operates as an inner join by default when the word INNER is omitted, so (c) is correct.

6.) The queries in (a), (b) and (c) all use a WHERE clause to filter the results, so even if they had used a CROSS JOIN they still won't return every row in one table for each row in the other making all three of those answers wrong. The query in (d) is correct, because it uses a CROSS JOIN and doesn't filter any of the results.

Bug Catcher Game

To play the Bug Catcher game run the BugCatcher_Chapter4.pps from the BugCatcher folder of the companion files. You can obtain these files from the www.Joes2Pros.com website.

[NOTES]

Chapter 5. Data Definition Language (DDL)

From our discussion so far, it is probably not surprising to know that in the database world, data is king because it's all about data. Databases are impressive tools that can be fun to use. Powerful programs like SQL Server exist because of the need for businesses and organizations to reliably store, organize, access and protect their mission-critical data. In this chapter we won't work with data at all. We will learn how to build the two basic structures that contain our valuable data: databases and tables.

READER NOTE: *Please run the SQLQueries2012Vol1Chapter5.0Setup.sql script in order to follow along with the examples in the first section of Chapter 5. All scripts mentioned in this chapter may be found at www.Joes2Pros.com.*

Creating and Dropping Databases

When a new database is created, it contains no data. In fact, it has no tables to hold data until we create them as well. Data is like cargo – it needs a container to hold it. The container itself is not really data, but a design or definition.

The columns within a table define what data they will hold. For example, if the EmpID field only accepts integer data, the table will not allow any other data type to be used. It would not be possible to place a name in the EmpID field, as it only accepts integer values (numbers). When creating a new object we must also define the data type for how the data will be stored. Any statement that starts with the keyword CREATE is known as a DDL statement (Data Definition Language). As the name implies, DDL statements are all about defining the structures we build to hold the data. The three DDL keywords are CREATE, DROP and ALTER. We will wait until Chapter 7 to discuss ALTER statements.

I am often asked by students if it is possible to have two databases named JProCo in SQL Server at the same time. The answer is no, as SQL Server will not allow two databases with the same name on the same SQL Server instance. If we already have a database named JProCo and try to create another JProCo, we will quickly be issued an error message.

We can have the same database name on many different servers. For instance, there can be a SQL Server named "Reno" and another SQL Server named "Tampa" that can each have a database named "JProCo".

There are two main ways to create a database. We can use the SSMS User Interface to "point-and-click" our way to a new database, or we can accomplish the same thing by writing some SQL code. While we should be aware of the "point-and-click" method, it is far more likely in a business setting and even more useful in individual study to be confident in writing reusable code to create a database.

It is easy to teach someone how to "point-and-click" their way to creating a database with the SSMS UI. This method, unlike coding by hand, does not leave us with a human readable path to trace our steps in case of a mistake. When any mistake is made the entire process must start over from scratch, since there isn't any way of knowing where the mistake was made. If we were asked to create the same database on 10 different servers, we would need to be extra careful using this method, as a single incorrect click can make a large difference. As mentioned in previous chapters, this is another case where reusable code is our friend.

Creating Databases with Management Studio

For this exercise, we are going to create a database named db1 by using the SQL Server Management Studio User Interface (SSMS UI). This will require us to navigate thru some windows in the Object Explorer pane. Look to the far left side of the SSMS UI immediately under the toolbar(s) to locate the Object Explorer window pane. Found it? Great, now right-click on the Databases folder and choose the 'New Database…' option in the pop-up menu, as seen in Figure 5.1.

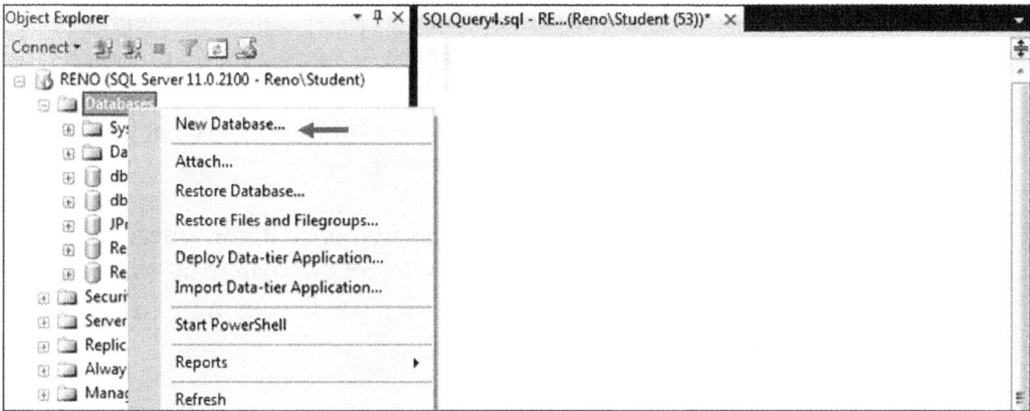

Figure 5.1 Creating a new database from Object Explorer.

The next few steps here are pretty simple. Enter the database name and then click on the 'OK' button. The program executes for a few seconds as the new user database goes thru the process of being registered with SQL Server instance.

Once this simple step is completed, we should notice a new gold cylinder in the Object Explorer with the name of db1. Since this is a brand new database, db1 has no tables, but is ready for us to add them whenever we choose.

What if we want to get rid of the database? This is called dropping a database. When it comes time to drop the db1 database, it's a simple process. We need to navigate the Object Explorer window to the Databases folder and then to the db1 database. Once we have located db1, simply right-click on it and choose the option for 'Delete'. We can confirm with the 'OK' button of the 'Delete Object' dialog box and the gold cylinder called db1 disappears from Object Explorer.

In the future, SSMS UI navigation instructions like those above will look like this:

Object Explorer > **Databases** > right-click **db1** > **Delete**

Creating Databases with SQL Code

We know SQL Server keeps track of all its databases. Most of our SQL Server setup and settings are stored in one location. Some applications like to store settings in a file or registry. Since SQL is a champ at storing data in tables, it has its own private collection of System tables. System tables are storage areas to keep track of what is going on in the system. When we add a new database like db2, it gets recorded in these special system tables.

Most of the system tables are stored in a System database called Master. In fact, the Object Explorer is talking to the System databases all the time and graphically displays what it has found. We can also talk directly with the Master database. We can use the Master database to make major changes on SQL Server or just look around at what has been created or set on the server.

To create a database named db2, we will need to first open a new query window to the Master database. Alternatively, we can write a USE statement to set the master database context. Write and execute the SQL code shown in Figure 5.2.

Remember the GO statement from Chapter 2? This separates our code into batches. Each batch finishes entirely before the next batch starts. This means we must be in the Master database context before trying to create the db2 database.

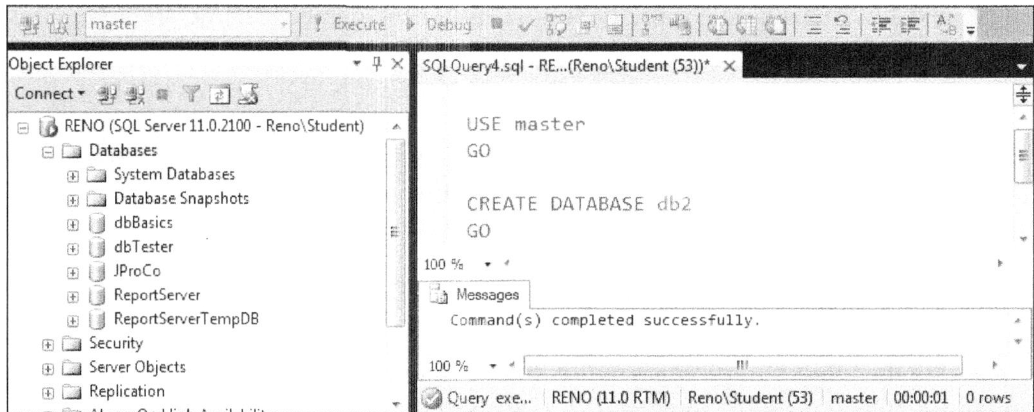

Figure 5.2 SQL Server creates db2 sucessfully, but Object Explorer must be refreshed to see it.

SQL Server tells us it successfully created db2 by displaying the message 'Command(s) completed successfully' shown in Figure 5.3. The Object Explorer needs to be refreshed to visually confirm the gold cylinder with db2 exists. Go to the Object Explorer window, right-click the Databases folder and select Refresh.

The Object Explorer now shows the db2 database in Figure 5.3. It appears along with our other user databases as a gold cylinder. This is an easy way to view all the databases in the SQL Server instance.

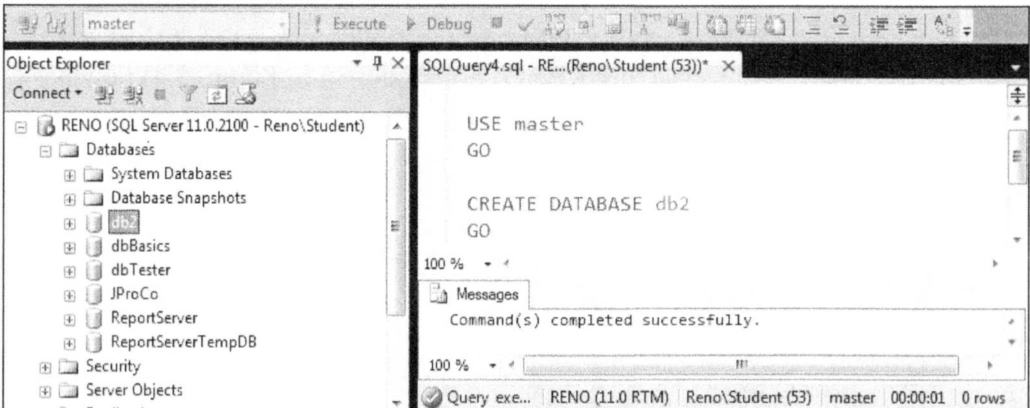

Figure 5.3 The db2 database appears after refreshing the Object Explorer.

Now that we have created a database, let's eliminate or remove it using this SQL statement:

```
USE master
GO

DROP DATABASE db2
GO
```

In the Object Explorer it appears that our db2 database is still present. Once again refresh the Databases folder in the Object Explorer window.

Object Explorer > right-click **Databases** > **Refresh**

We can now see that SQL Server has dropped the database from our system.

The keyword DROP is used by SQL Server to eliminate databases. Many students wonder why DROP is used instead of the keyword DELETE, hang on – we'll find the complete explanation in Chapter 6 on DML statements.

Verifying Which Databases Exist

Databases which we create, modify and drop are called *user databases*. They hold all the business data we need on SQL Server. When someone says "database" this tends to be shorthand for a user database.

There are databases that SQL Server itself uses for storing settings and other metadata it needs to operate. These System databases can tell us a lot about what is going on. They are not used to store user-generated information.

Create a new user database named dbMovie and Refresh the Object Explorer Databases folder. In this case, my RENO server (shown in Figure 5.4) now has seven user databases.

```
CREATE DATABASE dbMovie
GO
```

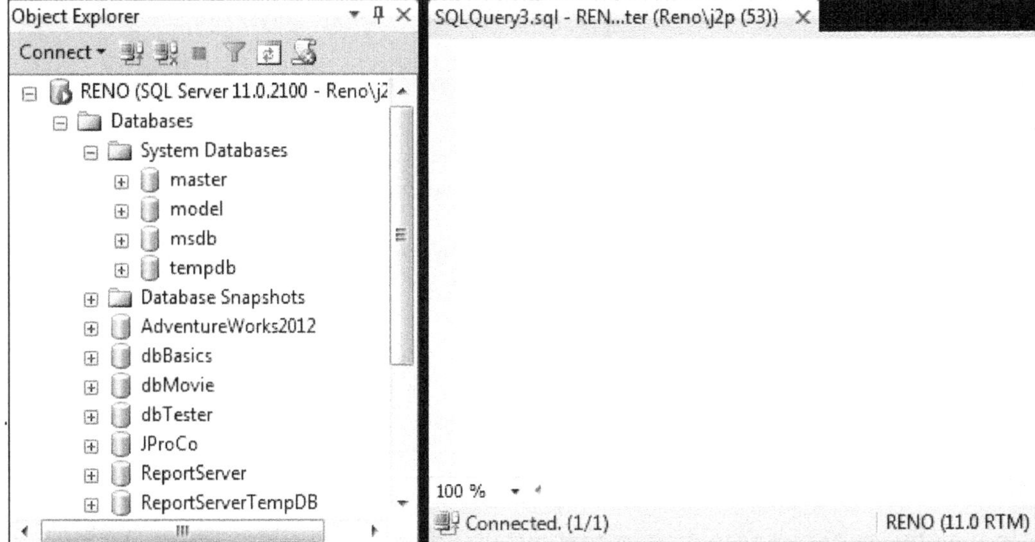

Figure 5.4 This SQL Server instance has seven user databases and four System databases.

The Object Explorer also shows four System databases for a total of eleven databases stored in my RENO SQL Server instance. Keep a mental note of this list for the next explanation.

The Object Explorer talks to SQL Server and asks for a list of databases to show the user. We can do the same thing by looking for the data directly. To see how many databases exist on our instance of SQL Server, query the system table directly. Type and run the code below:

```
USE master
GO

SELECT * FROM sys.sysdatabases
```

We will get a list of all system and user databases. Notice this list matches the same list we see in the Object explorer.

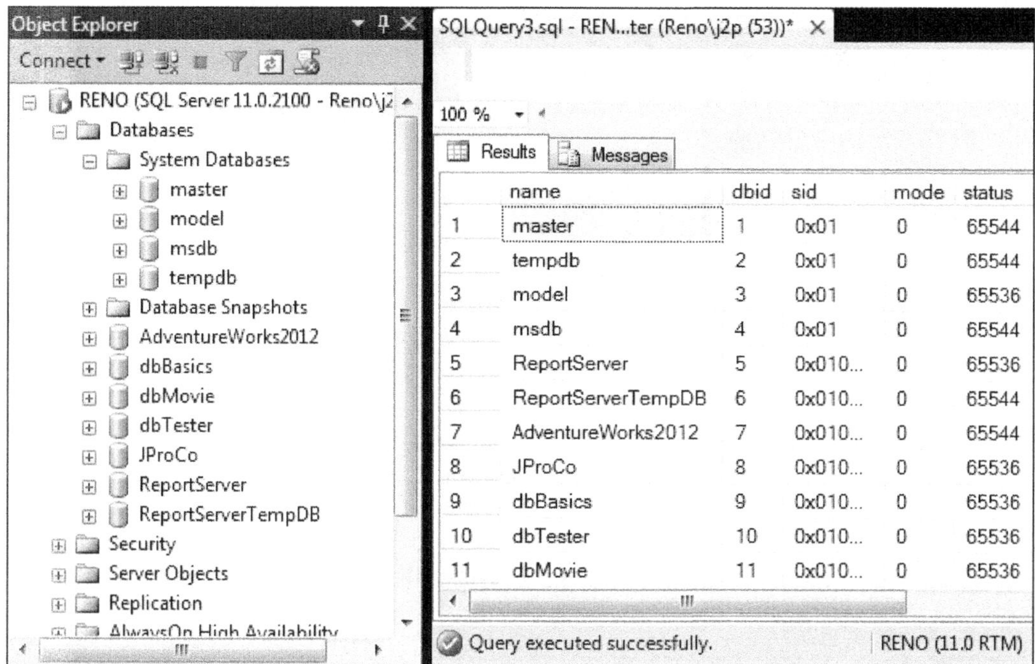

Figure 5.5 A query of the sys.sysdatabases catalog view shows all user and System databases.

Sys.sysdatabases acts like a table, but is actually called a Catalog View. A Catalog is a term that either means database or data storage area. If we wanted to find a specific database named JProCo, we can modify our earlier query:

```
SELECT *
FROM sys.sysdatabases
WHERE [name] = 'JProCo'
```

If a record is displayed, then JProCo exists. If there are no records, then there is no database named JProCo on our server. Remember that SQL Server is case insensitive, so we could have provided 'jproco', 'JPROCO' or any combination of upper/lower case letters for JProCo and received the same results.

We learned earlier in this chapter that if we attempted to create another JProCo database we would get an error. What if we tried to drop a database that does not exist? There is no dbJoes on our SQL Server. If we try to drop dbJoes and it's not there, we will also get an error message, as seen in Figure 5.6.

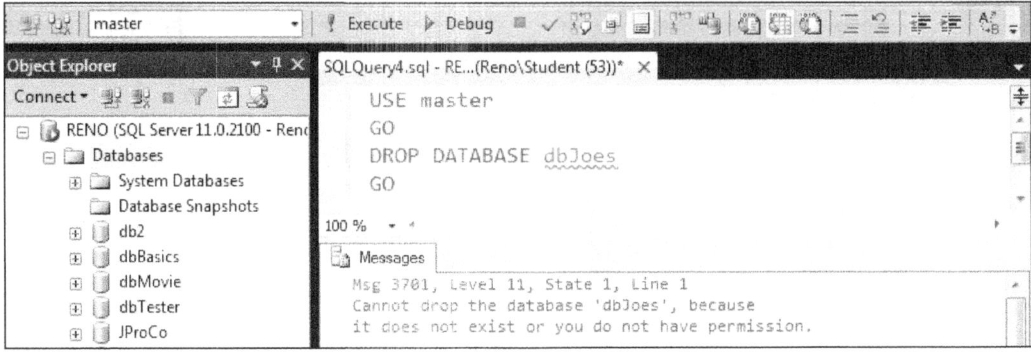

Figure 5.6 A database cannot be dropped that doesn't exist.

So, we can only drop a database if it already exists, and trying to affect an object that does not exist will give us an error message.

There is a way to make sure the database is gone: Drop it only if it exists. If it does not exist, there's no need to drop it. The following code will only drop the dbJoes database if it exists:

```
USE master
GO

IF EXISTS(
SELECT * FROM sys.sysdatabases
WHERE [name] = 'dbJoes')
DROP DATABASE dbJoes
GO
```

By the time the second GO has been hit, we know there is no dbJoes database on your system. How does the code accomplish this? This code first tells SQL Server to use the master database. GO ensures that the 'USE master' is completed before the code to DROP the database starts. IF EXISTS is a conditional statement.

IF EXISTS will evaluate what is inside the parentheses. If it finds any records in the SELECT statement, then it evaluates to true. If nothing is found, it becomes false. If the dbJoes database exists (true), then the DROP DATABASE statement will execute. If the dbJoes database does not exist (false), then code execution skips over the next line (DROP DATABASE dbJoes) and executes whatever comes after the next line (GO). In this case, there is no dbJoes database to be dropped, so the conditional statement skips the DROP statement and completes the code block with the GO command.

Creating User Databases

The need for ever dropping a production database is very rare, however; when we are building and testing a database to be deployed to production, we constantly make changes and improvements until we have a finished product. During the development cycle we need to test what happens when installing the database from scratch.

The only way we can install a database, is if it's not there already. When we want to install on a brand new system, we simply create the database. However; if we are trying to install on a system that might already have a version of the database on it, we need to drop and recreate the database. We can avoid having two different code scripts for these situations by writing the following SQL code that will work on either system:

```
USE master
GO

IF EXISTS(
SELECT * FROM sys.sysdatabases
WHERE [name] = 'dbMovie')
DROP DATABASE dbMovie
GO

CREATE DATABASE dbMovie
GO
```

The second code block (batch) contains a DROP statement, which will only execute if the database already exists. Once the second batch completes, regardless if the conditional statement resolves as true or false, the dbMovie database will not exist on this instance of SQL Server. Now that the second batch is complete, the third batch will create the database.

So, if the dbMovie database does exist at the beginning of the second batch, it will be dropped before completing the second batch. If the dbMovie database does not exist at the beginning of the second batch, the code immediately completes with the GO statement. Either way, there is no dbMovie database by the end of the second batch. This means the third batch will execute successfully with the creation of a new database (dbMovie).

Lab 5.1: Creating Databases

Lab Prep: Each lab has one or more Skill Checks. Start with Skill Check 1 and proceed until reaching the Points to Ponder section.

Before beginning this lab, verify that SQL Server 2012 is properly installed and operating. Before running the lab setup script for resetting the database (SQLQueries2012Vol1Chapter5.1Setup.sql), please make sure to close all query windows within SSMS. An open query window pointing to a database context can lock that database preventing it from updating when the script is executing. A simple way to assure all query windows are closed, is to exit out of SSMS, then open a new instance of SSMS, and lastly run the setup script.

Skill Check 1: Create a script using four separate code blocks (batches ending with the keyword GO). The first batch will use the master database. The second batch will drop the dbSkillCheck database only if it exists. The third batch will create the dbSkillCheck database. The final batch will set the database context to dbSkillCheck. When done, the System message should resemble Figure 5.7.

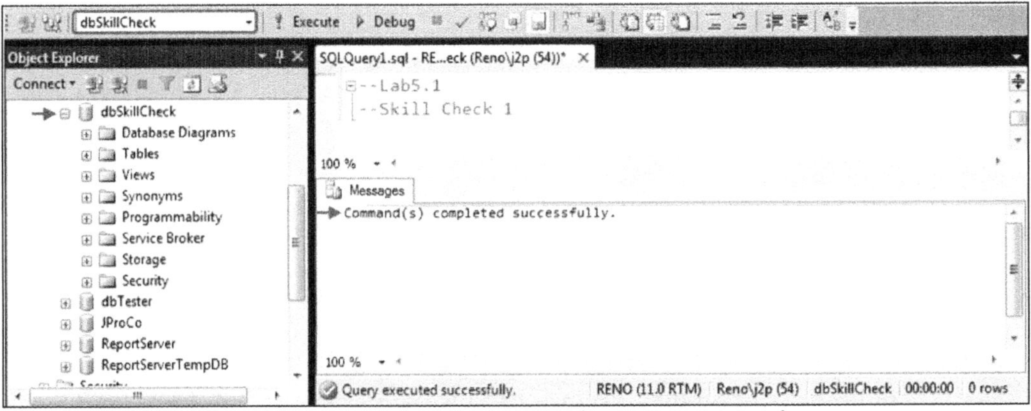

Figure 5.7 dbSkillCheck should be created and the database context set to it.

Answer Code: The T-SQL code to this lab can be found from the downloadable files named Lab5.1_CreatingDatabases.sql.

Points to Ponder - Creating Databases

1. CREATE is used to make new objects in SQL Server, including the database itself. The CREATE clause is part of a DDL statement.
2. DROP removes objects in SQL Server, including entire databases. The DROP clause is part of a Data Definition Language (DDL) statement.
3. System tables include information that SQL Server uses to define and maintain the database. The traditional abbreviation for database is DB or db.
4. Newer System table names begin with 'sys' followed by a dot and then the table name.
5. The Catalog Views sys.sysdatabases, sysdatabases and sys.databases will provide information about the databases on a SQL Server instance. The newest versions of SQL Server will use the sys.sysdatabases syntax. The other names are used to facilitate backward compatibility with older SQL code already in use on many installations.
6. The recommended way to view System metadata is with the Catalog View sys.sysdatabases. Metadata is information about how an individual installation of SQL Server is configured. Metadata is contained in the columns or fields of the sys.sysdatabases table.
7. A database that does not exist cannot be dropped.
8. A database cannot be created with the same name as an existing database.
9. An IF EXISTS statement will only run the next line of code when evaluating to True. SQL Server skips the next line when evaluating to False.
10. A batch is a set of SQL statements that are executed in their entirety before continuing on to further commands.
11. Batches are completed and separated by the word GO.

Creating Tables

The previous section ended by creating a new database named dbMovie. Since it doesn't yet have tables, let's create some and put this database to use.

To build a new table we will use the CREATE keyword. CREATE is a DDL statement. Set the database context to Master with a USE statement. Let's run the following code to ensure the dbMovie database is available before moving on:

```
USE master
GO

IF EXISTS(
SELECT * FROM sys.databases
WHERE [name] = 'dbMovie')
DROP DATABASE dbMovie
GO

CREATE DATABASE dbMovie
GO

USE dbMovie
GO
```

Remember that whatever our database context is set to will determine where the next command will attempt to run. If we create a table while in JProCo, that is the new table's home. If we do this in the dbMovie context, the new table will reside in dbMovie. Make sure the context is set to dbMovie and then use the code shown here to create our first table:

```
CREATE TABLE tblMovie (
m_ID INT PRIMARY KEY,
m_Title VARCHAR (30) NOT NULL,
m_Runtime INT NULL)
GO
```

The previous SQL code will create the tblMovie table. The field names and data types are enclosed in a set of parentheses. The ***m_ID*** field is the primary key for the table, which means we can't have two movies with the same m_ID value. The second field definition shows that the ***m_Title*** will not allow NULL values to be entered into this field. The ***m_Runtime*** field will accept integer (INT) data and can be NULL. We can create a movie name and enter the runtime at a later date when it is known.

Reader Note: *More details about the PRIMARY KEY are outside the scope of this book and will be covered in Volume 4 of this series.*

SQL Server creates the table definition with the CREATE statement. Query the table with a SELECT clause looking for all records and fields. Since this table is brand new, it has no records. The unpopulated table is seen in Figure 5.8 with the three fields we just created.

```
SELECT *
FROM tblMovie
```

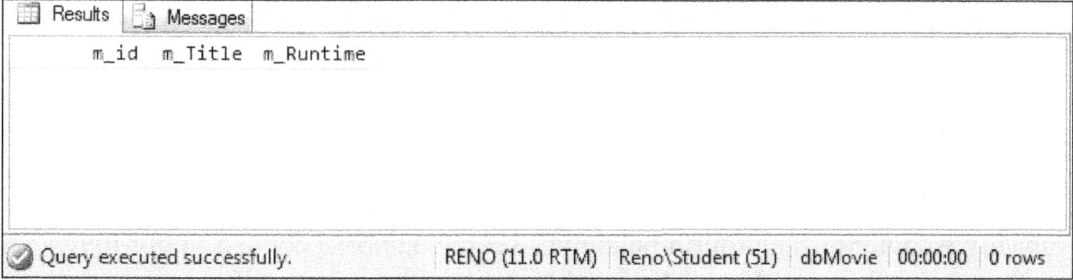

Figure 5.8 This query shows the tblMovie table, although it has not been populated with records.

No matter how much data we add, tblMovie will still have three fields unless we change the table definition later.

We currently have no data in this table. As promised, this chapter is all about the definition of objects and the next chapter will show us the many ways to INSERT, UPDATE and DELETE data from a table.

Lab 5.2: Creating Tables

Lab Prep: Each lab has one or more Skill Checks. Start with Skill Check 1 and proceed until reaching the Points to Ponder section.

Before beginning this lab, verify that SQL Server 2012 is properly installed and operating. Before running the lab setup script for resetting the database (SQLQueries2012Vol1Chapter5.2Setup.sql), please make sure to close all query windows within SSMS. An open query window pointing to a database context can lock that database preventing it from updating when the script is executing. A simple way to assure all query windows are closed, is to exit out of SSMS, then open a new instance of SSMS, and lastly run the setup script.

Skill Check 1: Write a script to create the tblMovie table in the dbMovie database in five batches. The first batch will use the master database. The second batch will drop the dbMovie database only if it exists. The third batch will create the dbMovie database. The fourth batch will set the database context to dbMovie. The fifth batch will create the tblMovie table. It should not matter if dbMovie database already exists, since the batches take care of dropping and creating this database.

When done, the Object Explorer window should resemble Figure 5.9.

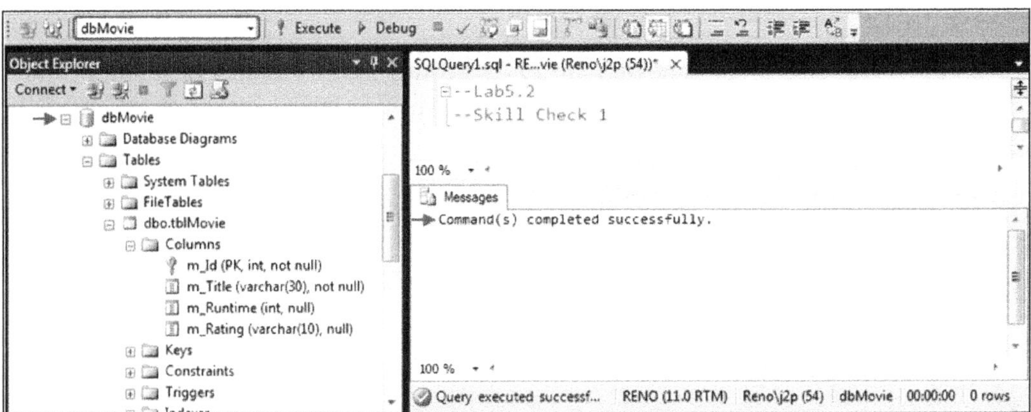

Figure 5.9 The tblMovie table is created in the dbMovie database and has four fields.

Reader Note: *The tblMovie table will now have four fields with these definitions:*

m_ID	INT	primary key
m_Title	VARCHAR(30)	null
m_Runtime	INT	null
m_Rating	VARCHAR(10)	null

Skill Check 2: Write a script to create the tblCar table in the dbCar database in five batches. The first batch will use the master database. The second batch will drop the dbCar database only if it exists. The third batch will create the dbCar database. The fourth batch will set the database context to dbCar. The fifth batch will create the tblCar table.

When done, the Object Explorer window should resemble Figure 5.10.

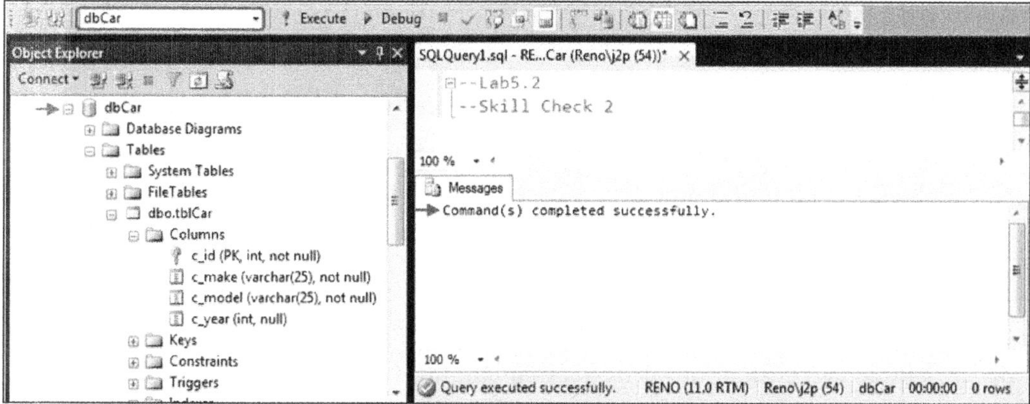

Figure 5.10 The tblCar table is created in the dbCar database and has four fields.

Reader Note: *The tblCar table will now have four fields with these definitions:*

c_id	INT	primary key
c_make	VARCHAR(25)	not null
c_model	VARCHAR(25)	not null
c_year	INT	null

Answer Code: The T-SQL code to this lab can be found from the downloadable files named Lab5.2_CreatingTables.sql.

Points to Ponder - Creating Tables

1. The CREATE TABLE statement is used to add a table object to a database.
2. A CREATE TABLE statement is a DDL statement.
3. The moment a table is created, the fields and data types should be specified.
4. When specifying a field during creation, the data type (integer, decimal or character) must be specified at the same time.
5. Column names for a table must be unique. SQL Server will not allow two fields named HireDate in the same table.
6. The same column name can be used in different tables. For example, the LocationID field may exist in both the Employee and Location tables.
7. When a field is defined as NOT NULL, the value for this field can never be empty, which means a value must be entered each time a new row is added.
8. A table is a collection of fields that can hold data. Each table is contained within a database.
9. A newly created database contains no tables, although any number of tables can be created at a later time to meet business requirements.
10. A table is unique within each database. SQL Server will not allow two Employee tables to exist in the JProCo database.
11. Once a table is created, it can be populated by adding records.
12. DDL is an acronym for Data Definition Language. Some DDL keywords are CREATE, DROP and ALTER.

Chapter Glossary

Catalog: A database or data storage area.

Catalog View: System information combined into a table-like view which can be queried with a SELECT statement.

CREATE: A DDL statement that creates an object or database.

DDL Statement: A statement that can CREATE, DROP, or ALTER a database or database objects.

DROP: A DDL statement that eliminates an object or database.

PRIMARY KEY: An attribute of a field that prevents records with duplicate values in this specific field.

System Table: A table created by SQL Server to track design and settings used by SQL Server.

Review Quiz - Chapter Five

1.) You want to see whether your dbMovie database exists. Which SQL code will achieve this?

O a. `IF(SELECT * FROM sysdatabases`
`WHERE [name] = 'dbMovie')`

O b. `WHEN EXISTS (SELECT * FROM sysdatabases`
`WHERE [name] = 'dbMovie')`

O c. `IF EXISTS (SELECT * FROM sysdatabases`
`WHERE [name] = 'dbMovie')`

O d. `WHEN EXISTS (SELECT * FROM sysdatabases`
`WHERE[ name] = 'dbMovie ')`

2.) What occurs if you try to DROP a database that is not present on SQL Server?

O a. You get an error message.

O b. It indicates it ran, but really did nothing.

O c. It drops the closest matching name.

3.) What is the purpose of the GO keyword?

O a. To speed up processing.

O b. To work with an IF statement when it evaluates to true.

O c. To run code in separate batches.

4.) Which SQL keyword goes first when you want to make a new database?

O a. NEW

O b. CREATE

O c. UPDATE

O d. INSERT

5.) At the time of table creation, you should add the fields you want because...

O a. You cannot add them later.

O b. It's considered a good practice.

6.) Can you create a table with zero fields?

O a. Yes – you can create a table with any number of fields including 0.

O b. No – You need at least one field to create a table.

Answer Key

1.) IF requires a Boolean expression and the SELECT statement within the parenthesis of answer (a) does not return a True or False value, so you will get an error message. The code in (b) and (d) will return an error message for incorrect syntax near the keyword WHEN. The IF EXISTS (SELECT * FROM sysdatabases WHERE [name] = 'dbMovie') will return a value of True, if the dbMovie database exists in the system tables, so (c) is correct.

2.) Because you get an error message when attempting to DROP a database that does not exist on SQL Server both (b) and (c) are incorrect. If you attempt to DROP a database that does not exist on SQL Server, an error message will be returned, so (a) is the correct choice.

3.) The GO keyword has nothing to do with speeding up processing, so (a) is incorrect. IF statements will determine whether the next piece of code is executed or not, so (b) is also wrong. The GO keyword tells SQL Server to finish executing the preceding code before continuing, so (c) is correct.

4.) NEW is not a SQL Server keyword, so (a) is not the right answer. UPDATE and INSERT both modify records in a table, so (c) and (d) are not correct either. CREATE is the first word in a statement when you want to make a new database, so (b) is the right answer.

5.) You can add fields later that you did not think of when creating the table, so (a) is incorrect. It is considered a good practice to add all the fields you want at the time of table creation making (b) the correct answer.

6.) When creating a table you must specify at least one field so (a) is not correct. Since you need at least one field specified at the time of table creation (b) is the correct answer.

Bug Catcher Game

To play the Bug Catcher game run the BugCatcher_Chapter5.pps from the BugCatcher folder of the companion files. You can obtain these files from the www.Joes2Pros.com website.

[NOTES]

Chapter 6. Data Manipulation Language (DML) Scripting

Databases contain tables, and tables contain the actual data. Queries turn data into information, which is what businesses need to see and use for decision-making. Manipulating data involves changing, deleting and viewing data. So far, all our Data Manipulation Language (DML) examples in the first five chapters use the SELECT keyword. In this chapter we learn the other DML statements. Besides selecting data, DML statements allow us to INSERT, UPDATE and DELETE data from tables.

READER NOTE: *Please run the SQLQueries2012Vol1Chapter6.0Setup.sql script in order to follow along with the examples in the first section of Chapter 6. All scripts mentioned in this chapter may be found at www.Joes2Pros.com.*

Inserting Data

Tables were created for the purpose of holding data. Every table begins its life as an unpopulated table. The only way to populate a table is by inserting data. SQL coding that starts with the INSERT keyword are DML statements that add new records to tables.

Currently, the dbMovie database has only one table, tblMovie. How much data we need to add depends on how many fields the table has. If the table has four fields we would likely need to add four pieces of information. A quick look at the tblMovie table shows we have four fields as in Figure 6.1.

```
SELECT *
FROM tblMovie
```

m_ID	m_Title	m_Runtime	m_Rating

0 rows

Figure 6.1 The tlbMovie table has no records in its four fields.

To fill the first record we need to supply a value for each of the four fields. An INSERT statement separates each entity value with a comma. The first movie record will have an id value of 1 called 'AList Explorers,' which is a PG-13 movie 96 minutes long. The code for doing this is shown here:

```
INSERT INTO tblMovie
VALUES (1,'AList Explorers',96,'PG-13')
```

If we want to insert two records at the same time, we always have the option to run multiple INSERTINTO statements. We can insert movie 2 and movie 3 at the same time as demonstrated by this code:.

```
INSERT INTO tblMovie
VALUES (2, 'Bonker Bonzo', 75, 'G')

INSERT INTO tblMovie
VALUES (3, 'Chumps to Champs', 75, 'PG-13')
```

Messages
(1 row(s) affected)
(1 row(s) affected)

0 rows

Figure 6.2 A SQL Server message after two INSERT INTO statements each inserted a record.

There was no need to run these INSERT INTO statements in separate batches with a GO statement. DML statements like INSERT INTO use Transaction Control Language (TCL) instead of batches. TCL will be discussed in Chapter 10.

Each statement ran its records once, resulting in two additional records in the tblMovie table. A quick look at all records and fields for the tblMovie table can confirm how many records we have inserted (Figure 6.3).

```
SELECT *
FROM tblMovie
```

	m_ID	m_Title	m_Runtime	m_Rating
1	1	AList Explorers	96	PG-13
2	2	Bonker Bonzo	75	G
3	3	Chumps to Champs	75	PG-13

3 rows

Figure 6.3 All three insert statements give you three new records.

Row Constructors

New features are invented so we may discover and use them. Since many of my students work or contract at Microsoft, homework is often done on beta software. One student was tasked to do a double insert like the one in Figure 6.2. She did a great innovative job and humbly I changed her grade from zero to a perfect 100.

That day the student taught me a new feature for SQL Server 2008 called *row constructors*. We can accomplish a double insert of data with one INSERT INTO statement using this feature. Simply separate each group of values with a comma. A row constructor looks exactly like the double INSERT INTO except that we can eliminate any additional INSERT INTO statements by replacing them with a comma. We can see how this is done with the following code.

```
INSERT INTO tblMovie VALUES
(4, 'Dare or Die', 110, 'R'),
(5, 'EeeeGhads', 88, 'G')
```

Messages
(2 row(s) affected)

0 rows

Figure 6.4 Row constructors are a feature introduced with SQL Server 2008.

The two records m_id 4 and m_id 5 were successfully inserted into tblMovie at the same time, with less typing than the two INSERT INTO statements we used with m_id 2 and 3. So, the first advantage of using row constructors is that we save time by not having to type an additional INSERT INTO statement. The second advantage is that SQL Server uses only one lock instead of two when using the row constructors feature. We can see the evidence of this by looking at the message provided by SQL Server in Figure 6.4 ("*2 row(s) affected*"). The message provided by SQL Server with the two individual INSERT INTO statements is shown in Figure 6.2 ("*1 row(s) affected*"). Each transaction gobbles up a bit of time by issuing a lock. We will learn more about why this is important later in Chapter 10.

Reader Note: *If we did not know the rating of the movie 'EeeeGhads' then we could insert a NULL value to indicate the rating is unknown. The code to do so is seen here:*

```
--example only: do not run
INSERT INTO tblMovie VALUES
(4,'Dare or Die', 110,'R'),
(5,'EeeeGhads', 88, NULL)
```

Lab 6.1: Inserting Data

Lab Prep: Each lab has one or more Skill Checks. Start with Skill Check 1 and proceed until reaching the Points to Ponder section.

Before beginning this lab, verify that SQL Server 2012 is properly installed and operating. Before running the lab setup script for resetting the database (SQLQueries2012Vol1Chapter6.1Setup.sql), please make sure to close all query windows within SSMS. An open query window pointing to a database context can lock that database preventing it from updating when the script is executing. A simple way to assure all query windows are closed, is to exit out of SSMS, then open a new instance of SSMS, and lastly run the setup script.

Skill Check 1: Create a table named Customer in the JProCo database. The table should contain the five fields shown here:

CustomerID	INT	primary key
CustomerType	VARCHAR(30)	not null
FirstName	VARCHAR(20)	null
LastName	VARCHAR(30)	null
CompanyName	VARCHAR(30)	null

Once the table is created, write five insert statements to add each field for the customer records shown in Figure 6.5.

```
SELECT * FROM Customer
```

	CustomerID	CustomerType	FirstName	LastName	CompanyName
1	1	Consumer	Mark	Williams	NULL
2	2	Consumer	Lee	Young	NULL
3	3	Consumer	Patricia	Martin	NULL
4	4	Consumer	Mary	Lopez	NULL
5	5	Business	NULL	NULL	MoreTechnology.com

5 rows

Figure 6.5 The Customer table of JProCo is created and populated.

Lab Self Checker 1: Skill Check 1 has a self-checker to see if all DML and DDL statements ran correctly. Open a query window and type the following code:

```
EXEC dbTester.dbo.Lab61SelfChecker
```

This displays a report card for each step in the lab. A perfect score is 1,000 points.

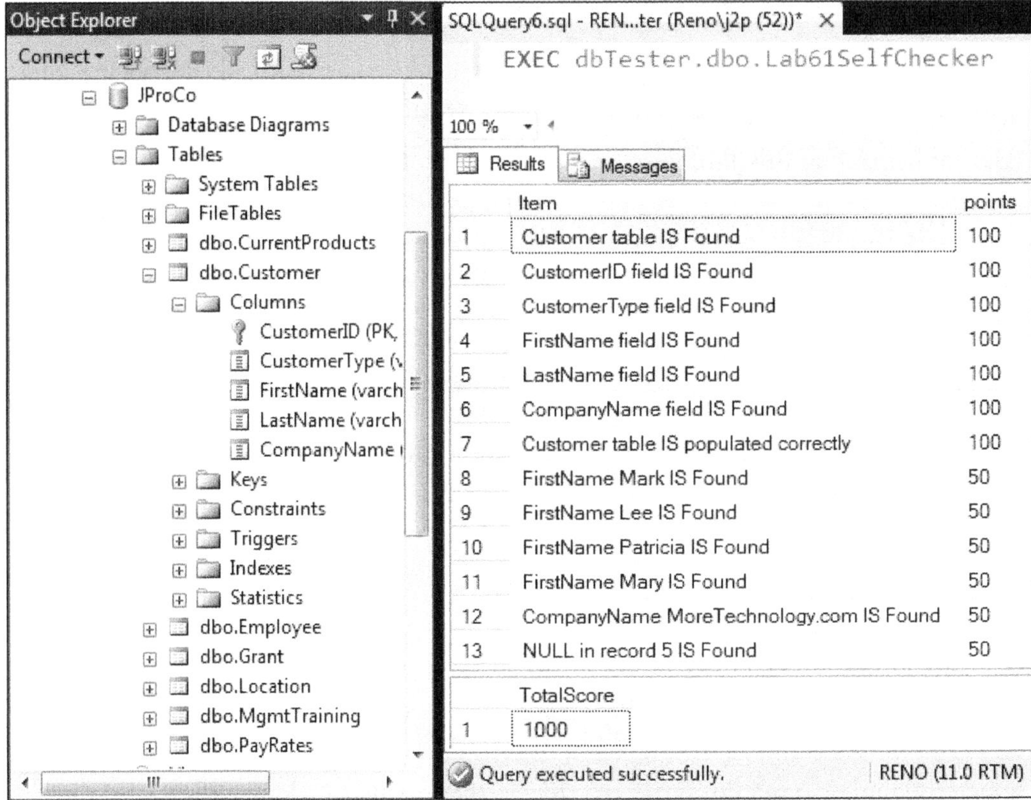

Figure 6.6 Execute the dbo.Lab61SelfChecker sproc to receive a test score for this lab.

Answer Code: The T-SQL code to this lab can be found from the downloadable files named Lab6.1_InsertingData.sql.

Points to Ponder - Inserting Data

1. Records can be added to a table by using an INSERT statement.
2. An INSERT statement is a DML statement.
3. Before SQL Server 2008 only 1 record could be added with a single INSERT statement.
4. Since SQL Server 2008 a feature called Row Constructors allows multiple records to be added with a single INSERT statement.

Updating Data

Whenever we move from one house to another, we normally notify our bank or credit card providers of our new address. Somewhere among their databases are tables that hold customer names and addresses. What if the address fields need to be updated? Changes over time mean Relational Database Management Systems (RDBMS) like SQL Server need the power to update existing data.

Think of UPDATE as a statement that changes, or manipulates existing data without adding any new records. Often, updates are needed so changes in our data, such as a new address, can be reflected. Sometimes changes happen because an error was found that must be corrected. In either case, the language of SQL offers us the UPDATE keyword. Any statement starting with the keyword UPDATE is a DML statement.

Before we make updates, it's a good idea to examine the existing data in our tblMovie table (Figure 6.7). In this example, we have five records showing five different movie names.

```
USE dbMovie
GO

SELECT *
FROM tblMovie
```

	m_ID	m_Title	m_Runtime	m_Rating
1	1	AList Explorers	96	PG-13
2	2	Bonker Bonzo	75	G
3	3	Chumps to Champs	75	PG-13
4	4	Dare or Die	110	R
5	5	EeeeGhads	88	G

5 rows

Figure 6.7 Using a SELECT statement is a good way to look at our data before making changes.

Single Table Updates

We have been notified that our tblMovie table needs the 'AList Explorers' value for the m_ Title field revised to have a hyphen in it. So, changing this value will appear as 'A-List Explorers'. We can make this modification without adding any new records by using an UPDATE statement.

An UPDATE statement offers a great deal of power, because we can update one or more records with a single statement. A common attempt to fix this might result in the following code:

```
UPDATE tblMovie
SET m_Title = 'A-List Explorers'
```

This may have worked a little too well. As the result set in Figure 6.8 reveals, field m_Title is now set to 'A-List Explorers'. Since we did not specify which record to update this field with, all of the records received this value. This is a very important point to remember. Always specify the record to be modified when using an UPDATE statement.

```
SELECT * FROM tblMovie
```

	m_ID	m_Title	m_Runtime	m_Rating
1	1	A-List Explorers	96	PG-13
2	2	A-List Explorers	75	G
3	3	A-List Explorers	75	PG-13
4	4	A-List Explorers	110	R
5	5	A-List Explorers	88	G

5 rows

Figure 6.8 An UPDATE statement without specific criteria changes all records.

Making this simple mistake can cause very big problems. With our data gone, the only way to get it back is either from an existing backup or a script. Since our database has only one table, we can easily recreate it. The following code should bring us back to the point just before we executed our first UPDATE statement:

```
USE master
GO

IF EXISTS (
SELECT * FROM Sys.sysdatabases
WHERE [name] = 'dbMovie')
DROP DATABASE dbMovie
GO

CREATE DATABASE dbMovie
GO

USE dbMovie
GO

CREATE TABLE tblMovie (
m_ID INT PRIMARY KEY,
```

```
m_Title VARCHAR(30) NOT NULL,
m_Runtime INT NULL,
m_Rating VARCHAR(10))

INSERT INTO tblMovie VALUES
(1,'A-List Explorers',96,'PG-13'),
(2,'Bonker Bonzo',75,'G'),
(3,'Chumps to Champs',75,'PG-13'),
(4,'Dare or Die',110,'R'),
(5,'EeeeGhads',88,'G')
```

***Reader Note**: The previous code works just fine if we have permissions to drop the dbMovie database and nobody else is using that database. If we have multiple query windows open and any one of them has the database context set to dbMovie, the DROP DATABASE statement will most likely fail.*

Now it's time to do just what we intended. The record with m_ID set to 1 should have its m_Title set to the hyphenated 'A-List Explorers' name.

```
UPDATE tblMovie
SET m_Title = 'A-List Explorers'
WHERE m_ID = 1
```

The criteria used in an UPDATE statement will utilize the same syntax and rules we have learned with queries. Fortunately, the syntax used with criteria has been standardized for all DML statements.

We can now take a look at our handiwork. We can see that each of the m_Title fields is unique and the tblMovie table still has five different records. We can also verify in Figure 6.9 that m_ID 1 now has the correct value for m_Title.

```
SELECT *
FROM tblMovie
```

	m_ID	m_Title	m_Runtime	m_Rating
1	1	A-List Explorers	96	PG-13
2	2	Bonker Bonzo	75	G
3	3	Chumps to Champs	75	PG-13
4	4	Dare or Die	110	R
5	5	EeeeGhads	88	G

5 rows

Figure 6.9 Only the first record is set to 'A-List Explorers' after the update has finished.

Setting all records to the same value is very rare. Therefore, using an update statement with criteria using the WHERE clause is an essential database development skill. Doing this correctly ensures you change only the records that need to be updated.

Multiple Table Updates

When updating records, it is vital to ensure that we are only changing the necessary records by using filtering criteria with a WHERE clause. Remember, that any available field can be used in the predicate for our criteria. Change the database context back to JProCo and look at the data to be updated in Figure 6.10.

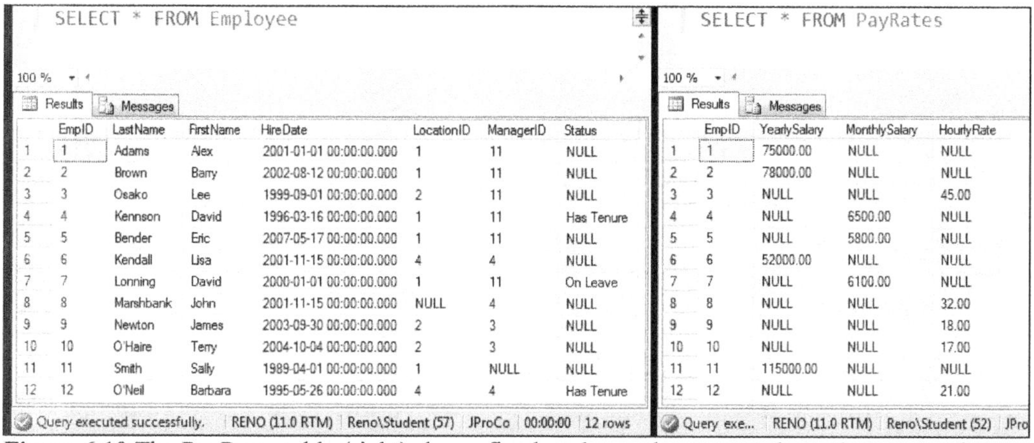

```
SELECT * FROM Employee
```

	EmpID	LastName	FirstName	HireDate	LocationID	ManagerID	Status
1	1	Adams	Alex	2001-01-01 00:00:00.000	1	11	NULL
2	2	Brown	Barry	2002-08-12 00:00:00.000	1	11	NULL
3	3	Osako	Lee	1999-09-01 00:00:00.000	2	11	NULL
4	4	Kennson	David	1996-03-16 00:00:00.000	1	11	Has Tenure
5	5	Bender	Eric	2007-05-17 00:00:00.000	1	11	NULL
6	6	Kendall	Lisa	2001-11-15 00:00:00.000	4	4	NULL
7	7	Lonning	David	2000-01-01 00:00:00.000	1	11	On Leave
8	8	Marshbank	John	2001-11-15 00:00:00.000	NULL	4	NULL
9	9	Newton	James	2003-09-30 00:00:00.000	2	3	NULL
10	10	O'Haire	Terry	2004-10-04 00:00:00.000	2	3	NULL
11	11	Smith	Sally	1989-04-01 00:00:00.000	1	NULL	NULL
12	12	O'Neil	Barbara	1995-05-26 00:00:00.000	4	4	Has Tenure

Query executed successfully. | RENO (11.0 RTM) | Reno\Student (57) | JProCo | 00:00:00 | 12 rows

```
SELECT * FROM PayRates
```

	EmpID	YearlySalary	MonthlySalary	HourlyRate
1	1	75000.00	NULL	NULL
2	2	78000.00	NULL	NULL
3	3	NULL	NULL	45.00
4	4	NULL	6500.00	NULL
5	5	NULL	5800.00	NULL
6	6	52000.00	NULL	NULL
7	7	NULL	6100.00	NULL
8	8	NULL	NULL	32.00
9	9	NULL	NULL	18.00
10	10	NULL	NULL	17.00
11	11	115000.00	NULL	NULL
12	12	NULL	NULL	21.00

Query exe... | RENO (11.0 RTM) | Reno\Student (52) | JPro

Figure 6.10 The PayRates table (right) shows five hourly employees. We learn the names of those hourly employees by examining the EmpID field in the Employee table (left).

Sally Smith is a member of management at JProCo. Sally has an EmpID of 11. There are six employees that report directly to Sally. Another way to say this is six employee records have a ManagerID of 11. To find all Employees who report to Sally, we can filter on just her ManagerID. The following query shows six records in the result set:

```
SELECT * FROM Employee
WHERE ManagerID = 11
```

Sally has decided that all of her yearly salaried employees will get a raise of $1,000 per year. How many of the employees reporting to Sally are on a yearly salary and how many are hourly? We can see the challenge here goes a bit beyond the last update example. We need to update a field in the PayRates table based on criteria (ManagerID) in the Employee table. To perform this update, we can use an inner join query from both tables.

In Figure 6.11 we see all the detailed information about the employees and their income information. Only the employees working for Sally appear in the result set. Two of Sally's six employees are paid yearly. To look at just those two employees, we need to find all records that have data for YearlySalary.

```
SELECT *
FROM Employee as e
INNER JOIN PayRates AS pr
ON e.EmpID = pr.EmpID
WHERE ManagerID = 11
```

	LastName	FirstName	HireDate	LocationID	ManagerID	Status	EmpID	YearlySalary	MonthlySalary	HourlyRate
1	Adams	Alex	2001-01-01 00:00:00.000	1	11	NULL	1	75000.00	NULL	NULL
2	Brown	Barry	2002-08-12 00:00:00.000	1	11	NULL	2	78000.00	NULL	NULL
3	Osako	Lee	1999-09-01 00:00:00.000	2	11	NULL	3	NULL	NULL	45.00
4	Kennson	David	1996-03-16 00:00:00.000	1	11	Has Tenure	4	NULL	6500.00	NULL
5	Bender	Eric	2007-05-17 00:00:00.000	1	11	NULL	5	NULL	5800.00	NULL
6	Lonning	David	2000-01-01 00:00:00.000	1	11	On Leave	7	NULL	6100.00	NULL

Query executed successfully. RENO (11.0 RTM) Reno\j2p (53) JProCo 00:00:00 6 rows

Figure 6.11 Joining the Employee and PayRates tables for ManagerID 11 shows the pay for all of Sally's workers.

A slight change to the code in Figure 6.11 will give us the records needed. A SELECT with a join type and an UPDATE with a join type are very similar. The good news is our work is almost done. Just change the first line of the code block from *SELECT* to *UPDATE*. We can see how this works here:

```
UPDATE pr
SET YearlySalary = YearlySalary + 1000
FROM Employee AS e
INNER JOIN PayRates AS pr
ON e.EmpID = pr.EmpID
WHERE ManagerID = 11
AND YearlySalary IS NOT NULL
```

This update statement takes the existing value of the YearlySalary and adds $1,000 dollars to that amount. If one of Sally's employees were making $75,000 before running this update, their annual income would now be $76,000. Using the query from the prior example, we can see that Alex Adams and Barry Brown each have salaries $1000 higher than before. Figure 6.12 reflects this annual increase.

```
SELECT * FROM Employee as e
INNER JOIN PayRates AS pr
ON e.EmpID = pr.EmpID
WHERE ManagerID = 11
AND YearlySalary IS NOT NULL
```

	EmpID	LastName	FirstName	HireDate	LocationID	ManagerID	Status	EmpID	YearlySalary	MonthlySalary	HourlyRate
1	1	Adams	Alex	2001-01-01 00:00:...	1	11	NULL	1	76000.00	NULL	NULL
2	2	Brown	Barry	2002-08-12 00:00:...	1	11	NULL	2	79000.00	NULL	NULL

Query executed successfully. RENO (11.0 RTM) Reno\j2p (53) JProCo 00:00:00 2 rows

Figure 6.12 The two employees with YearlySalary values $1000 higher than in Figure 6.11.

A multi-table UPDATE statement is used anytime our SET value is in a different table than some of the criteria necessary to make the change take place. Using the join syntax we learned from Chapter 3 allows us to run an UPDATE statement based on multiple tables.

Lab 6.2: Updating Data

Lab Prep: Each lab has one or more Skill Checks. Start with Skill Check 1 and proceed until reaching the Points to Ponder section.

Before beginning this lab, verify that SQL Server 2012 is properly installed and operating. Before running the lab setup script for resetting the database (SQLQueries2012Vol1Chapter6.2Setup.sql), please make sure to close all query windows within SSMS. An open query window pointing to a database context can lock that database preventing it from updating when the script is executing. A simple way to assure all query windows are closed, is to exit out of SSMS, then open a new instance of SSMS, and lastly run the setup script.

Skill Check 1: One of the movies in our tblMovie table was named incorrectly. m_ID 4 should be titled 'Dare the World to Try'. Write an UPDATE statement that makes this change. When done, the results should resemble Figure 6.13.

```
SELECT * FROM tblMovie
```

	m_ID	m_Title	m_Runtime	m_Rating
1	1	A-List Explorers	96	PG-13
2	2	Bonker Bonzo	75	G
3	3	Chumps to Champs	75	PG-13
4	4	Dare the World to Try	110	R
5	5	Eeee-Ghads	88	G

5 rows

Figure 6.13 m_id 4 has a new m_Title value.

Skill Check 2: The JProCo employee with EmpID 11 (Sally Smith) is getting married and wants her last name changed to Green. Write an UPDATE statement that will accomplish changing her maiden name to her married surname.

Skill Check 3: All JProCo employees from LocationID 4 (Spokane) are contractors. Change the value of the Status field to 'External' for all employee records of LocationID 4.

Skill Check 4: In the dbMovie database the tblMovie table needs a correction. The movie 'EeeeGhads' should be hyphenated to 'Eeee-Ghads' for m_ID 5.

Skill Check 5: In the JProCo database, we need to correct a typo in the Location table for Seattle. There is no First Street in Seattle. In the Street field of the Location table, change the value '111 First ST' to '111 1st Ave' for LocationID 1.

Skill Check 6: The Boston location manager of JProCo has called to request a change correcting some discovered errors. Boston has a standard form for all grants written to be in the amount of $20,000. Looking at all grants written by employees at LocationID 2 we see two grants have an amount entered incorrectly.

```
SELECT e.FirstName, e.LastName, e.LocationID,
g.GrantName, g.Amount
FROM [Grant] AS g
INNER JOIN Employee AS e
ON g.EmpID = e.EmpID
WHERE LocationID = 2
```

	FirstName	LastName	LocationID	GrantName	Amount
1	Lee	Osako	2	TALTA_Kishan International	18100.00
2	Terry	O'Haire	2	Ben@MoreTechnology.com	41000.00
					2 rows

Figure 6.14 There are two employees from Boston with grants.

Our challenge is to correctly UPDATE all Boston employees by making sure any grants found by them are set to $20,000. When done, our update should produce the result set seen in Figure 6.15.

```
SELECT e.FirstName, e.LastName, e.LocationID,
g.GrantName, g.Amount
FROM [Grant] AS G
INNER JOIN Employee AS e
ON G.EmpID = e.EmpID
WHERE LocationID = 2
```

	FirstName	LastName	LocationID	GrantName	Amount
1	Lee	Osako	2	TALTA_Kishan International	20000.00
2	Terry	O'Haire	2	Ben@MoreTechnology.com	20000.00
					2 rows

Figure 6.15 All Boston employees now have grant amount values of $20,000.

Answer Code: The T-SQL code to this lab can be found from the downloadable files named Lab6.2_UpdatingData.sql.

Points to Ponder - Updating Data

1. The UPDATE statement modifies existing data for columns in tables.
2. Statements starting with the word UPDATE are Data Manipulation Language (DML) statements.
3. Most queries pull data from multiple tables that relate to each other. Prior to SQL Server 2008, the limit was 256 tables in one query. The number of joined tables is now only limited by the available resources.
4. DML statements begin with the keywords SELECT, INSERT, UPDATE and DELETE.
5. During an UPDATE, the SET keyword assigns values to records in the selected columns. It is very important to use the WHERE clause, which limits the value changes by the SET statement to only the required records.
6. The WHERE clause is almost always used with the SET clause to limit the number of rows updated. It is rare to UPDATE an entire table with the same value in a column.
7. The SET command in the UPDATE statement assigns a new value to fields in the selected table rows.

Deleting Data

Knowing how to delete data is an essential skill that must be done carefully and correctly. With a little practice we can make sure only the required records are removed in our DELETE statement.

Reader Note: *We will practice our deletes on the dbMovie database, this way no harm comes to JProCo and we can experience deleting data without fear on a small sample database.*

The tblMovie table is already structured the way we need it. However, the data inside is only practice data used for testing before signing off officially for use by our company. When we need to delete all records, but the table structure must remain intact, we are depopulating the table. A DELETE statement with no criteria like the code below achieves this result.

```
DELETE tblMovie
```

After executing the code, SQL Server states exactly how many records have been affected (deleted), as seen in Figure 6.16. Any time we run a DML statement, the 'Messages' tab will show a '(***n*** row(s) affected)' confirmation.

```
Messages
(5 row(s) affected)
                                                    0 rows
```

Figure 6.16 Executing the Delete statement shows how many records were deleted.

We can now query tblMovie to verify it is empty, as shown in Figure 6.17.

```
SELECT * FROM tblMovie
```

m_ID	m_Title	m_Runtime	m_Rating

0 rows

Figure 6.17 All records have been deleted from this table (tblMovie).

This procedure is very common when we are working with test data and an actual table design. OK, let's geek it up a notch. We may be tasked into working with prototype databases soon to be used by the company. In order to test them, we might fill these databases with fictitious data. This is commonly known as a database testing environment. This means the DDL code for testing is identical to the DDL code for production. We use DML code for testing the data flow.

DELETE gets rid of all records that fit our criteria. If we have no criteria, all records of that table disappear. If we want to delete specific records, then we use a WHERE clause in the same way as all other DML statements. For example, let's place all the data for the tblMovie table back with the following code:

```
INSERT INTO tblMovie VALUES
(1,'A-List Explorers',96,'PG-13'),
(2,'Bonker Bonzo',75,'G'),
(3,'Chumps to Champs',75,'PG-13'),
(4,'Dare or Die',110,'R'),
(5,'EeeeGhads',88,'G')
```

After deleting all the records, we re-populate the table with the previous code. Now that we have five records in the tblMovie table, we will practice deleting one or more records that meet specific criteria.

Our goal is to delete every movie that is over 90 minutes long. To do this we find any m_Runtime value that is greater than 90. Using the code sample shown here will achieve this result.

```
DELETE tblMovie
WHERE m_Runtime > 90
```

Messages
(2 row(s) affected)
0 rows

Figure 6.18 The two movies with over 90 minutes of runtime are deleted.

The number of rows listed as affected (two rows in this case) in Figure 6.18 will be the same number of records removed from a populated table. The affected records are 'A-List Explorers' at 96 minutes and 'Dare or Die' at 110 minutes.

It will be easy to check the remaining records in our table. The most common DML statement is a SELECT query to view records. The query results for the following code shows we now have three records remaining (Figure 6.19).

```
SELECT *
FROM tblMovie
```

	m_ID	m_Title	m_Runtime	m_Rating
1	2	Bonker Bonzo	75	G
2	3	Chumps to Champs	75	PG-13
3	5	EeeeGhads	88	G

3 rows

Figure 6.19 After deleting two of the five movies, three records remain in the tblMovie table.

Like any other DML statement (SELECT, INSERT, UPDATE and DELETE), we can isolate the data in the result set by using joins plus criteria. If we use the DELETE keyword without criteria, all records in the table will be deleted.

Multiple Table Deletes

We need to restore the tblMovie table to have all five of its practice records in preparation for our next lab, so let's make sure we run the following code:

```
DELETE tblMovie

INSERT INTO tblMovie VALUES
(1,'A-List Explorers', 96,'PG-13'),
(2,'Bonker Bonzo', 75,'G'),
(3,'Chumps to Champs', 75,'PG-13'),
(4,'Dare or Die', 110,'R'),
(5,'EeeeGhads', 88,'G')
```

We can also use joins for deleting records. Let's use the JProCo database context to practice with an example of how this works. We have been asked to delete all employees that work in Chicago. To do this, we can construct our DELETE statement the same way as a SELECT statement. We begin by joining the Employee and Location tables together and then filtering on the City field equal to Chicago. Since this location is still under construction, there are no employees working in Chicago and this statement will run without affecting any records.

All join records that meet our criteria will be affected. As always, it is very important to test our code before running code that will delete any records. The easiest way to test a DELETE statement is to write it as a SELECT statement first and visually verify that the result set contains the records we expect to delete.

Once we have tested our code, we can run the following DELETE statement.

```
DELETE e
FROM Employee AS e
INNER JOIN Location AS l
ON e.LocationID = l.LocationID
WHERE City = 'Chicago'
```

Messages
(0 row(s) affected)
0 rows

Figure 6.20 Deletes can be used with joins and criteria to affect only the records you want.

Lab 6.3: Deleting Data

Lab Prep: Each lab has one or more Skill Checks. Start with Skill Check 1 and proceed until reaching the Points to Ponder section.

Before beginning this lab, verify that SQL Server 2012 is properly installed and operating. Before running the lab setup script for resetting the database (SQLQueries2012Vol1Chapter6.3Setup.sql), please make sure to close all query windows within SSMS. An open query window pointing to a database context can lock that database preventing it from updating when the script is executing. A simple way to assure all query windows are closed, is to exit out of SSMS, then open a new instance of SSMS, and lastly run the setup script.

Skill Check 1: Set the database context to dbMovie. We are told that there is a new KidsMovies database keeping track of 'G' rated movies. Our instructions are to delete all records in the tblMovie table with an m_Rating value of 'G' right away. Write a delete statement that deletes all such movies. When done, the tblMovie table should contain the three records seen in Figure 6.21.

```
SELECT * FROM tblMovie
```

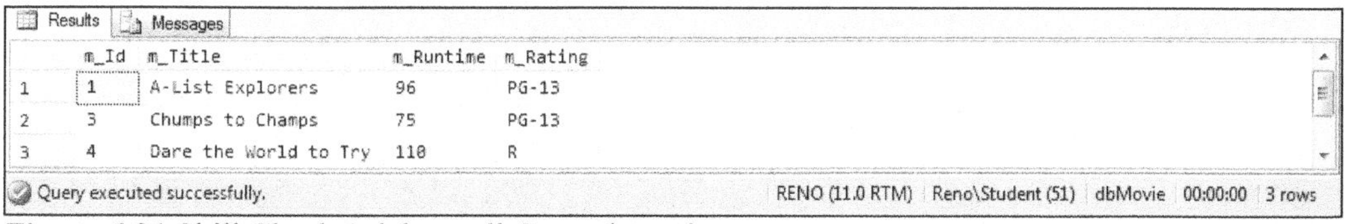

	m_Id	m_Title	m_Runtime	m_Rating
1	1	A-List Explorers	96	PG-13
2	3	Chumps to Champs	75	PG-13
3	4	Dare the World to Try	110	R

Query executed successfully. RENO (11.0 RTM) Reno\Student (51) dbMovie 00:00:00 3 rows

Figure 6.21 Skill Check 1 deletes all G-rated movies.

Skill Check 2: Set the context to the JProCo database. Delete all records from the MgmtTraining table that have a ClassDurationHours value greater than 20. This should delete one record. When done, there should be two records remaining.

Answer Code: The T-SQL code to this lab can be found from the downloadable files named Lab6.3_DeletingData.sql.

Points to Ponder - Deleting Data

1. Data Definition Language (DDL) statements handle the structure or design of database objects (e.g., databases and tables) whereas Data Manipulation Language (DML) statements affect the actual data content. SELECT, INSERT, UPDATE and DELETE are four DML keywords.
2. Statements starting with the word DELETE are DML statements.
3. DELETE is used to remove records from a table, but not the table itself.
4. The table and the table's structure remain intact when the data is removed using the DELETE statement without criteria.
5. All Data Manipulation Language (DML) statements start with SELECT, INSERT, UPDATE or DELETE.

DML Syntax

A big thank you goes to the loving pushback from the weekend spring VTE class of 2009 (VTE stands for Volt Technical Education). They reviewed this chapter and noticed the table below was removed. People told me how useful it was and so now it's back. When students tell me what works, future students benefit.

Because of them we now have the table below at our fingertips. This is a quick reference summary of what was covered in this chapter (Table 6.1). When this makes sense, we are sure to have a solid grasp of this topic.

Table 6.1 A summary of how to use the DML statements INSERT, UPDATE and DELETE.

Task	Explanation and code sample

Inserting data	This example shows how two records are added to the Location table. The table is in the JProCo database.
	`INSERT INTO Location`
	`VALUES (5 , '523 Elm', 'Portland', 'OR')`
	`INSERT INTO Location`
	`VALUES (6 , '678 Front', 'Yakima', 'WA')`

Update based on a single table	This example shows the data getting updated. The code will change the value for the Street field with the LocationID for Yakima, to be '699 Mead Street'.
	`UPDATE Location`
	`SET Street = '699 Mead Street'`
	`WHERE LocationID = 6`

Update based on many tables	In this example, the VacationTime in the Benefits table is being updated to 40 hours vacation based on the ManagerID in the Employee table.
	`UPDATE b SET VacationTime = 40`
	`FROM Employee AS e`
	`INNER JOIN Benefits AS b`
	`ON e.EmpID = b.EmpID`
	`WHERE ManagerID = 11`

Delete based on a single table	This example shows the record containing the City field value equal to Yakima being deleted from the Location table.
	`DELETE Location`
	`WHERE City = 'Yakima'`

Delete based on many tables	In this example, all employee records from the Employee table that work at the City field value equal to Yakima (Location table) will be deleted.
	`DELETE Emp`
	`FROM Employee AS Emp`
	`INNER JOIN Location AS Loc`
	`ON Emp.LocationID = Loc.LocationID`
	`WHERE Loc.City = 'Yakima'`

Creating SQL Scripts

Combining all the skills we have learned to create and populate the tblMovie table will bring us to an ability to write and understand the following code.

Reader Note: *The following code sample uses row constructors to insert values, which will only work with SQL Server 2008 or newer. Any attempt to run the INSERT statements, as written, on earlier versions of SQL Server will need to refer to a prior example for the precise code syntax.*

```
USE master
GO

IF EXISTS (
SELECT * FROM Sys.sysdatabases
WHERE [name] = 'dbMovie')
DROP DATABASE dbMovie
GO

CREATE DATABASE dbMovie
GO

USE dbMovie
GO

CREATE TABLE tblMovie (
m_ID INT PRIMARY KEY,
m_Title VARCHAR(30) NOT NULL,
m_Runtime INT,
m_Rating VARCHAR(10))
GO

INSERT INTO tblMovie VALUES
(1,'A-List Explorers',96,'PG-13'),
(2,'Bonker Bonzo',75,'G'),
(3,'Chumps to Champs',75,'PG-13'),
(4,'Dare or Die',110,'R'),
(5,'EeeeGhads',88,'G')
```

This code starts off with a DDL statement that drops and creates objects. Once the database is created, we populate the table with some DML statements starting with the INSERT keyword. When writing this much code, we have probably worked on it over time. It is very likely that someone will also run this code, thus benefiting from our work. In either case, it is a good idea to save our code as a file. When we save code as a file it has a .sql extension and is referred to as a *script* or a *sql script* in the SQL Server community.

For the Joes2Pros practices, we need to have a Joes2Pros folder existing on the root of the C:/ drive for the computer we are working on. If this folder does not already exist, then one will have to be created in order for the next set of exercises to work correctly. Refer to Figure 6.22 for doing this in the Windows 7 OS.

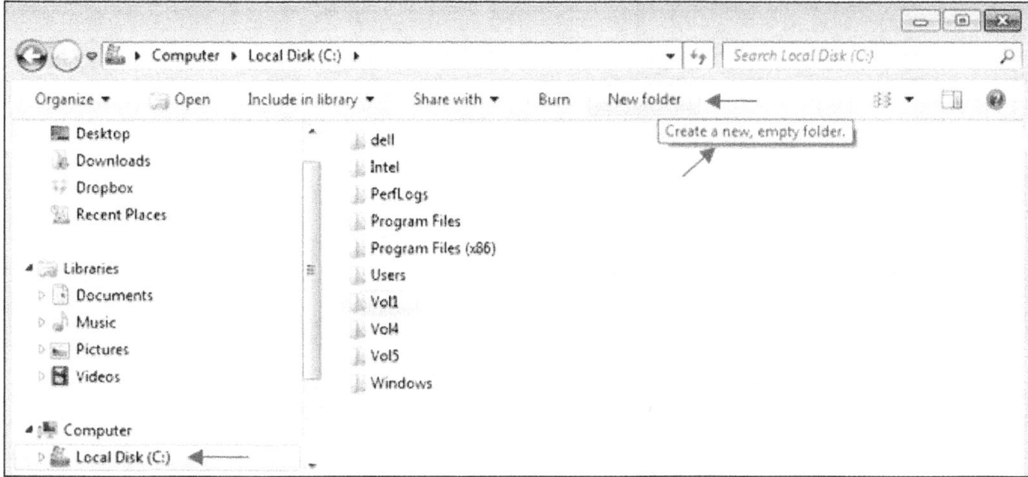

Figure 6.22 Shows the steps to create the C:\Joe2Pros folder.

After naming the folder 'Joes2Pros,' we will have an empty folder ready to hold anything we wish to save or store inside. Once our code has been tested, we can save the file as CreateDBMovie.sql in our C:\Joes2Pros folder (Figure 6-23).

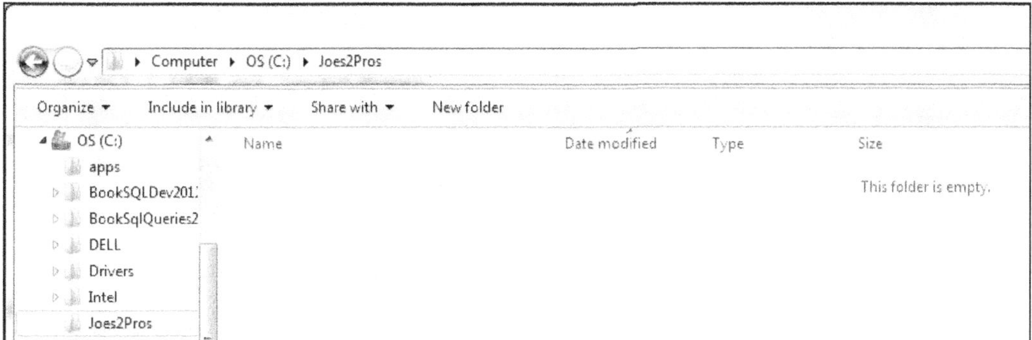

Figure 6.23 Saving your T-SQL code as a SQL script to the C:\Joes2Pros folder.

As soon as we save the SQL statements, they become SQL scripts (Figure 6.24). SQL Server scripts are all saved with the .sql extension. In our example we have one script saved in the C:\Joes2Pros folder named CreateDBMovie.sql script. Scripts eliminate the need to re-create SQL code that is used repeatedly. This script can be re-executed in our database testing environment. Another very useful purpose for scripts is to share with our team members or the SQL community.

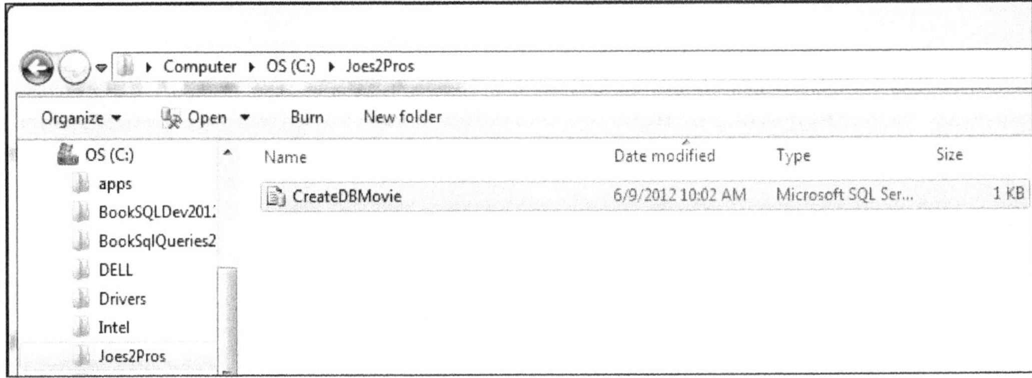

Figure 6.24 Verify the SQL script has been saved.

Executing SQL Scripts

Now that we have written our code to create the dbMovie database along with a tblMovie table that is populated with practice data and then saved it as a script named CreateDBMovie.sql in our Joes2Pros folder we are ready to use this code whenever the need arises.

Not surprisingly, as soon as we arrive at work in the morning, our manager asks us to demo the script for the entire team! A quick way to get our demo started is in Management Studio, using the toolbar to navigate to the file (Figure 6.25).

File > **Open** > left-click **File** to open a Windows Explorer window > > **Computer** > **Local Disk (C:)** > **Joes2Pros** > select **CreateDBMovie.sql** > click the '**Open**' button

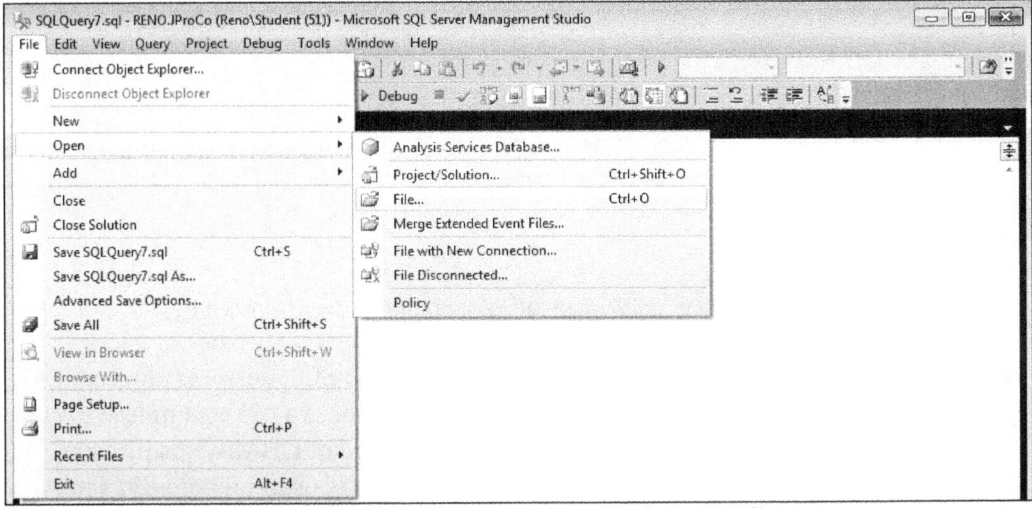

Figure 6.25 You can open a script from Management Studio from the File menu.

Choose the file location and click the Open button. The end result is our script will be loaded into a new Query Window (Figure 6.26). All we need to do now is execute the code with the F5 button on the keyboard, or the '**! Execute**' button in the SSMS toolbar.

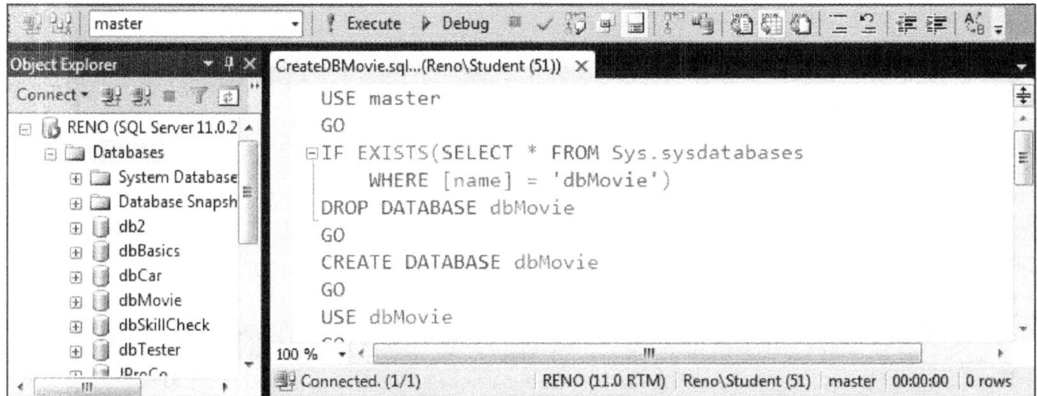

Figure 6.26 The CreateDBMovie script is open in a query window of Management Studio.

From Management Studio we can open a script. First, close completely out of Management Studio to a blank desktop. We will see how to force the script to open inside of Management Studio in a single step. To accomplish this, we will use a technique known as invocation.

Open the Windows Explorer window we use to navigate the folders and files on our computer every day. Locate the CreateDBMovie.sql script and double-click on the name of the file. SQL Server Management Studio will open with our script inside a new Query Window. We must press the 'Connect' button in order to run the script. Notice that when we open SQL Server with this process, the Object Explorer is not displayed, only a big Query Window with our script (Figure 6.27).

Reader Note: *If we need access to the Object Explorer, we simply press the 'F8' button on our keyboard, and then use the 'Connect' drop-down menu to select the 'Database Engine…' option. This will open the '**Connect to Server**' dialog box. Press the 'Connect' button and the Object Explorer will now be available to use.*

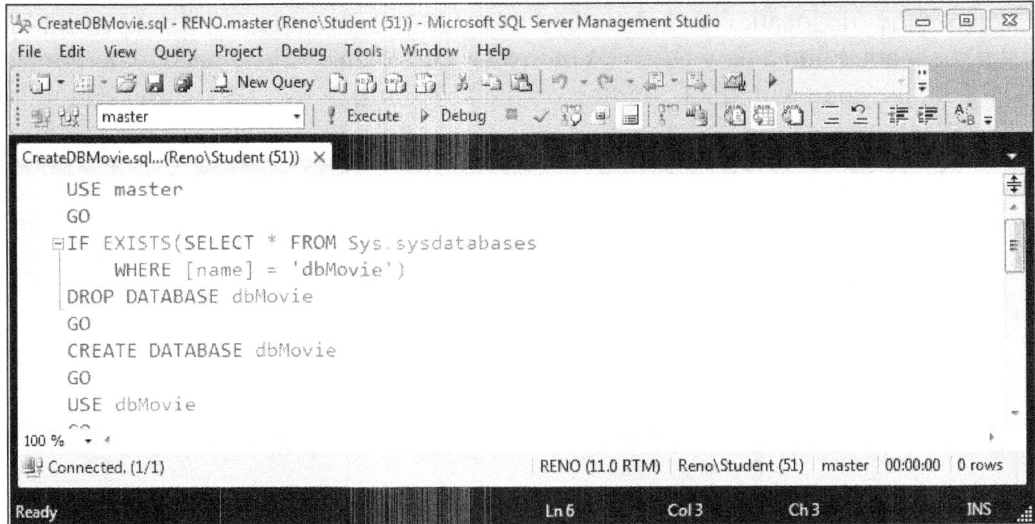

Figure 6.27 Our script opens in SSMS by double-clicking the file in Windows Explorer.

SQLCMD Utility

There is another way to invoke a script without touching Management Studio. We can use the *SQLCMD* utility window. Since our script creates a database, a good demonstration of this method will be to execute this script. Let's drop our dbMovie database by highlighting the first two batches of the script and executing it. Notice in Figure 6.28 that our code ran and the dbMovie database is gone.

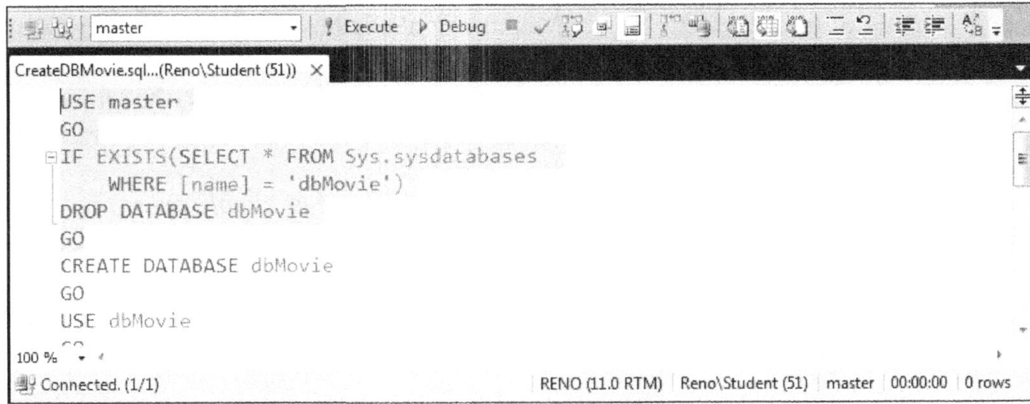

Figure 6.28 Run just the DROP portion of our script by highlighting the first two batches.

Now that dbMovie is gone, minimize Management Studio to the taskbar, then press the keyboard combination '⊞ + R' (Windows key plus R key). In the '***Run***' dialog box type the word '**cmd**' and then press 'OK' (Figure 6.29).

Caution: *SQL Express Users… please keep reading, but don't do any of the steps until reaching Figure 6.34.*

Run

Type the name of a program, folder, document, or Internet resource, and Windows will open it for you.

Open: cmd

OK Cancel Browse...

Figure 6.29 Type CMD from the start menu command.

We need to change to the C:\ drive root directory by typing the command '**cd**' at the flashing cursor and press 'Enter'. Now we set the folder context to Joes2Pros by typing the command '**cd Joes2Pros**' and press the 'Enter' button. We are now in the Joes2Pros folder and can view the contents by typing the command '**dir**' and pressing the 'Enter' button on our keyboard (Figure 6.30).

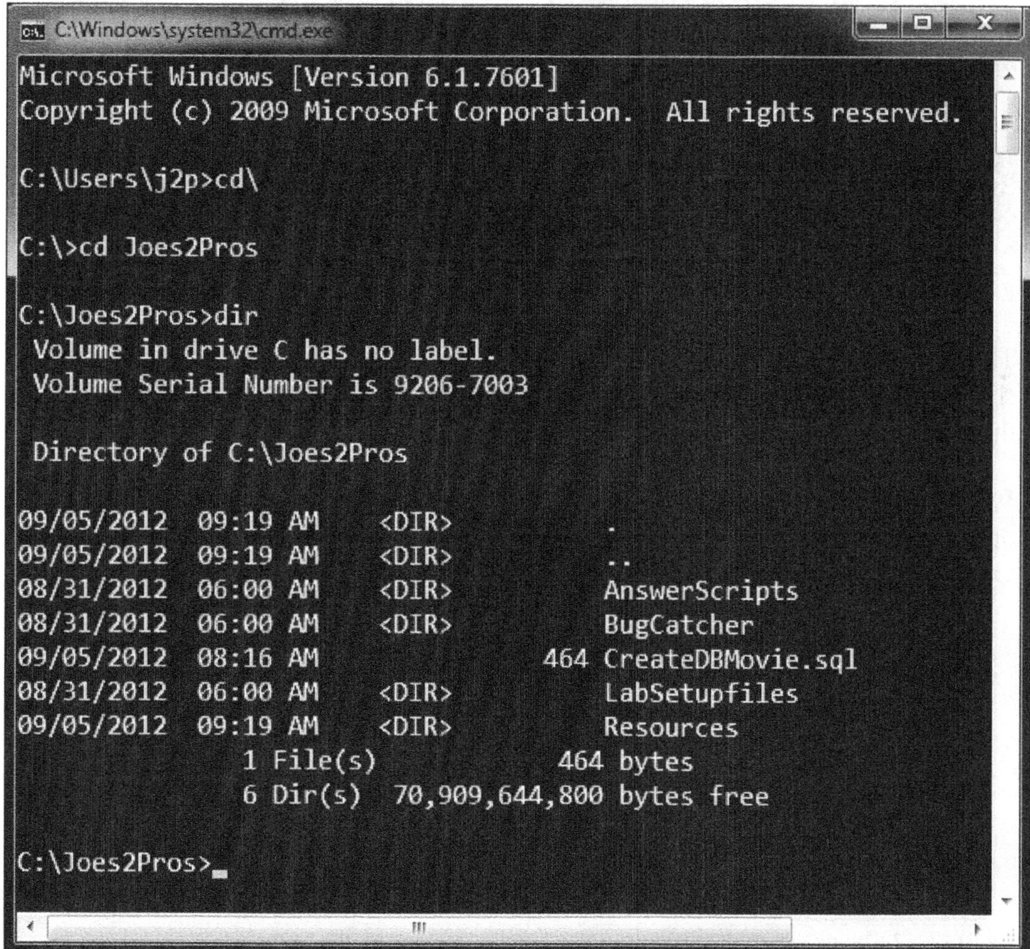

Figure 6.30 Using the command prompt to show the script existing in the C:\Joes2Pros folder.

At this point, we are going to use the command-line tool known as SQLCMD. We can use SQLCMD to connect to the SQL Server service on our computer, or to connect with another SQL Server service on the network. There are different options that we have with this tool called *switches*. We can see a list of all the *switches* displayed in Figure 6.33.

For example, to run on our local server, we specify a capital 'S' and the server name like this '**-S(local)**'. Be mindful that the command line is case sensitive. If we specify a lowercase 's', trying to access the server it will not work properly, as this is the column separator switch in this utility. The command to run our script is '**SQLCMD -S(local) -E -i CreateDBMovie.sql**' (Figure 6.31).

```
C:\Windows\system32\cmd.exe

C:\Joes2Pros>SQLCMD -S(local) -E -i CreateDBMovie.sql
Changed database context to 'master'.
Changed database context to 'dbMovie'.

(5 rows affected)

C:\Joes2Pros>_
```

Figure 6.31 SQLCMD runs CreateDBMovie.sql file on local server using a Trusted Connection.

The '**-S**' must be a capital 'S', which stands for Server. The '**-E**' must be a capital 'E', which stands for trusted connection. The '**-i**' (must be a lower case) specifies the input file we want to run.

We can verify that this script has created and populated the dbMovie database, by opening Management Studio to a new Query Window using the dbMovie context. Query the tblMovie table to display all records and fields (Figure 6.32).

```
SELECT * FROM tblMovie
```

	m_ID	m_Title	m_Runtime	m_Rating
1	1	A-List Explorers	96	PG-13
2	2	Bonker Bonzo	75	G
3	3	Chumps to Champs	75	PG-13
4	4	Dare or Die	110	R
5	5	EeeeGhads	88	G

5 rows

Figure 6.32 The dbMovie database is created and populated by the SQLCMD.

We know the '-S' switch is for the Server and we have used some other switches, but what if we forget these and want some help? To learn what a given SQLCMD code switch symbol or letter means, type the command 'SQLCMD /?' and then press the 'Enter' button. The SQL Server command line help window will appear, as shown in Figure 6.33.

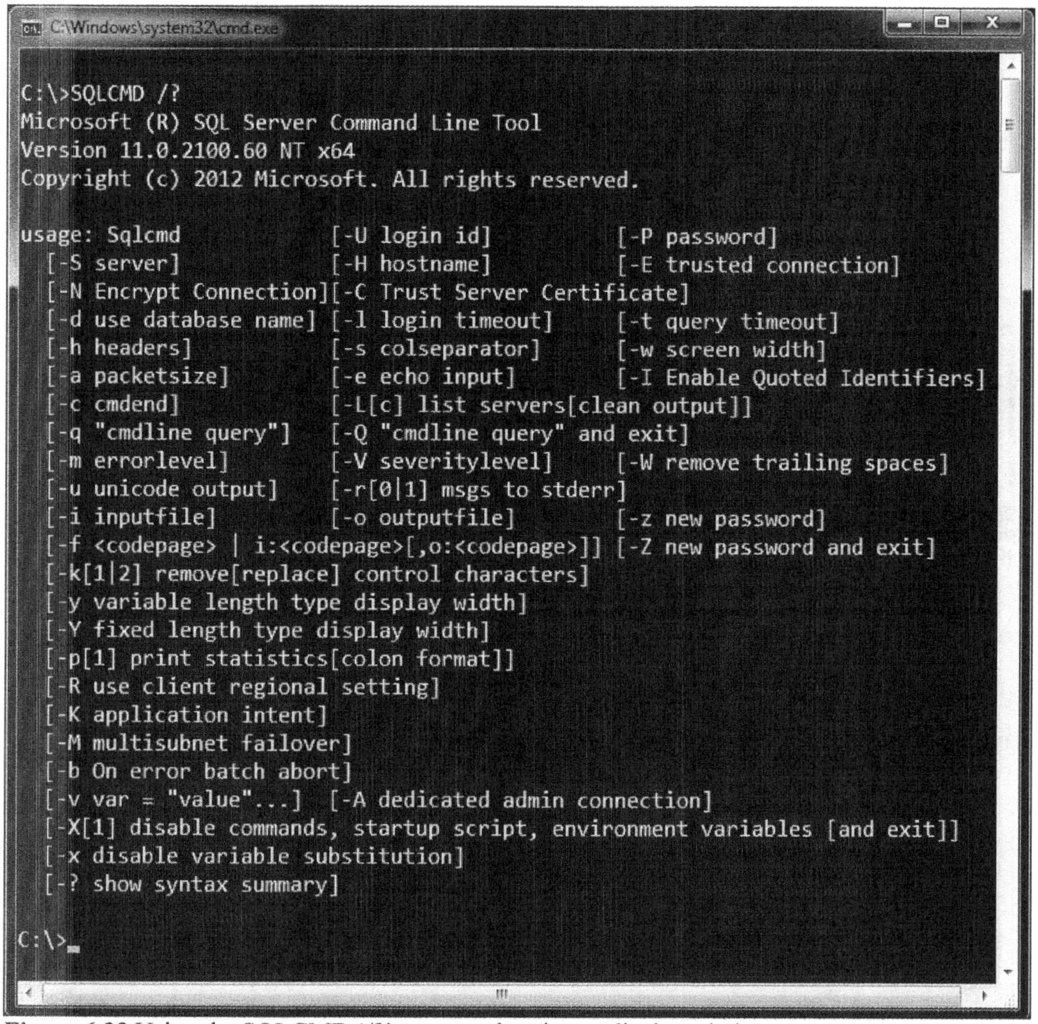

```
C:\Windows\system32\cmd.exe

C:\>SQLCMD /?
Microsoft (R) SQL Server Command Line Tool
Version 11.0.2100.60 NT x64
Copyright (c) 2012 Microsoft. All rights reserved.

usage: Sqlcmd               [-U login id]          [-P password]
  [-S server]               [-H hostname]          [-E trusted connection]
  [-N Encrypt Connection][-C Trust Server Certificate]
  [-d use database name] [-l login timeout]     [-t query timeout]
  [-h headers]              [-s colseparator]      [-w screen width]
  [-a packetsize]           [-e echo input]        [-I Enable Quoted Identifiers]
  [-c cmdend]               [-L[c] list servers[clean output]]
  [-q "cmdline query"]      [-Q "cmdline query" and exit]
  [-m errorlevel]           [-V severitylevel]     [-W remove trailing spaces]
  [-u unicode output]       [-r[0|1] msgs to stderr]
  [-i inputfile]            [-o outputfile]        [-z new password]
  [-f <codepage> | i:<codepage>[,o:<codepage>]] [-Z new password and exit]
  [-k[1|2] remove[replace] control characters]
  [-y variable length type display width]
  [-Y fixed length type display width]
  [-p[1] print statistics[colon format]]
  [-R use client regional setting]
  [-K application intent]
  [-M multisubnet failover]
  [-b On error batch abort]
  [-v var = "value"...]  [-A dedicated admin connection]
  [-X[1] disable commands, startup script, environment variables [and exit]]
  [-x disable variable substitution]
  [-? show syntax summary]

C:\>_
```

Figure 6.33 Using the SQLCMD '/?' command option to display a help screen.

Reader Note: *Typing '/?' is the universal command to display a help screen. This command can be typed after a utility name (SQLCMD, BCP), or after a command line tool name (HOSTNAME, SYSTEMINFO, DIR, etc…) to quickly show basic information on how to use the tool or utility.*

We now know that there are several ways to run scripts on SQL Server.

- Open a script from within Management Studio (SSMS).
- Invoke a script from Windows Explorer by double-clicking it.
- Use the SQLCMD utility to run a script from the command-line.

SQL Server Express Users: To complete this exercise with SQL Server Express edition, we will need to know the exact name of our SQL Server instance. To do this, verify our server name at the top of the Object Explorer. For example, we can see in Figure 6.34 the instance name is Reno. The full path name for this instance is 'SQL Server 11.0.2100 - Reno\Student'.

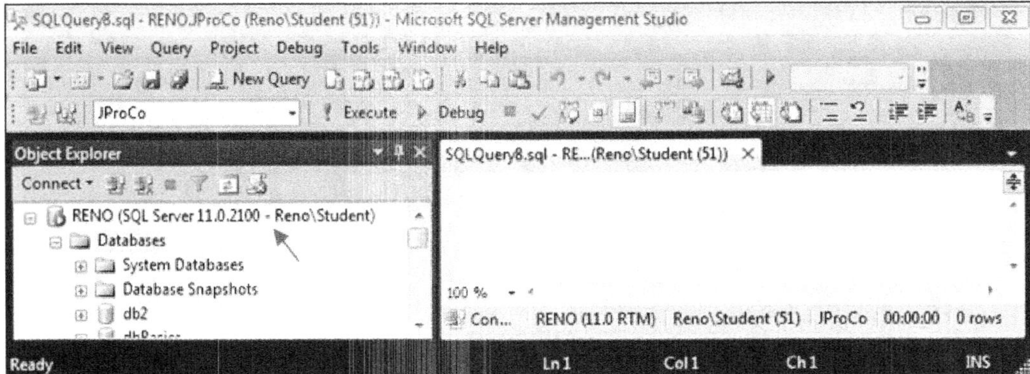

Figure 6.34 SQL Express on the Reno server will have the instance name of Reno\SQLExpress.

Users of SQL Server Express need to explicitly name their server. So, to run our CreateDBMovie.sql script with SQLCMD, use the correct Server switch '**-S**' and then type the name of our SQL Server instance (found in Object Explorer) followed by a backslash '\' sign and then the word '**sqlexpress**'. An example of what this looks like is shown in Figure 6.35.

```
C:\Joes2Pros>SQLCMD -S Reno\sqlexpress -E -iCreateDBMovie.sql
Changed database context to 'master'.
Changed database context to 'dbMovie'.

(0 rows affected)

C:\Joes2Pros>_
```

Figure 6.35 SQL Server Express users must explicitly identify the server name in SQLCMD.

Lab 6.4: Using Scripts

Lab Prep: Each lab has one or more Skill Checks. Start with Skill Check 1 and proceed until reaching the Points to Ponder section.

Before beginning this lab, verify that SQL Server 2012 is properly installed and operating. Before running the lab setup script for resetting the database (SQLQueries2012Vol1Chapter6.4Setup.sql), please make sure to close all query windows within SSMS. An open query window pointing to a database context can lock that database preventing it from updating when the script is executing. A simple way to assure all query windows are closed, is to exit out of SSMS, then open a new instance of SSMS, and lastly run the setup script.

Skill Check 1: Before we can begin the lab, exit out of SSMS and create a folder on the C: drive named Joes2Pros.

In the Resources folder, there is a file named Chapter6.4SetupAll.sql. Copy this file to the C:\Joes2Pros folder.

Use the SQLCMD utility, to run the C:\Joes2Pros\Chapter6.4SetupAll.sql script.

Reader Note: *The screenshot displayed in Figure 6.36 has been altered with image manipulation software to show the majority, but not all, of the information returned in the Command Prompt utility window when this exercise is complete.*

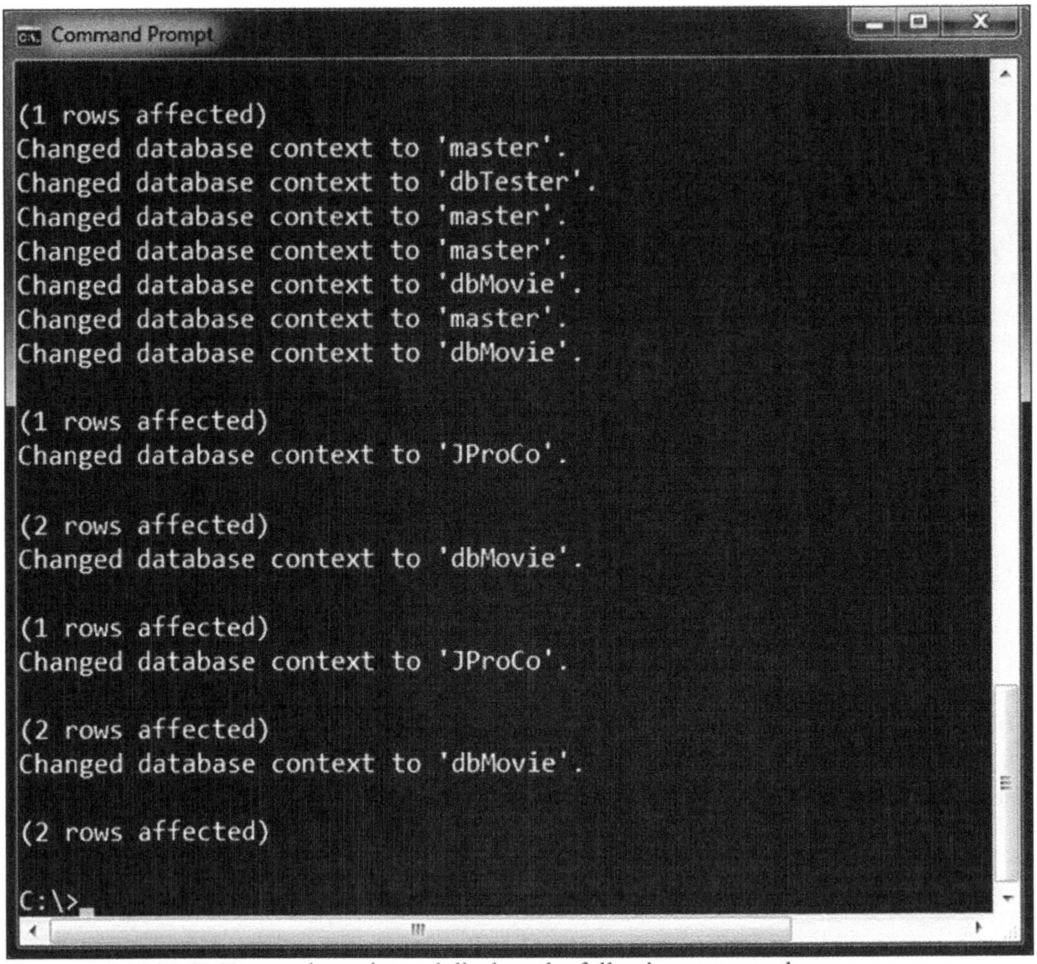

```
(1 rows affected)
Changed database context to 'master'.
Changed database context to 'dbTester'.
Changed database context to 'master'.
Changed database context to 'master'.
Changed database context to 'dbMovie'.
Changed database context to 'master'.
Changed database context to 'dbMovie'.

(1 rows affected)
Changed database context to 'JProCo'.

(2 rows affected)
Changed database context to 'dbMovie'.

(1 rows affected)
Changed database context to 'JProCo'.

(2 rows affected)
Changed database context to 'dbMovie'.

(2 rows affected)

C:\>_
```

Figure 6.36 SQLCMD runs the script and displays the following status to the screen.

Answer Code: There is no answer code, but we recommend opening SSMS and verifying database records. Steps can be found in the Lab6.4_RunningScripts file in the Answer Scripts folder.

Points to Ponder - Scripts

1. A SQL script is a collection of lines of SQL code saved as a file.
2. A single script can create a database, create all of that database's tables, and even populate those tables with records.
3. Scripts are useful for re-running the same code repeatedly on the local computer, or on a network computer with the same database.
4. A script file for SQL Server has the '.SQL' or '.sql' extension. This is because file extensions are not case sensitive.
5. SQLCMD is a command-line utility that allows SQL scripts or code to run.
6. SQLCMD has optional runtime parameters like '-E' for trusted connection, or '-P' for password.
7. SQLCMD is case sensitive, so the '-p' and '-P' switches are different.
8. To find all optional runtime parameters that SQLCMD accepts, type the command 'SQLCMD /?' in the command prompt window.

Chapter Glossary

DDL: Data Definition Language.

DELETE: Removes records from a table, without changing the structure of the table, or removing the table itself from the database.

DML: Data Manipulation Language.

INSERT: A DML keyword used to add new records to tables.

Populate: The process of adding data to a table.

Row Constructors: Allow multiple records in one INSERT INTO statement.

Script: SQL code saved as a file with a '.sql' file extension.

SET: A SQL keyword that assigns values to variables.

SQLCMD: A command-line tool to run SQL scripts or SQL statements.

Unpopulated Table: A table with no records.

UPDATE: A statement that changes, or *manipulates* existing data without adding any new records.

Review Quiz - Chapter Six

1.) Insert, update and delete belong to what family of language statements?

O a. DDL

O b. XML

O c. DML

2.) Which is the appropriate SQL code to add records to a table?

O a. `INSERT INTO tblSports VALUE(1,'Football')`

O b. `INSERT INTO tblSports VALUES (1,'Football')`

3.) What is a script?

O a. Any SQL code.

O b. SQL code saved as a file.

O c. It's another name for a stored procedure.

4.) Which is the newest recommended command line utility that enables running of SQL scripts?

O a. OSQL

O b. ISQL

O c. SQLCMD

5.) Which of the following is not a way to run a SQL script?

O a. Run it in a query window.

O b. Use the script file in a command-line utility.

O c. Open Windows Explorer and double-click the .sql file.

O d. Double click .mdb (Microsoft Database File) file in Windows Explorer.

6.) Your Employee table holds all employees and their work LocationID. Your [Grant] table contains a list of grants and the employee ID number of the person who found the grant in an EmpID field. Your Boston location only accepts grants in the exact amount of $50,000 from each donor. You have noticed incorrectly entered values in the Amount field of the [Grant] table for your Boston employees. You need to set the amount to $50,000 for all entries in the [Grant] table to correspond to employees at Location 2 (Boston). You must not change the grant amounts of the other locations. Which SQL statement should you use?

O a.
```
UPDATE [Grant] SET Amount = 50000
WHERE EXISTS (SELECT * FROM Employee E
              WHERE E.LocationID = 2)
```

O b.
```
UPDATE G SET Amount = 50000
FROM [Grant] G
INNER JOIN Employee E
ON G.EmpID = E.EmpID
WHERE E.LocationID = 2
```

7.) Which of the following is the correct way to name a SQL script?

O a. .jpg
O b. .sql
O c. .trc
O d. .SqlPlan

Answer Key

1.) DDL (Data Definition Language), as we learned in Chapter 5, is all about defining the structures to hold data with CREATE, ALTER or DROP, so (a) is incorrect. XML (Extensible Markup Language) is a set of rules for encoding documents electronically and does not do anything within an RDBMS, so (b) is not correct either. INSERT, UPDATE and DELETE are statements which make changes to, or manipulates the data so they are part of DML (Data Manipulation Language), making (c) the correct answer.

2.) *INSERT INTO tblSports VALUE(1,'Football',)* is missing an 's' at the end of 'values' and will result in a syntax error, so (a) is incorrect. *INSERT INTO tblSports VALUES(1,'Football')* is written correctly, so (b) is correct.

3.) Not just any SQL code is a script; it must be saved as a file with a .sql extension, so (a) is incorrect. A stored procedure (see Chapter 8) is SQL code saved to SQL Server rather than its own file, so (c) is also incorrect. SQL code saved as a file is a script, so (b) is the correct answer.

4.) OSQL and ISQL are both command line utilities provided with SQL Server 2000 so they are not the newest recommended command line utility that enables running of SQL scripts, making both (a) and (b) wrong answers. SQLCMD is the newest recommended command line utility that enables running of SQL scripts, making (c) the correct answer.

5.) SQL scripts can be run in a Query Window, with a command line query or by double-clicking the .sql file in Windows Explorer, so (a), (b) and (c) are all wrong. Double-clicking an .mdb (Microsoft Database File) file in Windows Explorer will open Microsoft Access if it is installed, so (d) is the correct answer.

6.) Using EXISTS as a predicate in the WHERE clause, will update either all or none of the records in the Grant table, so (a) is incorrect. Correct use of an INNER JOIN and predicating the WHERE clause to filter on Employee records with a LocationID of 2 will ensure that only Grant records that have a related Employee record will be updated, making (b) the correct answer.

7.) The .jpg extension is for pictures, so (a) is incorrect. SQL Server Profiler Stored Procedures create files using the .trc extension, making (c) an incorrect answer too. The .SqlPlan extension identifies SSMS Execution Plan files, so (d) is also a wrong answer. SQL Scripts are created with the .sql extension by default, making (b) the correct answer.

Bug Catcher Game

To play the Bug Catcher game run the BugCatcher_Chapter6.pps from the BugCatcher folder of the companion files. You can obtain these files from the www.Joes2Pros.com website.

[NOTES]

Chapter 7. Maintaining Tables

Tables get lots of attention. After all, they hold all of the data. Since data is added or removed constantly, designing the table correctly with the right number of fields and data types is part of good planning. We may also need to re-design tables that already have data in them. This chapter will discuss the choices we have for setting up and maintaining tables.

READER NOTE: *Please run the SQLQueries2012Vol1Chapter7.0Setup.sql script in order to follow along with the examples in the first section of Chapter 7. All scripts mentioned in this chapter may be found at www.Joes2Pros.com.*

DELETE vs. DROP

In previous chapters we encountered the DELETE command, which is a DML statement that eliminates some records from an existing table. We also learned the DROP command, which is a DDL statement eliminating a database or table. While intuitively they both have the effect of eliminating items, it's vital to be clear on the distinct usage of each command with tables.

```
DELETE tblMovie
```

```
SELECT * FROM tblMovie
```

m_ID	m_Title	m_Runtime	m_Rating

0 rows

Figure 7.1 A DELETE statement with no criteria tells SQL to delete all records from a table.

In Chapter 6, we learned the DELETE statement removes entire records, so we must be especially careful with how we use it. In most instances, we use filter criteria to remove only one record or a specific subset of records. For example, if we specify the ***m_ID*** field, SQL Server will remove just that record:

```
DELETE tblMovie WHERE m_ID = 1
```

Recall when we accidentally changed all the movie names to 'A-List Explorers', we needed to take the drastic step of using DELETE without any criteria (DELETE tblMovie) to get rid of **all** records in the tblMovie table. Any future queries on a table after deleting all records returns an empty result set.

DROP is an even more drastic step. It's the most severe thing we can do to a table. *Besides getting rid of all our records, the drop command goes a step further and removes the entire table and its design!* In other words, all the DDL and DML statements we used to build the structure of this table and then populate it with data will be wiped out with a DROP statement. The following code syntax will drop a table:

```
DROP TABLE tblMovie
GO
```

Trying to query the table after it is dropped gives an error message (Figure 7.2).

```
DROP TABLE tblMovie
GO
```

```
SELECT * FROM tblMovie
```

```
Messages
Msg 208, Level 16, State 1, Line 1
Invalid object name 'tblMovie'.
                                                    0 rows
```

Figure 7.2 The DROP statement removes the entire table and its contents from your database.

DROP does not accept criteria since DROP is a DDL statement. Since the tblMovie table has been dropped, there is no table to query. We can refresh the Object Explorer window to confirm the table is gone. This is why SQL Server returns an error when we try to query the table.

The next section titled ***Altering Table Design*** uses the tblMovie table, so we will need to run the following code and save it as a script to create and populate the tblMovie table when we reach this section:

```
USE master
GO

IF EXISTS(
SELECT * FROM sys.sysdatabases
WHERE [name] = 'dbMovie')
DROP DATABASE dbMovie
GO

CREATE DATABASE dbMovie
GO

USE dbMovie
GO

CREATE TABLE tblMovie (
m_ID INT PRIMARY KEY,
m_Title VARCHAR(30) NOT NULL,
m_Runtime INT,
m_Rating VARCHAR(10))
GO

INSERT INTO tblMovie VALUES
(1,'A-List Explorers',96,'PG-13'),
(2,'Bonker Bonzo',75,'G'),
(3,'Chumps to Champs',75,'PG-13'),
(4,'Dare or Die',110,'R'),
(5,'EeeeGhads',88,'G')
```

Altering Table Design

We have a populated table and just learned we must add a new field called ***m_Description***. Every new movie will now have a marketing description. One option is to drop and rebuild the table from scratch. We saved our code as a script, so we could modify the code to include the new field and add description values for those five existing records to the script. However, we haven't yet received descriptions for the five records and the manager wants this field added ASAP before anyone can add more movies into the database.

A better way to succeed in this scenario is to simply use an ALTER TABLE statement and add the new field. If records already exist and we want to populate them later, it's a good idea to have the field accept NULL data types. While we might consider rebuilding a five-record table that has just a few columns, we certainly wouldn't want to rebuild a table that contained hundreds of records. Run the following code to add the ***m_Description*** field:

```
ALTER TABLE tblMovie
ADD m_Description VARCHAR(100) NULL
```

A quick look at our table with a SELECT query will show us several things. We now have a field called ***m_Description***. We also haven't yet specified a value for any of the old records. The unknown value is currently set as NULL (Figure 7.3).

```
SELECT * FROM tblMovie
```

	m_ID	m_Title	m_Runtime	m_Rating	m_Description
1	1	A-List Explorers	96	PG-13	NULL
2	2	Bonker Bonzo	75	G	NULL
3	3	Chumps to Champs	75	PG-13	NULL
4	4	Dare or Die	110	R	NULL
5	5	EeeeGhads	88	G	NULL

5 rows

Figure 7.3 All five existing records are NULL for the new m_Description field until you add data.

Adding fields after we've already designed a database and its tables can be tricky. For example, we have allowed this field to be nullable only because we already had records in the table. However, we now risk someone entering additional NULL records to the table by using the following code:

```
INSERT INTO tblMovie VALUES
(6,'Fire Shaft',75,'R',NULL)
```

Our manager has also told us that any new movies must be entered with a description. We can't change this field to NOT NULL because our five existing records would violate this rule. Fortunately, there are ways to restrict NULL values from being added to future records, while giving us some freedom with the existing records. First off, let's DELETE the record created by the last INSERT statement, since it doesn't meet the manager's requirements, then we will need to DROP the existing field with the following code:

```
DELETE FROM tblMovie
WHERE m_ID = 6

ALTER TABLE tblMovie
DROP COLUMN m_Description
```

In order to add a new, non-nullable field to tblMovie, we need to think about what description the existing records should get. We have the option to assign a default value at the time the field is created. The first five movies need a description that reads 'Description Coming Soon'. The following code creates the non-nullable ***m_Description*** field with our default value:

```
ALTER TABLE tblMovie
ADD m_Description VARCHAR(100) NOT NULL
DEFAULT 'Description Coming Soon'
```

The new field is now in place and our existing records show a default description (Figure 7.4). This also means future movies entered must have some value for the description since ***m_Description*** will not accept a NULL. To insert new records with a default value just use the **DEFAULT** keyword in the INSERT statement:

```
--Example of how to insert default values
INSERT INTO tblMovie VALUES
(6,'Fire Shaft',75,'R',DEFAULT)

SELECT * FROM tblMovie
```

	m_ID	m_Title	m_Runtime	m_Rating	m_Description
1	1	A-List Explorers	96	PG-13	Description Coming Soon
2	2	Bonker Bonzo	75	G	Description Coming Soon
3	3	Chumps to Champs	75	PG-13	Description Coming Soon
4	4	Dare or Die	110	R	Description Coming Soon
5	5	EeeeGhads	88	G	Description Coming Soon
6	6	Fire Shaft	75	R	Description Coming Soon
					6 rows

Figure 7.4 The existing records get the default value 'Description Coming Soon' for the new field.

In addition to adding new fields to existing tables, we can also rename fields. SQL Server issues a caution message when changing field names. To change the title of ***m_Description*** to ***m_Teaser***, we would run the following code:

```
EXEC sp_rename 'tblMovie.m_Description', 'm_Teaser'
```

Reader Note: *Changing an object name already in use is considered risky. Many users and calling applications may be expecting a field, or other object name that is no longer there. This can cause a dependent process to break. Therefore, expect a caution message similar to this when executing the sp_rename command.*

Messages
Caution: Changing any part of an object name could break scripts and stored procedures.
0 rows

A query of the tblMovie table confirms the field name has changed (Figure 7.5).

```
SELECT * FROM tblMovie
```

	m_ID	m_Title	m_Runtime	m_Rating	m_Teaser
1	1	A-List Explorers	96	PG-13	Description Coming Soon
2	2	Bonker Bonzo	75	G	Description Coming Soon
3	3	Chumps to Champs	75	PG-13	Description Coming Soon
4	4	Dare or Die	110	R	Description Coming Soon
5	5	EeeeGhads	88	G	Description Coming Soon
6	6	Fire Shaft	75	R	Description Coming Soon
					6 rows

Figure 7.5 The last field in this query has been renamed to m_Teaser.

With sp_rename we have wandered outside the SQL language and into a Microsoft specific stored procedure. However, this is a curiosity point that frequently comes up in class, so we will demo it here. Stored procedures are discussed more in the next chapter. Next, we want to change our tblMovie table to just be called Movie. This can be achieved with the following code:

```
EXEC sp_rename 'tblMovie', 'Movie'
```

Now we can query the Movie table. Change our SELECT statement after the FROM clause to use the name Movie and we will see the same result set as the one we are familiar with for tblMovie.

```
SELECT *
FROM Movie
```

	m_ID	m_Title	m_Runtime	m_Rating	m_Teaser
1	1	A-List Explorers	96	PG-13	Description Coming Soon
2	2	Bonker Bonzo	75	G	Description Coming Soon
3	3	Chumps to Champs	75	PG-13	Description Coming Soon
4	4	Dare or Die	110	R	Description Coming Soon
5	5	EeeeGhads	88	G	Description Coming Soon
6	6	Fire Shaft	75	R	Description Coming Soon
					6 rows

Figure 7.6 The new table name Movie produces the same results as the old name tblMovie.

Altering Columns

One more thing we can do is to change column properties without having to drop and re-create the column. For example, some movie teasers actually go over 100 letters in length. This field has a VARCHAR(100) data type and needs to become a VARCHAR(200). If we dropped and re-created the fields all our existing data would be lost. We can avoid this problem by simply running the code shown here to change the ***m_Teaser*** column to have a length of 200.

```
ALTER TABLE Movie
ALTER COLUMN m_Teaser VARCHAR(200) NOT NULL
```

DDL Syntax

The table shown in this section is a quick reference summary of what has been covered in this chapter (Table 7.1). When this makes sense, we are sure to have a solid grasp of this topic.

Table 7.1 A summary of SQL code for table definitions.

Task	Explanation and code sample
DROP a table	In this example, we remove the entire tblMovie table. `DROP TABLE tblMovie`

ALTER a table Adding a nullable column	In this example, we add a new field to the tblMovie table that allows nulls.
	`ALTER TABLE tblMovie`
	`ADD m_Description VARCHAR(100) NULL`

ALTER a table Adding a non-nullable column	In this example, we add a new non-nullable field to the tblMovie table with a default value.
	`ALTER TABLE tblMovie`
	`ADD m_Description VARCHAR(100) NOT NULL`
	`DEFAULT 'Description Coming Soon'`

DROP a column from a table	In this example, we remove the m_Description field from tblMovie.
	`ALTER TABLE tblMovie`
	`DROP COLUMN m_Description`

Rename a Table	In this example, we rename the Location table to Locations. `sp_rename 'Location', 'Locations'`
Rename a Column in a Table	In this example, we rename the Street field in the Location table to Address. `sp_rename 'Location.Street', 'Location.Address'`

Lab 7.1: Altering Tables

Lab Prep: Each lab has one or more Skill Checks. Start with Skill Check 1 and proceed until reaching the Points to Ponder section.

Before beginning this lab, verify that SQL Server 2012 is properly installed and operating. Before running the lab setup script for resetting the database (SQLQueries2012Vol1Chapter7.1Setup.sql), please make sure to close all query windows within SSMS. An open query window pointing to a database context can lock that database preventing it from updating when the script is executing. A simple way to assure all query windows are closed, is to exit out of SSMS, then open a new instance of SSMS, and lastly run the setup script.

Skill Check 1: Add a new non-nullable integer field called ***m_Release*** to the Movie table. The default value for this new field should be 2000. When done, the results should resemble Figure 7.7.

```
SELECT * FROM Movie
```

	m_ID	m_Title	m_Runtime	m_Rating	m_Teaser	m_Release
1	1	A-List Explorers	96	PG-13	Description Coming Soon	2000
2	2	Bonker Bonzo	75	G	Description Coming Soon	2000
3	3	Chumps to Champs	75	PG-13	Description Coming Soon	2000
4	4	Dare or Die	110	R	Description Coming Soon	2000
5	5	EeeeGhads	88	G	Description Coming Soon	2000
6	6	Fire Shaft	75	R	Description Coming Soon	2000
						6 rows

Figure 7.7 Skill Check 1.

Answer Code: The T-SQL code to this lab can be found from the downloadable files named Lab7.1_AlteringTables.sql.

Points to Ponder - Altering Tables

1. DROP removes the entire table from the database. Statements starting with DROP are DDL statements.
2. New fields can be added to a table even after the table is initially created.
3. ALTER TABLE can be used to add new columns. For example:

```
ALTER TABLE tblMovie
ADD m_Description VARCHAR(300) NULL
```

4. ALTER TABLE can be used to remove columns. For example:

```
ALTER TABLE Employee
DROP COLUMN m_Runtime
```

5. ALTER TABLE statements are DDL statements. DDL statements never use filtering criteria.

Bulk Copy Program (BCP)

There are many ways to get data into a SQL server database. We have discussed scripts extensively and have also seen many ways to run these scripts. Most of the time, the source of our data will be plain, raw data. Raw data often comes to us as a block of values separated by commas with no SQL code whatsoever. In our SQL career, we will no doubt receive inputs in the form of spreadsheets, text files, Microsoft Access databases or another company's database.

There are utilities that understand data, and SQL Server can manage the inserting of data for us by using these different utilities and services. Some programs like *SQL Server Integration Services* (SSIS) can take just about any source of data and move it into or out of SQL Server. In this chapter, we explore how to use the *Bulk Copy Program* (BCP) utility, which was designed for the flow of data between SQL Server and text files. It's a simple utility that does one of the most common types of bulk copying.

Before we can practice importing records with the BCP utility, we need to delete the record containing m_ID 6. Run this code before moving to the next section.

```
DELETE FROM Movie
WHERE m_ID = 6
```

Importing Data

If we have data in a text file and need to move it into a SQL table, then we are ready to import that file into SQL Server using the BCP utility. A quick visual comparison of data in the input file and destination table will really help. We must confirm that the text data supply can populate each field by matching the design of the destination table.

Let's start off by looking at the destination where we intend to import this new data into. Usually this will be an existing table. In this example let's look at the Movie table of the dbMovie database to examine the records (Figure 7.8).

```
SELECT * FROM Movie
```

	m_ID	m_Title	m_Runtime	m_Rating	m_Teaser	m_Release
1	1	A-List Explorers	96	PG-13	Description Coming Soon	2000
2	2	Bonker Bonzo	75	G	Description Coming Soon	2000
3	3	Chumps to Champs	75	PG-13	Description Coming Soon	2000
4	4	Dare or Die	110	R	Description Coming Soon	2000
5	5	EeeeGhads	88	G	Description Coming Soon	2000

6 rows

Figure 7.8 The destination of the data will be the Movie table of the dbMovie database.

We currently have six fields, which can also be stated as "We need six values for each record in this table". There are also five records in our Movie table and two records in the file called Ch7MovieFeed.txt (Figure 7.9). Our goal is to import movies 6 and 7 into the Movie table using the BCP utility.

```
SELECT * FROM Movie
```

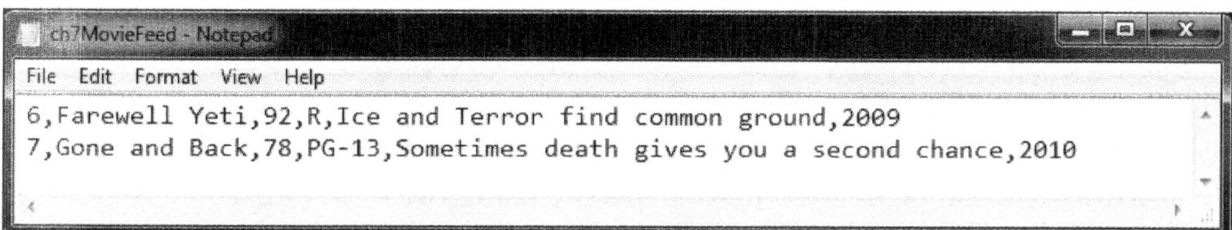

ch7MovieFeed - Notepad

File Edit Format View Help

```
6,Farewell Yeti,92,R,Ice and Terror find common ground,2009
7,Gone and Back,78,PG-13,Sometimes death gives you a second chance,2010
```

Figure 7.9 A text file with data is used to copy two records into the Movie table.

Locate the file Ch7MovieFeed.txt inside the Resources folder of the C:\Joes2Pro folder location. Copy this file directly into the C:\Joes2Pros folder.

The first record of the text file is m_id 6. Note the value 6 is terminated with a comma to separate it from the second field value of 'Farewell Yeti', which is separated by a comma from the third field, which shows a runtime of 92 minutes. The pattern repeats until the final field in each record is reached. At that point, a return (a carriage return or the equivilant of pressing the 'Enter' key) signals the end of the record. Keep in mind that *commas separate fields*, and after each line the *carriage return separates records.*

OK, we've confirmed the data in the source file and now are confident the data conforms to the destination format of our Movie table. The BCP utility should be able to run without a problem. We need to provide a few logistical items to BCP:

- The filepath of the source file.
- Which table we want the data copied into (Destination).
- The type of field terminators designated (commas, tabs, hash mark).

Close any Query Window that is open to the Movie database and minimize the Management Studio window to the taskbar, then press the keyboard combination '⊞ + R' (Windows key plus R key). This will open a dialog box. In the '***Run***' dialog box type the word '**cmd**' and then press 'OK' (Figure 7.10).

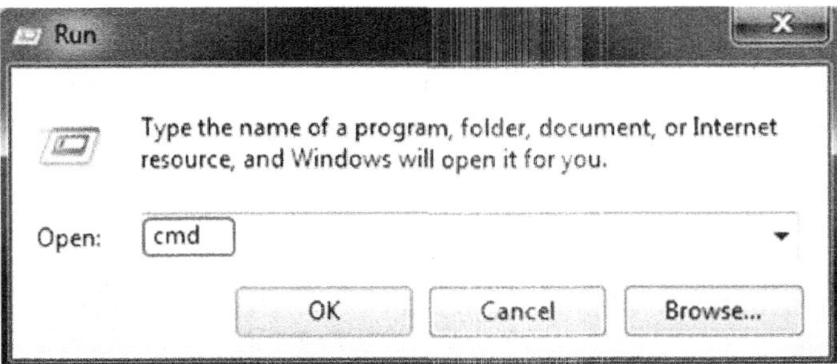

Figure 7.10 Starting the command prompt.

With the command prompt open (Figure 7.11), we can go to the root of the C:\ drive with a '**cd**' command and then press 'Enter'. Set the folder context to C:\Joes2pros with the command '**cd Joes2Pros**' then press 'Enter'. While in the folder, a good practice is to make sure the Ch7MovieFeed.txt is actually located in the directory. We can verify this by simply typing the command '**dir**', which will show us all the folders and files in the Joes2Pros folder. Once this is confirmed, we can proceed to invoke the file using the BCP utility.

We want to tell BCP to expect character data '**-c**' with fields terminated by commas '**-t,**'. The Windows Operating System has already authenticated our password, and SQL Server trusts Windows authentication. Since we are logged on as a user with permissions, we don't need to re-type our password. Use the Trusted connection switch by typing an upper case '**-T**'. Lastly, we have multiple records in the text file. Each record is separated by a new line '**\n**' or a carriage return '**r\n**' (carriage return\newline) in our text file. Place all these command switches together in the command line shown in Figure 7.11.

Caution: *SQL Express Users... to successfully complete this exercise, the '-S' switch will require the SQL Server instance name (found in Object Explorer) followed by a backslash '\' sign and then the word '**sqlexpress**'. Please look to Figure 6.34 and Figure 6.35 and the accompanying paragraphs as an example.*

```
Command Prompt
Microsoft Windows [Version 5.2.3790]
(C) Copyright 1985-2003 Microsoft Corp.

C:\Documents and Settings\Student>cd\

C:\>cd Joes2Pros

C:\Joes2Pros>BCP dbMovie.dbo.Movie IN ch7MovieFeed.txt -c -t, -T -r\n

Starting copy...

2 rows copied.
Network packet size (bytes): 4096
Clock Time (ms.) Total     : 10      Average : (200.00 rows per sec.)

C:\Joes2Pros>
```

Figure 7.11 Context is C:\Joes2Pros, run BCP to add two new records into the Movie table.

Query the Movie table and notice the two new records for a total of seven. This verifies that the m_id 6 and m_id 7 records were successfully added via BCP.

```
SELECT * FROM Movie
```

	m_ID	m_Title	m_Runtime	m_Rating	m_Teaser	m_Release
2	2	Bonker Bonzo	75	G	Description Coming Soon	2000
3	3	Chumps to Champs	75	PG-13	Description Coming Soon	2000
4	4	Dare or Die	110	R	Description Coming Soon	2000
5	5	EeeeGhads	88	G	Description Coming Soon	2000
6	6	Farewell Yeti	75	R	Ice and Terror find a…	2009
7	7	Gone and Back	75	R	Sometimes death gives…	2010

7 rows

Figure 7.12 The result set after running BCP shows there are now seven movie records.

Exporting Data

We are now being asked to share this information with a parent company. That company needs all seven records from our Movie table. Since they do not have permissions to our SQL Server, they have requested that we send them the data in a text file terminated (delimited) by hash # marks.

Essentially, we will be reversing the import process we just completed using the BCP utility. So, we will be moving data from our table in SQL Server and then saving it as a text file in the file system. In the command prompt window we will use BCP to specify the Movie table is going out to the Ch7PartnerFeed.txt using character data terminated by hash marks (Figure 7.13).

```
Command Prompt
Microsoft Windows [Version 5.2.3790]
(C) Copyright 1985-2003 Microsoft Corp.

C:\Documents and Settings\Student>cd\

C:\>cd Joes2Pros

C:\Joes2Pros>BCP dbMovie.dbo.Movie OUT ch7PartnerFeed.txt -c -t# -T -r\n

Starting copy...

7 rows copied.
Network packet size (bytes): 4096
Clock Time (ms.) Total     : 10      Average : (700.00 rows per sec.)

C:\Joes2Pros>_
```

Figure 7.13 The BCP process is saving all seven files as a text file.

Next, we will open the file C:\Joes2Pros\Ch7PartnerFeed.txt and examine its contents. We can do this by locating the file with Windows Explorer and then double-clicking on the file name. We can use the command line and type the command '**notepad C:\Joes2Pros\Ch7PartnerFeed.txt**'. We can easily see that our file uses hash marks as delimiters and has seven records in total (Figure 7.14).

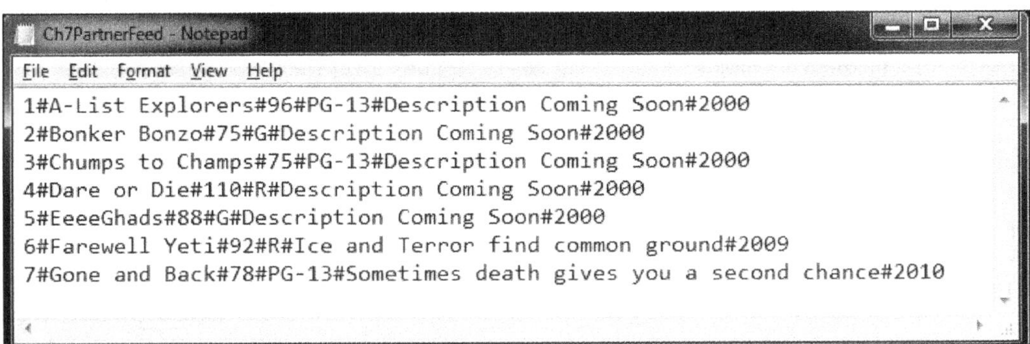

Figure 7.14 The seven records from the Movie table were exported to a text file.

There are many options to tell BCP how to perform a task. Different file types and security settings are among the choices. To view the list of all command line switches for the BCP utility we can type this command '**BCP /?**' and then press the 'Enter' button on our keyboard. The results are shown in Figure 7.15.

```
C:\>BCP /?
usage: BCP {dbtable | query} {in | out | queryout | format} datafile
  [-m maxerrors]            [-f formatfile]          [-e errfile]
  [-F firstrow]             [-L lastrow]             [-b batchsize]
  [-n native type]          [-c character type]      [-w wide character type]
  [-N keep non-text native] [-V file format version] [-q quoted identifier]
  [-C code page specifier]  [-t field terminator]    [-r row terminator]
  [-i inputfile]            [-o outfile]             [-a packetsize]
  [-S server name]          [-U username]            [-P password]
  [-T trusted connection]   [-v version]             [-R regional enable]
  [-k keep null values]     [-E keep identity values]
  [-h "load hints"]         [-x generate xml format file]
  [-d database name]        [-K application intent]

C:\>_
```

Figure 7.15 All the options of the BCP can be seen with the BCP help command '**BCP /?**'.

In order for BCP to communicate with SQL Server, it needs the right password or credential. This means we must either supply it with a trusted connection or a password.

If we want to see what the text file would look like if we accidently missed specifying a terminator in the previous example (Figure 7.13), we can type in the following command at the flashing cursor.

```
BCP dbMovie.dbo.Movie OUT Ch7TabFeed.txt -c -T -r\n
```

If a field terminator is not specified, a tab-delimited text file is created by default. A best practice is to specify a delimiter, otherwise BCP will choose the default tab delimiter.We can see what this looks like in Figure 7.16. With tab delimited files, it can be difficult to see where fields of varying lengths end, since columns don't line up uniformly and sometimes the gap for a tab is the same as a single space. In this case, a comma-delimited text file would be easier to visually scan and verify.

```
Ch7TabFeed - Notepad
File  Edit  Format  View  Help
1       A-List Explorers        96      PG-13   Description Coming Soon 2000
2       Bonker Bonzo    75      G       Description Coming Soon 2000
3       Chumps to Champs        75      PG-13   Description Coming Soon 2000
4       Dare or Die     110     R       Description Coming Soon 2000
5       EeeeGhads       88      G       Description Coming Soon 2000
6       Farewell Yeti   92      R       Ice and Terror find common ground       2009
7       Gone and Back   78      PG-13   Sometimes death gives you a second chance       2010
```

Figure 7.16 A tab-delimited text file is the default for BCP without specifying a terminator type.

Lab 7.2: Using BCP

Lab Prep: Each lab has one or more Skill Checks. Start with Skill Check 1 and proceed until reaching the Points to Ponder section.

Before beginning this lab, verify that SQL Server 2012 is properly installed and operating. Before running the lab setup script for resetting the database (SQLQueries2012Vol1Chapter7.2Setup.sql), please make sure to close all query windows within SSMS. An open query window pointing to a database context can lock that database preventing it from updating when the script is executing. A simple way to assure all query windows are closed, is to exit out of SSMS, then open a new instance of SSMS, and lastly run the setup script.

Skill Check 1: The Customer table of JProCo has five test records inside. The Lab72CustomerFeed.txt in the C:\Joes2Pros\Resources folder has 775 verified records.

```
SELECT * FROM Customer
```

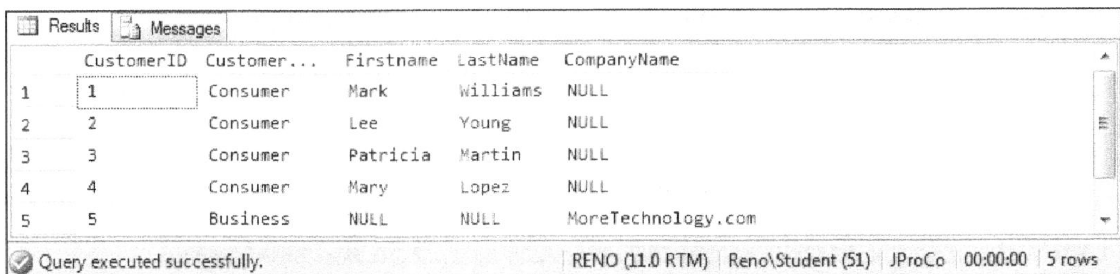

	CustomerID	Customer...	Firstname	LastName	CompanyName
1	1	Consumer	Mark	Williams	NULL
2	2	Consumer	Lee	Young	NULL
3	3	Consumer	Patricia	Martin	NULL
4	4	Consumer	Mary	Lopez	NULL
5	5	Business	NULL	NULL	MoreTechnology.com

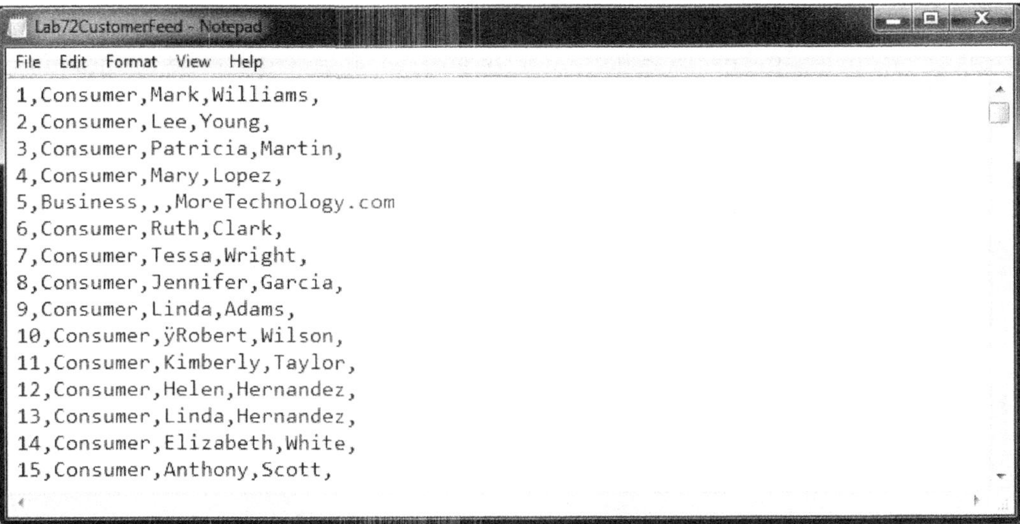


```
1,Consumer,Mark,Williams,
2,Consumer,Lee,Young,
3,Consumer,Patricia,Martin,
4,Consumer,Mary,Lopez,
5,Business,,,MoreTechnology.com
6,Consumer,Ruth,Clark,
7,Consumer,Tessa,Wright,
8,Consumer,Jennifer,Garcia,
9,Consumer,Linda,Adams,
10,Consumer,ÿRobert,Wilson,
11,Consumer,Kimberly,Taylor,
12,Consumer,Helen,Hernandez,
13,Consumer,Linda,Hernandez,
14,Consumer,Elizabeth,White,
15,Consumer,Anthony,Scott,
```

Figure 7.17 Lab72CustomerFeed.txt is a comma-delimited file ready to import to the Customer table.

We need to delete all five test records from the Customer table and then import the 775 comma-delimited rows of data from the Lab72CustomerFeed.txt file. When done, the Command Prompt window will resemble the BCP utility results shown here in Figure 7.18.

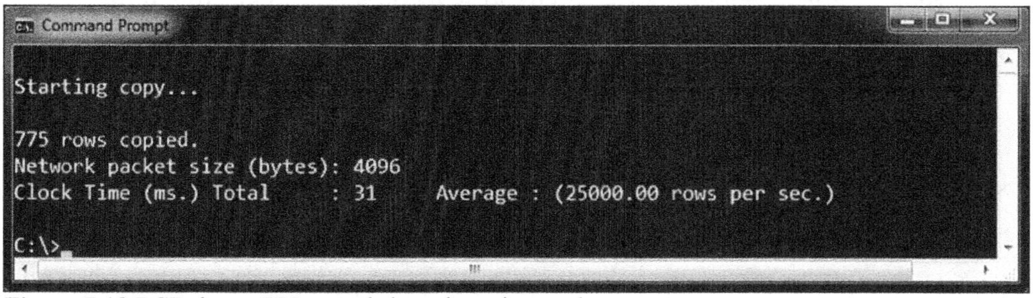

```
Command Prompt

Starting copy...

775 rows copied.
Network packet size (bytes): 4096
Clock Time (ms.) Total     : 31      Average : (25000.00 rows per sec.)

C:\>
```

Figure 7.18 BCP shows 775 records have been inserted.

Answer Code: There is no answer code for the BCP process.

Points to Ponder - Using BCP

1. BCP stands for Bulk Copy Program.
2. BCP performs data imports and exports using a command-line utility.
3. In BCP, the '-t' switch is used to specify how fields are terminated. For example, if commas are used between each field, use **'-t',** and if ampersands are used between fields, use the **'-t&'** switch.
4. To see all the available switches for BCP run the command **'BCP /?'**
5. A script is one or many lines of working SQL statements stored in a .sql file.
6. Upper and lower case switches have different meanings in BCP and all other Command Prompt utilities.

Chapter Glossary

ALTER: A DDL statement that changes the design or properties of a database or database object.

BCP: Bulk Copy Program is a command-line utility for importing or exporting data from a delimited text file.

DROP: A DDL statement that removes a database or database object.

Export: A process to take data from a table and save it with another type of data storage.

Import: A process to bring data into a SQL table.

Tab-Delimited Text File: A text file where each field is separated by a tab character.

Terminator: This type of marker designates the ending of a column or a row.

Review Quiz - Chapter Seven

1.) Which code correctly adds a new field called Status to the Location table?

O a. `ALTER TABLE Location ADD Status VARCHAR(300) NULL`

O b. `CREATE TABLE Location ALTER Status VARCHAR(300) NULL`

O c. `CREATE FIELD Location ADD Status VARCHAR(300) NULL`

O d. `ALTER FIELD Location ADD Status VARCHAR(300) NULL`

2.) What is the correct way to insert a default value in the third field of the Activity table?

O a. `INSERT INTO Activity VALUES (1,100, NULL)`

O b. `INSERT INTO Activity VALUES (1,100, DEFAULT)`

O c. `INSERT INTO Activity VALUES (1,100, 'NULL')`

O d. `INSERT INTO Activity VALUES (1,100, 'Default')`

3.) BCP is a command-line utility that does what?

O a. It runs SQL scripts.

O b. It installs SQL Server.

O c. It imports data from any type of file.

O d. It imports data from a text file.

4.) What does the –t switch in BCP do?

O a. It specifies a trusted connection.

O b. It specifies a row terminator.

O c. It specifies a field terminator.

O d. It specifies the time out in seconds.

O e. It specifies the terminal connection.

5.) If you do not specify a way to delimit your fields what does BCP do?

O a. You get an error message.

O b. It picks the most recently used delimiting option.

O c. You don't get any delimited file.

O d. You get a comma delimited file.

O e. You get a tab delimited file.

6.) You receive text files with updated movie data from across the country. Columns are separated by # signs. You need to import them into your database. What do you do?

O a. Re-create the text file in a custom format.
O b. Import them with BCP and specify the # as the field terminator.
O c. Import them with BCP and don't specify a terminator. It will be picked automatically.

7.) You receive text files with updated movie data from across the country. Columns are separated by tab characters. You need to import them into your database. What do you do?

O a. Re-create the text file in a custom format.
O b. Use BCP and specify the # as the field terminator.
O c. Use BCP and don't specify a terminator. It will be picked automatically.
O d. Re-create the text file as an Excel spreadsheet.

8.) Which statement describes the difference between the DROP and DELETE clauses for tables?

O a. They do exactly the same thing.
O b. DROP leaves you with an empty table and DELETE removes the table.
O c. DELETE empties the table and DROP eliminates the table.

9.) You are modifying a table named [Product] in a SQL Server 2012 database. You want to add a new column named FriendlyName to the product table. A friendly name for each product will be stored in this column. The table currently contains data. The sales department has not yet created a friendly name for each product. Friendly names are a required value for each product. You want to add this new column by using the least amount of effort. What should you do?

O a. Define the new column as NOT NULL with a default value of Undefined.
O b. Define the new column as NULL with a default value of Undefined.
O c. Define the new column as NULL and update the records later.
O d. Define the new column as NOT NULL without a default.

Answer Key

1.) Since the CREATE statement is used to initially define a new object, both (b) and (c) are incorrect. The ALTER statement is used on existing tables not fields, so (d) is also wrong. The correct answer is (a), because the ALTER statement is altering the table to add a new field.

2.) Inserting a NULL is not the same as inserting the default value, so (a) is wrong. Both (c) and (d) attempt to insert a string contained within quotes rather than the default values, so they are incorrect. To insert the default value, use the word default without quotes, making (b), the correct answer.

3.) SQL Server runs SQL scripts, so (a) is incorrect. Installation discs are used for installing SQL Server, so (b) is wrong. Programs like SSIS can import data from most types of files, so (c) is wrong. The correct answer is (d) because BCP (Bulk Copy Program) imports data from text files.

4.) The '-T' switch specifies a trusted connection and the '-r' switch specifies the row terminator making (a) and (b) incorrect. The BCP utility doesn't have switches for specifying a time out or the terminal connection, so (d) and (e) are wrong. Since the '-t' switch specifies a field terminator, (c) is the correct answer.

5.) Since, by default, a tab delimited file is used when a delimiter is not specified with the '-t' switch, then (a), (b), (c), and (d) are wrong. BCP will create a tab delimited file if the '-t' switch is not used, making (e) correct.

6.) Re-creating the text file in a custom format is a waste of valuable time by creating unnecessary work, so (a) is incorrect. The default field terminator is a tab, so (c) will not work. If the columns in the text file are separated by # signs then a '#' delimiter must be specified, therefore (b) is correct.

7.) Re-creating the text file in a custom format is a waste of valuable time by creating unnecessary work, so (a) is incorrect. If the columns in the text file are not separated by a tab then the field terminator must be specified, so (b) is also incorrect. Tab is the default field terminator, so (c) is correct.

8.) DROP removes the table from the database while DELETE removes records from the table, so (a) and (b) are incorrect. The correct answer is (c), since DROP eliminates the table and DELETE empties the table.

9.) Defining the new column as NULL will not satisfy the requirement, so (b) and (c) will not work. Not assigning a default value when adding the field will cause an error because of the records that already exist, so (d) will not work. The correct answer is (a) because it will require each record to have a friendly name and assigns existing records to something that can be changed.

Bug Catcher Game

To play the Bug Catcher game run the BugCatcher_Chapter7.pps from the BugCatcher folder of the companion files. You can obtain these files from the www.Joes2Pros.com website.

[NOTES]

Chapter 8. Stored Procedures

One of my fondest childhood memories is that of my father building a tree house with me. That was my first true practice with real tools. Using an actual hammer and nails was far superior to just grabbing the nearest rock. My aim and efficiency got better with each use as I figured out my swing. Soon I was able to brag about getting a nail to go flush into the wood using four or fewer swings – AND with no misses or bent nails!

Compare the first swing of a hammer with the first run of a brand new SQL query. Behind the scenes, SQL Server evaluates the new query and attempts to guess the fastest way to accomplish it. Each time it runs, it gets faster. Code simply saved as a script won't retain the execution history and optimization. However, if we save your code as a ***stored procedure*** instead of a script, the preserved execution history and optimization are quite beneficial. This chapter explores the value of saving our code as a stored procedure.

READER NOTE: *Please run the SQLQueries2012Vol1Chapter8.0Setup.sql script in order to follow along with the examples in the first section of Chapter 8. All scripts mentioned in this chapter may be found at www.Joes2Pros.com.*

Creating Stored Procedures

Creating our first stored procedure is done by simply creating a query and then giving it a name. Oftentimes this will be a query we intend to reuse. Using the following query, we can find all JProCo employees who work in Washington as seen in Figure 8.1.

```
SELECT e.FirstName, e.LastName, l.City, l.[State]
FROM Employee AS e
INNER JOIN Location AS l
ON e.LocationID = l.LocationID
WHERE l.[State] = 'WA'
```

	FirstName	LastName	City	State
1	Alex	Adams	Seattle	WA
2	Barry	Brown	Seattle	WA
3	David	Kennson	Seattle	WA
4	Eric	Bender	Seattle	WA
5	Lisa	Kendall	Spokane	WA
6	David	Lonning	Seattle	WA

8 rows

Figure 8.1 Employee table inner joined with the Location table returns Washington employees.

This query will yield all the Washington employee records. Knowing what it does helps us to come up with an intuitive name. Let's create a stored procedure called GetWashingtonEmployees that is built around this query.

Place a CREATE PROCEDURE statement before the name we wish to give it and follow with the keyword AS right before the query begins. By using the code shown below, we can run it to create the new procedure.

```
CREATE PROCEDURE GetWashingtonEmployees AS
SELECT e.FirstName, e.LastName, l.City, l.[State]
FROM Employee AS e
INNER JOIN Location AS l
ON e.LocationID = l.LocationID
WHERE l.[State] = 'WA'
GO
```

Messages
Command(s) completed successfully.

0 rows

Figure 8.2 The GetWashingtonEmployees stored procedure is created, but not yet executed.

Executing Stored Procedures

The stored procedure has now been successfully created. It is ready for use and reuse right away. Use the EXECUTE or the shorter EXEC statement followed by the stored procedure's name to run the procedure (Figure 8.3).

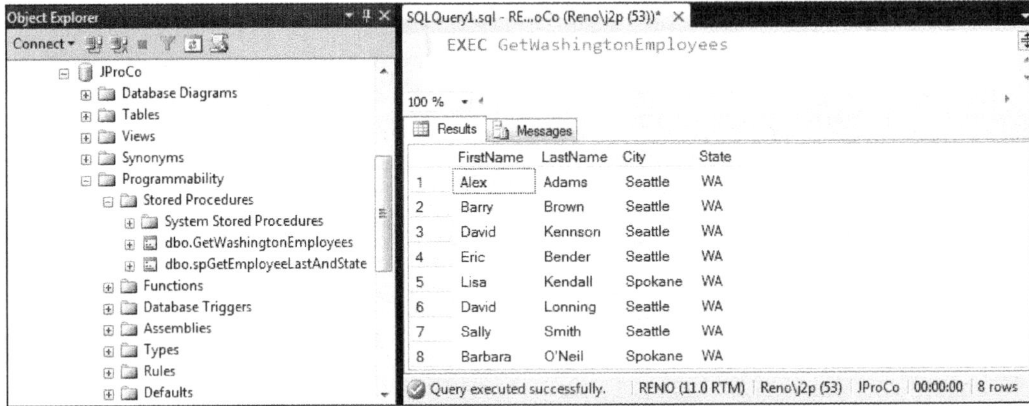

Figure 8.3 The GetWashingtonEmployees stored procedure is executed with the EXEC command.

Let's make a slight change and only get employees *not* working in Washington. We have the option of shortening CREATE PROCEDURE with CREATE PROC in our statement. Create GetNonWashingtonEmployees with the following code:

```
CREATE PROC GetNonWashingtonEmployees AS
SELECT e.FirstName, e.LastName, l.City, l.[State]
FROM Employee AS e
INNER JOIN Location AS l
ON e.LocationID = l.LocationID
WHERE l.[State] != 'WA'
GO
```

The GetNonWashingtonEmployees stored procedure is executed with the EXEC command, as seen in Figure 8.4.

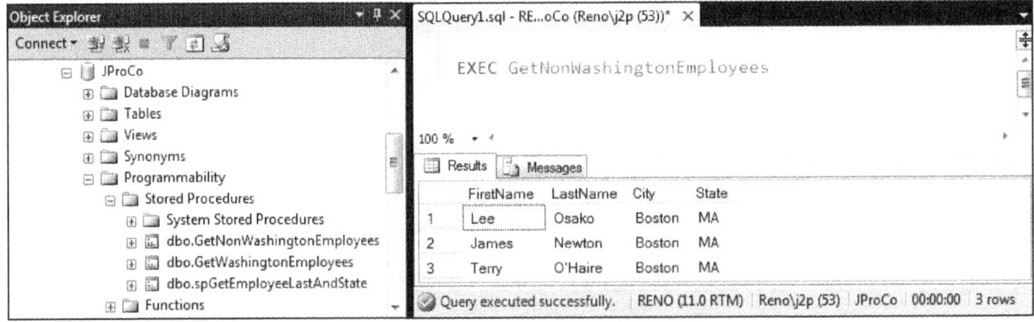

Figure 8.4 Results from Executing the GetNonWashingtonEmployees.

Lab 8.1: Stored Procedures

Lab Prep: Each lab has one or more Skill Checks. Start with Skill Check 1 and proceed until reaching the Points to Ponder section.

Before beginning this lab, verify that SQL Server 2012 is properly installed and operating. Before running the lab setup script for resetting the database (SQLQueries2012Vol1Chapter8.1Setup.sql), please make sure to close all query windows within SSMS. An open query window pointing to a database context can lock that database preventing it from updating when the script is executing. A simple way to assure all query windows are closed, is to exit out of SSMS, then open a new instance of SSMS, and lastly run the setup script.

Skill Check 1: Create a stored procedure in JProCo called GetOvernightProducts that shows all the Overnight-Stay records from the CurrentProducts table. When done, the results should resemble Figure 8.5.

```
EXEC GetOvernightProducts
```

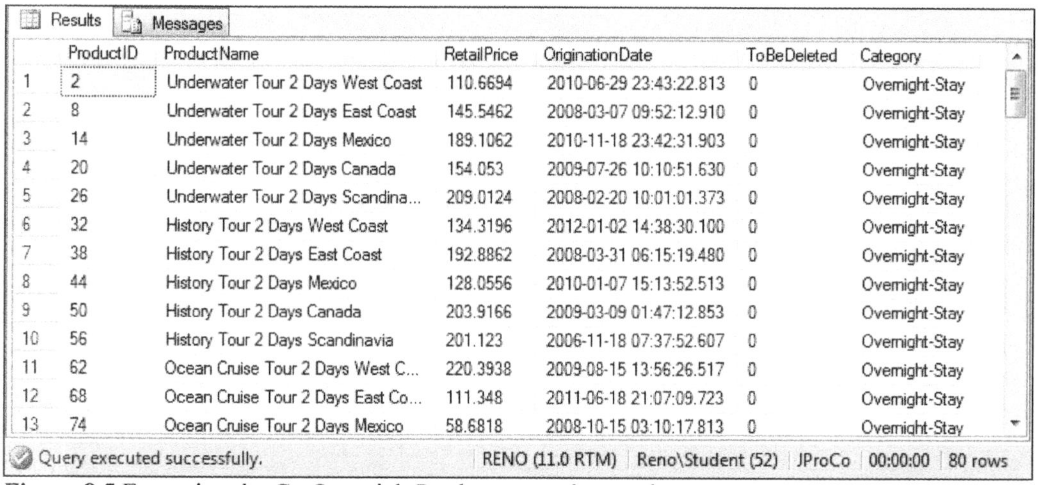

	ProductID	ProductName	RetailPrice	OriginationDate	ToBeDeleted	Category
1	2	Underwater Tour 2 Days West Coast	110.6694	2010-06-29 23:43:22.813	0	Overnight-Stay
2	8	Underwater Tour 2 Days East Coast	145.5462	2008-03-07 09:52:12.910	0	Overnight-Stay
3	14	Underwater Tour 2 Days Mexico	189.1062	2010-11-18 23:42:31.903	0	Overnight-Stay
4	20	Underwater Tour 2 Days Canada	154.053	2009-07-26 10:10:51.630	0	Overnight-Stay
5	26	Underwater Tour 2 Days Scandina...	209.0124	2008-02-20 10:01:01.373	0	Overnight-Stay
6	32	History Tour 2 Days West Coast	134.3196	2012-01-02 14:38:30.100	0	Overnight-Stay
7	38	History Tour 2 Days East Coast	192.8862	2008-03-31 06:15:19.480	0	Overnight-Stay
8	44	History Tour 2 Days Mexico	128.0556	2010-01-07 15:13:52.513	0	Overnight-Stay
9	50	History Tour 2 Days Canada	203.9166	2009-03-09 01:47:12.853	0	Overnight-Stay
10	56	History Tour 2 Days Scandinavia	201.123	2006-11-18 07:37:52.607	0	Overnight-Stay
11	62	Ocean Cruise Tour 2 Days West C...	220.3938	2009-08-15 13:56:26.517	0	Overnight-Stay
12	68	Ocean Cruise Tour 2 Days East Co...	111.348	2011-06-18 21:07:09.723	0	Overnight-Stay
13	74	Ocean Cruise Tour 2 Days Mexico	58.6818	2008-10-15 03:10:17.813	0	Overnight-Stay

Query executed successfully. | RENO (11.0 RTM) | Reno\Student (52) | JProCo | 00:00:00 | 80 rows

Figure 8.5 Executing the GetOvernightProducts stored procedure.

Skill Check 2: Create two more stored procedures called GetMediumProducts and GetLongTermProducts.The GetMediumProducts stored procedure should get all products categorized as Medium-Stay from the CurrentProducts table. The GetLongTermProducts should get all products categorized as LongTerm-Stay from the CurrentProducts table.

Answer Code: The T-SQL code to this lab can be found from the downloadable files named Lab8.1_StoredProcedures.sql.

Points to Ponder - Stored Procedures

1. A script is a file that consists of a series of SQL code with the .sql extension.
2. Stored procedures are also saved SQL statements, but they are saved to SQL Server rather than to their own file.
3. A stored procedure makes it possible to save SQL code to the database and give it an easy to reference name.
4. A CREATE PROCEDURE statement can be shortened to CREATE PROC.
5. To call a stored procedure, use the EXEC *ProcedureName* statement.

Introducing Variables

Many computer concepts are borrowed from the everyday non-computer world. Perhaps the biggest one we have not yet put a name to is *variables*. Think back to grade school when the teacher handed out a test. In the upper-right corner of the paper was an empty box for a student's name. The teacher did not pre-fill or order the tests with any of the student names on it. The empty box held the space for a *variable*, and every student would complete that *variable* by filling the box with his or her own name.

A job application is just a big sheet full of declared empty variables for each individual applicant to set. The employer has declared the variables it wants to see in order to consider each person for hire. When we fill out the application, we are actually setting values to the variables.

This relates in computer terms as well. This section shows us how to pick a variable, set the value, and have the query show records related to what we picked. We have done something similar to this in the first three chapters. At first, people see the use of variables as taking extra steps in writing their queries, but it is worth the work because we can make the same query work for different people without re-coding every query.

Before we use a variable with queries, we need to see how they work on their own. If we wanted to capture someone's first and last names, we will be setting two values. We would likely name these variables after what we want to capture. When deciding what type of information we are going to store, it's time to declare the data type and the name of the variable. All variables in SQL Server begin with the '@' sign.

We begin by declaring the @FirstName and @LastName variable to hold variable length characters. We will use the name John Smith for the above variables. By setting the @FirstName to John and the @LastName to Smith these variables now hold these specific values. Once set, these values can be used in queries or other SQL statements. The results are shown in Figure 8.6.

```
DECLARE @FirstName VARCHAR
DECLARE @LastName VARCHAR

SET @FirstName = 'John'
SET @LastName = 'Smith'

SELECT @FirstName, @LastName
```

	(No column name)	(No column name)
1	J	S

1 rows

Figure 8.6 Variables declared and set. A VARCHAR with a size not specified holds only the first character.

This works pretty well except for the size of the variable length characters (VARCHAR). Notice that the result set only returns the first character of the first and last names. Why did this happen? Well, SQL Server has a rule that when the length is not specified in a variable declaration statement the default character length will be 1. Thus, we only get the first letter of the character string returned by these two undefined length variables.

We can fix this by specifying that the @FirstName will hold up to 20 characters and the @LastName will hold up to 30 characters with this code. We can see the effect this has had right away in Figure 8.7.

```
DECLARE @FirstName VARCHAR(20)
DECLARE @LastName VARCHAR(30)

SET @FirstName = 'John'
SET @LastName = 'Smith'

SELECT @FirstName, @LastName
```

	(No column name)	(No column name)
1	John	Smith

1 rows

Figure 8.7 The declare statements of VARCHAR(20) and VARCHAR(30) now hold John and Smith.

Variables most frequently come in the form of numbers. Let's say we are planning for a vacation and the travel company asks for our maximum price limit. Perhaps we are willing to pay no more than $1,000 for the trip. In effect, the travel company asked for a @MaxPrice variable and we set it at $1,000 with our response. Use the code here for this example and view the results in Figure 8.8.

```
DECLARE @MaxPrice INT
SET @MaxPrice = 1000
SELECT @MaxPrice
```

	(No column name)
1	1000

1 rows

Figure 8.8 We are declaring and setting the @MaxPrice variable to 1000.

Later they would use this number to help identify good trips we might be interested in around this price. The next customer might come in and set $500 as their maximum price. The same variable with a different set of values can change how a company responds. In SQL Server, we use variables the same way we use them in everyday life.

Using Variables with Queries

We know how to write queries and we know how to use variables. Knowing how to use them both together will make for robust code, which is an essential skill in the workplace. Why? We can get millions of different requests from customers that are all a bit different. If we would rather write one query with variables versus a million rigid ones (i.e., hard-coded), then variables are the answer.

If a customer came in to see all our high-end products, we would want to oblige. What is defined as high-end to this customer is a useful piece of information. They ask to see all products costing more than $1,000 dollars. To pull up this list, we run a query for the RetailPrice to be greater than 1,000.

The next person might want to see all products over $800. Before learning how to use variables, we would have to re-write the WHERE clause of the query to adapt to this new amount. The code would look something like this:

```
SELECT * FROM CurrentProducts
WHERE RetailPrice > 800
```

The goal is to change our criterion without touching any code after the SELECT keyword. The solution is to use a variable in the query and set the variable ***before*** the SELECT keyword.

The next customer wants to see everything above the $800 minimum. Without changing the actual query itself, we can use a variable to change it to run correctly for the next customer. Let's try the following code:

```
DECLARE @MinPrice INT

SET @MinPrice = 800

SELECT * FROM CurrentProducts
WHERE RetailPrice > @MinPrice
```

We still had to make a change, so this may seem like only a slight improvement. What if we are not the one making the change? If the value is passed through an automated web process, this query would work for any e-commerce customer who wanted to see minimum price amounts.

We can use as many variables in our query as we like. For example, consider the following query:

```
SELECT * FROM CurrentProducts
WHERE RetailPrice BETWEEN 900 AND 1000
```

This uses two numbers and could easily be converted to use two variables instead. We can say 900 is the minimum price and 1,000 is the maximum price. We can then DECLARE the @MinPrice and the @MaxPrice before the query and then use the variable in place of the hard-coded amounts for the criterion (Figure 8.9).

```
DECLARE @MinPrice INT
DECLARE @MaxPrice INT

SET @MinPrice = 900
SET @MaxPrice = 1000

SELECT * FROM CurrentProducts
WHERE RetailPrice BETWEEN @MinPrice AND @MaxPrice
```

Results | Messages

	ProductID	ProductName	RetailPrice	OriginationDate	ToBeDeleted	Category
1	18	Underwater Tour 2 Weeks Mexico	945.531	2004-12-20 14:17:02.213	0	LongTerm-Stay
2	42	History Tour 2 Weeks East Coast	964.431	2010-05-17 23:20:28.873	0	LongTerm-Stay
3	90	Ocean Cruise Tour 2 Weeks Scandinavia	964.575	2008-03-29 19:25:18.263	0	LongTerm-Stay
4	120	Fruit Tasting Tour 2 Weeks Scandinavia	984.438	2009-11-07 15:00:38.513	0	LongTerm-Stay
5	228	Tiger Watching Tour 2 Weeks Mexico	946.089	2005-08-20 01:59:51.337	0	LongTerm-Stay
6	288	Acting Lessons Tour 2 Weeks Mexico	909.612	2007-04-27 18:19:07.007	0	LongTerm-Stay
7	312	Cherry Festival Tour 2 Weeks East Coast	976.968	2008-12-09 21:45:41.527	0	LongTerm-Stay
8	414	River Rapids Tour 2 Weeks Canada	978.858	2004-08-06 18:21:42.790	0	LongTerm-Stay

Query executed successfully. | RENO (11.0 RTM) | Reno\j2p (53) | JProCo | 00:00:00 | 8 rows

Figure 8.9 Two variables are used to set the minimum and maximum price range.

Variables allow the user to customize the same query for different processes that call on it for information. It does this because the criteria can change without having to make any code changes to the query. It may appear a little messy at the beginning of the query, but when used with a stored procedure as a parameter(s) we can clean this up significantly.

Variables in SQL Server

In all the versions previous to SQL Server 2008 it was essential to DECLARE the variable on one line and SET the value on another. A good example of this is the code sample shown here:

```
DECLARE @MinPrice INT

SET @MinPrice = 800

SELECT * FROM CurrentProducts
WHERE RetailPrice > @MinPrice
```

New to SQL Sever 2008 as well as all versions after, is the ability to DECLARE the variable and SET the value on the same line, as seen in this code sample:

```
DECLARE @MinPrice INT = 800

SELECT * FROM CurrentProducts
WHERE RetailPrice > @MinPrice
```

Variable Scope

We have all heard the story about someone locking themselves out of their own car or house and can even see their keys through a window. They are basically stuck as these keys are sadly of no use, since they are out of your reach. That is what happens when someone locks the door first and then decides to grab keys. We know from experience to grab the keys first and then lock the door. How can it be that the keys are within sight, but they are out of reach, or scope of use?

So what happens if we SET a variable before the DECLARE statement? A common question I help readers with who are learning about variables, is why the DECLARE statement for a variable seems to not work correctly all the time. More often than not, either the DECLARE statement was not written correctly, or it was not within the scope of the SET statement.

Look at Figure 8.10 for an example of this. The figure on the right is an obvious failure since we are trying to use a variable that has never been declared. The figure on the left does have a DECLARE statement, but still fails with the same error. The reason for this is the highlighted part of the query is being run without the DECLARE statement setting the @MinPrice variable.

This means the @MinPrice used as the criterion in the WHERE clause is out of scope during execution from the DECLARE statement, since SQL Server is unable to set aside memory and a value for this variable. In other words, both queries are not using the DECLARE statement, making @MinPrice out of scope.

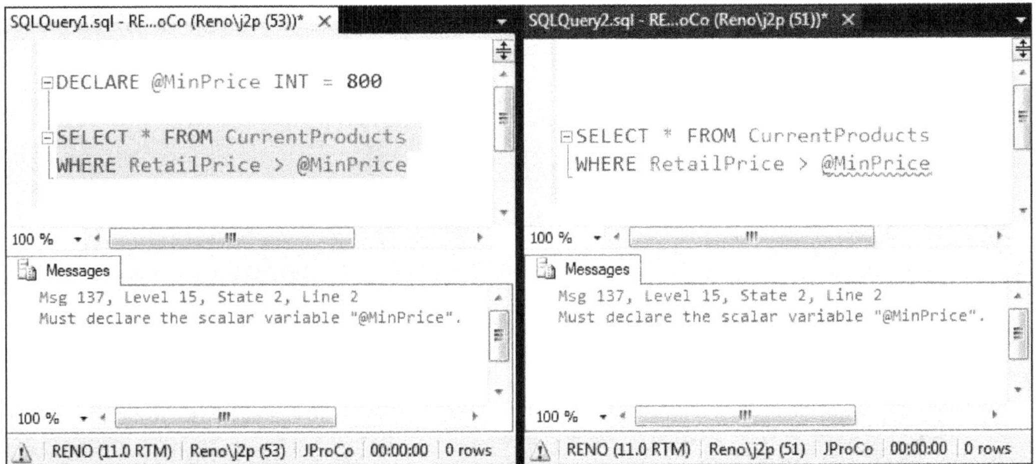

Figure 8.10 The DECLARE statement is not being used, when either of these queries is run, which makes the @MinPrice variable out of scope as the criteria in the WHERE clause.

Lab 8.2: Using Variables

Lab Prep: Each lab has one or more Skill Checks. Start with Skill Check 1 and proceed until reaching the Points to Ponder section.

Before beginning this lab, verify that SQL Server 2012 is properly installed and operating. Before running the lab setup script for resetting the database (SQLQueries2012Vol1Chapter8.2Setup.sql), please make sure to close all query windows within SSMS. An open query window pointing to a database context can lock that database preventing it from updating when the script is executing. A simple way to assure all query windows are closed, is to exit out of SSMS, then open a new instance of SSMS, and lastly run the setup script.

Skill Check 1: Go to the JProCo database and declare two integers called @MinGrant and @MaxGrant. Set these integers to 20,000 and 40,000, respectively. Use both variables in the criteria to find all grants in the range of 20,000 to 40,000. When done, the results should resemble Figure 8.11.

```
--Insert skill check 1
--variable declaration code here
SELECT * FROM [Grant]
WHERE Amount BETWEEN @MinGrant AND @MaxGrant
```

	GrantID	GrantName	EmpID	Amount
1	004	Norman's Outreach	NULL	21000.00
2	005	BIG 6's Foundation%	4	21000.00
3	006	TALTA_Kishan International	3	20000.00
4	007	Ben@MoreTechnology.com	10	20000.00
5	008	@Last-U-Can-Help	7	25000.00
6	009	Thank you @.com	11	21500.00

6 rows

Figure 8.11 Skill Check 1 shows the results of using two integer variables to filter the result set.

Answer Code: The T-SQL code to this lab can be found from the downloadable files named Lab8.2_UsingVariables.sql.

Points to Ponder - Using Variables

1. Variables are named placeholders for values.
2. Local variables begin with a single '@' sign.
3. Values and results of a query can be changed without changing any code inside the query itself by passing in variable(s) and performing filtering or calculations against those variable(s).
4. A data type must be specified when declaring a variable.
5. A variable must be declared before setting the value.
6. Variables can change, like the integer *@CurrentTemperature* would change throughout the day.
7. Declaring a variable allocates computer memory space that will be used when the value is set.
8. Think of DECLARE as reserving a seat ahead of time in a nice restaurant. Think of SET as actually taking a seat at the table.
9. The identifier for the variable in the code below is called @MinGrant:

   ```
   DECLARE @MinGrant INT
   ```

10. Reserved words like OUTER can never be used as object identifiers, although keywords like GRANT can be used as object identifiers if they are enclosed in square brackets. However, variables starting with '@' can use any reserved word or keyword in combination with the '@' sign.

Parameterized Stored Procedures

When executing a stored procedure (sproc or 'sp_') the code we specify in its definition is run. For example, look at the code below which will create the sproc GetEmployeesFromSeattle:

```
CREATE PROC GetEmployeesFromSeattle AS
SELECT e.FirstName, e.LastName, l.City, l.[State]
FROM Employee AS e
INNER JOIN Location AS l
ON e.LocationID = l.LocationID
WHERE l.City = 'Seattle'
GO
```

We will run – or *invoke* – a stored procedure like this by using EXEC followed by the sproc name (Figure 8.12).

```
EXEC GetEmployeesFromSeattle
```

	FirstName	LastName	City	State
1	Alex	Adams	Seattle	WA
2	Barry	Brown	Seattle	WA
3	David	Kennson	Seattle	WA
4	Eric	Bender	Seattle	WA
5	David	Lonning	Seattle	WA
6	Sally	Smith	Seattle	WA

6 rows

Figure 8.12 Executing the stored procedure runs the defined code and it returns a result set.

If we wanted to create a stored procedure for each city in the Location table, we are free to do so. Alternatively, we can get one stored procedure to work for each city by using variables. When we define variables in stored procedures they are called *parameters*.

Let's pick a descriptive name for a new stored procedure. Its name should imply that we will get the results by city and for each employee in that city. The stored procedure should be ready to accept a variable length of characters up to the longest city name we could expect. To create the GetEmployeesByCity stored procedure, which will accept up to 50 characters, use the following code:

```
CREATE PROC GetEmployeesByCity @City VARCHAR(50) AS
SELECT e.FirstName, e.LastName, l.City, l.[State]
FROM Employee AS e
INNER JOIN Location AS l
ON e.LocationID = l.LocationID
WHERE l.City = @City
GO
```

To call this stored procedure, SQL Server expects a VARCHAR value to be passed into it as a *parameter*. Simply put the word 'Boston' in single quotes after the stored procedure name (Figure 8.13).

```
EXEC GetEmployeesByCity 'Boston'
```

	FirstName	LastName	City	State
1	Lee	Osako	Boston	MA
2	James	Newton	Boston	MA
3	Terry	O'Haire	Boston	MA

3 rows

Figure 8.13 Boston is passed into GetEmployeesByCity sproc to get the Boston employees.

This same stored procedure can be used for all cities. By changing the parameter to 'Spokane' we get the two resulting employees from Spokane.

```
EXEC GetEmployeesByCity 'Spokane'
```

	FirstName	LastName	City	State
1	Lisa	Kendall	Spokane	WA
2	Barbara	O'Neil	Spokane	WA

2 rows

Figure 8.14 Spokane is passed into GetEmployeesByCity sproc to get the Spokane employees.

If we choose a city that does not exist in the database, such as Tampa, then we get no employees (Figure 8.15). This is not an error since we passed in a valid VARCHAR value. The query critera found there were no records in the result set.

```
EXEC GetEmployeesByCity 'Tampa'
```

FirstName	LastName	City	State

0 rows

Figure 8.15 Passing a valid parameter with no matching records gives back an empty record set.

If a stored procedure requires a parameter, we must supply it with one. By calling this sproc without a parameter, SQL Server will issue us an error message stating that it expects to have a paramater supplied to the sproc (Figure 8.16).

```
EXEC GetEmployeesByCity
```

```
Messages
Msg 201, Level 16, State 4, Procedure GetEmployeesByCity, Line 0
Procedure or function 'GetEmployeesByCity' expects parameter '@City',
which was not supplied.
                                                                0 rows
```

Figure 8.16 The GetEmployeesByCity will not run, without supplying the parameter.

Default Parameter Values

Imagine that we have created the GetEmployeesByCity stored procedure weeks ago and we now need to make a change. To view the code that created the stored procedure, use the ***sp_helptext*** with the procedure name (Figure 8.17).

```
EXEC sp_helptext GetEmployeesByCity
```

	Text
1	CREATE PROC GetEmployeesByCity @City VARCHAR(50)
2	AS
3	SELECT E.FirstName, E.LastName,
4	L.City, L.[State]
5	FROM Employee AS E
6	INNER JOIN Location AS L
7	ON E.LocationID = L.LocationID
8	WHERE L.City = @City

8 rows

Figure 8.17 The sp_helptext shows the code that created the object.

By copying and pasting these lines into a new query window, we can see the original code that created the stored procedure. If we try to create the stored procedure using this exact code, SQL Server will issue an error that this object already exists in the database. To re-create it we must first DROP the sproc before using a CREATE PROCEDURE statement, as shown in the following code:

```
DROP PROC GetEmployeesByCity
GO

CREATE PROC GetEmployeesByCity @City VARCHAR(50) AS
SELECT E.FirstName, E.LastName, L.City, L.[State]
FROM Employee AS E
INNER JOIN Location AS L
ON E.LocationID = L.LocationID
WHERE City = @City
GO
```

We want to make a single change that will allow the process that is calling on this sproc to be able to get a result, even if it does not specify a City value for the parameter (avoiding any error messages being sent back to the application). We will set the default value to look for Seattle. It is easy to set the Seattle value with the following code:

```
DROP PROC GetEmployeesByCity
GO

CREATE PROC GetEmployeesByCity @City VARCHAR(50)='Seattle'
AS
SELECT E.FirstName, E.LastName, L.City, L.[State]
FROM Employee AS E
INNER JOIN Location AS L
ON E.LocationID = L.LocationID
WHERE City = @City
GO
```

This tells the stored procedure to use Seattle unless the caller of the stored procedure uses another value. Test this stored procedure by omitting the parameter (Figure 8.18).

```
EXEC GetEmployeesByCity
```

	FirstName	LastName	City	State
1	Alex	Adams	Seattle	WA
2	Barry	Brown	Seattle	WA
3	David	Kennson	Seattle	WA
4	Eric	Bender	Seattle	WA
5	David	Lonning	Seattle	WA
6	Sally	Smith	Seattle	WA

6 rows

Figure 8.18 The GetEmployeesByCity sproc uses the default parameter if one isn't supplied.

Notice it still uses a city parameter of Seattle that was self-supplied. If a stored procedure is most often run with the same parameter, we can save the calling code some work. Seattle can now be called on by either of the code choices below:

```
EXEC GetEmployeesByCity

EXEC GetEmployeesByCity 'Seattle'
```

Lab 8.3: Stored Procedure Parameters

Lab Prep: Each lab has one or more Skill Checks. Start with Skill Check 1 and proceed until reaching the Points to Ponder section.

Before beginning this lab, verify that SQL Server 2012 is properly installed and operating. Before running the lab setup script for resetting the database (SQLQueries2012Vol1Chapter8.3Setup.sql), please make sure to close all query windows within SSMS. An open query window pointing to a database context can lock that database preventing it from updating when the script is executing. A simple way to assure all query windows are closed, is to exit out of SSMS, then open a new instance of SSMS, and lastly run the setup script.

Skill Check 1: In the JProCo database context, create a stored procedure called GetProductListByCategory that expects a VARCHAR(50) parameter called @Category and returns the ProductID, ProductName and RetailPrice for records in the CurrentProducts table for the category specified by @Category.

Run and test the code and then call on this stored procedure by passing it 'No-Stay' as a parameter. When done, the result set should have 80 records and resemble those shown in Figure 8.19.

```
EXEC GetProductListByCategory 'No-Stay'
```

	ProductID	ProductName	RetailPrice
1	1	Underwater Tour 1 Day West Coast	61.483
2	7	Underwater Tour 1 Day East Coast	80.859
3	13	Underwater Tour 1 Day Mexico	105.059
4	19	Underwater Tour 1 Day Canada	85.585
5	25	Underwater Tour 1 Day Scandinavia	116.118
6	31	History Tour 1 Day West Coast	74.622
			80 rows

Figure 8.19 The GetProductListByCategory stored procedure will return these results.

Skill Check 2: In the JProCo database context, create a stored procedure called GetGrantsByEmployee that expects a VARCHAR(50) parameter called @LastName and returns the GrantName, Amount, EmpID, FirstName and LastName for all grants found by the @LastName employee.

The GrantName and Amount will come from the [Grant] table. The EmpID, FirstName and LastName fields will come from the Employee table.

Run and test the code and then call the stored procedure by passing in 'Lonning' as the parameter. When done, the results should resemble Figure 8.20.

```
EXEC GetGrantsByEmployee 'Lonning'
```

	GrantName	Amount	EmpID	FirstName	LastName
1	92 Purr_Scents %% team	4750.00	7	David	Lonning
2	Robert@BigStarBank.com	18100.00	7	David	Lonning
3	@Last-U-Can-Help	25000.00	7	David	Lonning
					3 rows

Figure 8.20 The GetProductListByCategory stored procedure will return these results.

Answer Code: The T-SQL code to this lab can be found from the downloadable files named Lab8.3_StoredProcedureParameters.sql.

Points to Ponder - Stored Procedure Parameters

1. Stored procedures can take parameters.
2. The code within a stored procedure treats the parameter as a variable.
3. The declaration of a parameter in a stored procedure is implicit. This means a DECLARE statement is not necessary.
4. Once a stored procedure is designed to use a parameter, it must use an explicit or default parameter during execution.
5. To set stored procedures to have default parameter values, use the '=' sign and the value after the parameter declaration.

Chapter Glossary

Data Type: A safety mechanism on a field that allows only the correct type of data to be entered. For example, an integer data type will not allow a name for a person to be entered into this field. Only numbers with no decimals are allowed.

DECLARE: Allocates the use of computer memory that will be used when the value is set.

Default Parameter: A value chosen if one is not explicitly specified.

EXECUTE or EXEC: Command used to execute a stored procedure.

Parameter: Data supplied to, or passed into, a stored procedure to set the value(s) of the variables defined in the sproc.

Stored Procedure: Defined, precompiled SQL code that is then stored in a SQL Server instance for use in a specific database.

Variables: Named placeholders for re-use in code.

Review Quiz - Chapter Eight

1.) A variable in SQL begins with which character?

O a. %

O b. *

O c. @

O d. #

2.) What is the proper way to declare an integer variable named Minimum?

O a. `DECLARE *Minimum INT`

O b. `DECLARE @Minimum INT`

O c. `DECLARE INT *Minimum`

O d. `DECLARE INT @Minimum`

3.) How is a script different from a stored procedure?

O a. Stored Procedures are saved code. Scripts have no code inside them.

O b. Scripts are saved code. Stored Procedures have no code inside them.

O c. Scripts are saved to a file, stored procedures as saved to the SQL data file.

O d. Stored Procedures are saved to a file, scripts as saved to the SQL data file.

4.) How do you execute a stored procedure?

O a. Double-click the stored procedure's name.

O b. Run the SQL statement EXEC *StoredProcedureName*.

O c. Use the SQL setup.exe file.

5.) What family of language statements do you use to create a stored procedure?

O a. DDL

O b. DML

O c. DCL

6.) You want to create a stored procedure called GetWagesByManager that takes a parameter called EmpID. What would be the first line of your statement?

O a. `CREATE PROC GetWagesByManager @EmpID INT`

O b. `CREATE PROC @EmpID INT AS GetWagesByManager`

O c. `CREATE PROC GetWagesByManager WHERE @EmpID = EmpID INT`

Answer Key

1.) Since variables in SQL begin with the '@' character (a), (b) and (d) are incorrect. The correct answer is (c), because all variable in SQL begin with the '@' character.

2.) The proper syntax is DECLARE @*VariableName*DataType so (a), (c), and (d) are all incorrect. The statement in (b) is using the correct syntax.

3.) Both stored procedures and scripts are saved SQL code, so (a) and (b) are incorrect. The difference between the two is that stored procedures are saved to the SQL data file while scripts are saved to a file system file, making (d) incorrect too. Scripts are saved to a file while stored procedures are saved to the SQL data file, so (c) is the correct answer.

4.) Double-clicking the stored procedure name will only expand that node, so (a) is incorrect. The SQL setup.exe file is used to install SQL Server components, so (c) is also wrong. Since running the SQL statement EXEC *StoredProcedureName* will execute a stored procedure, (b) is correct.

5.) The CREATE statement is a member of the Data Definition Language (DDL) of SQL, so both (b) and (c) are incorrect. Because the CREATE statement is used to define new objects, it belongs to the Data Definition Language, making (a) the correct answer.

6.) The correct syntax for creating a stored procedure is CREATE PROC *StoredProcedureName* @*VariableName*DataType, making (b) and (c) both wrong. Since the correct syntax for creating a stored procedure is CREATE PROC *StoredProcedureName* @*VariableName*DataType, (a) is correct.

Bug Catcher Game

To play the Bug Catcher game run the BugCatcher_Chapter8.pps from the BugCatcher folder of the companion files. You can obtain these files from the www.Joes2Pros.com website.

[NOTES]

Chapter 9. Transaction Control Language (TCL)

There are several rules that systems like SQL Server must measure up to before they can be called a Relational Database Management System (RDBMS). The Rule of Durability means the database needs to safely be on a permanent storage location, such as a hard disk. That way, a reboot (or system or power failure) does not cause the database to lose data. To take it one step further, anytime SQL Server says "Row(s) affected" after a DML statement executes, it confirms the data was accepted and stored. The process to go from a request to a completion is known as a transaction. You have some options to control transactions through the use of Transaction Control Language or TCL.

READER NOTE: *Please run the SQLQueries2012Vol1Chapter9.0Setup.sql script in order to follow along with the examples in the first section of Chapter 9. All scripts mentioned in this chapter may be found at www.Joes2Pros.com.*

The Transaction Process

First of all, only DML statements run transactions. DDL statements run in batches separated with the keyword GO. However, we don't need to separate transactions with GO.

The simplest way to describe the steps of a transaction is to use an example of updating an existing record into a table. When the insert runs, SQL Server gets the data from storage, such as a hard drive, and loads it into memory and the CPU. The data in memory is changed and then saved to the storage device. Finally, a message is sent confirming the rows that were affected.

This is an oversimplification of the real checks and steps that happen under the hood, but that is the basic principle. Until the change is permanently stored or saved, the transaction is considered incomplete. During the time a record has been changed in memory, but not yet committed to storage, it is in a condition known as a *dirty record.* While making changes to a record, no other process can access that record until the change is permanently committed to storage. For example, the following two statements will not be allowed to run at the same time:

```
UPDATE Location SET Street = '123 First Ave'
WHERE LocationID = 1

UPDATE Location SET Street = '199 First Blvd'
WHERE LocationID = 1
```

The first UPDATE statement locks the record, while the second UPDATE statement waits for the lock to finish and release the record. This usually takes a fraction of a second to complete. Each of the statements above is its own auto committed transaction. By default each DML statement is a transaction.

Explicit Transactions

Explicit transactions are something we experience every day. When we are at a gas station and go to pay the cashier before putting fuel into our car, we are completing an explicit transaction. This process involves two main steps, which must be completed for an explicit transaction to occur:

1) We pay for the fuel
2) We fill the gas tank with fuel.

An explicit transaction is one where all events of the transaction either happen together, or they don't take place at all. In the previous example, if we don't pay money upfront, we will not receive any fuel. If our credit card is approved, we get fuel and can continue to drive our car.

When we transfer money from savings to checking accounts, we are performing another explicit transaction. A transfer from savings to checking is actually two separate events. If we transfer $500 to checking, we expect to see a $500 withdrawal from savings and a $500 deposit to checking. Our bank would not call us the next day to say they successfully withdrew $500 from savings, but did not manage to credit our checking account.

Would we say one out of two is not bad? No, because either the money was transferred or not. The code below is vulnerable to failure during a transfer from savings to checking:

```
UPDATE SavAccount
SET Balance = Balance - 500
WHERE CustomerID = 18568

UPDATE CkAccount
SET Balance = Balance + 500
WHERE CustomerID = 18568
```

If SQL Server fails after the first update, but before the second one, we would have a loss of data. We need to specify that both statements above will either succeed or fail as a single unit. The problem is that each UPDATE statement is by default, an individual transaction.

The example of a checking account transfer is a very simplified version of a transaction. Naturally a bank would have more code in place than just what is seen here. For example, they might have a condition to check for a negative balance and purposefully abort the transaction if there are any negative numbers. This type of logic can be found in the *SQL Queries 2012 Volume 4* book. We can place many DML statements into one transaction if they need to run together. To make sure the two statements above run as a single explicit transaction, we can use the following code:

```
BEGIN TRAN

UPDATE SavAccount
SET Balance = Balance - 500
WHERE CustomerID = 18568
```

```
UPDATE CkAccount
SET Balance = Balance + 500
WHERE CustomerID = 18568

COMMIT TRAN
```

A failure taking place before the COMMIT TRAN statement can mean that the records never get committed to permanent storage. The TRAN keyword is short for transaction.

Lab 9.1: Explicit Transactions

Lab Prep: Each lab has one or more Skill Checks. Start with Skill Check 1 and proceed until reaching the Points to Ponder section.

Before beginning this lab, verify that SQL Server 2012 is properly installed and operating. Before running the lab setup script for resetting the database (SQLQueries2012Vol1Chapter9.1Setup.sql), please make sure to close all query windows within SSMS. An open query window pointing to a database context can lock that database preventing it from updating when the script is executing. A simple way to assure all query windows are closed, is to exit out of SSMS, then open a new instance of SSMS, and lastly run the setup script.

Skill Check 1: An agreement between charity conglomerate foundations Norman's Outreach and new donor Seasons Outreach means they never give to the same organization. Seasons Outreach has approached JProCo about a grant contribution of $85,000. They noticed we already have one from Norman's Outreach and thus can't donate.

Both foundations have agreed that if we delete the record for Norman's Outreach, we may enter the following values for a new grant:

GrantID	GrantName	EmployeeID	Amount
011	Seasons Outreach	NULL	85000

Create two DML statements. One is to remove the Norman's Outreach record and another is to create the Seasons Outreach record. Make sure the INSERT and DELETE statements succeed or fail as a unit by using an explicit transaction. When done, run the following query to produce the results shown in Figure 9.1.

```
SELECT * FROM [Grant]
```

	GrantID	GrantName	EmpID	Amount
1	001	92 Purr_Scents %% team	7	4750.00
2	002	K_Land fund trust	2	15750.00
3	003	Robert@BigStarBank.com	7	18100.00
4	011	Seasons Outreach	NULL	85000.00
5	005	BIG 6's Foundation%	4	21000.00
6	006	TALTA_Kishan International	3	20000.00
				10 rows

Figure 9.1 Seasons Outreach has replaced Norman's Outreach with an explicit transaction.

Answer Code: The T-SQL code to this lab can be found from the downloadable files named Lab9.1_ExplicitTransactions.sql.

Points to Ponder - Explicit Transactions

1. A transaction is a group of SQL statements treated as a single unit. Transactions ensure data integrity.
2. Transaction statements will either execute completely together, or they will not execute at all.
3. If one statement can't run then the transaction is not committed.
4. A failed statement in a transaction means all data in the intermediate state gets discarded and none of the records will be committed.
5. The BEGIN TRANSACTION statement marks the beginning of a group of SQL statements in a transaction.
6. The COMMIT TRANSACTION statement marks the end of the transaction and saves all the changes to SQL's permanent storage.

Using Commit and Rollback

By putting a series of DML statements between the BEGIN TRAN and COMMIT TRAN we ensure all statements succeed or fail as a single unit. Any failure means the final COMMIT statement is never reached because the transaction is aborted, thus the records are never saved to storage in a database.

Encountering an error is one way to cause a running transaction to discard all of its changes. When a transaction does this, it is called *rolling back the transaction.* Sometimes we want to intentionally rollback a transaction through code logic. The code below does a rollback partway through an explicit transaction:

```
CREATE PROC Add500ToChecking @CustID INT AS

BEGIN TRAN

UPDATE SavAccount SET Balance = Balance - 500
WHERE CustomerID = @CustID

IF( (
SELECT Balance FROM SavAccount
WHERE CustomerID = @CustID) < 0)
ROLLBACK TRAN
RETURN

UPDATE CkAccount SET Balance = Balance + 500
WHERE CustomerID = @CustID
COMMIT TRAN
RETURN
GO
```

In this example, we deducted $500 from savings. If the customer only had $400 in savings, then they would be overdrawn. The IF statement checks the @CustID parameter for a negative value, before crediting the checking account the full amount of $500. When the result of this IF statement is True, then the transaction is rolled back and neither of the updates is committed to the database. When the result of this IF statement is False, the transfer is made to the checking account with an UPDATE statement before committing the entire transaction.

In other words, the first UPDATE statement places the data into an intermediate state, **not** a permanent state. The second UPDATE statement is never called upon if a negative balance occurs (IF statement evaluates as 'True').

Transaction Locking

During the time a DML statement is changing data, no other process can access that data. This is because the data has a lock on it until it is completed. Typically this waiting process is usually a few milliseconds at the most.

We can slow down a simple transaction when updating the price of ProductID 1 to $75.95. Normally this would take about 10 milliseconds. Now it will take a full ***two minutes, 30 seconds*** with the following code sample:

```
BEGIN TRAN
UPDATE CurrentProducts
SET RetailPrice = 75.95
WHERE ProductID = 1

WAITFOR DELAY '00:02:30'
COMMIT TRAN
```

The two statements above will take a combined two minutes, thirty seconds to complete. No other process will be able to use ProductID 1 during this time. Let's try running the previous code that has the time delay, while we open a new Query Window and run another query against the CurrentProducts table looking for the same records equal to ProductID 1. The code for the second query is shown here:

```
SELECT * FROM CurrentProducts
WHERE ProductID = 1
```

Notice this very simple query appears to be running (right side of Figure 9.2). In reality, it is waiting for the lock on ProductID 1 to be released. It does not know if the RetailPrice value is the current 61.483 or the updated value of 75.95. The query doesn't know which value to return until the UPDATE commits or fails.

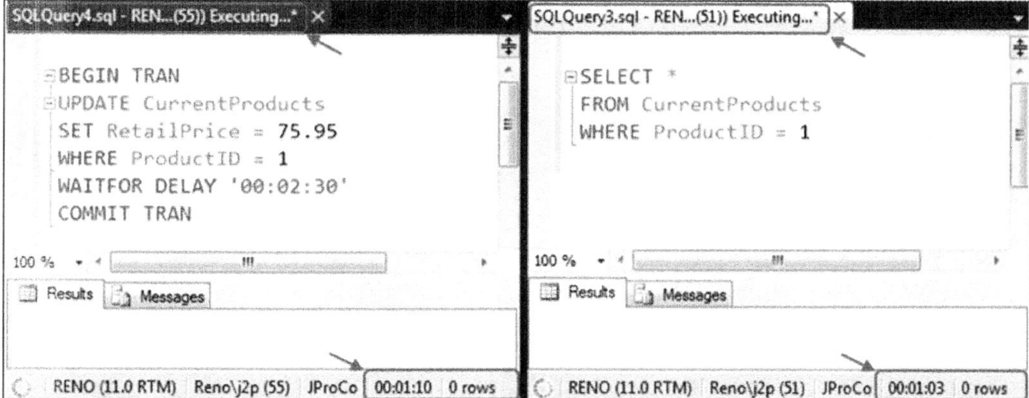

Figure 9.2 The query on the right is waiting for the UPDATE statement (left) to release the lock.

Table Hints (Locking Method)

For every data change to a table there is a brief moment where the change is in the intermediate state, but is not yet permanently committed. During this time, any other DML statement needing that data waits until the lock is released. This is a safety feature so that SQL Server evaluates only official data.

Some transactions take time and then rollback. In other words, the changes never become official data and in essence never took place. The example below shows a transaction that takes 15 seconds and then rolls back:

```
BEGIN TRAN

UPDATE dbo.Employee SET HireDate = '1/1/1992'
WHERE EmpID = 1

WAITFOR DELAY '00:00:15'

ROLLBACK TRAN
```

If EmpID 1 was really hired in 1989 and we run the previous code, there is incorrect data in the intermediate state for fifteen seconds before it is rolled back to its original value. During those fifteen seconds, if a 401K vesting program ran an evaluation on all employees hired before 1990, the process would wrongfully overlook EmpID 1. The safety catch makes the 401K process wait until this transaction is completed in order to get the official data.

A great deal of data can be changed in the intermediate state, but never gets to the state of being permanently committed. ***Locking*** prevents other processes from making decisions on *dirty data.* The result is that transactions are isolated because they only use permanently committed data. The drawback is that some processes that could benefit from running instantly now have to wait. Locking lowers the level of ***concurrency***, which is the ability to allow software to run many processes at the same time.

A SELECT query can now pull out any record being changed in the intermediate state. It could be said that a query will not show any dirty records because all transactions are isolated from each other. By simply making a change to one record in our CurrentProducts table, any query looking for records from that table will have to wait (right side of Figure 9.3) until the change is complete.

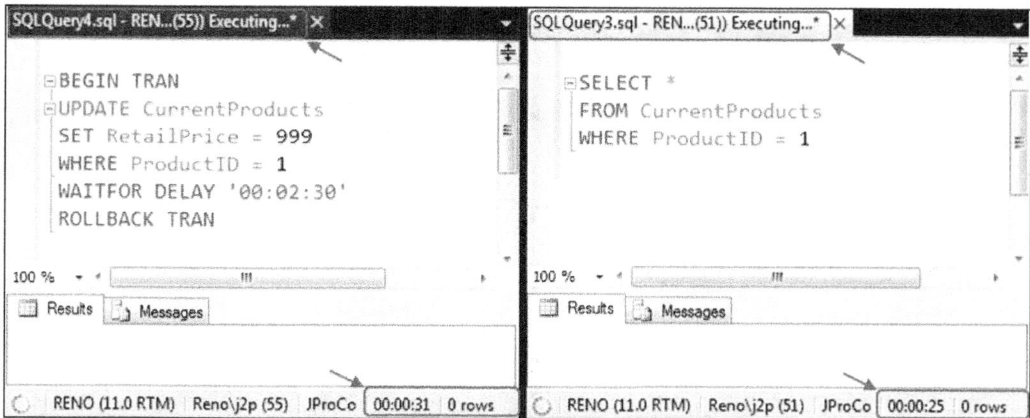

Figure 9.3 The UPDATE statement was executed first and puts data into an intermediate state. The query on the right waits for the transaction to be committed.

In Figure 9.3 we see the UPDATE statement has been running for 31 seconds and the query in the second window was started six seconds later. The committed value for RetailPrice is $75.95 and the price in the intermediate state is $999 for the next 00:01:59 until this transaction is rolled back. When the UPDATE transaction on the left of Figure 9.3 is finished, the RetailPrice is never changed. The query on the right waits until the data becomes official. The downside to the safety catch is that this SELECT query takes much longer to run.

If we don't want the query on the right of Figure 9.3 to wait, we have some options available to us when we write the SELECT query. Suppose that we are fine with the query on the right accessing dirty data, we can issue a table hint for the query. The following code tells the query to run without waiting:

```
SELECT *
FROM CurrentProducts (READUNCOMMITTED)
```

In this code example, the query would run without waiting. The result is the query would show the RetailPrice value of $999.00 as soon as it runs (Figure 9.4).

The query shows ProductID 1 to have a value in the RetailPrice field of 999.00 in the result set. However, the 999.00 value was never a committed value in the database. Any reports requiring accurate information that are based on the data retrieved by this query could give us a false report.

If we run this same query three minutes later, we will get a different result. This is because the UPDATE transaction has been rolled back, wiping out the 999.00 value held in the intermediate state and returning the 75.95 value held in the permanent state stored by SQL Server.

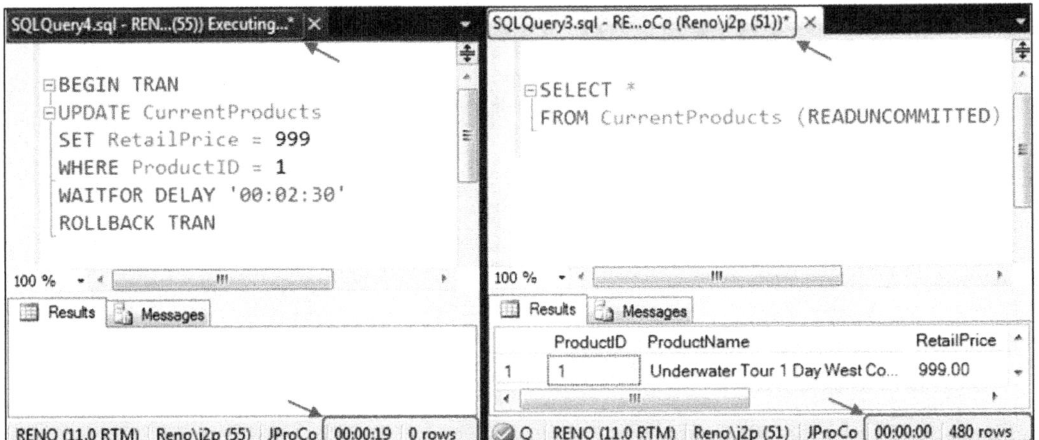

Figure 9.4 The UPDATE statement was executed first and puts data into an intermediate state. The query on the right returns the intermediate data with the READUNCOMMITED hint.

The READUNCOMMITTED table hint allows the query to show uncommitted *dirty data*. The advantage of this table hint is that the query will run much faster. Queries used for evaluation, such as tracking general trends, commonly use this type of table hint.

The following statements are equivalent and show more than one way of accomplishing the same result. In this case, SQL Server allows the query to run without waiting. This type of query is simply looking to see how many records are in a table, the data itself doesn't need to be exact.

```
SELECT COUNT(*)
FROM CurrentProducts (READUNCOMMITTED)

SELECT COUNT(*)
FROM CurrentProducts (NOLOCK)
```

Lab 9.2: Table Hints

Lab Prep: Each lab has one or more Skill Checks. Start with Skill Check 1 and proceed until reaching the Points to Ponder section.

Before beginning this lab, verify that SQL Server 2012 is properly installed and operating. Before running the lab setup script for resetting the database (SQLQueries2012Vol1Chapter9.2Setup.sql), please make sure to close all query windows within SSMS. An open query window pointing to a database context can lock that database preventing it from updating when the script is executing. A simple way to assure all query windows are closed, is to exit out of SSMS, then open a new instance of SSMS, and lastly run the setup script.

Skill Check 1: Write a transaction that updates all grant amount values to one dollar. Include a delay of three minutes as the second step of the transaction. End the transaction with a ROLLBACK TRAN.

Open a new Query Window and query the Grant table for all records in the intermediate state. When done, the results should resemble Figure 9.5.

```
SELECT * -- code to complete Skill Check
```

	GrantID	GrantName	EmpID	Amount
1	001	92 Purr_Scents %% team	7	1.00
2	002	K_Land fund trust	2	1.00
3	003	Robert@BigStarBank.com	7	1.00
4	011	Seasons Outreach	NULL	1.00
5	005	BIG 6's Foundation%	4	1.00
6	006	TALTA_Kishan International	3	1.00
7	007	Ben@MoreTechnology.com	10	1.00
8	008	@Last-U-Can-Help	7	1.00
9	009	Thank you @.com	11	1.00
10	010	Call Mom @Com	5	1.00

10 rows

Figure 9.5 A query for all grants runs instantly and gets dirty records with an Amount of 1.00.

Reader Note: *Wait three minutes and rerun this same query, since the original amount never changed it should be displayed in the result set.*

Answer Code: The T-SQL code to this lab can be found from the downloadable files named Lab9.2_TableHints.sql.

Points to Ponder - Table Hints

1. Locking is used to protect changes in a database and only allows committed (official) data to be viewed in a result set.
2. Use the READUNCOMMITTED table hint in a query to view a result set that might contain data that has not been committed (official).
3. The NOLOCK and READUNCOMMITTED table hints operate identically. Since NOLOCK is easier to type, it is used more often.
4. The advantage to the NOLOCK or READUNCOMMITTED table hints is the query will run without waiting for another process to release its locks.

Chapter Glossary

Committed: A record that is changed in the database, temporarily loaded into memory and then permanently saved back into the database.

Dirty Record: A record that is changed in the database, temporarily loaded into memory in an intermediate state, and may not ever become a permanent record.

Explicit Transaction: One or more SQL statements grouped in a transaction that must all occur at once to succeed, or none of them takes place at all.

Intermediate State: The state a record is in after it has been loaded into memory and before it is committed to permanent storage in the database.

Locking: Exclusive use of data within a table, that ensures any changes to the data occur without conflicts or loss.

NOLOCK: A table hint that allows a query to view data in the intermediate state. NOLOCK means the same as READUNCOMMITTED.

Transaction: A group of actions treated as a single unit to ensure data integrity.

READUNCOMMITTED: A table hint that allows a query to view data in the intermediate state. READUNCOMMITTED means the same as NOLOCK.

ROLLBACK: Data in the intermediate state of a transaction is discarded.

TCL: Transaction Control Language provides options to control transactions.

TRAN: The TRAN keyword is short for transaction.

Review Quiz - Chapter Nine

1.) Explicit transactions ensure that all their statements do what?

O a. Succeed or fail together

O b. Run faster

O c. Save data one DML statement at a time

2.) What is a dirty record?

O a. A record that can't be accepted for violating the database constraints.

O b. A record that replaced the original record in permanent storage.

O c. A record that has been changed, but not yet saved to permanent storage.

3.) If you want to throw away a dirty record, which keyword do you use?

O a. BEGIN TRAN

O b. COMMIT TRAN

O c. ROLLBACK TRAN

O d. THROWBACK TRAN

4.) What happens when you try to query records in the intermediate state?

O a. Your query waits until the data is no longer in the intermediate state.

O b. Your query runs normally.

O c. Your query splits the results into permanent and intermediate results.

5.) What is the shorter equivalent to the READUNCOMMITTED table hint?

O a. LOCK

O b. NOLOCK

O c. UNLOCK

6.) BEGIN, COMMIT and ROLLBACK are part of which family of language statements?

O a. DML

O b. DDL

O c. DCL

O d. TCL

Answer Key

1.) Explicit transactions do not affect the speed at which the statements execute, so (b) is incorrect. Since auto committed transactions save data one DML statement at a time, (c) is also incorrect. Because explicit transactions ensure that all their statements succeed or fail together, (a) is the correct answer.

2.) Because a dirty record does not violate any database constraints, but is just not committed to permanent storage yet, both (a) and (b) are incorrect. A dirty record is a record that has been changed, but not yet saved to permanent storage; therefore (c) is the right answer.

3.) BEGIN TRAN starts an explicit transaction, so (a) is incorrect. COMMIT TRAN saves data to permanent storage, so (b) is incorrect. THROWBACK has no special meaning in SQL Server, so (d) is also wrong. To throw away a dirty record use ROLLBACK TRAN, making (c) the correct choice.

4.) Since the query may be waiting for data to leave the intermediate state and the results will not contain intermediate results, both (b) and (c) are incorrect. Because SQL needs to ensure data integrity the query waits until the data is no longer in the intermediate state, so (a) is correct.

5.) Since LOCK has no special meaning in SQL Server and UNLOCK applies only to SQL Server logins, both (a) and (c) are incorrect. The shorter equivalent to the READUNCOMMITTED table hint is NOLOCK, making (b) the correct answer.

6.) Because BEGIN, COMMIT and ROLLBACK control Transactions, and not Data (a), (b) and (c) are all wrong answers. BEGIN, COMMIT and ROLLBACK all control transaction processing so they belong to the TCL family of language statements, thus (d) is the correct answer.

Bug Catcher Game

To play the Bug Catcher game run the BugCatcher_Chapter9.pps from the BugCatcher folder of the companion files. You can obtain these files from the www.Joes2Pros.com web site.

[NOTES]

Chapter 10. Data Control Language (DCL)

All the chapters up to this point have dealt with creating objects and manipulating data. DML and DDL statements, such as those we've seen in this book, comprise the lion's share of the code we are expected to know in the workplace. When it comes time to hire a new person to work with SQL Server, we need to create an account for them and understand how permissions and security work. This chapter discusses how to set the level of access to SQL Server using Data Control Language (DCL) statements.

READER NOTE: *Please run the SQLQueries2012Vol1Chapter10.0Setup.sql script in order to follow along with the examples in the first section of Chapter 10. All scripts mentioned in this chapter may be found at www.Joes2Pros.com.*

Introduction to Security

Security in SQL Server starts by creating types of accounts such as *logins* and *users*. Since this chapter covers the basics of security, we will focus on SQL Server logins. It is essential to know how to create logins and then GRANT or DENY them the required permissions. There are different types of logins for different networks and different ways to set security. That subject in itself is an entire book! In this section, we get familiar with the most common security terms.

Securables and Permissions

When Greg logs onto his computer at work and then tries to print to the network printer, several things happen. The printer checks its own list of who's who to see if Greg has permission. Most of us are familiar with the term permission. This chapter will add a few other words to our arsenal that will be a help when we are involved in security discussions.

Greg wants access to the printer. The printer does not need access to Greg, but it does need to know who is making the request. Since Greg wants access, he is known as the *principal*. The printer is what he wishes to access, so the printer is known as the *securable*. Permissions control the level of access principals have to securables.

In reality the principal, Greg, has no permissions. The list of permissions resides with the securable. The printer is the securable and contains a list of principals and permissions. When a match is found, the securable allows its use by the authorized principal.

There are many types of principals in SQL Server. The type of principal we will learn about is called a login. Logins will want access to securables such as resources, databases and tables.

Creating SQL Logins

Logins are the principals for the SQL Server security scope. To create logins, we use the CREATE keyword. The following code creates the login named Murray with the ABC password:

```
USE master
GO

CREATE LOGIN Murray
WITH PASSWORD = 'ABC'
```

The previous code may or may not work, depending on the operating system this instance of SQL Server is running on. Beginning with SQL Server 2005 (*when installed on a Windows 2003 server or higher*), SQL Server likes to enforce the same level of password policies that Windows Server is running. Windows Server does not consider passwords secure if they contain only alphabetical characters. If SQL Server is enforcing password complexity, it will issue an error message similar to the one in Figure 10.1.

```
USE master
GO

CREATE LOGIN Murray
WITH PASSWORD = 'ABC'
```

```
Messages
Msg 15116, Level 16 State 1, Line 2
Password validation failed. The password does not meet
Windows policy requirements because it is too short.
                                                    0 rows
```

Figure 10.1 SQL Server will not accept simple passwords by default when installed on a Windows Server 2003 or later Windows Server Operating System.

Most password complexity requirements call for at least seven characters with at least one numeral and one capital letter. The code sample shown here will create the Murray login without an error:

```
USE master
GO

CREATE LOGIN Murray
WITH PASSWORD = 'ABC$$123'
```

Once the Murray login is created, we can verify it with the Object Explorer. We simply need to navigate to the Logins folder located inside the Security folder to see the login named Murray amongst several others (Figure 10.2).

Object Explorer > **Security** > **Logins** > Murray

Reader Note: *It might be necessary to refresh the Object Explorer window to visually see this change has taken effect.*

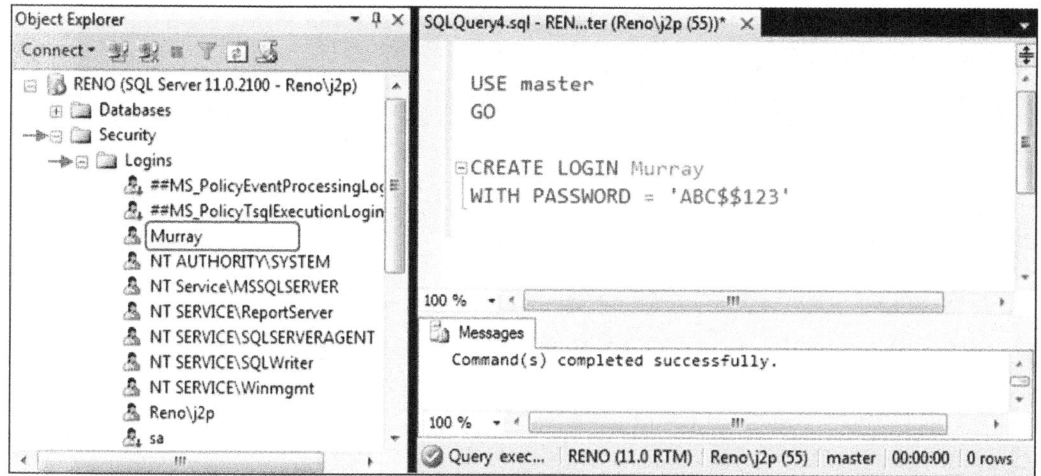

Figure 10.2 The Security node of Object Explorer shows the new Murray login in the Logins folder.

Currently SQL Server knows about Murray and his password, but no permissions to securables have yet been granted to him. By default, new accounts get public level permissions, which means Murray can login and browse the database list. However, he would have no permissions to open, use or query databases or tables.

Authentication Modes

When we open Management Studio, SQL Server wants to know who we are. One way to do this is with a password like the one given to Murray. If we are already logged into a Windows Operating System with a password, SQL Server can ask Windows for our login token for authentication and not ask us again while it is running. This is Geek Speak for saying SQL Server can authenticate us manually, or trust that Windows has already effectively done this.

When SQL Server is configured for Windows Authentication mode, we will not be allowed access when logging in with a SQL Server password. We can try this out for ourselves by logging in as Murray with the ABC$$123 password using the SQL Server Authentication mode.

Before attempting this next exercise, we must close Management Studio and get back to a blank desktop. Once this is accomplished, we will open Management Studio, but pause at the 'Connect to Server' dialog box before taking any action.

While in the '***Connect to Server***' dialog box, use the 'Authentication:' drop-down list to choose SQL Server Authentication as shown in Figure 10.3.

Figure 10.3 Change to SQL Server Authentication mode with 'Connect to Server' dialog box.

The dialog box will refresh immediately and enable the Login and Password text entry boxes. Type 'Murray' into the 'Login:' box and type 'ABC$$123' into the 'Password:' text box and then click the 'Connect' button (Figure 10.4).

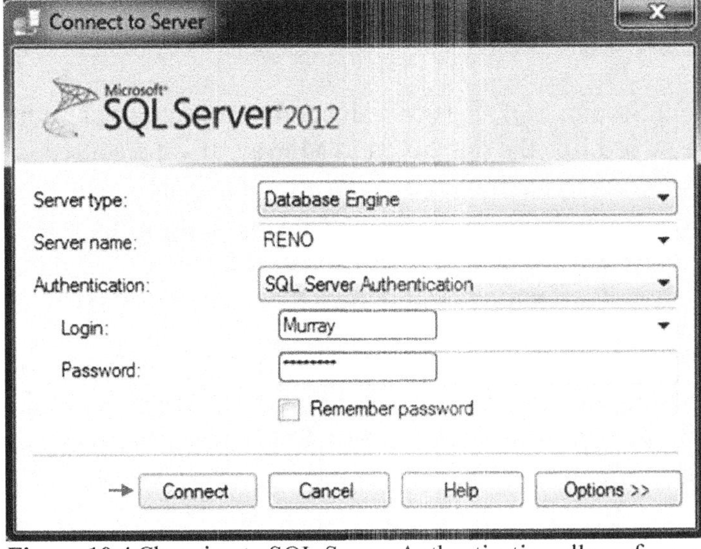

Figure 10.4 Changing to SQL Server Authentication allows for a specific login and password.

The Login and Password boxes were not enabled previously when Windows Authentication was selected. That's because the Windows Operating System relayed the authentication credentials to the SQL Server service automatically when we signed into Windows.

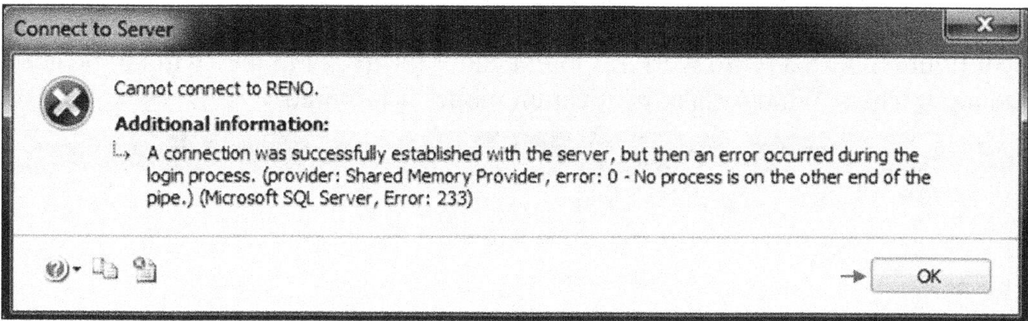

Figure 10.5 SQL Server Authentication may not work if SQL Server is not configured to use this type of authentication mode.

The SQL Server error message, similar to the one shown in Figure 10.5, will most likely be issued during this exercise. Take a moment to read the message and then click on the 'OK' button to exit out of this dialog box.

Let's change back to the Windows Authentication mode and login to SQL Server the way that we normally do each day. Once the 'Authentication:' drop-down list displays Windows Authentication, click on the 'Connect' button (Figure 10.6).

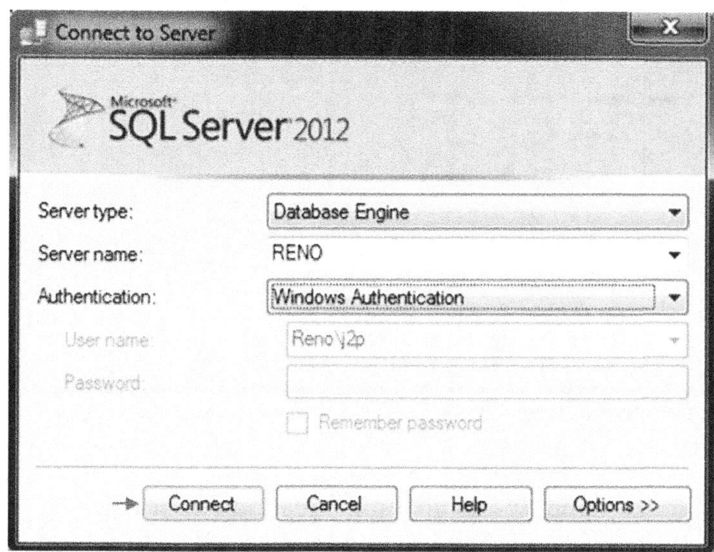

Figure 10.6 Change back to Windows Authentication and log in.

To find out why we received an error message with SQL Server Authentication, we will need to use the Object Explorer to access the System properties. Locate the gold cylinder-shaped server icon at the top of the pane. My server is named Reno. Right-click the icon, then select the 'Properties' option at the bottom of the list. Select the 'Security' page and the '***Server Properties***' dialog box will come up as seen in Figure 10.7.

The settings shown in Figure 10.7 will not allow SQL Server logins. We can configure SQL Server to work for logins like Murray's, but they will not be able to login when 'Windows Authentication mode' is required.

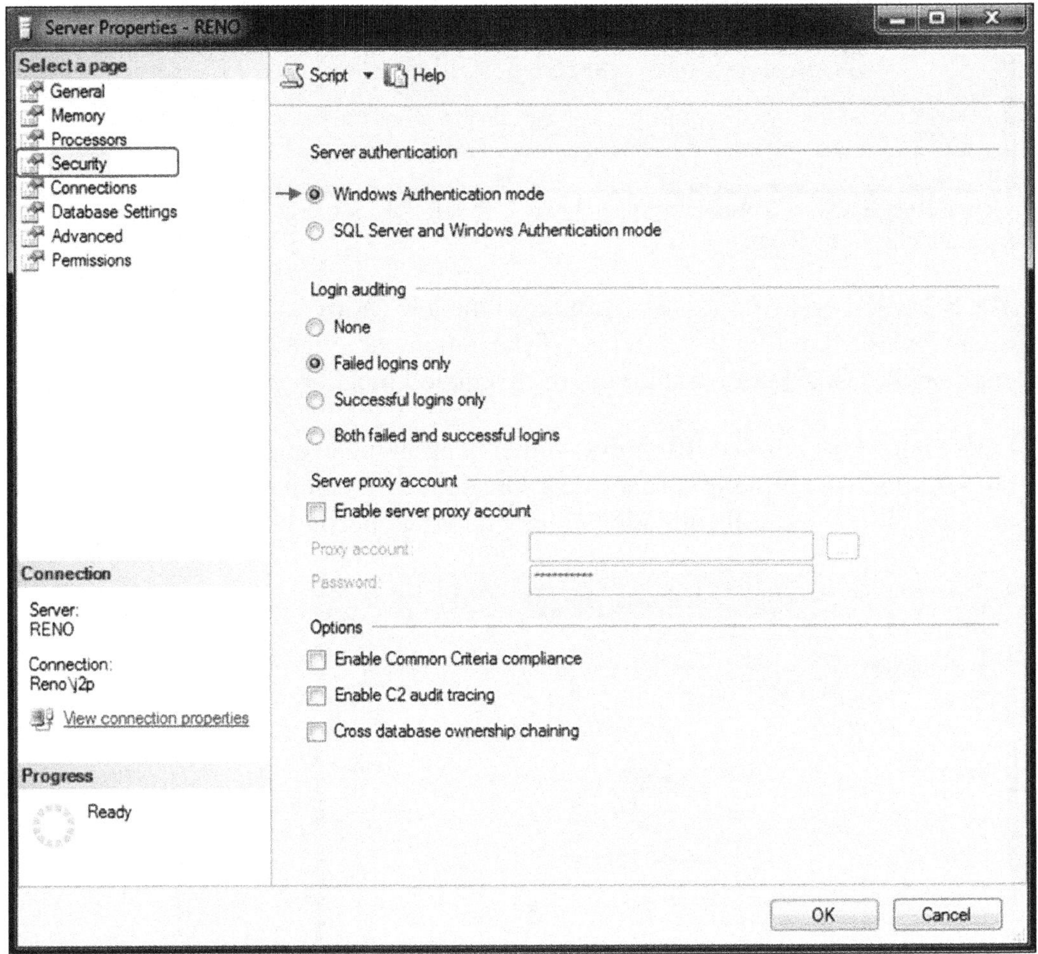

Figure 10.7 The Server Properties Security page shows that the Server authentication is set to 'Windows Authentication Mode'.

SQL Server is often set up to let Windows do all authentications, so it will recognize us by our Windows login. If we want SQL Server to only allow logins to be authenticated by Windows, then we would set the 'Server authentication' to 'Windows Authentication mode'. Likewise, if we wanted SQL Server to handle all login authentication for non-Windows accounts, we would use the setting for 'SQL Server and Windows Authentication mode'.

It is possible to configure SQL Server to allow Murray to login via his account. We can make this change while still on the 'Security' page by simply clicking on the '*SQL Server and Windows Authentication mode*' radio button and then clicking the 'OK' button to register this change with SQL Server. Another dialog box will open stating that our SQL Server configuration changes will not take effect until we restart the service, click 'OK' to acknowledge this statement.

In the Object Explorer window locate the gold cylinder-shaped server icon at the top of the pane (this icon is labeled with the name of our server). Right-click on this icon and choose the 'Restart' option from the pop-up menu.

Reader Note: *Windows Vista, Windows 7 and Windows 8 users will most likely see a 'User Account Control' dialog box appear asking if it is okay for the program named SQL Server 2012 from the Microsoft Corporation to make changes to our computer. Click 'Yes' and proceed to the next step.*

Another dialog box will open with a message to confirm that we really do want to restart the SQL Server service. Click the 'Yes' button to confirm (Figure 10.8).

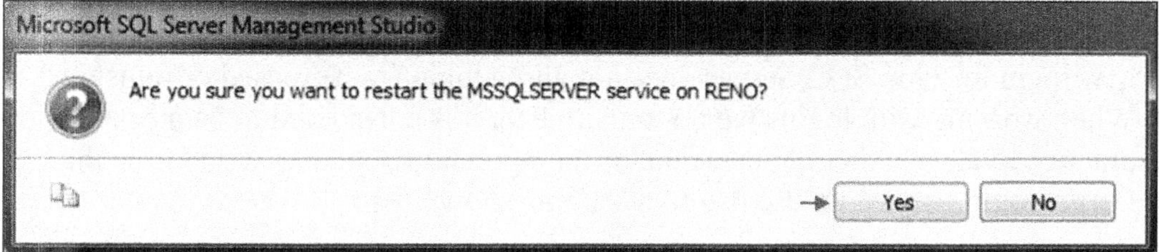

Figure 10.8 A confirmation dialog box appears after choosing the Restart option.

Close completely out of Management Studio and try to log back in as Murray. Notice he can now log into the server. The server node of Object Explorer shows Murray is currently logged in and can see the databases, although he does not have permission to use them (Figure 10.9).

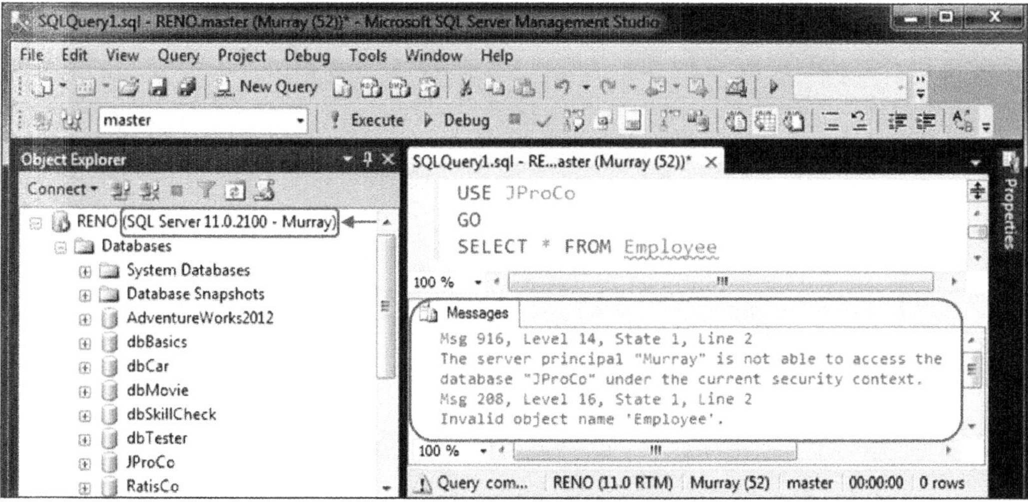

Figure 10.9 The Object Explorer shows Murray is logged into SQL Server and can see the databases, although he is denied access because he does not have any permission to them.

Dropping SQL Logins

If we wanted to get rid of a login, we only need to know the name of the login. Let's say we had created a login named Bernie with the following code:

```
CREATE LOGIN Bernie
WITH PASSWORD = 'ABC$$123'
```

Time goes by and now Bernie no longer works for our organization, so we want to remove his access to SQL Server. This is as easy as writing the following code:

```
DROP LOGIN Bernie
```

Dropping a login is rare and must be done carefully. Once a login has been dropped, there is no way to get it back. If we made a mistake and learned that Bernie was actually still with the organization, we would need to recreate a brand new login for him. SQL Server does not allow logins to be reused or reinstated. When working with logins we no longer need, it is considered to be a best practice to disable them, rather than dropping them altogether. To disable the Bernie login, we would use the code sample shown here:

```
ALTER LOGIN Bernie DISABLE
```

Lab 10.1: SQL Logins

Lab Prep: Each lab has one or more Skill Checks. Start with Skill Check 1 and proceed until reaching the Points to Ponder section.

Before beginning this lab, verify that SQL Server 2012 is properly installed and operating. Before running the lab setup script for resetting the database (SQLQueries2012Vol1Chapter10.1Setup.sql), please make sure to close all query windows within SSMS. An open query window pointing to a database context can lock that database preventing it from updating when the script is executing. A simple way to assure all query windows are closed, is to exit out of SSMS, then open a new instance of SSMS, and lastly run the setup script.

Skill Check 1: Create a login named Sara, with the password ABC$$123. Change the SQL Server configuration to 'SQL Server and Windows Authentication', which is also known as mixed authentication. Take the necessary steps to open Management Studio and login with the Sara account.

When done, the Object Explorer will resemble the one shown in Figure 10.10.

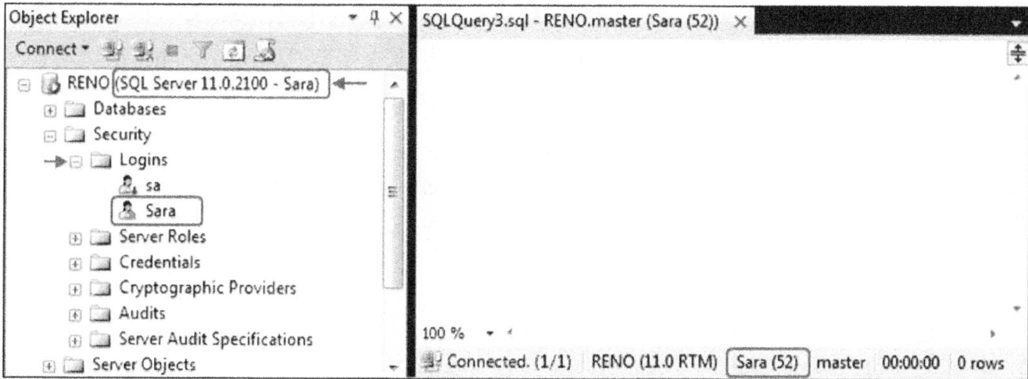

Figure 10.10 The Sara login has been created.

Answer Code: The T-SQL code to this lab can be found from the downloadable files named Lab10.1_SQLLogins.sql.

Points to Ponder - SQL Logins

1. To log into SQL Server, an account needs a server-level login.
2. To create a SQL Server login, use the CREATE keyword followed by the login information in this example:
   - `CREATE LOGIN Sally WITH PASSWORD = 'ABC$$123'`
3. There are two types of server level logins:
   - SQL Server
   - Windows
4. SQL Server has two authentication modes:
   - Windows Authentication mode
     - Principals who have been authenticated by the Windows operating system will be the only ones able to connect to SQL Server.
   - SQL Server and Windows Authentication mode (mixed mode)
     - Principals pre-authenticated by Windows or logins with a password authenticated by SQL Server will be allowed to log into the server.
5. SQL Server's default configuration is to only allow Windows logins that have proper permissions to SQL Server. Allowing SQL Server logins is optional and can be turned on and off.
6. Only use '*SQL Server and Windows Authentication mode*' when accounts or applications that do not have Windows credentials must be allowed to connect to SQL Server.

Granting Permissions

In the section and lab examples thus far, we have created the Murray and Sara logins recognized by SQL Server. These two accounts can log into SQL Server, but can do virtually nothing after that point. When we logged in as Murray and then tried to expand the JProCo database, we are denied access (Figure 10.11).

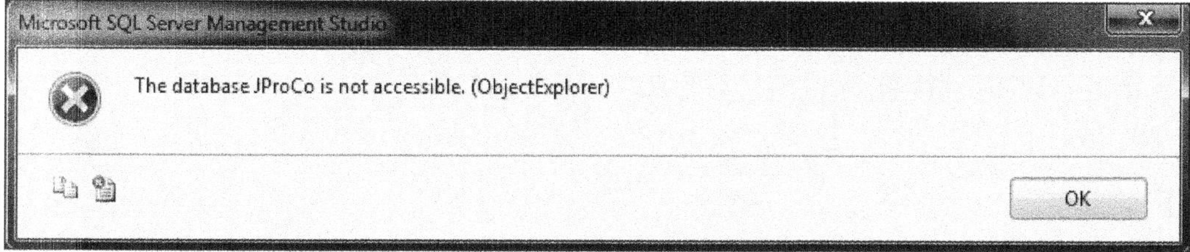

Figure 10.11 The Murray account is denied access to the JProCo database in Object Explorer.

We might try another way to gain access to JProCo by coding a USE statement in a new Query Window. Once again, SQL Server denies access to the Murray account, with a message stating the Murray principal does not have the necessary level of security (Figure 10.12).

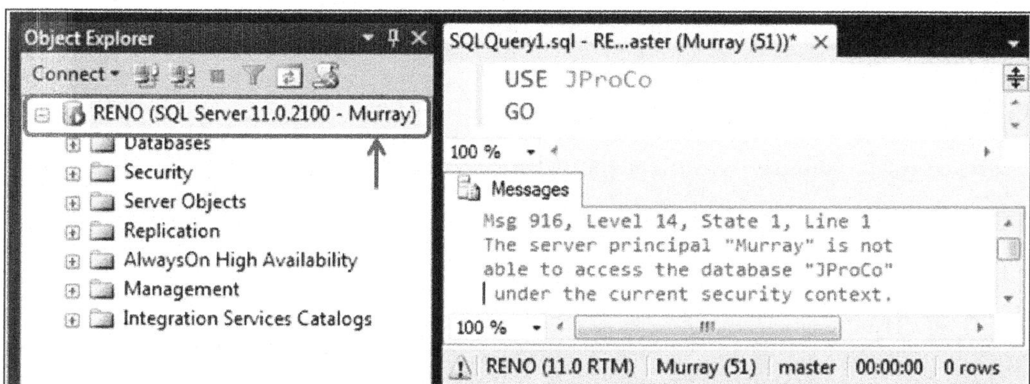

Figure 10.12 The Murray principal has no access to JProCo through any means.

Murray has access to the master database, but will be unable to access any user databases until appropriate permissions are granted (Figure 10.13).

```
USE MASTER
GO
```

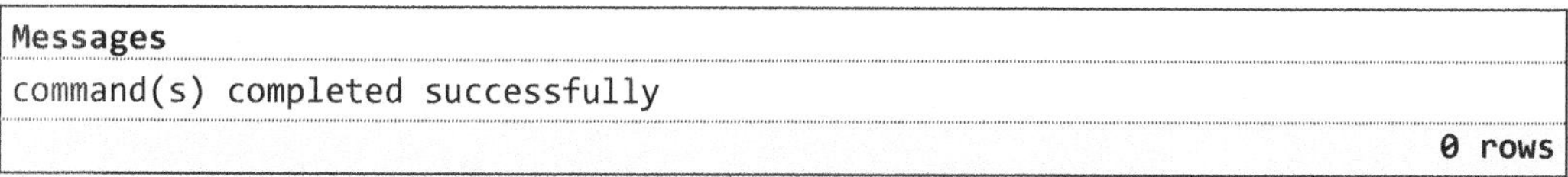

Messages
command(s) completed successfully
0 rows

Figure 10.13 The Murray account login can access the master database.

The master database is a powerful database. From there we can drop other databases. Let's see if Murray has the power to drop the dbBasics database from within the master database context.

Murray may use the master database context, but may not perform any DDL statements (CREATE, ALTER or DROP), as seen in Figure 10.14.

```
USE MASTER
GO

DROP DATABASE dbBasics
GO
```

```
Messages
Msg 3701 Level 11, State 1, Line 2
Cannot drop the database 'dbBasics',
because it does not exist or you do not have permission
                                                  0 rows
```

Figure 10.14 Murray does not have permission to ALTER or DROP databases from the server.

JProCo is a securable, and the Murray principal wants some level of access to it. We can change the securable to authorize Murray by giving him permissions. The GRANT keyword adds permission listings that allow principals access to these securables.

There are different levels of permissions for each securable. We might want total control for a database while another user just needs to make DDL changes.

Caution: *The following example is for a fictitious login and will not run.*

The sample shown here will GRANT the Rick login control of the entire server:

```
USE Master
GO

GRANT CONTROL SERVER TO Rick
GO
```

The principal is Rick and the securable is the server. The level of permission that the server is granting to Rick is called *control*. Control allows a login account to run all DML, DDL and DCL statements for any database on the server. Log in as an administrator (Windows login) to issue DCL statements, such as GRANT.

Oftentimes the control level of permissions is higher than an employee really needs. For Murray, we want to allow him to CREATE, ALTER or DROP databases. GRANT Murray the ability to alter any database with this code:

```
USE master
GO

GRANT ALTER ANY DATABASE TO Murray
GO
```

Log back in as Murray with the password ABC$$123. Let's try to DROP the dbBasics database with the following code:

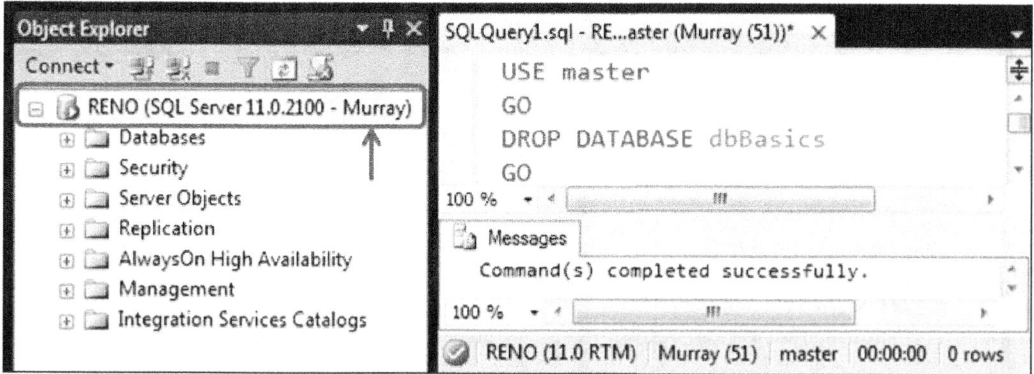

Figure 10.15 The Murray login now has permissions to drop a database.

Murray is now able to drop the database (Figure 10.15). All databases reside on the server. Therefore, any permission that works on all databases means it is a server-level securable.

Murray is able to run DDL statements on databases, but not on tables or other objects. When Murray attempts to access the JProCo database, the permissions still do not allow this action.

```
USE JProCo
GO
```

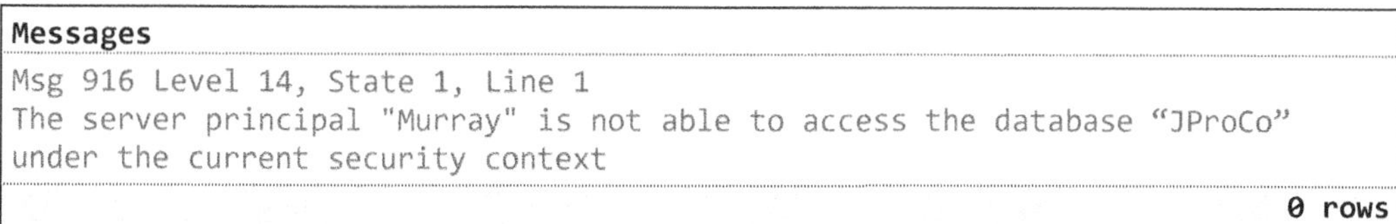
Messages
Msg 916 Level 14, State 1, Line 1
The server principal "Murray" is not able to access the database "JProCo" under the current security context
0 rows

Figure 10.16 Murray can ALTER databases, but still can't use their context.

Murray has important work to do. Let's give Murray the ultimate server-level permission of *control*. Log back in as an administrator (Windows login) so we can issue some additional DCL statements. To GRANT the login Murray to CONTROL the entire server, the following code would be used:

```
USE Master
GO

GRANT CONTROL SERVER TO Murray
GO
```

Log back in with the Murray account and password (ABC$$123) and notice he has unlimited access to all server and database resources.

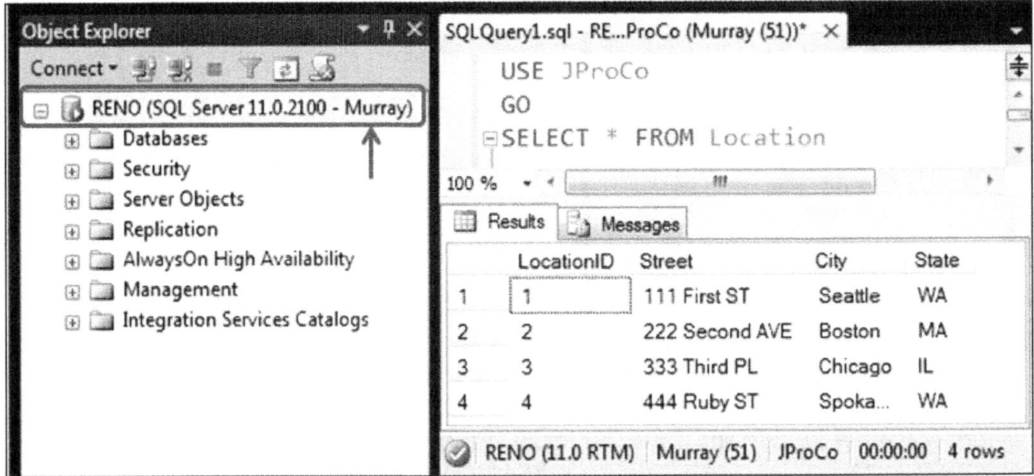

Figure 10.17 The Murray login can now run all DDL, DML and DCL statements on the server.

Lab 10.2: Granting Permissions

Lab Prep: Each lab has one or more Skill Checks. Start with Skill Check 1 and proceed until reaching the Points to Ponder section.

Before beginning this lab, verify that SQL Server 2012 is properly installed and operating. Before running the lab setup script for resetting the database (SQLQueries2012Vol1Chapter10.2Setup.sql), please make sure to close all query windows within SSMS. An open query window pointing to a database context can lock that database preventing it from updating when the script is executing. A simple way to assure all query windows are closed, is to exit out of SSMS, then open a new instance of SSMS, and lastly run the setup script.

Skill Check 1: Grant Sara the CONTROL SERVER permission. Once the permission is in place, log in with the Sara account and password (ABC$$123).

Use the JProCo database context to write a query displaying all records and fields from the Location table.

When done, the results should resemble those shown this figure.

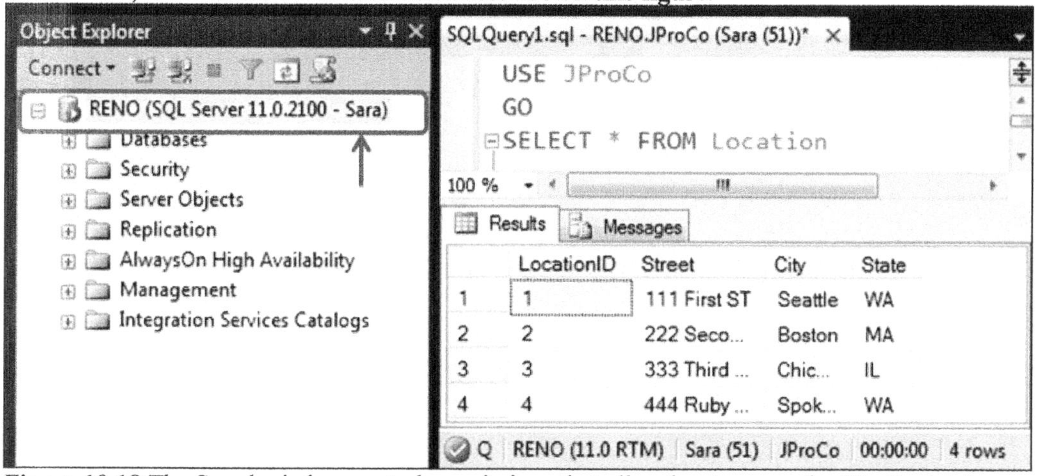

Figure 10.18 The Sara login has control permissions that allow her to query the JProCo database.

Answer Code: The T-SQL code to this lab may be found in the script Lab10.2_GrantingPermissions.sql (downloadable files from Joes2Pros.com).

Points to Ponder - Granting Permissions

1. To add server permissions to a login, use the GRANT keyword.
2. GRANT is a DCL (Data Control Language) permission statement.
3. Immediately after the GRANT keyword is the permission type to be issued to the login account. For example, to GRANT CONTROL SERVER permission to Josh, use the following syntax:
    - `GRANT CONTROL SERVER TO Josh`

Revoking and Denying Permissions

We learned that the GRANT keyword is a DCL statement that creates permissions on a securable and grants these permissions to a principal. OK, that is geek speak again, so let's use an example.

With the GRANT keyword, we can instruct the server (securable) to allow control (permission level) to Murray (principal). In the steps leading up to this point, we set the following permissions (Table 10.1).

Table 10.1 Shows all permissions granted to Murray and Sara.

Principal	Securable	Permission Level
Murray	SQL Server	Control Server = GRANT Alter Any Database = GRANT
Sara	SQL Server	Control Server = GRANT

We have granted two permissions from the server to Murray and one to Sara. Despite this, they have the same level of resource access. That's because a login account with the CONTROL SERVER permission can do everything including altering databases. Sara can effectively do everything at the same level as Murray.

Let's test this by closing Management Studio. Open it again, only this time using Server Authentication and logging in as Sara, as we will be creating a database named dbSara from this account. After running the code sample shown here, SQL Server should issue a successful completion message (Figure 10.19).

```
USE Master
GO

CREATE DATABASE dbSara
GO
```

```
Messages
command(s) completed successfully
                                                        0 rows
```

Figure 10.19 While logged in as Sara, we can CREATE the dbSara database.

With full control over the server, Sara can also DROP databases. Close the query window and open a new one. In the new query window, let's have Sara DROP the dbSara database (Figure 10.20).

```
USE Master
GO

DROP DATABASE dbSara
GO
```

Messages
command(s) completed successfully
0 rows

Figure 10.20 Sara is able to DROP the dbSara database.

Log out and log back in as an administrator. If we want Sara to be able to do everything except alter any database, we can keep the control server permission in place and then deny her that permission and issue the following DCL statement:

```
DENY ALTER ANY DATABASE TO Sara
```

Close Management Studio and log back in as Sara. She can still query all the databases and do pretty much the work she was able to do before (Figure 10.21).

```
USE JProCo
GO

SELECT * FROM Location
```

	LocationID	Street	City	State
1	1	111 First ST	Seattle	WA
2	2	222 Second AVE	Boston	MA
3	3	333 Third PL	Chicago	IL
4	4	444 Ruby ST	Spokane	WA
				4 rows

Figure 10.21 Sara has DML permissions for all the databases from Control Server permissions.

Sara has been granted control to the server, but denied permission to alter any database, preventing Sara from creating the dbSara database (Figure 10.22).

```
USE MASTER
GO

CREATE DATABASE dbSara
GO
```

Messages
Msg 262 Level 14, State 1, Line 2 CREATE DATABASE permission denied in database 'master'.
0 rows

Figure 10.22 Sara does not have database-level DDL permissions.

To summarize what has been done with the permission levels for Murray and Sara, review Table 10.2. The most recent change for the Sara account login has been made in ***bold italics*** to make it easier to find.

Table 10.2 A list of all permissions issued to Murray and Sara.

Principal	Securable	Permission Level
Murray	SQL Server	Control Server = GRANT Alter Any Database = GRANT
Sara	SQL Server	Control Server = GRANT ***Alter Any Database = DENY***

Murray has control of the server and no permissions have been denied. He has a second permission granting altering databases that appears redundant and his account would be unaffected if his 'Alter Any Database' permission didn't exist.

We need to remove the 'Alter Any Database' permission for Murray from the server's access list. We don't want to DENY or GRANT this permission. We want it to be unspecified or *revoked* by issuing the following DCL statement:

```
REVOKE ALTER ANY DATABASE TO Murray
GO
```

The REVOKE keyword simply removes an existing GRANT or DENY. After running the REVOKE, your permission structure is as seen in Table 10.3.

Table 10.3 After revoking Alter Any Database permission from Murray, one permission remains.

Principal	Securable	Permission Level
Murray	SQL Server	Control Server = GRANT
Sara	SQL Server	Control Server = GRANT Alter Any Database = DENY

Log in as Murray and try creating the dbMurray database. Notice his account still has this level of permission (Figure 10.23).

```
USE Master
GO

CREATE DATABASE dbMurray
GO
```

Messages
command(s) completed successfully
0 rows

Figure 10.23 Murray can alter databases with Control Server after revoking Alter Any Databases.

Revoke sounds like a penalty or a roadblock to someone's permissions. This indeed can be the case, as REVOKE takes away Grants. REVOKE also removes denied permissions. In reality, the REVOKE would free up Sara. The following code would again give Sara complete control over the server:

```
REVOKE ALTER ANY DATABASE TO Sara
GO
```

The end result is that Sara has server control and no more denied permissions. The Revoke freed her account up to use more server resources.

Table 10.4 After revoking the "Alter Any Database" permission from both logins, only the Control Server permission remains.

Principal	Securable	Permission Level
Murray	SQL Server	Control Server = GRANT
Sara	SQL Server	Control Server = GRANT

There are several permissions granted at the server level. Table 10.5 lists the most common ones and a description of their uses.

Table 10.5 Common server-level permissions.

Permission Level	Description
ALTER ANY LOGIN	Permission allows changing a login name and password.
ALTER ANY DATABASE	Permission to run any DDL statement against a database (CREATE, ALTER or DROP).
CONTROL SERVER	Permission to perform all operations.
SHUTDOWN	Permission allows the SQL Server service to be shut down.

A full detailing of all the possibilities with security would easily warrant an entire book. This chapter aims to familiarize us with the basic security concepts of SQL Server, along with the DCL statements. Any statement starting with keywords GRANT, REVOKE or DENY will set the level of control to principals and are therefore called Data Control Language statements.

Lab 10.3: Revoking and Denying Permissions

Lab Prep: Each lab has one or more Skill Checks. Start with Skill Check 1 and proceed until reaching the Points to Ponder section.

Before beginning this lab, verify that SQL Server 2012 is properly installed and operating. Before running the lab setup script for resetting the database (SQLQueries2012Vol1Chapter10.3Setup.sql), please make sure to close all query windows within SSMS. An open query window pointing to a database context can lock that database preventing it from updating when the script is executing. A simple way to assure all query windows are closed, is to exit out of SSMS, then open a new instance of SSMS, and lastly run the setup script.

Skill Check 1: Create a SQL Server login account named Alan with the password of ABC$$123. GRANT Alan a server-level permission that allows him full control of the server. Login as Alan and CREATE the dbAlan database.

When done, the Object Explorer should resemble the one shown in Figure 10.24.

Figure 10.24 The new login "Alan" has control permissions and can create the dbAlan database.

Skill Check 2: Create a SQL Server login named Bruce with the password of ABC$$123. Grant Bruce a server-level permission that allows him full control to the server. Deny Bruce the ability to ALTER databases. Login with the Bruce account and CREATE a database named dbBruce.

When done, the results from running the CREATE DATABASE statement should resemble (Figure 10.25).

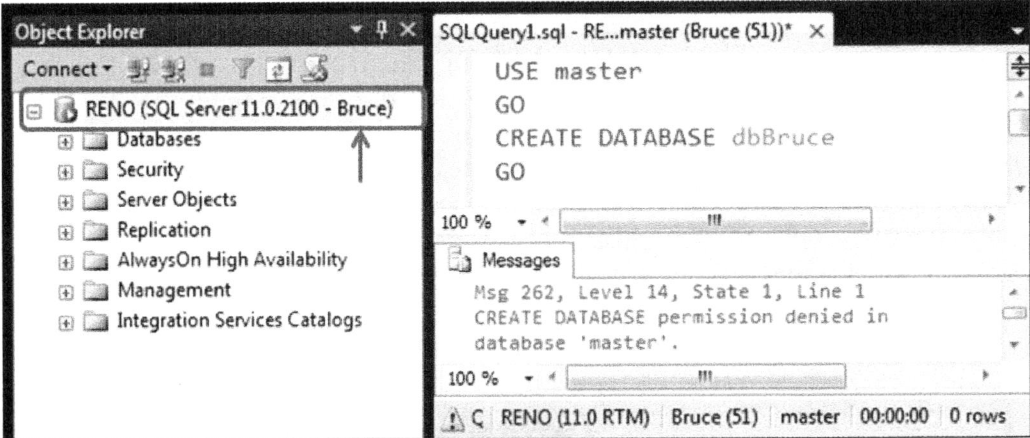

Figure 10.25 Bruce can do anything except alter databases.

Answer Code: The T-SQL code to this lab can be found from the downloadable files named Lab10.3_RevokingAndDenyingPermissions.sql.

Points to Ponder - Denying Permissions

1. Permissions can be manipulated with these DCL statements: GRANT, DENY and REVOKE.
2. DCL stands for Data Control Language.
3. To reduce a login account's permission, use a DENY *permission* statement.
4. A DENY permission trumps any other permissions to that object or scope. For example: GRANT control and DENY control, the user would have no access to the securable.
5. Use the REVOKE keyword to remove an existing granted or denied permission.
6. Sometimes a REVOKE will not reduce the overall effective permission of a principal if that principal receives its permissions from other sources.
7. When using REVOKE, all explicit and collection principal permissions must fully take away the permission.

Chapter Glossary

Authentication Mode: A security setting on SQL Server that specifies what types of logins are allowed access to the server.

Control: Permission that allows full control.

DCL: Data Control Language, a statement that affects the permissions a principal has to a securable.

DENY: A DCL statement that forbids permission to a securable.

GRANT: A DCL statement that allows permission to a securable.

LOGIN: A server-level principal in SQL.

Permission: A level of access to a securable given to a principal.

Principal: Any account or entity that is trying to access a resource.

REVOKE: A DCL statement to undo the last Grant or Deny for that permission.

Securable: A resource that controls access by setting security limits. Databases and tables are examples of securables.

SQL Login: A SQL server-level principal.

Windows Authentication: All logins are part of a Windows domain.

Review Quiz - Chapter Ten

1.) The server-level principal account is called?

O a. A User

O b. A Login

O c. A Password

2.) How do you create a login named Dexter with the QAZ123ZZ password?

O a. `CREATE LOGIN DEXTER WITH PASSWORD = 'QAZ123ZZ'`

O b. `CREATE USER DEXTER WITH PASSWORD = 'QAZ123ZZ'`

O c. `CREATE LOGIN DEXTER AS PASSWORD = 'QAZ123ZZ'`

O d. `CREATE USER DEXTER AS PASSWORD = 'QAZ123ZZ'`

O e. `CREATE LOGIN DEXTER FOR PASSWORD = 'QAZ123ZZ'`

O f. `CREATE USER DEXTER FOR PASSWORD = 'QAZ123ZZ'`

3.) How do you grant full control of the server to Phil?

O a. `GRANT CONTROL SERVER TO Phil`

O b. `GRANT SERVER CONTROL TO Phil`

O c. `REVOKE CONTROL SERVER TO Phil`

O d. `REVOKE SERVER CONTROL TO Phil`

4.) If you granted Phil control to the server, but denied his ability to create databases, what would his effective permissions be?

O a. Phil can do everything.

O b. Phil can do nothing.

O c. Phil can do everything except create databases.

5.) If you granted Phil control to the server and revoked his ability to create databases, what would his effective permissions be?

O a. Phil can do everything.

O b. Phil can do nothing.

O c. Phil can do everything except create databases.

6.) Granting permissions is in what family of language statements?

O a. DML

O b. DDL

O c. DCL

O d. TCL

7.) You have a login named James who has Control Server permission. You want to elimintate his ability to Create databases without affecting any other permissions. What SQL statement would you use?

O a. `ALTER LOGIN James DISABLE`

O b. `DROP LOGIN James`

O c. `DENY CREATE DATABASE TO James`

O d. `REVOKE CREATE DATABASE TO James`

O e. `GRANT CREATE DATABASE TO James`

Answer Key

1.) Because the server-level principal account is called a login, (a) and (c) are incorrect. The server-level principal is a login, so (b) is the correct answer.

2.) Being that the correct syntax to create a login is CREATE LOGIN *LoginName* WITH PASSWORD = '*Password*', (b), (c), (d), (e) and (f) are all incorrect. Since (a) is the only one that has the correct syntax it is correct.

3.) GRANT SERVER CONTROL will result in a syntax error because SERVER and CONTROL are reversed, so (b) is incorrect. REVOKE undoes the last GRANT or DENY for a permission, so (c) and (d) are also incorrect. The correct answer is (a), because it is the only one to use the correct syntax of GRANT CONTROL SERVER TO Phil.

4.) Phil cannot do everything because he was denied the ability to create databases, so (a) is wrong. Phil can do some things because he was granted control of the server before being denied only the permission to create databases, so (b) is also incorrect. Because Phil was granted control of the server and only denied permission to create databases, (c) is correct.

5.) Because Phil is still allowed to create databases through the CONTROL SERVER permission (b) and (c) are incorrect. Phil can do everything because even though his permission to create databases was revoked, he still has the ability through the CONTROL SERVER permission, so (a) is the correct answer.

6.) Granting permissions does not manipulate, define data, nor will it affect transaction control, making (a), (b) and (d) all wrong answers. Because granting permissions affects the level of access or control a principal has over data it belongs to the DCL (Data Control Language) family of statements, making (c) the correct answer.

7.) Disabling or dropping a login would affect all permissions that a login had available to it, so (a) and (b) are both wrong. REVOKE only undoes the last DENY or GRANT on a permission, and since CREATE DATABASE was never granted, revoking it will have no effect, so (d) is also incorrect. GRANT CREATE DATABASE would give James the ability to create databases rather than eliminate the ability, so (e) is incorrect too. To eliminate the ability to create databases, a DENY CREATE DATABASE must be used, so (c) is the correct answer.

Bug Catcher Game

To play the Bug Catcher game run the BugCatcher_Chapter10.pps from the BugCatcher folder of the companion files. You can obtain these files from the www.Joes2Pros.com website.

[NOTES]

Chapter 11. Workplace Tips

While at work as a SQL Developer, knowing how to get around the databases and tables we are responsible for will help a great deal when the time comes to find and fix problems within existing code. Being able to correctly design SQL Server objects using industry best practices, while meeting business requirements and timelines is another task that is in demand in today's workplace. It is common to collaborate with others in order to accomplish these varied tasks, and presenting or watching demos is all part of the daily routine to make sure the team is on the same page and everything is working as expected.

There are a few main tools and practices that greatly enhance these daily tasks that have very little to do with actually writing code. One of these comes in the form of sharing and clarifying code and data with other people in the company that may, or may not, have any background knowledge of SQL. Knowing how to navigate through the various tools or features within the SQL Server Management Studio and being able to use some of the basic coding tricks for collaborating is a must for a sought after SQL Developer.

This chapter will focus on the most common non-running code parts used on a regular basis by every good SQL Developer around the world. Some of the skills and tools covered include: Code Commenting, Automated Code Generation for basic tasks, as well as Importing and Exporting to Microsoft Excel files.

READER NOTE: *Please run the SQLQueries2012Vol1Chapter11.0Setup.sql script in order to follow along with the examples in the first section of Chapter 11. All scripts mentioned in this chapter may be found at www.Joes2Pros.com.*

Code Comments

Old classic movies utter this famous phrase "Gentlemen, this is off the record". In movies this is used when talking to the press and letting them know a certain comment or two will be said, however it is not meant for publication in the media. Sometimes, we want to use words or phrases within a query window that we want SQL Server to ignore when executing the code.

Fortunately, SQL Server allows us to write words or phrases that are "off the record", with a coding technique called a **comment**. When writing a query in the SQL Server query window, we can use special symbols to instruct the Query Engine to ignore these portions of the code when the query is run.

These special symbols also allow comments to visually look different than the rest of our code, which makes it much easier for the human eye to distinguish from the rest of the code as being something unique, and indicates this portion has a special purpose meant specifically for a human to read and for the computer to ignore.

Thus the main purpose of commenting techniques is to allow us to write words or phrases that are often descriptive notes or warnings of what the code is doing, when to run it and why it is necessary. This is a big benefit when other people, such as our team members, supervisors, or software testers are reviewing the code for their own purposes. In other words, ***comments*** are commonly used as a mini informational 'readme' file allowing other people reading it to learn more about the code being used.

Another great use of commenting techniques is to troubleshoot or test smaller segments of code without needing to modify or delete surrounding blocks of code that are around the segment we want to run by itself. This is a more specialized use of comments that every good SQL Developer needs to know.

Single-Line Comments

How can we make just one line in a query window not run, while the other lines of code still run as expected? Typing two hyphen signs '--', one after the other without a space, will instruct SQL Server to ignore every character that follows it on the same line. This coding technique is known as a single-line comment.

In Figure 11.1, we see a query with a single-line comment written as the first line, describing the purpose of the code below it. The comment in this example shows other developers and testers what action the code is expected to accomplish.

Indeed, when we run this code block, the result set contains all the fields from the Employee table and the Location table based on the matching LocationID field using the INNER JOIN keyword.

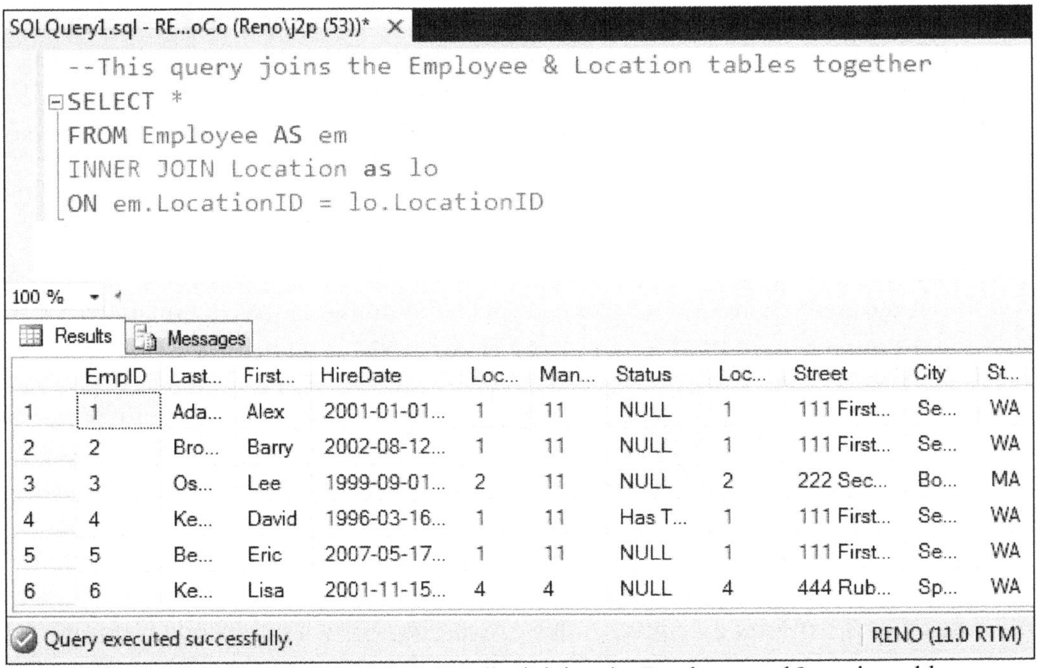

SQLQuery1.sql - RE...oCo (Reno\j2p (53))*

```
--This query joins the Employee & Location tables together
SELECT *
FROM Employee AS em
INNER JOIN Location as lo
ON em.LocationID = lo.LocationID
```

100 %

Results | Messages

	EmpID	Last...	First...	HireDate	Loc...	Man...	Status	Loc...	Street	City	St...
1	1	Ada...	Alex	2001-01-01...	1	11	NULL	1	111 First...	Se...	WA
2	2	Bro...	Barry	2002-08-12...	1	11	NULL	1	111 First...	Se...	WA
3	3	Os...	Lee	1999-09-01...	2	11	NULL	2	222 Sec...	Bo...	MA
4	4	Ke...	David	1996-03-16...	1	11	Has T...	1	111 First...	Se...	WA
5	5	Be...	Eric	2007-05-17...	1	11	NULL	1	111 First...	Se...	WA
6	6	Ke...	Lisa	2001-11-15...	4	4	NULL	4	444 Rub...	Sp...	WA

Query executed successfully. | RENO (11.0 RTM)

Figure 11.1 A query using comments to describe joining the Employee and Location tables.

However; the description is overly simple, as it does not explain why the two tables are being joined together, and what service or department might need the results from this query.

It is important to use comments wisely, by considering who, what, when, where, and why for describing the purpose of the code. The challenge is to write notes that balance being descriptive and brief, so anyone else that may read it days, weeks, months or even years from now can understand why it exists and what it is meant to achieve.

A better example of how comments can be used to describe code in a work environment is shown in Figure 11.2. This example describes a query similar to the one in Figure 11.1, while adding in more detail by indicating who the code is written for (HR), the specific purpose of why the code exists (Employee Report) and also draws attention to which fields from each table need to be included in the results (all Employee fields and the Address, City and State Location fields).

Since the comments in this example take up two lines in the Query Window, it is necessary to start each new line of comments with a new set of double hyphen signs, so SQL Server will know to ignore the first two lines of the query.

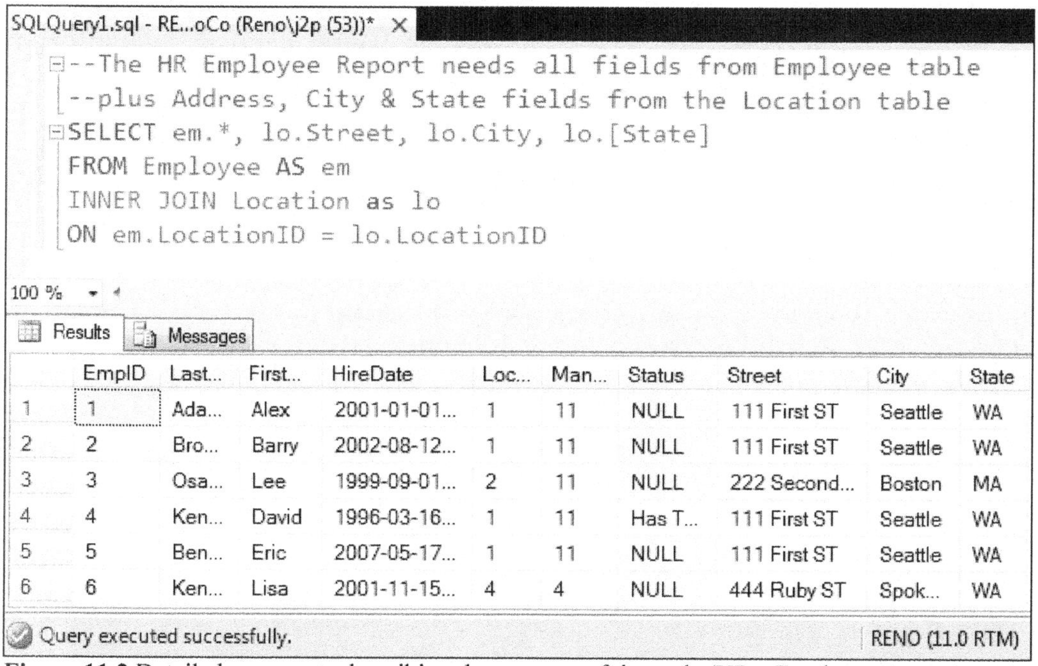

SQLQuery1.sql - RE...oCo (Reno\j2p (53))* ×

```
--The HR Employee Report needs all fields from Employee table
--plus Address, City & State fields from the Location table
SELECT em.*, lo.Street, lo.City, lo.[State]
FROM Employee AS em
INNER JOIN Location as lo
ON em.LocationID = lo.LocationID
```

100 %

Results | Messages

	EmpID	Last...	First...	HireDate	Loc...	Man...	Status	Street	City	State
1	1	Ada...	Alex	2001-01-01...	1	11	NULL	111 First ST	Seattle	WA
2	2	Bro...	Barry	2002-08-12...	1	11	NULL	111 First ST	Seattle	WA
3	3	Osa...	Lee	1999-09-01...	2	11	NULL	222 Second...	Boston	MA
4	4	Ken...	David	1996-03-16...	1	11	Has T...	111 First ST	Seattle	WA
5	5	Ben...	Eric	2007-05-17...	1	11	NULL	111 First ST	Seattle	WA
6	6	Ken...	Lisa	2001-11-15...	4	4	NULL	444 Ruby ST	Spok...	WA

Query executed successfully. RENO (11.0 RTM)

Figure 11.2 Detailed comments describing the purpose of the code (HR - Employee Report).

It is also possible to use single-line comments for testing specific segments of code. This commenting technique gives us the ability to temporarily prevent a segment of the code block from being able to execute, while the remaining code we want to inspect closer is able to run.

Let's say that while building the code for the HR Employee Report, something was not working right. We suspect there is a problem with the join to the Location table and believe that the code for the Employee table segment is correct. We want to test our theory by only running the segment of code with the SELECT statement for the Employee table, without having to rewrite it as a separate query, or deleting any of the code in the INNER JOIN segment.

This can be accomplished by commenting out the last two lines of the code, which will instruct the SQL Server query engine to ignore these two lines of code and only run the first two lines of code. The following code will not execute the INNER JOIN for the Location table and will only return the records from the Employee table, as shown in Figure 11.3.

```
SELECT *
FROM Employee AS em
--INNER JOIN Location as lo
--ON em.LocationID = lo.LocationID
```

	EmpID	LastName	FirstName	HireDate	LocationID	ManagerID	Status
1	1	Adams	Alex	2001-01-01...	1	11	NULL
2	2	Brown	Barry	2002-08-12...	1	11	NULL
3	3	Osako	Lee	1999-09-01...	2	11	NULL
4	4	Kennson	David	1996-03-16...	1	11	Has Tenure
5	5	Bender	Eric	2007-05-17...	1	11	NULL
6	6	Kendall	Lisa	2001-11-15...	4	4	NULL

12 rows

Figure 11.3 Using single-line comments to disable the INNER JOIN segment of a code block.

This next query calls on the [GRANT] table but has filtered the record set with criteria. This filter is looking for one of three things: EmpID is NULL, or Amounts that are less than 10000, or an EmpID that is equal to 7:

```
SELECT GrantID, GrantName, EmpID, Amount
FROM [Grant]
WHERE EmpID IS NULL
OR Amount < 10000
OR EmpID = 7
```

	GrantID	GrantName	EmpID	Amount
1	001	92 Purr_Scents %% team	7	4750.00
2	003	Robert@BigStarBank.com	7	18100.00
3	004	Norman's Outreach	NULL	21000.00
4	008	@Last-U-Can-Help	7	25000.00
5	010	Call Mom @Com	5	7500.00

5 rows

Figure 11.4 The Grant table with the GrantID field and limiters present.

One of the records in Figure 11.4 shows an EmpID of 5. Since the criterion seems to be looking for an EmpID with a value of 7 or NULL, why does the record for EmpID 5 show up in the results? Simple, the Amount field for EmpID 5 has a value less than 10,000, which matches the second criteria of the WHERE clause.

Even though this query is run every day for a department head at JProCo, a different manager is insisting on a report that only includes records for EmpID 7 or NULL. This is a report that will only be used once by this manager. What are our choices for giving the manager what they are asking for?

1) We could rewrite the query and save it in case it was ever needed again.
2) We could delete the line with OR Amount < 10000 criteria, run the query, and then re-type the line to put the query in its original state.
3) We could simply comment out the line with the OR Amount < 10000, run the query, and uncomment the line to put the query in its original state.

The first two options require a great deal of additional work and introduce the opportunity for making a mistake that might go unnoticed until a critical situation arises. The third option is both the simplest to implement and the safest, as any mistake that is made by commenting out a line of code can quickly be fixed by uncommenting the line of code.

So, the best choice here is option #3, since it requires the least amount of changes to the current code, is easily undone, and meets the needs of this one-time event.

We can see how easy it is to put option #3 into action by examining the following code and the results shown in Figure 11.5. By commenting out this line of code, we as humans can see it, even though SQL Server will ignore it during execution.

```
SELECT GrantID, GrantName, EmpID, Amount
FROM [Grant]
WHERE EmpID IS NULL
-- OR Amount < 10000
OR EmpID = 7
```

	GrantID	GrantName	EmpID	Amount
1	001	92 Purr_Scents %% team	7	4750.00
2	003	Robert@BigStarBank.com	7	18100.00
3	004	Norman's Outreach	NULL	21000.00
4	008	@Last-U-Can-Help	7	25000.00
				4 rows

Figure 11.5 The OR Amount < 10000 criterion is now non-executing code.

Reader Note: *Be cautious to avoid placing the double hyphen commenting sign in front of, and on the same line as, code that must be executed in order for a query to run. Remember that every character following the double hyphen signs on the same line will be ignored by the SQL Server query engine.*

Multi-Line Comments

There are times when we want to run part of a query or just a few lines for a quick test. Once the test is over we want all of the code back in its original state. For these purposes many SQL developers choose to highlight (select) only the segment of code they are interested in executing and ignore the remaining code block.

This next code example demonstrates how it is possible to run a segment of code that is part of a larger code block without using any commenting techniques.

Notice that the SELECT and FROM lines of the query are highlighted in blue for the Employee table. While the INNER JOIN is part of our query, since it is not highlighted (selected) this segment of code will not run at the same time as the segment of code that is highlighted in blue. When we run the highlighted segment of the query, we see that only the fields from the Employee table are returned. The segment of code with the INNER JOIN is ignored by the Query Engine.

```
--This query joins the Employee & Location tables together
SELECT *
FROM Employee AS em
INNER JOIN Location AS lo
ON em.LocationID = lo.LocationID
```

	EmpID	LastName	FirstName	HireDate	LocationID	ManagerID	Status
1	1	Adams	Alex	2001-01-01…	1	11	NULL
2	2	Brown	Barry	2002-08-12…	1	11	NULL
3	3	Osako	Lee	1999-09-01…	2	11	NULL
4	4	Kennson	David	1996-03-16…	1	11	Has Tenure
5	5	Bender	Eric	2007-05-17…	1	11	NULL
6	6	Kendall	Lisa	2001-11-15…	4	4	NULL

12 rows

Figure 11.6 Running code that has been highlighted in the SSMS query window.

When we want to comment out many consecutive lines of code, we have two different commenting techniques to accomplish this goal. Use single-line comments for each and every line to be prevented from running, or use the more efficient multi-line commenting technique to disable small or large segments of code with an easy to use beginning and ending sign.

The first option is to use single-line comments by placing the double hyphen sign at the beginning of each line we want to prevent running when the query is executed. We used this technique in the previous section, so the following code should look familiar.

```
SELECT *
FROM Employee AS em
```

```
--INNER JOIN Location as lo
--ON em.LocationID = lo.LocationID
```

With the INNER JOIN and ON clauses commented out, this query will return the exact same result set shown earlier in Figure 11.3. Every time we put two hyphens at the beginning of a line, this line becomes non-executing code (a comment).

The second option is to use multi-line comments by placing a '/*' (forward slash, asterisk with no spaces) sign at the start of the segment to be commented out and then close the comment with a '*/' (asterisk, forward slash with no spaces). Let's see how this works by using the same query we have been practicing with. The results of using this multi-line commenting technique are the same as those returned by using single-line comments in Figure 11.3.

```
SELECT *
FROM Employee AS em
/*INNER JOIN Location as lo
ON em.LocationID = lo.LocationID*/
```

In this example of commenting out only two lines of code, typing two sets of '--' signs, is about the same amount of work as typing a matching set of '/*' and '*/' signs. If this is the case, why choose one technique over the other?

The amount of effort to type the '--' signs for a single-line comment increases dramatically as the number of continuous lines to be commented out grows. What if we wanted to disable the last 300 lines of code? Typing '/*' and '*/' signs one time each, is definitely easier than typing the '--' signs, 300 times to achieve the exact same result. Unlike the double hyphen, which can only instruct SQL Server to ignore one line of code at a time, the '/*' '*/' signs (delimiters) are more efficient for multi-line commenting as there can be an infinite number of lines of code between the opening and closing delimiters.

Imagine if we had needed to comment out these 300 lines of code for testing purposes and as soon as we completed our test, it was necessary to uncomment the same 300 lines of code for the next member of our team to review. Removing one set of opening and closing '/*' '*/' delimiters is much simpler and faster than removing 300 sets of double hyphens!

In-Line Comments

What if we wanted to disable a specific part of code located on the same line as other code that we wanted to remain unaffected? The goal might be to disable one word in a long line of words within the code. We can achieve this goal by using an in-line commenting technique. In-line comments are best accomplished by using the same delimiters we used for making multi-line comments. We simply mark the beginning and ending of the word, or words, that we need to comment out of the code when the query is run. To make this clearer we will practice using in-line comments with some of the techniques we have already learned.

Let's use the code from one of our earlier queries, however; in this example, we want to display a report without the GrantID field. If we try to accomplish this by placing the '--' (double hyphens) delimiter, in front of the GrantID field, it's going to prevent all the fields in the SELECT statement from being seen by SQL Server. Since, every SELECT statement must have at least one field for the Query Engine to find results; we get an error message when running this query (Figure 11.7).

```
SELECT --GrantID, GrantName, EmpID, Amount
FROM [Grant]
WHERE EmpID IS NULL
-- OR Amount < 10000
OR EmpID = 7
```

Messages
Msg 156, Level 15, State 1, Line 2 Incorrect syntax near the keyword 'FROM'
0 rows

Figure 11.7 Commenting out all the fields in a SELECT statement will result in an error message.

Using the '--', as a delimiter will always result in everything following them on the same line to be commented out and instruct SQL Server to ignore this code. Since GrantID was the first field listed on the line and no other lines of code between the SELECT and FROM keywords have any fields listed, SQL Server has nothing to search for in this query.

If GrantID were on its own line and the other fields were on the next line below it, using the '--', as a delimiter would only comment out the GrantID field. This works just fine, although it can become tedious doing and undoing this procedure. An example of what this technique looks like is shown in the following code.

```
SELECT --GrantID,
GrantName, EmpID, Amount
FROM [Grant]
WHERE EmpID IS NULL
-- OR Amount < 10000
OR EmpID = 7
```

In the previous example we needed to change the code by moving part of the field selection list to the next line, in order to make our test work. This is generally not considered a best practice for commenting techniques, as one of the goals with commenting is to be able to run tests without changing the code.

The best way to accomplish the task of preventing the GrantID field from being displayed in our result set is to use the '/*' '*/' delimiters. Using this technique, we can easily prevent the smallest elements of a code block from executing, without moving or affecting the code surrounding it. The following example demonstrates how this is achieved and the results are shown in Figure 11.8.

```
SELECT /*GrantID,*/ GrantName, EmpID, Amount
FROM [Grant]
WHERE EmpID IS NULL
-- OR Amount < 10000
OR EmpID = 7
```

	GrantName	EmpID	Amount
1	92 Purr_Scents %% team	7	4750.00
2	Robert@BigStarBank.com	7	18100.00
3	Norman's Outreach	NULL	21000.00
4	@Last-U-Can-Help	7	25000.00

4 rows

Figure 11.8 The Grant table without the GrantID field as part of the result set.

Notice the result set shown in Figure 11.8 displays the GrantName, EmpID, and Amount fields and does not include the GrantID field. Success! The '/*' '*/' delimiters have allowed us to comment out the GrantID field, thus instructing the Query Engine to return results without affecting the remaining three fields, or changing any code.

Lab 11.1: Code Comments

Lab Prep: Each lab has one or more Skill Checks. Start with Skill Check 1 and proceed until reaching the Points to Ponder section.

Before beginning this lab, verify that SQL Server 2012 is properly installed and operating. Before running the lab setup script for resetting the database (SQLQueries2012Vol1Chapter11.1Setup.sql), please make sure to close all query windows within SSMS. An open query window pointing to a database context can lock that database preventing it from updating when the script is executing. A simple way to assure all query windows are closed, is to exit out of SSMS, then open a new instance of SSMS, and lastly run the setup script.

Skill Check 1: Use the single-line commenting technique to make the following query return all records from the Employee and PayRates tables for LocationID 1. Do not delete, or make changes to any of the code. When done, results should resemble those shown in Figure 11.9.

```
SELECT em.EmpID, em.LastName, em.FirstName, em.LocationID,
em.ManagerID, pr.YearlySalary, pr.MonthlySalary
FROM Employee AS em
INNER JOIN PayRates AS pr
ON em.EmpID = pr.EmpID
WHERE LocationID = 1
AND ManagerID IS NOT NULL
```

	EmpID	LastName	FirstName	LocationID	ManagerID	YearlySalary	MonthlySalary
1	1	Adams	Alex	1	11	76000.00	NULL
2	2	Brown	Barry	1	11	79000.00	NULL
3	4	Kennson	David	1	11	NULL	6500.00
4	5	Bender	Eric	1	11	NULL	5800.00
5	7	Lonning	David	1	11	NULL	6100.00
6	11	Smith	Sally	1	NULL	115000.00	NULL

6 rows

Figure 11.9 Skill Check 1 results return all records for LocationID 1.

Skill Check 2: When running the following query, only 3 of the 12 employees with PayRates are shown. Use multi-line commenting to show all 12 employees. Results should resemble Figure 11.10. ***Hint:*** *Disable the last four lines of code.*

```
SELECT em.EmpID, em.LastName, em.FirstName, em.LocationID,
em.ManagerID, pr.YearlySalary, pr.MonthlySalary
FROM Employee AS em
INNER JOIN PayRates AS pr
ON em.EmpID = pr.EmpID
WHERE LocationID = 1
AND ManagerID IS NOT NULL
AND HireDate > '1/1/2000'
AND [Status] IS NULL
```

	EmpID	LastName	FirstName	LocationID	ManagerID	YearlySalary	MonthlySalary
1	1	Adams	Alex	1	11	76000.00	NULL
2	2	Brown	Barry	1	11	79000.00	NULL
3	3	Osako	Lee	2	11	NULL	NULL
4	4	Kennson	David	1	11	NULL	6500.00
5	5	Bender	Eric	1	11	NULL	5800.00
6	6	Kendall	Lisa	4	4	52000.00	NULL
							12 rows

Figure 11.10 Skill Check 2 results return all 12 records from the Employee table.

Skill Check 3: Use in-line commenting to display just the FirstName, LastName, and City fields from the following query, as shown in Figure 11.11.

```
SELECT em.EmpID, em.FirstName, em.LastName, lo.City
FROM Employee AS em
INNER JOIN Location AS lo
ON em.LocationID = lo.LocationID
```

	FirstName	LastName	City
1	Alex	Adams	Seattle
2	Barry	Brown	Seattle
3	Lee	Osako	Boston
4	David	Kennson	Seattle
5	Eric	Bender	Seattle
6	Lisa	Kendall	Spokane
			11 rows

Figure 11.11 Skill Check 3 displays just three fields from the query's SELECT list.

Answer Code: The T-SQL code to this lab can be found in the downloadable files in a file named Lab11.1_CodeComments.sql.

Points to Ponder - Code Comments

1. A code comment is also called Non-Executing code.
2. Code Comments can be used to make code more readable to other people in the organization who may or may not have backgrounds in SQL.
3. Code Comments can be used to test and disable parts of written code. The code that has been commented out can be uncommented at a later time when testing has been completed.
4. Single line comments in SQL start with a double hyphen.
5. Single line comments don't need an ending comment; SQL Server recognizes that the end of the comment is the end of the line it is on.
6. Use multi-line comments to comment out many consecutive lines at once.
7. To start a multi-line comment use '/*' (forward slash followed by the asterisk signs together, in that order).
8. To end a multi-line comment use '*/' (asterisk followed by the forward slash signs together, in that order).
9. The '/* */' (forward slash asterisk and asterisk forward slash) pair can be used for in-line comments to comment out a portion of a code line.

Automatic Script Generation

Almost everyone these days feels comfortable with using a "point and click" process to get things done with a computer. Only a small percentage of us have ventured into writing code or working with command line utilities to create the programs that perform these tasks. Weather we write code or use 'clicks', what really matters is getting the job done. Computers will respond to their instructions, regardless of how they receive them. Whether we copy a file with a drag and drop operation, or use the copy command in a console window, the end result is the same; the file has been copied from one place to another.

With the SQL Server Management Studio User Interface (SSMS UI), we can create a table by writing code in a Query Window, or use the "point and click" method. Point and click allows us to create a table without writing any code ourselves. It is much easier to send someone the code script to accomplish a task with SQL Server than it is to send step-by-step instructions on how to "point and click" their way to accomplish the same task. For this reason, code script is the most common method used to consistently and reliably deploy new databases and objects the exact same way on many systems.

It is much faster to run code that has already been written and tested by someone else than it is to accurately and consistently navigate with the user interface. There are times when creating long constructions of code is faster with the SSMS UI than it is to write out each line of code by hand. In addition, some people simply prefer to "point and click" their way to creating objects in SQL Server.

In either case, it is possible to instruct SQL Server to convert all the "point and click" steps into T-SQL code scripts. There is a handy feature within SQL Server known as a "Code Generator", which automatically generate T-SQL scripts to perform specific actions for objects that already exist in the database, including the database itself.

Code Generators

To demonstrate how code generators work in SQL Server Management Studio let's start by expanding the dbBasics database folder in the Object Explorer and looking at some of the tables it contains (Figure 11.12).

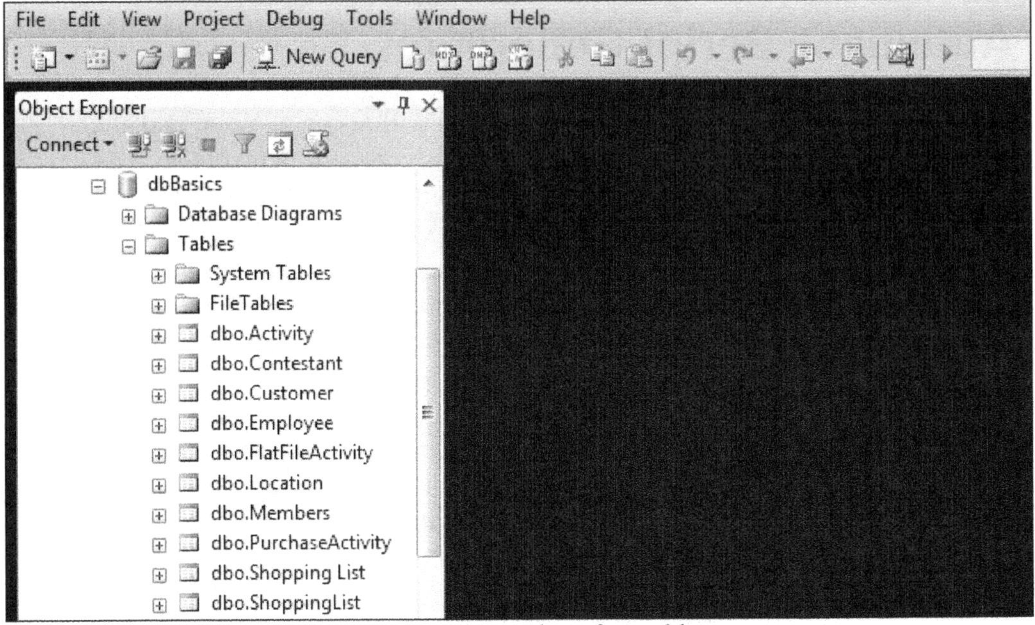

Figure 11.12 The dbBasics database currently consists of ten tables.

There are two tables in the dbBasics database which appear to be duplicates.

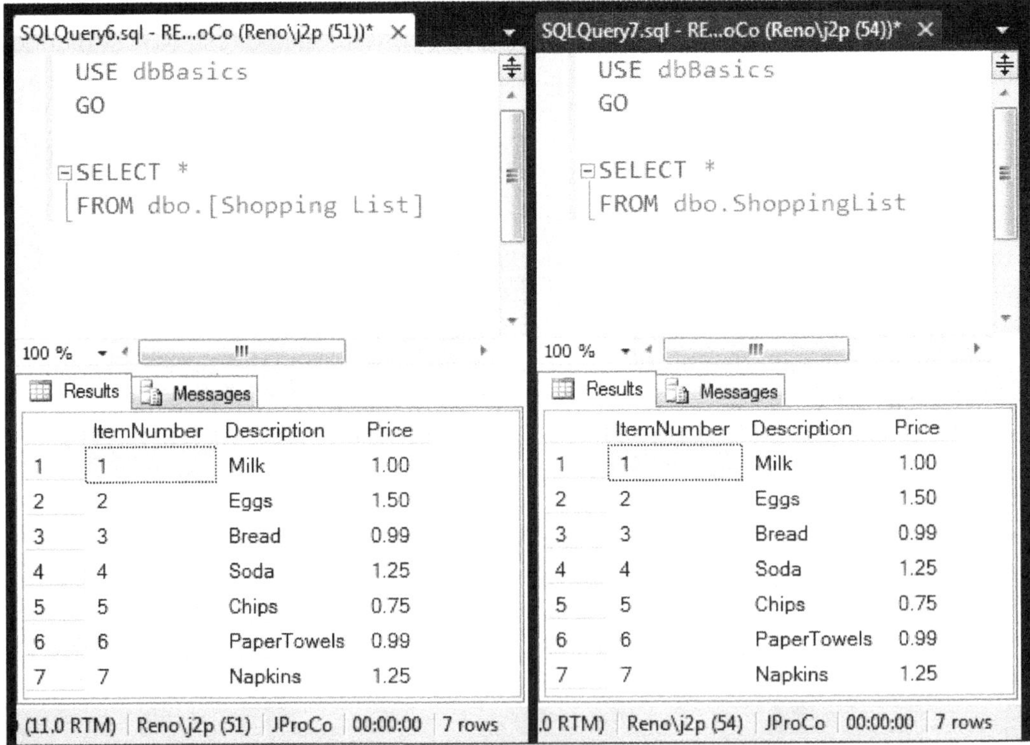

Figure 11.13 The [Shopping List] and ShoppingList tables appear to be duplicates.

There is a [Shopping List] table (with a space between the words), as well as a [ShoppingList] table (without a space between the words). When we look at the two queries in Figure 11.13 our suspicions are confirmed, in addition to having similar names, these two tables share the exact same data and we don't need both of them in the database at the same time.

One way to solve this dilemma is by using the "point and click" method. We can right-click on the [Shopping List] table, and then choose the 'Delete' option from the pop-up menu. This will open a Delete Object dialog box that gives us several choices, including pressing the 'OK' button to confirm we want the table deleted, or pressing the 'Cancel' button to exit out of the operation. What many SQL users are not aware of is that when we press the 'OK' button, SQL Server will actually execute T-SQL code in the background, relieving us from having to write the code to delete this table for ourselves.

What if we are asked to help delete this table on a server that someone else owns, and that we are not allowed to access directly? This is a common situation. When a SQL Server is being used in a production environment, very few people have access for security purposes. Since our job is to provide the code that will be run on this production SQL Server, it will be up to someone else to perform the action to delete the [Shopping List] table either with code or a "point and click" solution.

Years of personal experience tells us that if we try to talk someone thru all of the "point and click" steps necessary to accomplish this task there is a chance for a misunderstanding. A simple misunderstanding when deleting a table could have an immediate negative effect on mission critical readiness, which is definitely not a desirable outcome. It will be far easier and safer to create this action as a script that we could send to the company's SQL Operations team. This would allow another person to run the scripted action on their machine with the exact same results as the code we have already safely tested. This is also a better result as the other person can complete their work with just one execution step.

A task like the one just described is a great use of the code generator feature. The SSMS UI, as the T-SQL code generated for these types of actions will always be consistent and safe. It is the exact same code that SQL Server runs when we perform a task via the "point and click" method.

We can discover how to use the code generator by going through each of the "point and click" steps (plus one to generate code). Instead of pressing 'OK' as the last step to delete the table, we will press 'Cancel' to prevent the table from being deleted until we test the code that has been generated for us by SQL Server.

We have been asked to write a script that can be used to delete the Members table at some point in the future. Of course, we are tasked to write this script when we are already in the middle of an important test. The quickest and safest way to write this new script is to use the SSMS UI to generate the code for us.

The first step is to right-click the Members table of the dbBasics database shown in Figure 11.14, then choose the 'Delete' option from the pop-up menu. This will open a 'Delete Object' dialog box giving us several options to choose from.

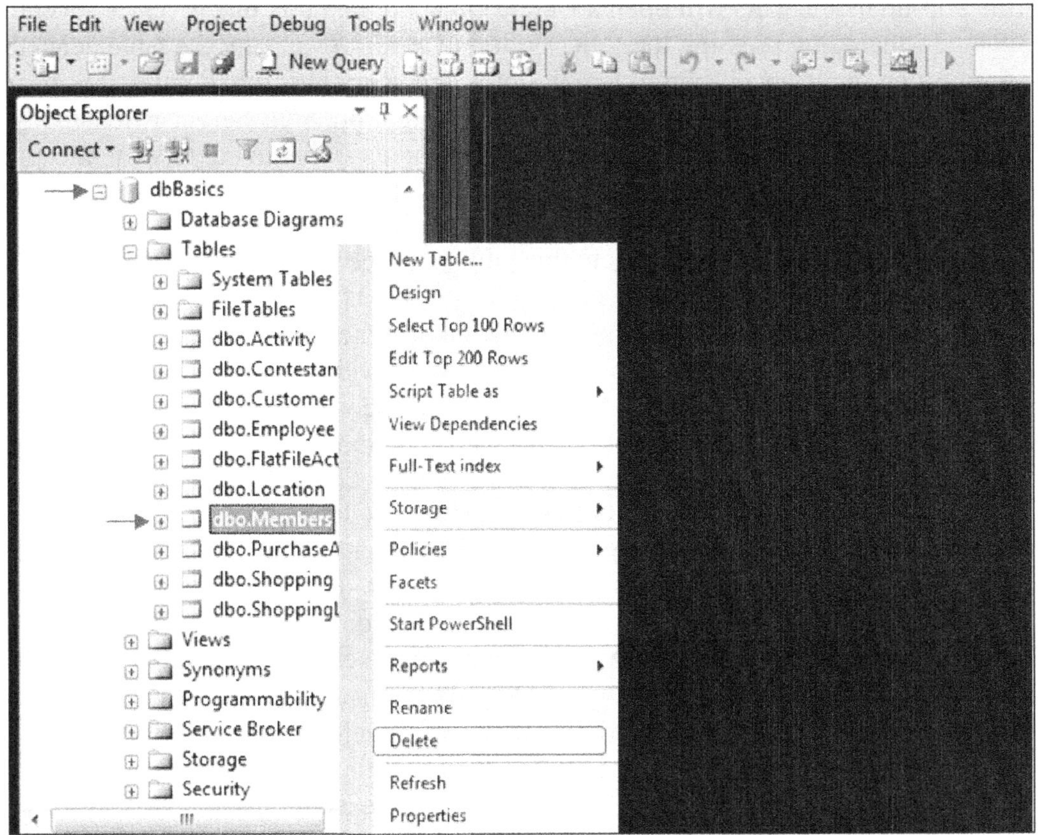

Figure 11.14 Right-click on the Members table and choose the 'Delete' option from the menu.

Warning: *<u>DO</u> <u>NOT</u> left-click the 'OK' button during any of these steps as it will instruct SQL Server to execute the code which will delete the Members table, preventing this exercise to work correctly.*

The next step is to find the 'Script' drop-down menu button located at the top of the right-hand pane in the 'Delete Object' dialog box (Figure 11.15). Simply left-click on the drop-down menu arrow and then choose the 'Script Action to New Query Window' option. Finish the process, by left-clicking on the 'Cancel' button to exit the dialog box and view the code generated in the new Query Window.

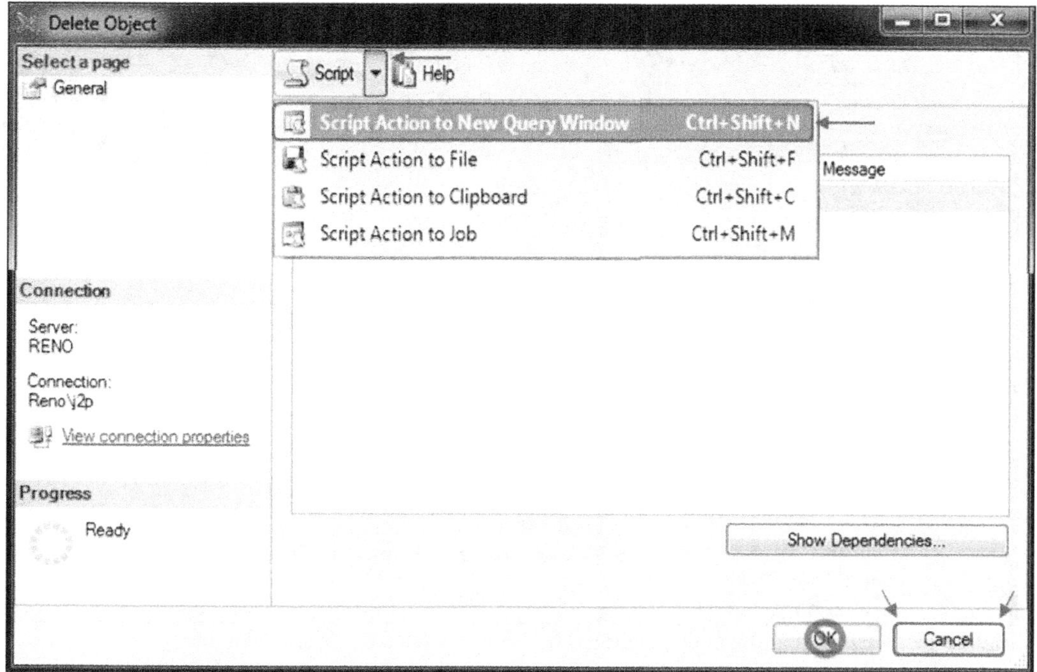

Figure 11.15 Choose the 'Script Action to New Query Window' option and then click Cancel.

A new Query Window will open in SSMS containing the code generated to delete the Members table of the dbBasics database. An example of what this code will look like is shown here:

```
USE [dbBasics]
GO

/****** Object:  Table [dbo].[Members]    Script Date:
8/29/2012 2:15:19 PM ******/

DROP TABLE [dbo].[Members]
GO
```

We can verify that this code works properly, by clicking on the '! Execute' button to run the code. When this is complete, it will be necessary to refresh the 'Tables' folder (should still be expanded from when we started this exercise) inside the dbBasics database (right-click the 'Tables' folder, then select the 'Refresh' option in the pop-up menu). Once this folder is refreshed we can visibly see that the Members table no longer exists in the dbBasics database (Figure 11.16).

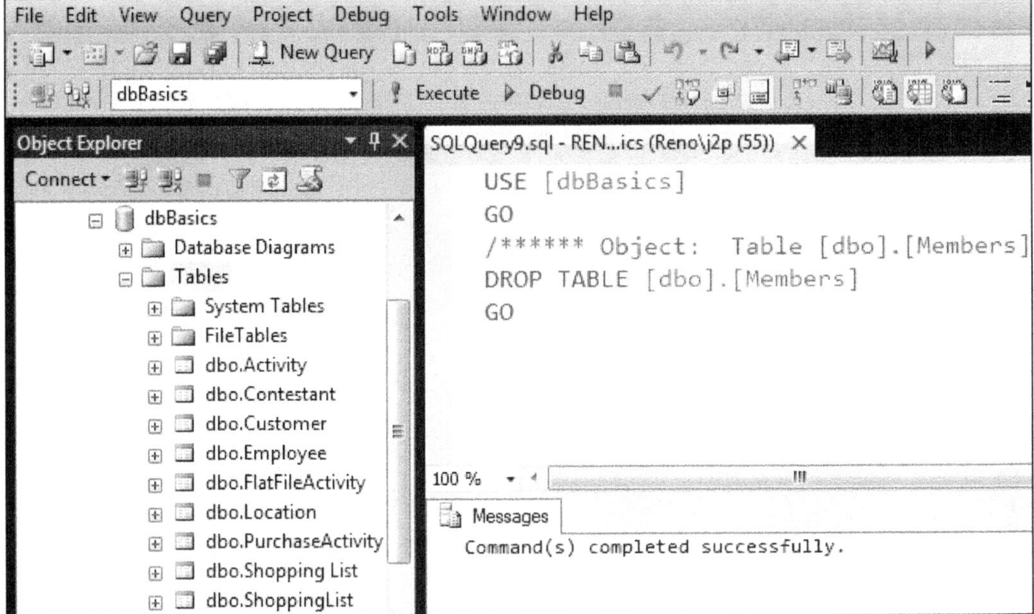

Figure 11.16 Executing the code generated by SSMS deletes the Members table.

The SSMS code generator is very useful in these types of situations, as it will quickly produce reliable code to perform basic database maintenance actions. It also comes in handy for those times when it is difficult to remember exactly what syntax is necessary to write certain T-SQL code. It can even serve as an excellent learning tool to show what code will accomplish certain actions that we have yet to work with.

Leveraging from Generated Code

There are certain tasks that a SQL Developer performs on a regular, if not a daily basis. At the top of this list is creating, altering and deleting database objects. Any good coder is always looking for ways to make common or mundane tasks easier to accomplish, even if it means a great deal of work today, if it saves hours and hours of work later and helps to prevent mistakes, then the effort is deemed to be worthwhile.

Fortunately for all of us today, there have been many versions of SQL Server prior to the SQL Server 2012 edition we are working with now. Each version is the end result of many dozens of people programming code with the end goal of achieving a better product than the one before it and to incorporate as many shortcuts and features as possible to help the next generation of SQL Developers.

One of the great benefits of the Code Generator is being able to leverage the code it produces for one object into using it, with slight modifications, to work with a new or existing object. This is a great timesaver in a SQL Developers work day.

Let's take a look at the Employee table of the dbBasics database by using this simple query to view the results shown in Figure 11.17.

```
USE dbBasics
GO

SELECT *
FROM Employee
```

	EmpNo	LastName	FirstName	Dept	Position	Salary	LocationID
1	101	Smith	Sarah	Admin	Manager	54000.00	2
2	102	Brown	Bill	Sales	Clerk	25200.00	2
3	103	Fry	Fred	Admin	Clerk	21900.00	1
4	104	Thomas	Tina	Admin	Secretary	26700.00	1
5	105	Gregg	Gary	Sales	Manager	48000.00	2
6	106	Davies	Diana	Admin	Clerk	23400.00	1

16 rows

Figure 11.17 The Employee table of the dbBasics database has 16 records.

When looking at Figure 11.17 a little closer, we can see the Employee table has seven fields. This is important because we need to create an EmployeeArchive table that is identical in structure to the Employee table. In other words, we need to create a duplicate table with the exact same design, without any records in it yet (table is empty).

The purpose of this new EmployeeArchive table will be to hold all the records of employees who are no longer employed by the company. This new table needs to have the exact same fields and data types as the existing Employee table in order to easily move the data from the Employee table to the EmployeeArchive table without any problems.

Since the Employee table already exists, we can use the Code Generator to help us leverage the code it produces to accomplish this task. To do this, we simply right-click on the Employee table in the Object Explorer window and make the following selections from the pop-up menu(s) shown in Figure 11.18:

Object Explorer > Employee > Script Table as > CREATE To > New Query Editor Window

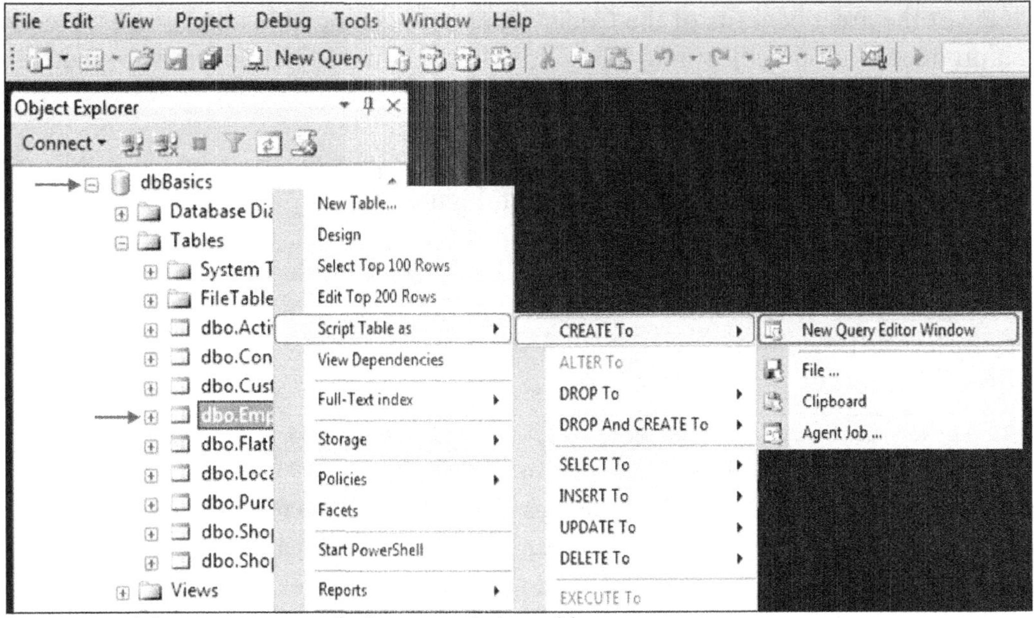

Figure 11.18 Steps to create code from an existing table.

A new query window will open with the code necessary for creating the existing Employee table before it had any records. An example of the generated code for creating the Employee table, including the declaration for the Primary Key, and its seven fields is shown here:

```
USE [dbBasics]
GO

/****** Object:  Table [dbo].[Employee]    Script Date:
8/29/2012 2:30:12 PM ******/

SET ANSI_NULLS ON
GO

SET QUOTED_IDENTIFIER ON
GO

SET ANSI_PADDING ON
GO

IF NOT EXISTS (SELECT * FROM sys.objects WHERE object_id =
OBJECT_ID(N'[dbo].[Employee]') AND type in (N'U'))
BEGIN
```

```
CREATE TABLE [dbo].[Employee](
      [EmpNo] [INT] NOT NULL,
      [LastName] [VARCHAR](25) NOT NULL,
      [FirstName] [VARCHAR](35) NOT NULL,
      [Dept] [VARCHAR](25) NULL,
      [Position] [VARCHAR](40) NULL,
      [Salary] [MONEY] NULL,
      [LocationID] [INT] NULL,
PRIMARY KEY CLUSTERED
(     [EmpNo] ASC
)WITH (PAD_INDEX = OFF, STATISTICS_NORECOMPUTE = OFF,
IGNORE_DUP_KEY = OFF, ALLOW_ROW_LOCKS = ON,
ALLOW_PAGE_LOCKS = ON) ON [PRIMARY]
) ON [PRIMARY]
END
GO

SET ANSI_PADDING OFF
GO
```

A simple ***change*** to the first line of the CREATE TABLE statement and we can have our new EmployeeArchive table created with the exact same structure as the Employee table within seconds! Run the following code and verify the new EmployeeArchive table exists in the Object Explorer window (Figure 11.19).

```
USE [dbBasics]
GO

CREATE TABLE [dbo].[EmployeeArchive](
      [EmpNo] [INT] NOT NULL,
      [LastName] [VARCHAR](25) NOT NULL,
      [FirstName] [VARCHAR](35) NOT NULL,
      [Dept] [VARCHAR](25) NULL,
      [Position] [VARCHAR](40) NULL,
      [Salary] [MONEY] NULL,
      [LocationID] [INT] NULL,
PRIMARY KEY CLUSTERED
(     [EmpNo] ASC
)WITH (PAD_INDEX = OFF, STATISTICS_NORECOMPUTE = OFF,
IGNORE_DUP_KEY = OFF, ALLOW_ROW_LOCKS = ON,
ALLOW_PAGE_LOCKS = ON) ON [PRIMARY]
) ON [PRIMARY]
GO
```

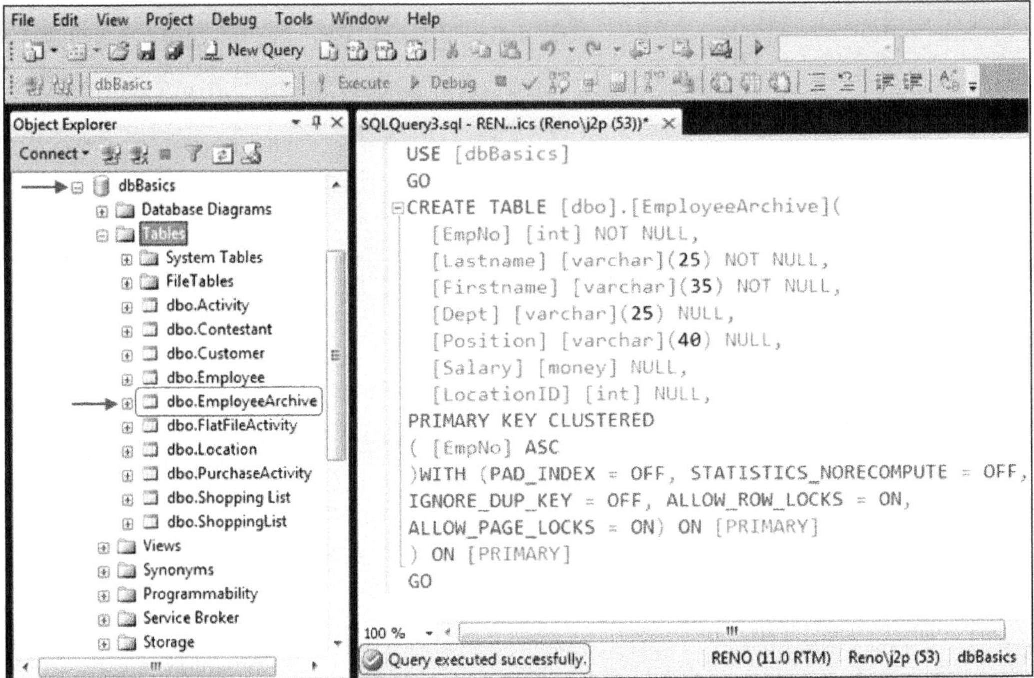

Figure 11.19 The EmployeeArchive table, created by leveraging code generated by SSMS.

It might be necessary to refresh the 'Tables' folder (should still be expanded from when we started this exercise) inside the dbBasics database (right-click the 'Tables' folder, then select the 'Refresh' option in the pop-up menu). Once this folder is refreshed we can visibly see that the EmployeeArchive table has been created in the dbBasics database, as shown in Figure 11.19.

Great, we have now successfully experienced the power of leveraging the Code Generator to create a new database object (EmployeeArchive table) from an existing database object (Employee table), within a matter of seconds and without making any mistakes writing the required T-SQL code!

Lab 11.2: Automatic Script Generation

Lab Prep: Each lab has one or more Skill Checks. Start with Skill Check 1 and proceed until reaching the Points to Ponder section.

Before beginning this lab, verify that SQL Server 2012 is properly installed and operating. Before running the lab setup script for resetting the database (SQLQueries2012Vol1Chapter11.2Setup.sql), please make sure to close all query windows within SSMS. An open query window pointing to a database context can lock that database preventing it from updating when the script is executing. A simple way to assure all query windows are closed, is to exit out of SSMS, then open a new instance of SSMS, and lastly run the setup script.

Skill Check 1: Use the Code Generator to leverage the code used for creating the existing Employee table in the JProCo database to create a new table named EmployeeArchive in JProCo with the identical structure as the Employee table. After executing the code to create the new table, refresh the Object Explorer to verify that the EmployeeArchive table exists, as shown in Figure 11.20.

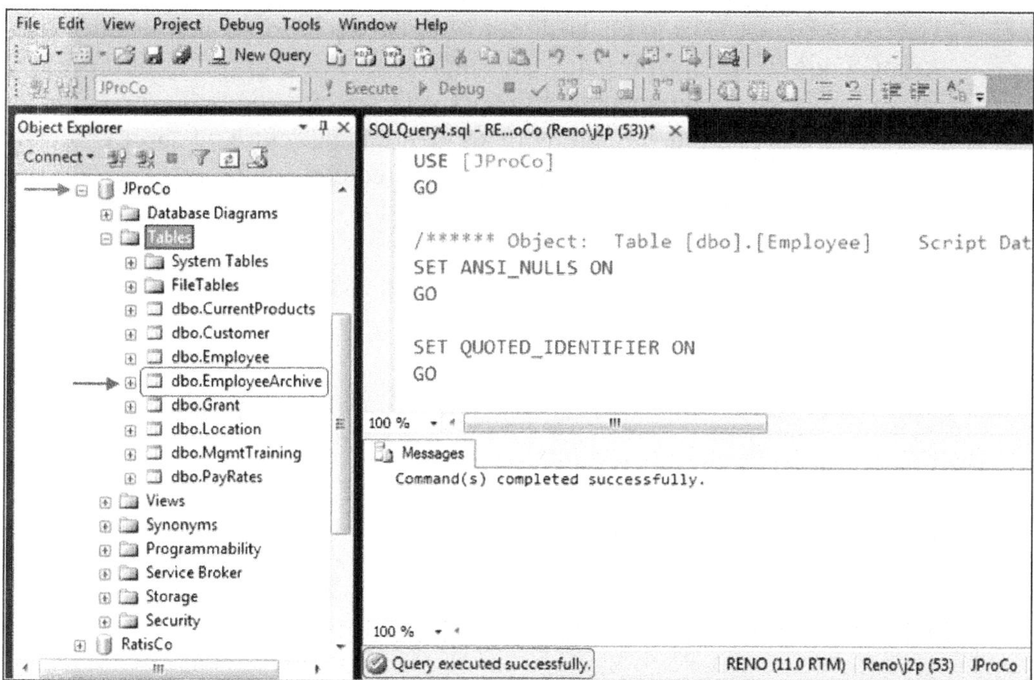

Figure 11.20 Skill Check1 leverages the code generated by SSMS to create EmployeeArchive.

Answer Code: The T-SQL code to this lab can be found in the downloadable files in a file named Lab11.2_CodeComments.sql.

Points to Ponder - Automatic Script Generation

1. Selections made while performing 'point and click' steps in the SSMS UI is a user friendly method of creating and running T-SQL code.
2. SQL Server accepts commands in several ways:
   - Running code written in a Query Window
   - Executing a saved .sql script
   - Using the SSMS UI to perform 'point and click' steps
3. If someone is requesting the 'point and click' steps necessary to perform a database action, it is both easier and safer to use the code generator and then provide them with the script. This way they only have to execute a trusted script and possibly avoid making a mistake in the 'point and click' process.
4. The Code Generator records the 'point and click' actions when using the SSMS UI and then converts them into valid, reliable T-SQL code.
5. The Code Generator can be used to leverage existing objects to create sample code for performing the same action on a new or different object. For example, the code generated to CREATE an existing table can be used to easily CREATE a new table with an identical structure by simply changing the name of the table in the generated code and then executing it.

Import/Export Wizard

In Chapter 7 of this volume, we learned how to use the BCP utility (Bulk Copy Program) to Import and Export text files for SQL Server. If BCP can perform Import/Export actions for SQL Server, why use an Import/Export Wizard? Since, the BCP utility is only capable of working with text and binary files it has many limitations in a work environment that uses data stores such as Microsoft Excel, XML, Oracle, Microsoft Access, and just about any other data store available.

This is where the SQL Server Import/Export Wizard becomes a valuable tool, as it is capable of moving and working with nearly every type of data store there is.

BCP Recap

On the C: drive there should be a C:\Joes2Pros folder containing the folders and files copied from the Sql2012Vol1CompanionFiles.zip file we downloaded earlier from the www.Joes2Pros.com website.

We can verify that this folder exists on our C:\ drive by using the Command Prompt utility. Press the keyboard button with the Windows symbol ⊞ + the letter 'R' to open the 'Run' dialog box (typically opens in the lower left-hand corner of the desktop window). Type the word 'cmd' in this dialog box to open the Command Prompt utility.

Once the Command Prompt window appears on the screen type the command '**DIR C:**' where the flashing cursor is located and then press the 'Enter' button to view a directory listing of all the folders and files in the root of the C:\ drive. The results of executing this command should resemble those shown in Figure 11.21. Look for a folder named Joes2Pros in the directory list.

If a folder named Joes2Pros does not already exist in the root directory of the C:\ drive for the computer these exercises are being run on, then it will be necessary to create one in order to complete this section for importing and exporting data. If the Joes2Pros folder is missing from the list, follow the instructions in the next ***Reader Note***; otherwise skip to the text after Figure 11.21 to begin this exercise.

Reader Note: *While in the Command Prompt utility window type the following command at the flashing cursor, '**MD C:\Joes2Pros**' (this command will **M**ake a **D**irectory folder named Joes2Pros in the root of the C:\ drive). Verify the folder was created by once again typing the command '**DIR C:**' at the flashing cursor and locate the Joes2Pros folder in the directory list results shown on the screen.*

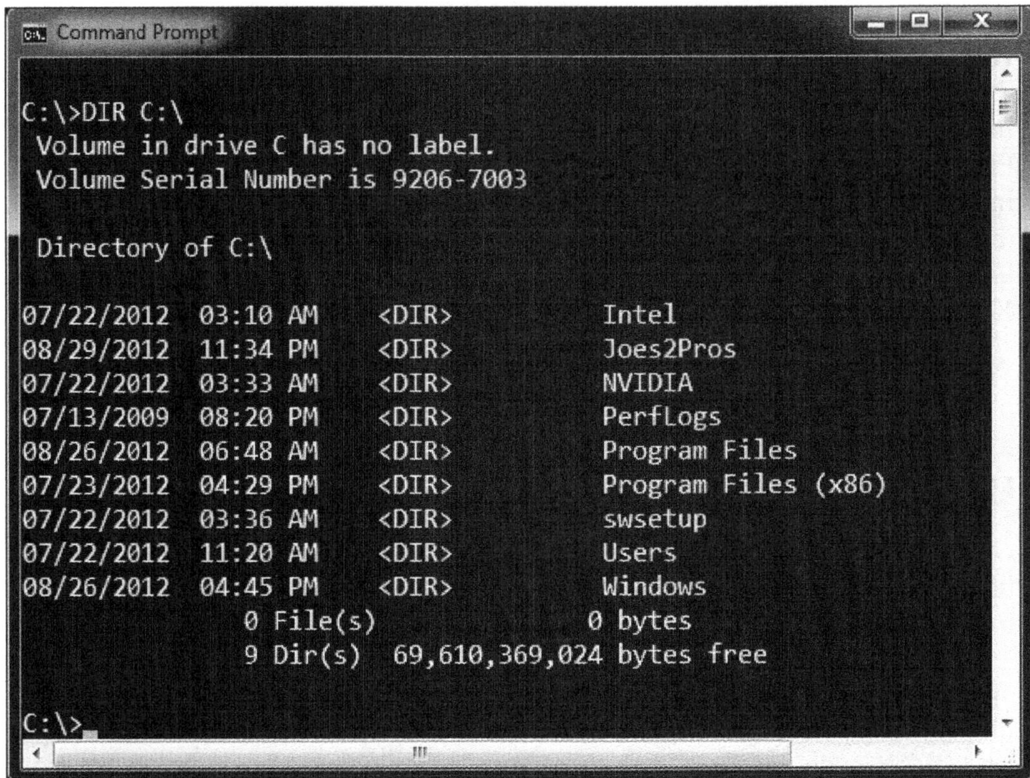

Figure 11.21 Verifying the Joes2Pros folder does exist in the root C:\ drive directory list.

BEGIN EXERCISE: Recall that we can use the BCP utility to import and export data to and from SQL Server. Let's use a simple query to look at all the records in the Location table of the JProCo database (Figure 11.22).

```
SELECT *
FROM Location
```

	LocationID	Street	City	State
1	1	111 First ST	Seattle	WA
2	2	222 Second AVE	Boston	MA
3	3	333 Third PL	Chicago	IL
4	4	444 Ruby ST	Spokane	WA

4 rows

Figure 11.22 There are currently 4 records in the Location table.

If we used the BCP utility to export the Location table, we would create a new file with a .txt file extension (text). Type the first command shown in Figure 11.23, '**BCP JProCo.dbo.Location OUT C:\Joes2Pros\Location.txt –T –c**' and then press the 'Enter' button to export the records from the Location table in the JProCo database into the C:\Joes2Pros folder with a file named Location.txt.

```
C:\>BCP JProCo.dbo.Location OUT C:\Joes2Pros\Location.txt -T -c

Starting copy...

4 rows copied.
Network packet size (bytes): 4096
Clock Time (ms.) Total     : 1      Average : (4000.00 rows per sec.)

C:\>
```

Figure 11.23 The BCP command export the records of the Location table to the Location.txt file.

Verify that the Location.txt file was created in the C:\Joes2Pros\ folder by typing the command shown on the first line of Figure 11.24 '**DIR C:\Joes2Pros**' and then press the 'Enter' button to retrieve a directory list of the Joes2Pros folder. The Location.txt file should be in the list of results (Figure 11.24).

```
C:\>DIR C:\Joes2Pros\
 Volume in drive C has no label.
 Volume Serial Number is 9206-7003

 Directory of C:\Joes2Pros

08/29/2012  11:34 PM    <DIR>          .
08/29/2012  11:34 PM    <DIR>          ..
08/29/2012  11:37 PM               108 Location.txt
               1 File(s)            108 bytes
               2 Dir(s)  69,579,997,184 bytes free

C:\>
```

Figure 11.24 Using the Command Prompt to verify Location.txt is in the C:\Joes2Pros folder.

An easy way to view the contents of the Location.txt folder while still in the Command Prompt window is to type the following command at the flashing cursor, '**notepad C:\Joes2Pros\Location.txt**' and then press the 'Enter' button. This will immediately open the Location.txt file using the Notepad application that comes with all Microsoft Windows Operating Systems. The results of this command should resemble those shown in Figure 11.25.

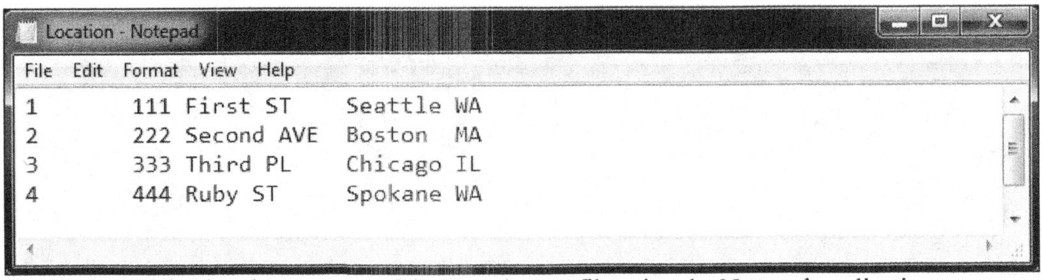

```
Location - Notepad
File  Edit  Format  View  Help
1        111 First ST     Seattle WA
2        222 Second AVE   Boston  MA
3        333 Third PL     Chicago IL
4        444 Ruby ST      Spokane WA
```

Figure 11.25 Viewing the contents of the Location.txt file using the Notepad application.

If we wanted to export the data from the Location table into a Microsoft Excel spreadsheet, the BCP utility will not be able to handle this request. There are some import/export tasks that the BCP utility simply isn't capable of performing. This is when we need to implement the SQL Server Import/Export Wizard.

Reader Note: *Keep the Command Prompt window open, as we will use it again.*

Running the Wizard

When we want to import and export to other types of data stores, we will need to use the SQL Server Import/Export Wizard. This will allow us to export the data from the JProCo.dbo.Location table into a Microsoft Excel spreadsheet file. The first step begins with the Object Explorer, as shown below and in Figure 11.26.

Object Explorer > right-click **JProCo** > **Tasks** > left-click (select) **Export Data**

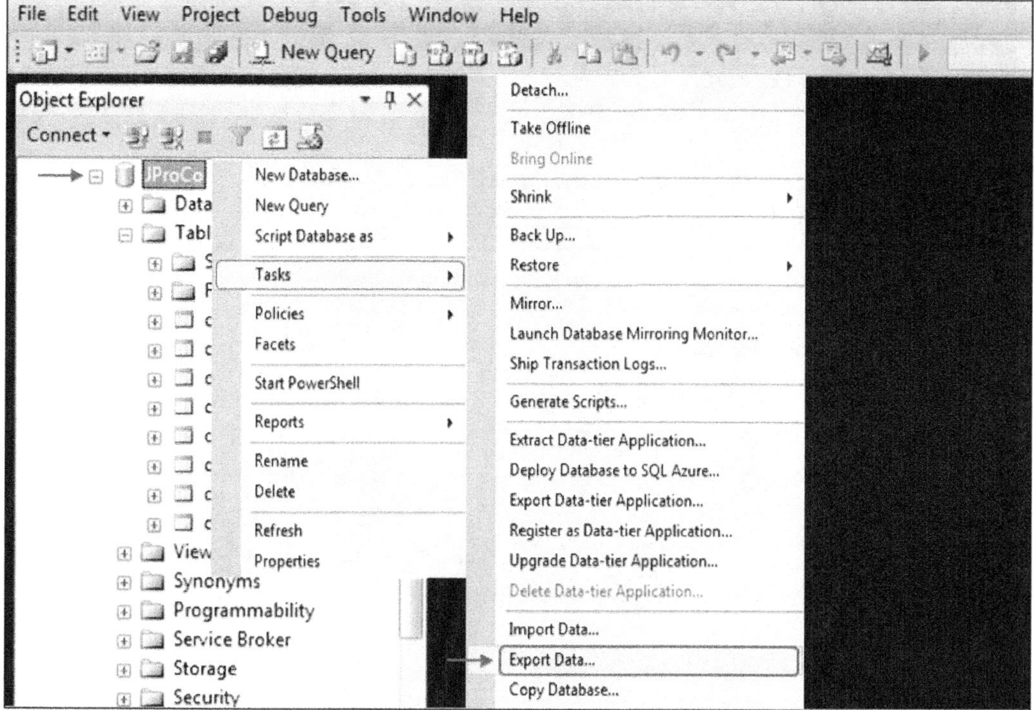

Figure 11.26 Start the Export process by choosing the Tasks > Export Data option in SSMS.

The ***Welcome to SQL Server Import and Export Wizard*** (splash screen) opens, with a brief description of what actions this interface is capable of performing. Click on the 'Next' button to go to the ***Choose a Data Source*** dialog box, as shown in Figure 11.27. Since, this Wizard was started by right-clicking on the JProCo database, from inside a SQL Server 2012 SSMS application, the Data Source, Server Name, Authentication and Database will default to these settings.

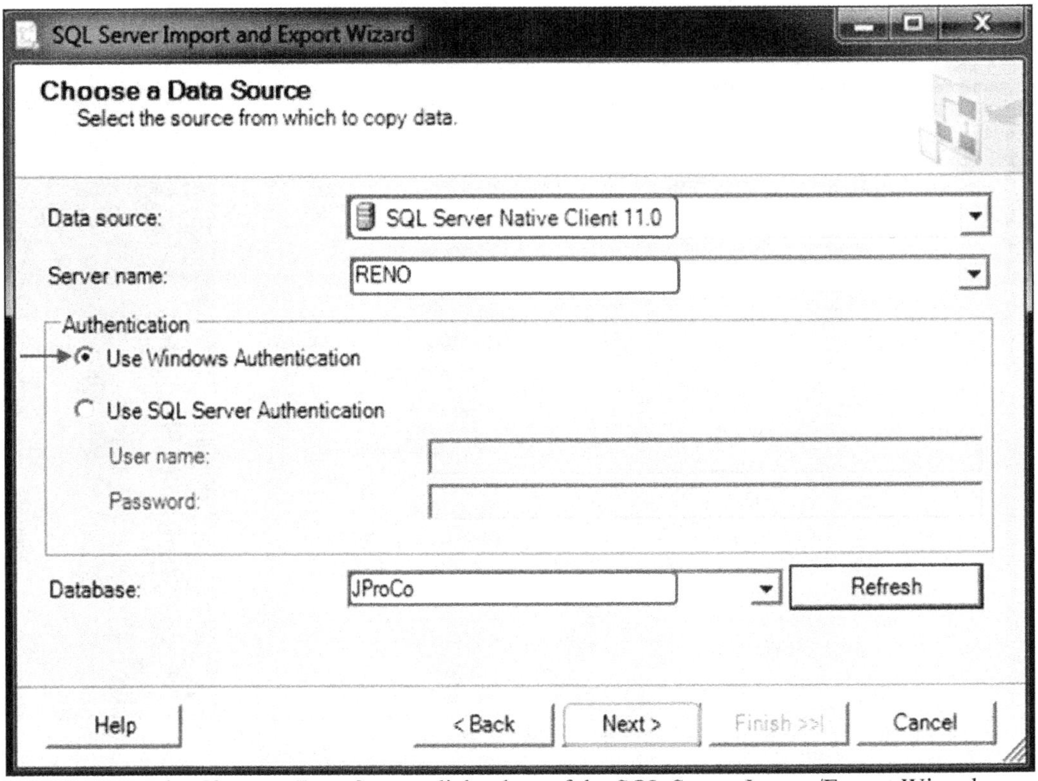

Figure 11.27 The Choose a Data Source dialog box of the SQL Server Import/Export Wizard.

Reader Note: *If the SQL Server Import/Export Wizard is accidently started in a different database, or if it is necessary to connect to a different Data Source or Server, it is possible to change any of the settings in the Choose Data Source dialog box, prior to clicking on the 'Next >' button.*

The default Data Source settings chosen by the Wizard are correct, so we need to click on the 'Next >' button to choose where the data will go to with the ***Choose a Destination*** dialog box. Our goal is to send the data to Microsoft Excel, so we will need to locate and select this option from the 'Destination' drop-down menu, as seen in Figure 11.28.

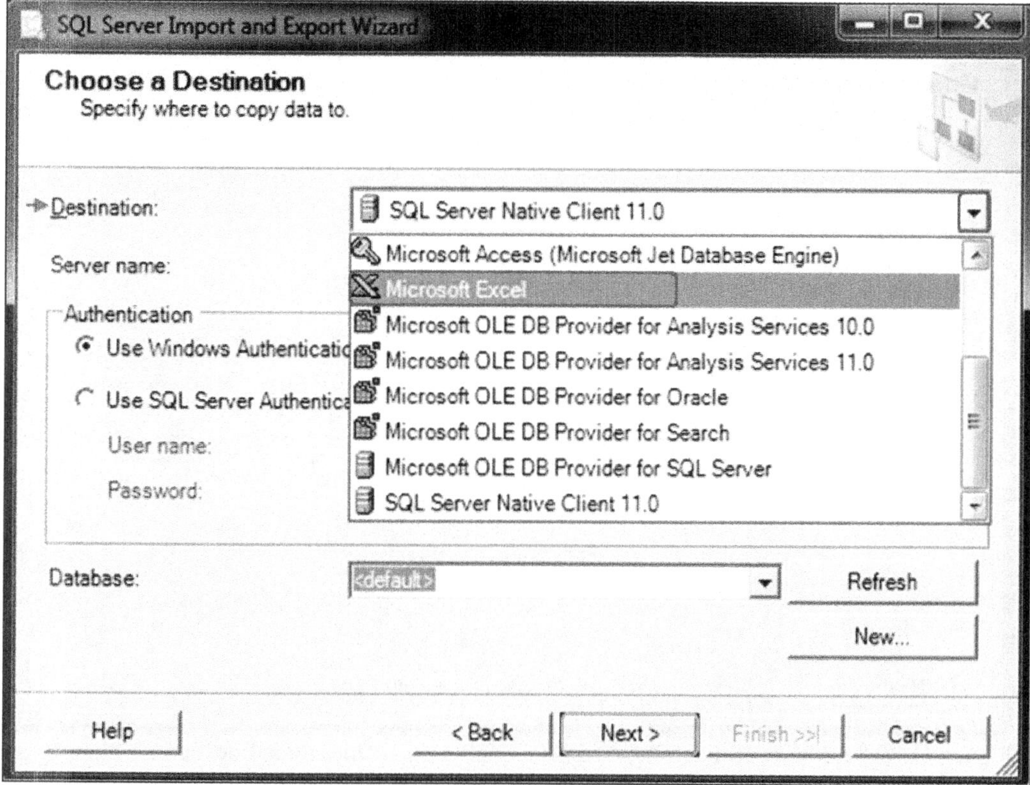

Figure 11.28 Choose Microsoft Excel as the destination for our exported data.

Once the 'Destination' has been set to Microsoft Excel, the dialog box will refresh the screen to allow for us to determine three additional settings:

- 'Excel file path' = **C:\Joes2Pros\Location.xls**
- 'Excel version' = **Microsoft Excel 97-2003**
- 'First row has column names' = ☑

Confirm these settings are correct by comparing them to those in Figure 11.29. When everything has been confirmed, click on the 'Next >' button.

In the ***Specify Table Copy or Query*** dialog box, choose the 'Copy data from one or more tables or views' option, as shown in Figure 11.30. This option will instruct SQL Server to create the necessary T-SQL code for populating the Location.xls file with all the records from the table that we are going to select in the next dialog box. *The other option in this dialog box allows us to write the T-SQL code ourselves.* Click on the 'Next >' button to advance to the ***Select Source Tables and Views*** dialog box.

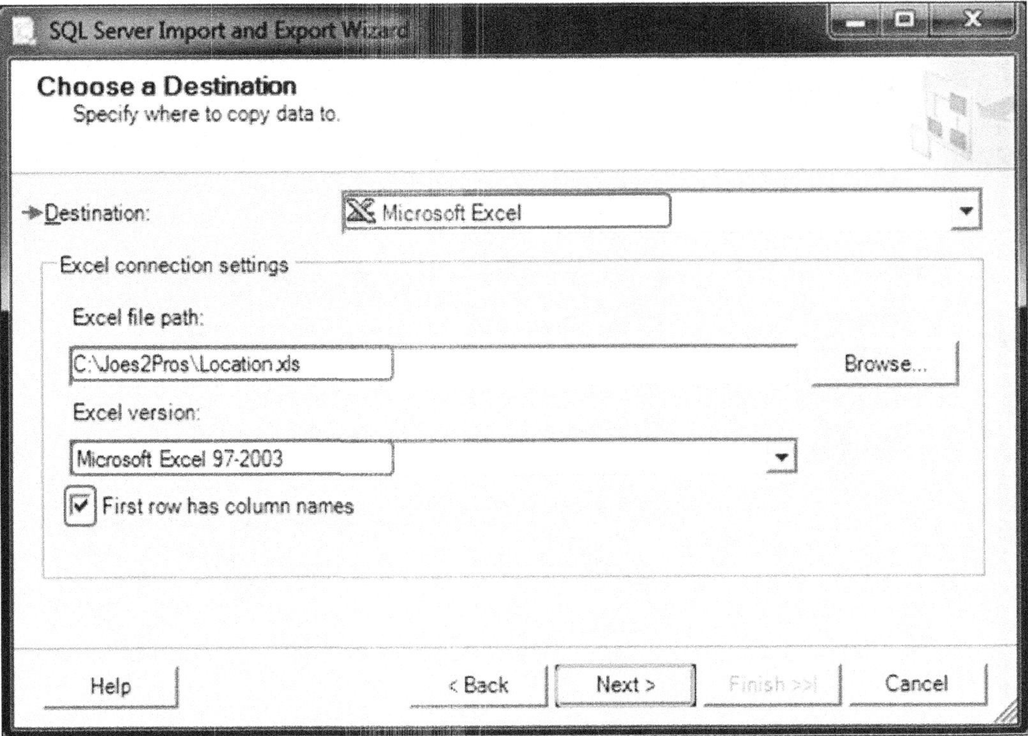

Figure 11.29 Set Microsoft Excel as the destination with a C:\Joes2Pros\Location.xls path.

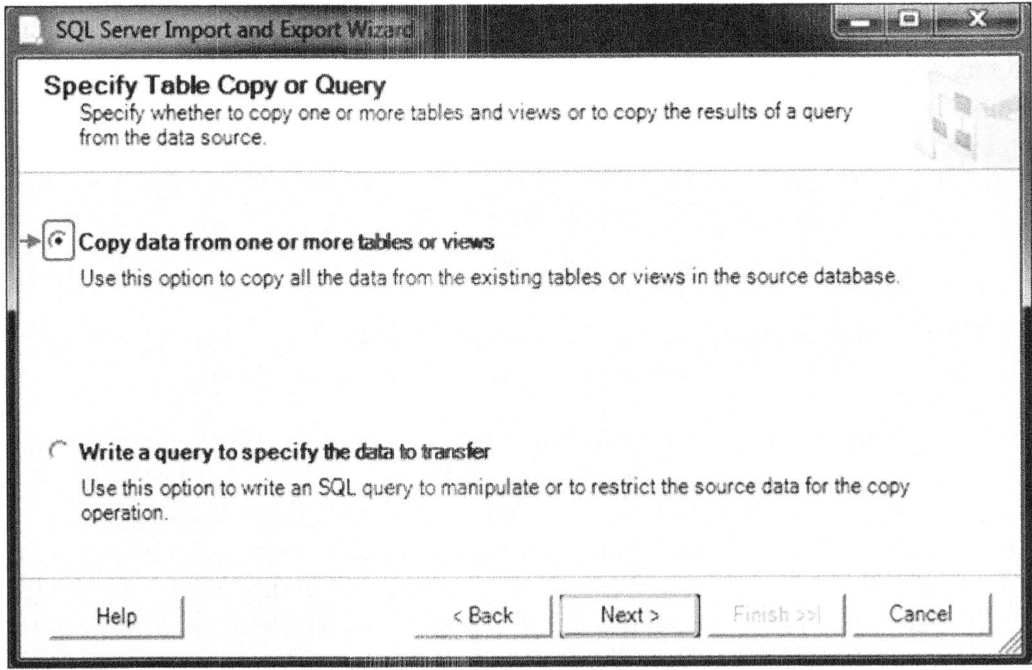

Figure 11.30 Choose the 'Copy data from one or more tables or views' option.

In the ***Select Source Tables and Views*** dialog box, mark '☑' the dbo.Location table, choose it as our source table and export to the C:\Joes2Pros\Location.xls destination, as shown in Figure 11.31. When done, click on the 'Next >' button.

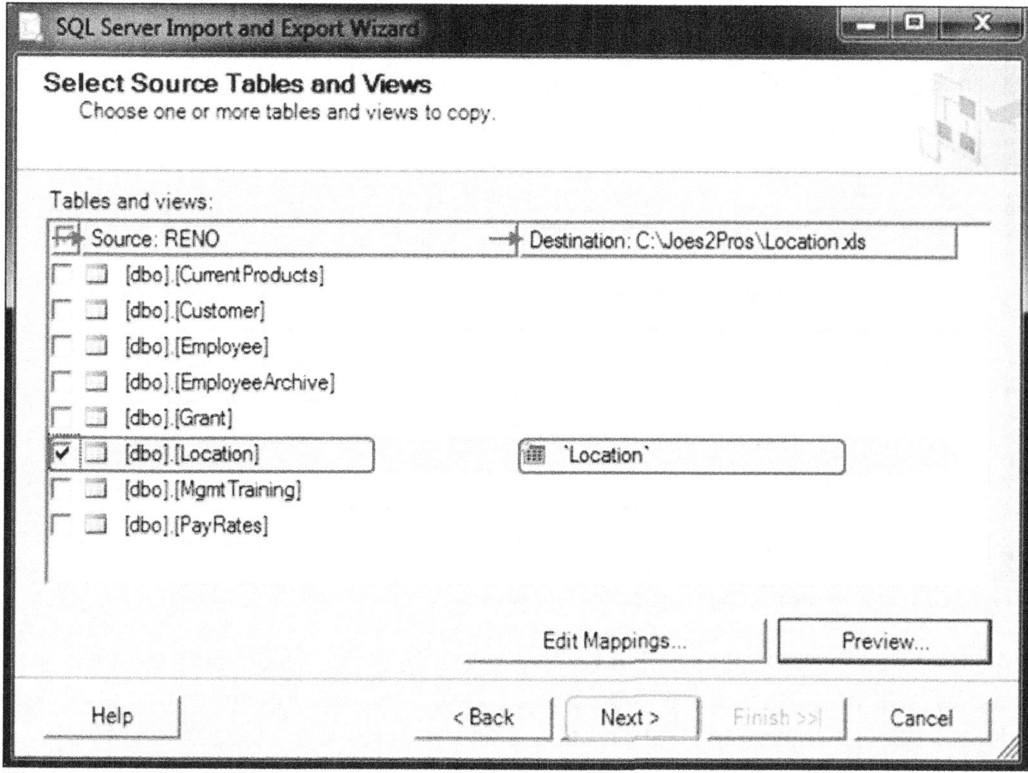

Figure 11.31 Choose the dbo.Location source table to export to C:\Joes2Pros\Location.xls.

Behind the scenes, SQL Server is verifying the source and destination paths and then creates the T-SQL code to export all records from the JProCo.dbo.Location table to the C:\Joes2Pros\Location.xls file.

As soon as this is complete, the ***Review Data Type Mapping*** dialog box opens. Do not make any changes here and simply click the 'Next >' button. This opens the ***Save and Run Package*** dialog box. We will choose the 'Run immediately' option, by marking it with a '☑', since we are not interested in creating a SSIS package at this time. We can confirm this dialog box is configured correctly by comparing it to Figure 11.32. When ready, click the 'Next >' button.

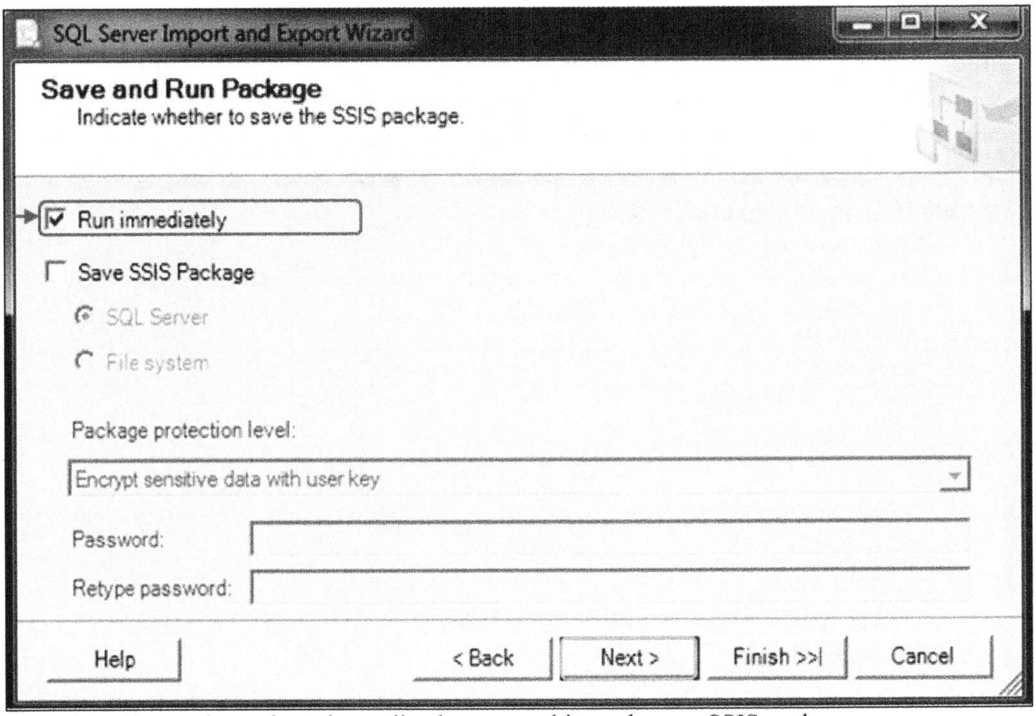

Figure 11.32 Run the package immediately or save this work as an SSIS package.

Another dialog box opens called ***Complete the Wizard***, which outlines what actions will be performed by SQL Server as soon as the 'Finish' button is clicked. This is the last chance to verify all the previous steps were performed correctly. If anything doesn't look right when reviewing this information, it is possible to click on the 'Back' button as many times as necessary to return to the dialog box that needs to be corrected and continue with each dialog box again from that point.

Everything should be okay here, so let's click on the 'Finish' button and watch what happens!

A new dialog box will open to display the progress for each step of the export process in an easy to read format. Icons will appear on the left-hand side of the description for each action. A green circle with a '✓' mark indicates the action completed successfully and a red circle with an '✖' mark indicates the action has failed with an error.

When all of the steps have completed, a brief message and report will appear at the top of the dialog box indicating the overall status of the export process. We can look at Figure 11.33 to see what the expected results are for exporting this data using the ***SQL Server Import and Export Wizard***.

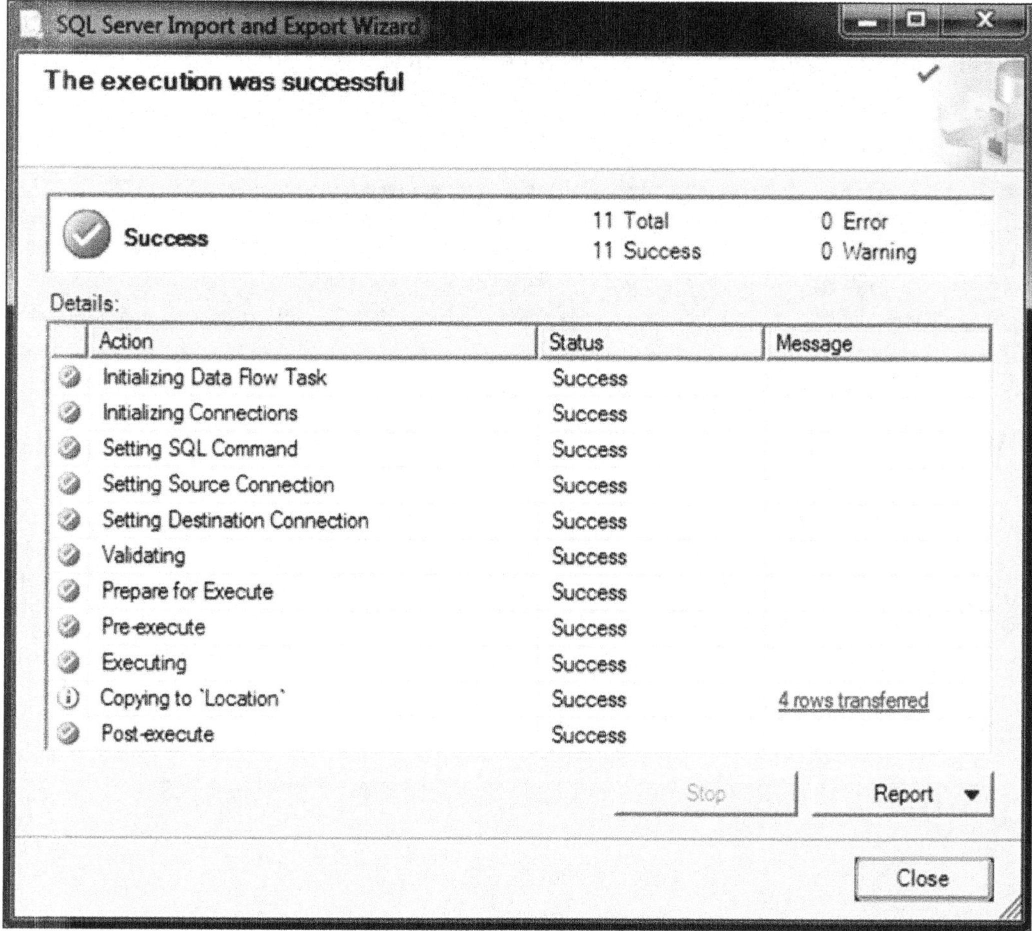

Figure 11.33 The final stage of the export process using the SQL Server Import/Export Wizard.

There are several ways to locate and open the newly created Location.xls file to verify it is populated with the records from the JProCo.dbo.Location table. Since we already have the Command Prompt window open, let's have some fun and learn a new trick that will come in handy at work.

We already know that we can verify the file is in the Joes2Pros folder by typing the command '**DIR C:\Joes2Pros**' and observing that the Location.xls file is in this folder along with the Location.txt file that we created with the BCP utility.

If we know the location of an executable file, like a Microsoft Excel spreadsheet, we can type a special command followed by the path to the file to open the application. Opening an application in the Command Prompt is very close to what an Operating System is doing behind the scenes when we double-click on a file to begin working with it. So, if our mouse ever quits working, and it will, we can always use the Command Prompt to open our files and applications for us!

Type the following command at the flashing cursor in the Command Prompt window: '**START C:\Joes2Pros\Location.xls**' (Figure 11.34)

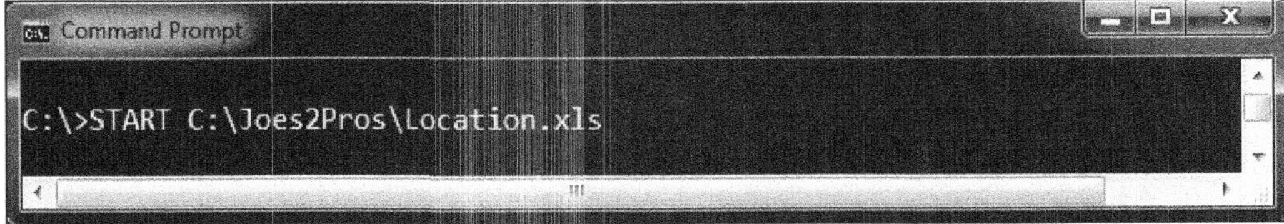

Figure 11.34 Opening the Location.xls file directly from the Command Prompt.

As soon as we press the 'Enter' button, we are instructing the Operating System to start Microsoft Excel (or whatever the default application is for opening .xls file extensions) and open the Location.xls file for viewing at the same time.

We can see in Figure 11.35 that the Location.xls file has indeed opened up inside of the Microsoft Excel application. It appears that the export process has been successful, as this file now contains all four records (with column headers) from the JProCo.dbo.Location table. Notice that the tab for this worksheet has been labeled with the name of our table, Location (lower left corner of this image).

Location [Compatibility Mode] - Microsoft Excel

	A	B	C	D
1	LocationID	Street	City	State
2	1	111 First ST	Seattle	WA
3	2	222 Second AVE	Boston	MA
4	3	333 Third PL	Chicago	IL
5	4	444 Ruby ST	Spokane	WA

Location

Figure 11.35 All four records from the Location table are now populated in the Location.xls file.

Lab 11.3: Import/Export Wizard

Lab Prep: Each lab has one or more Skill Checks. Start with Skill Check 1 and proceed until reaching the Points to Ponder section.

Before beginning this lab, verify that SQL Server 2012 is properly installed and operating. Before running the lab setup script for resetting the database (SQLQueries2012Vol1Chapter11.3Setup.sql), please make sure to close all query windows within SSMS. An open query window pointing to a database context can lock that database preventing it from updating when the script is executing. A simple way to assure all query windows are closed, is to exit out of SSMS, then open a new instance of SSMS, and lastly run the setup script.

Skill Check 1: Use the SQL Server Import/Export Wizard to export all records from the JProCo.dbo.Employee table into the C:\Joes2Pros\Employee.xls file.

When done, the results should resemble those in Figure 11.36 and Figure 11.37.

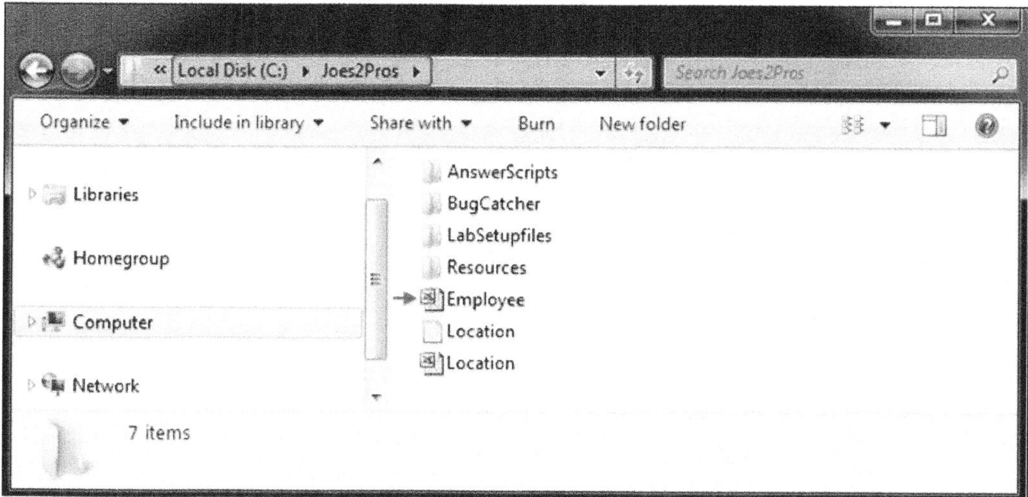

Figure 11.36 Verification that the Employee.xls file is located in the C:\Joes2Pros folder.

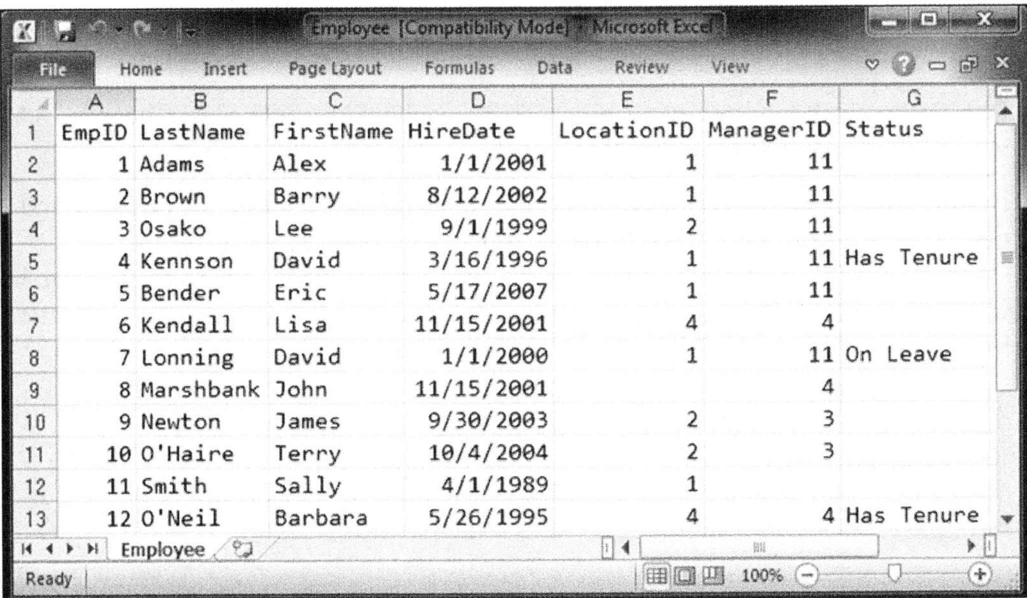

EmpID	LastName	FirstName	HireDate	LocationID	ManagerID	Status
1	Adams	Alex	1/1/2001	1	11	
2	Brown	Barry	8/12/2002	1	11	
3	Osako	Lee	9/1/1999	2	11	
4	Kennson	David	3/16/1996	1	11	Has Tenure
5	Bender	Eric	5/17/2007	1	11	
6	Kendall	Lisa	11/15/2001	4	4	
7	Lonning	David	1/1/2000	1	11	On Leave
8	Marshbank	John	11/15/2001		4	
9	Newton	James	9/30/2003	2	3	
10	O'Haire	Terry	10/4/2004	2	3	
11	Smith	Sally	4/1/1989	1		
12	O'Neil	Barbara	5/26/1995	4	4	Has Tenure

Figure 11.37 All 12 records from the Employee table have populated the Employee.xls file.

Answer Code: The T-SQL code to this lab can be found in the downloadable files in a file named Lab11.3_CodeComments.sql.

Points to Ponder - Import/Export Wizard

1. Importing and Exporting to and from SQL Server is a common workplace requirement.
2. BCP can only import and export to text files and BCP native files.
3. BCP cannot import from, or export to, Microsoft Excel.
4. The Import/Export Wizard uses easy to follow dialog boxes to help us import or export to/from many types of data stores, such as Microsoft Excel.

Chapter Glossary

BCP: Bulk Copy Program is a command-line utility for importing or exporting data from a delimited text file.

Code Generators: A mechanism built into the SSMS UI that converts "point and click" actions into T-SQL code that can be compiled and executed by any application capable of doing so.

Data Source: A storage type that can be imported from or exported to a location.

Import/Export Wizard: A wizard within SQL server that creates simple SSIS packages that will integrate with many types of data sources.

In-line Comments: A comment that spans the middle part of a line of code.

Multi-line Comments: A comment that marks the beginning and ending of a block or blocks of code that should not execute.

Non-Executing code: Code that can be seen and read by humans, but will be ignored by SQL Server.

Script: T-SQL code saved as a .sql file extension.

Single-line Comments: A point marked on a line of code to turn the rest of that line into non-executing code.

Review Quiz - Chapter Eleven

1.) Which two types of signs are used for marking comments when coding with SQL Server?

☐ a. *

☐ b. --

☐ c. /* */

☐ d. _

2.) Multi-Line Comments are also called:

O a. Single-Line Comments

O b. In-Line Comments

O c. DML Comments

3.) BCP can import and export to native BCP files and text files. What files can the Import/Export Wizard work with? (choose all that apply)

☐ a. Text Files

☐ b. Excel Files

☐ c. MS Access

☐ d. XML

Answer Key

1.) The '*' (asterisk) is used to instruct SQL Server to search for all fields in a table, so (a) is incorrect. The '_' (underscore) instructs SQL Server to look for a single character in a WHERE clause, so (d) is incorrect. Using the '--' (two hyphens for single-line comments) and the '/* */' (asterisk and forward slash pair combinations for multi-line comments) are acceptable to instruct SQL Server to treat any text bound by them as comments, therefore (b) and (c) are the correct answers.

2.) Multi-line and single-line comments are different and there is no such thing as a DML comment, so (a) and (c) are incorrect. Since '/* */' have a beginning and ending marker they can also be used as in-line comments, making (b) the correct answer.

3.) The Import/Export Wizard can work with nearly any kind of data store integration, therefore (a), (b), (c) and (d) are all correct answers.

Bug Catcher Game

To play the Bug Catcher game, run the BugCatcher_Chapter11.pps from the BugCatcher folder of the companion files. These files can be obtained from the www.Joes2Pros.com website.

[NOTES]

Chapter 12. Summary: SQL Queries Volume 1

Learning SQL Server is a journey and it never gets old no matter how many times we walk on the same route. When the traveler walks on a long journey, they often pick up new learning and experiences along the way.

Whenever a journey is very long, the duration can differ from traveler to traveler as their individual goals and their capacity to adapt are different. Changes to the path of the journey can also occur over time, such as the road is upgraded, or new facilities like rest-areas are built. This can also change the comfort from traveler to traveler during the journey. When taking the same route more than once, the traveler starts learning the lessons to deal with the scenarios better than before. The traveler has the advantage of added experience when he walks the road again.

The journey to learn technology is the same, as one will benefit from repeating steps multiple times to become really familiar with how to use the information. In this book we are the traveler and are on the journey to learn SQL Server. While you have been provided with a comprehensive introduction to the subject, you should refer to it whenever you are in need of SQL education. We promise that this book will present you with an excellent learning experience every time.

Having finished this book, you are ready to isolate and annihilate your next goal. In my experience, this often includes writing more advanced queries using DML statements, or administration functions involving DCL and TCL statements. You can place a feather in your cap and build upon it with this next logical step.

SQL Server works with more than just data. You need to protect data, structure data, and process data. A quick recap of what we covered and how it is used in the workplace wraps up this final chapter.

This SQL book covered the broad core of the language and how it works. If you finished this book and want to work towards your certification you can go directly to ***SQL Queries 2012 Joes 2 Pros Volume 2***. With a solid understanding of SQL, you can delve deeper into the next discipline; advanced DML statements.

Reader Note: *You can find more detail and keep in touch with the Joes 2 Pros community at www.Joes2Pros.com.*

SQL Language Statement Types

The SQL language is comprised of four major parts shown here in Figure 12.1.

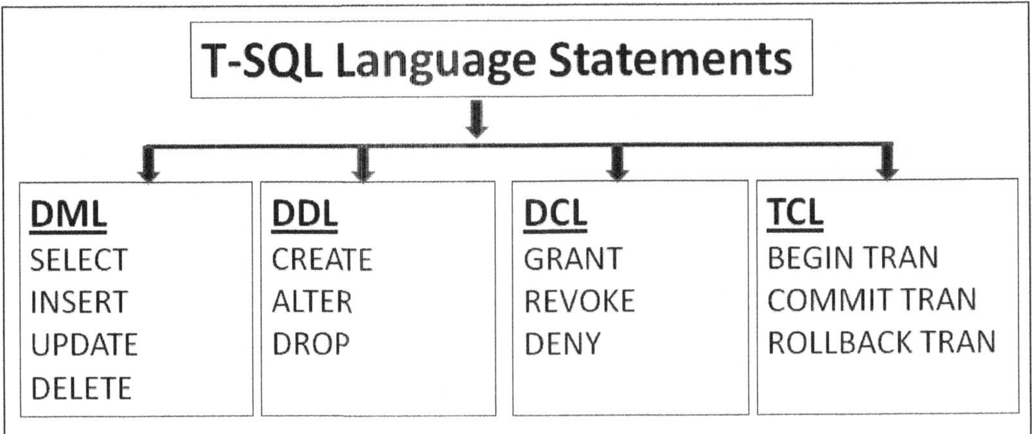

Figure 12.1 The breakdown of different language family statements which SQL supports.

There are a few SQL Server statements that support the four major types above. For example, setting the database context with USE JProCo tells the next DDL statement into which database the object(s) will be created. Also, statements like IF and IF EXISTS will conditionally run the next statement. For example, we might not want to create the Bruce login if it already exists. By putting an IF EXISTS above that DCL statement, it will support the code by only running when a certain condition is met, which helps to avoid errors.

SQL has evolved and grown from just a data language to support many more programming concepts. At its core are data, and how to use and protect it by using DML, DDL, DCL and TCL statements. Remember the following:

- DML is about getting data in and out of a database and returning information in result sets.
- DDL is about the structure and design of database objects, which help protect the data by setting the fields and the data types they can hold.
- DCL allows only the right logins to do certain actions by controlling the level of access any account has to securables.
- TCL protects data by keeping transactions consistent.

When browsing books on SQL queries or advanced query techniques, they typically offer a deep dive into writing DML statements. This is because getting data in and out of a database is performed more often than the other three types of SQL statements combined.

What's Next

SQL Queries 2012 Joes 2 Pros Volume 1 provides a sound foundation of the fundamental knowledge necessary to become a SQL developer. Whether your goal is to learn how to solve challenging problems, create critical business reports, or to become a master in SQL Server you will need to learn the skills of an expert to succeed.

The next book in this series will take you beyond the fundamentals of how SQL Server works and becoming a SQL developer. It will address more advanced T-SQL concepts with a focus on the practical knowledge necessary to be a highly skilled professional.

SQL Queries 2012 Joes 2 Pros Volume 2 will teach the skills necessary to be amongst those developers who know how to get the most out of writing scripts using the SELECT, INSERT, UPDATE and DELETE statements well enough to build and power amazing applications. In addition, you will have the necessary knowledge and skills to become a highly sought after developer who routinely builds solid data structure and impeccable reusable T-SQL code.

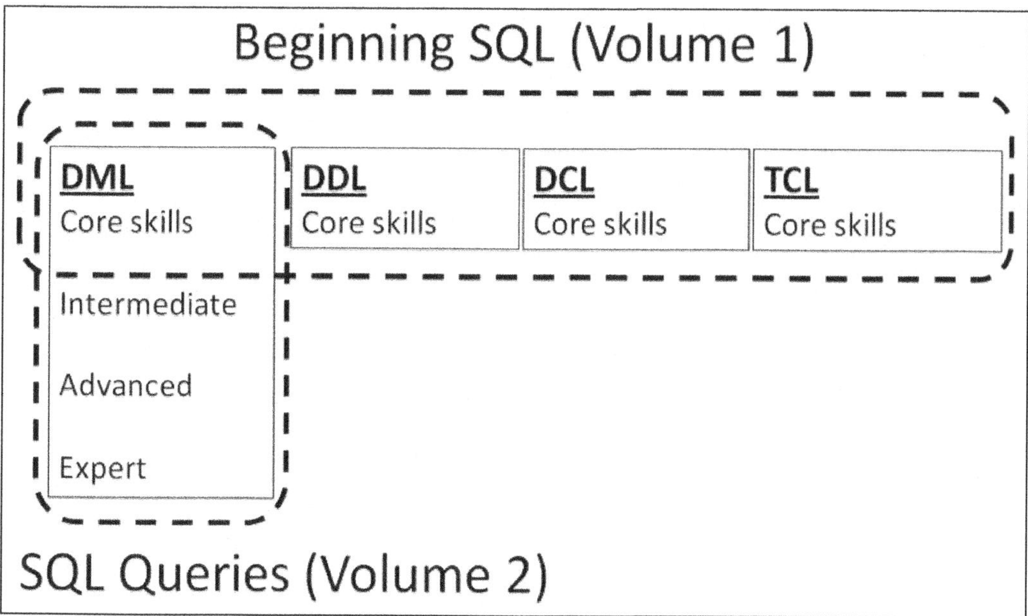

Figure 12.2 SQL Queries 2012 Volume 2 is a deeper study of the DML component in SQL.

You will be learning more advanced concepts of how to use DML statements to solve the difficult problems and create reports that business users need every day. A critical part is to know how to use the proper syntax as well as the practical implementation of writing queries, subqueries, recursive queries, merging data, ranking functions and aggregation strategies to meet these business data needs. Experienced SQL developers can make decisions such as, whether to use joins or subqueries to best achieve the required results by analyzing various data points.

SQL Queries 2012 Joes 2 Pros Volume 2 will be very important to advance your career as a SQL Server developer or tester, as most interview questions will be based on skills related to the DML statement skills covered with this book.

Remember the three keys of success to your career:

1) Learn
2) Practice and Apply Skills
3) Repeat steps 1 and 2

INDEX

E

F

G

I

J

[NOTES]

CPSIA information can be obtained
at www.ICGtesting.com
Printed in the USA
LVOW03s1327031215
465210LV00015B/307/P

9 781939 666123